MW01166611

The Desktop Encyclopedia of

Corporate Finance & Accounting

The Desktop
Encyclopedia of
Corporate
Finance &
Accounting

CHARLES J. WOELFEL

PROBUS PUBLISHING COMPANY
Chicago, Illinois

Library of Congress Cataloging in Publication Data Available

ISBN 0-917253-65-5

Printed in the United States of America

1 2 3 4 5 6 7 8 9 0

To Colette

Preface

The *Desktop Encyclopedia of Corporate Accounting and Finance* is a reference and sourcebook which explains major concepts in accounting, finance, and economics. Over 270 major accounting and financial entries (short articles) and more than 2,500 related concepts are presented in detail.

This book was written for individuals who must have immediate access to authoritative accounting and financial information on a day-to-day basis—managers, executives, bankers, accountants and more. It is designed specifically to be a convenient reference. This one-volume sourcebook is alphabetized and indexed for easy use. Each entry is cross-referenced to enable the reader to explore a topic in greater depth. Many of the entries contain bibliographies which offer easy access to primary or secondary sources on the same general topic. Over seventy-five exhibits are included to provide examples and illustrations of more complex concepts. A detailed and analytical General Index lists topics and subtopics.

The *Desktop Encyclopedia of Corporate Accounting and Finance* is more than mere definitions. Accounting and financial reporting theory, principles and practices are described. The conceptual foundations of financial reporting are dealt with in a manner that provides the basis for an in-depth understanding of financial statements.

While accounting and finance for the corporate form of business enterprise are featured in the reference, special situations are also discussed: personal financial statements; partnerships; service enterprises; development stage companies; nonprofit enterprises; estates and trust; and bankrupt and insolvent enterprises and governmental entities.

The author appreciates the cooperation of the Financial Accounting Standards Board for allowing him to quote from their pronouncements. The author also wants to express his personal thanks to Probus Publishing Company for encouragement and support throughout this project.

Charles J. Woelfel

Introduction

There are various ways to use this book. For someone who needs to know what a particular accounting or finance concept or term means, the book will normally provide a particular entry that will satisfy this need. When the entry is located, carefully prepared cross-references are available to enable the reader to pursue the topic further. In addition, most entries also contain references to available books and other source documents. An extensive index is also available for additional guidance.

For someone interested in pursuing a systematic approach to accounting and finance, it is suggested that the following outline be used in the order presented to become acquainted with the basic structure of accounting and finance.

Underlying Principles

Accounting
Finance
Economics
Accounting associations
Accounting profession
Certified Public Accountants
Accounting theory
Accounting functions
Financial accounting

Accounting assumptions
Generally accepted accounting
   principles
Accounting principles
Accounting policies
Accounting procedures
Events, transactions, exchanges,
   and circumstances
Financial statements

Underlying Principles (continued)

Financial reporting
Economic environment of
   accounting
Financial Accounting Standards
   Board
Conceptual framework of
   accounting
Objectives of financial reporting
Statements of financial account-
   ing concepts (plus specific
   Statements)

Statements of financial account-
   ing standards
Economic consequences of
   accounting
Information system
Accounting system
Accounting period
Accounting cycle
Accounting equation
Accrual basis
Other comprehensive basis of
   accounting

Major Concepts

Measurement
Recognition
Realization
Allocation

Conservatism
Consistency
Materiality
Full disclosure
Objectivity

Capital maintenance theories:
   Financial capital
   Physical capital
Asset/liability assumption and
   Revenue/expense assumption

Cost-benefit analysis
Elements of accounting
   Asset
   Liability
   Revenue
   Expense

Capital
Income
Shareholders' equity

Statement of financial position
Income statement
Statement of changes in financial
   position
Financial statement analysis
Ratios

Cost and Managerial Accounting

Cost Accounting
   Job order
   Process cost
   Standard cost (variance
   analysis)
Direct cost and full absorption
   cost
Cost-volume-profit analysis

Planning and control
Budgeting
Capital budgeting
Return on Investment (ROI)
Discounted cash flow
Inventory model
Contribution margin analysis
Break-even analysis

Auditing

Audit	Peer review
Compilation (and review)	Fraud
Ethics	Related party transactions
Opinion	Foreign Corrupt Practices Act
	Privileged communications

Terms such as *capital, income, wealth, revenue,* and many others have a variety of meanings in various disciplines. The focus of terms included in this volume is directed primarily on their use in accounting and finance.

The user of this *Encyclopedia* can be assured that the discussions presented herein are authoritative, relevant, and reliable. This reference was prepared with the user in mind and so offers a practical and accessible guide to the current theory and practice of accounting and finance.

ACCOUNT

A ledger account is an accounting form used to assemble information that affects one specific asset, liability, owners' equity, revenue, or expense. In its simplest form, a ledger account can be represented in the form of a T as shown in Exhibit A–1 for the Cash account. The account contains the date of the transaction or event, the source of the item, and the dollar amount. Space is also available for an explanation or comment.

Exhibit A–1
Typical General Ledger Account in "T" Account Format

CASH   Account no. 1101

Date		Explanation	Ref.	Amount	Date		Explanation	Ref.	Amount
1991					1991				
June	1	Cash sales		40,000	June	5	Equipment		12,000
	15	S.M. Smith		35,000		10	Advertising		12,000
	25	A.P. Jones		60,000		15	Wages		75.000

The left side of an account is called the debit side; the right side is called the credit side. The dollar difference between

7

the debit side and the credit side is called the account balance. The rules for increasing and decreasing an account are summarized as follows:

Debit an account to	Credit an account to
1. increase an asset	1. decrease an asset
2. decrease a liability	2. increase a liability
3. decrease owners' equity	3. increase owners' equity

These rules can be graphically illustrated as follows for asset, liability, owners' equity, revenue, and expense accounts.

ASSETS		LIABILITIES		OWNERS' EQUITY	
Additions	Subtractions	Subtractions	Additions	Subtractions	Additions

EXPENSES		REVENUES	
Additions	Subtractions	Subtractions	Additions

Accounts are classified as real, nominal, or mixed accounts. Real accounts include asset, liability, and owners' equity accounts. Real (or permanent) accounts remain open after the books are closed at the end of a fiscal period; that is, account balances are carried forward from period to period. Real accounts appear on the balance sheet. Nominal (or temporary) accounts include revenue, expense, and dividends accounts. Nominal accounts are closed at the end of an accounting period to prepare these accounts for the next fiscal period. Nominal accounts determine the change in retained earnings of a corporation during an accounting period. Nominal accounts are also used by partnerships, sole proprietorships, and other accounting entities. Nominal accounts appear on the income statement. Mixed accounts contain both real and nominal components. At the end of an accounting period, mixed accounts are separated into either real or nominal accounts when adjusting entries are made.

A contra account is frequently used to show a reduction in a related account. For example, the accumulated depreciation account can be used as a contra (offsetting) account to the building account. Certain accounts relate to other accounts but must be added on the statements. Such accounts are referred to as adjunct accounts. For example, the Additional Paid-in Capital account is added to the Capital Stock account balance in the stockholders' equity section of the balance sheet.

A control account is frequently used in the general ledger for a group of specific accounts contained in a subsidiary ledger. The balance in the control account on a balance sheet date equals the total balance of its related subsidiary ledger.

See also Ledger; Journal; Accounting equation; Chart of accounts; Accounting system; Double-entry system; Contra account; Valuation account.

ACCOUNTANCY
Accountancy is a term that applies to the theory and practice of accounting, especially as it relates to the activities of an accountant. Accountancy is used in England to mean accounting. An accountant is a person educated and trained in accounting, especially in matters relating to accounting assumptions, conventions, principles, standards, and practices. Accountability is the condition of being accountable, liable, or responsible.

See also Accounting; Certified Public Accountant.

ACCOUNTING
Accounting is an information system that accumulates, processes, and communicates information, primarily financial in nature, about a specific economic entity.

Accounting was defined in Accounting Terminology Bulletin No. 2 of the American Institute of Certified Public Accountants as follows:

"Accounting is the art of recording, classifying, and summarizing in a significant manner and in terms of money, transactions and events which are, in part at least, of a financial character, and interpreting results thereof."

This definition emphasizes the work that the accountant does and makes little reference to the users of the information that the accountant provides.

The American Accounting Association defined accounting in a Statement of Basic Theory, 1966, as follows:

"Accounting is the process of identifying, measuring and communicating economic information to permit informed judgments and decisions by users of the information. . . .The objectives of accounting are to provide for the following purposes:

1. *Making decisions concerning the use of limited resources including crucial decision areas, and determination of goals and objectives.*

2. *Effectively directing and controlling an organization's human and material resources.*

3. *Maintaining and reporting on the custodianship of resources.*

4. *Facilitating social functions and controls."*

This definition identifies the major role of accounting as providing information for those who use the information. The definition specifies three major functions of accounting: identifying, measuring, and communicating economic information.

In 1970 the Accounting Principles Board of the American Institute of Certified Public Accountants developed the following definition of accounting:

"Accounting is a service activity. Its function is to provide quantitative information, primarily financial in

nature, about economic activities that is intended to be useful in making economic decisions—in making reasoned choices among alternative courses of action."

This definition of accounting is goal-oriented rather than process-oriented or function-oriented. It emphasizes economic decision-making activities rather than the functions of accounting as the major objectives of accounting.

In a popular sense, accounting has been referred to as *the language of business*, since it is the basic tool for recording and reporting economic events and transactions that affect business enterprises. Other concepts of accounting view accounting as an historical record, a mirror of current economic reality, a subset of a total business information system, and as a commodity that is the product of economic activity.

See also Accountancy; Accounting theory; Accounting assumptions; Accounting principles; Generally accepted accounting principles; Accounting policies; Accounting procedures; Accounting system; Economic environment of accounting; Events, transactions, exchanges, and circumstances; Economic consequences of accounting; Accounting functions; Accountancy; Certified Public Accountant; Bookkeeping; Controller.

REFERENCES
Carey, John L., *Getting Acquainted with Accounting* (Houghton Mifflin, Boston, 1973).
Seidler, Lee, and Carmichael, D. R., eds. *Accountants' Handbook* (John Wiley & Sons, N.Y., 1981).
Nicherson, Clarence B., *Accounting Handbook for Nonaccountants* (Van Nostrand Reinhold, N.Y., 1985).

ACCOUNTING ASSOCIATIONS

A number of accounting organizations have been established to promote the interests of their members and of the accounting profession in general. Many of these organizations play an active role in the development of financial accounting and reporting standards in the United States.

The American Institute of Certified Public Accountants is a national organization of professional accountants who have been certified by state law to practice public accounting. The Institute was organized to unite the accounting profession in the United States and to promote and maintain high professional and ethical standards within the profession. It also acts to safeguard the interests of CPAs, to advance accounting research, and to develop and improve accounting education. The Institute is concerned primarily with public accounting. The Institute established two divisions of accounting firms within the Institute—an SEC practice section (SECPS) for firms with an SEC practice and a private companies practice section (PCPS) for other CPA firms. A firm can be associated with both divisions. The AICPA has established two major technical committees—The Accounting Standards Executive Committee (AcSEC) and the Auditing Standards Committee (AuSEC). AcSEC deals with matters associated with financial and cost accounting issues. AuSEC deals primarily with auditing issues. These committees issue Statements of Position (SOP) on accounting and auditing issues which serve as guidelines for accounting practice. The AICPA has played an influential role in the establishment of generally accepted accounting principles (GAAP). Its Committee on Accounting Procedures (CAP) was organized in 1938 to "narrow the areas of difference in corporate reporting" which it proceeded to do by issuing 51 Accounting Research Bulletins (ARB) which represented the single source of GAAP in the United States. In 1959 the AICPA established a new body called the Accounting Principles Board (APB) "to advance the written expression of what constitutes generally accepted accounting principles." The APB issued Opinions which served as guidelines for accounting practice along with four statements and a series of Accounting Interpretations which dealt with accounting problems. The APB functioned until 1973 when it was replaced by the Financial Accounting Standards Board (FASB) as the major standard-setting body in the United States. The FASB is not a committee of the AICPA. The Institute publishes the *Journal of Accountancy*.

The American Accounting Association is an organization of individuals who are interested in the development of accounting theory, practice, and education. The major objectives of the AAA include the following: to encourage and sponsor research in education, to develop accounting principles and standards, and to improve methods of accounting instruction. The AAA publishes a quarterly journal called The Accounting Review.

The National Association of Accountants (NAA) is an organization of accountants concerned primarily with managerial accounting problems and practices. Its primary focus is on internal reporting rather than external reporting. The NAA publishes *Management Accounting*.

The Financial Executive Institute (FEI) is an organization composed primarily of controllers, treasurers, and chief accountants of an enterprise. The Institute publishes *The Financial Executive*.

Other major accounting associations include the following. The American Woman's Society of Certified Public Accountants is an organization established to advance the professional interests of women CPAs. The Institute of Internal Auditors (IIA) was established to promote the interests of those concerned with the practice of internal auditing. The Institute publishes *The Internal Auditor*. The EDP Auditor's Association is concerned primarily with the advancement and dissemination of EDP auditing knowledge and skills. The Association publishes the *EDP Auditor*. The Association of Government Accountants (AGA) is a national organization involved in accounting, auditing, and financial management in the public sector. The Association's major objectives are to assist professional managers in government service to perform effectively and efficiently. The Association publishes the *Government Accountants Journal*

Beta Alpha Psi is the national honorary fraternity of students majoring in accounting.

See also Accounting profession; Financial Accounting Standards Board.

ACCOUNTING ASSUMPTIONS

Accounting assumptions are those broad concepts that underlie generally accepted accounting principles and serve as a foundation for these principles. Accounting assumptions are statements accepted without proof that also serve as the basis for accounting activities. The major accounting assumptions include: the business entity assumption, the continuity assumption, the periodic and timely reporting assumption, and the monetary unit assumption.

A basic assumption in accounting is that economic activity can be identified with a particular unit or entity of accountability. This unit or entity is the one to be accounted for. A committee of the American Accounting Association reported on the business entity assumption as follows:

> *"In Accounting, the entity with which we are concerned may be defined as an area of economic interest to a particular individual or group. The boundaries of such economic entity are identifiable (1) by determining the interested individual or group, and (2) by determining the nature of that individual's or that group's interest."*

The business entity assumption determines the nature and scope of the reporting that is required for the unit or entity. For example, where the corporation is considered as the entity, the accounting system would be designed to account only for the economic activities of the corporation and not for those of the individual stockholders. The entity for accounting purposes is identified as the economic unit that controls resources, incurs obligations, and otherwise is involved in directing economic activities which relate to a specific accountability unit. The accounting records and reports would be developed for this entity. Accounting units or entities include corporations, partnerships, proprietorships, not-for-profit entities, trusts, and others.

Accounting is based on the assumption that the accounting unit or entity is engaged in continuous and ongoing activities. The accounting unit or entity is assumed to remain in operation into the foreseeable future to achieve its goals and objectives. This assumption is referred to as the continuity or going-concern assumption. The going-concern assumption implies indefinite continuance of the accounting entity and that the business will not be liquidated within a time period required to carry out existing contractual commitments or to consume assets according to current plans. The going-concern assumption extends the boundaries of accounting beyond the limitations of liquidation values and strict legal rights and obligations. For example, the application of depreciation accounting to buildings and equipment requires the assumption that the business will operate at least as long as the estimated useful life of the assets. If evidence indicates that the entity has a limited life, modifications in accounting principles, methods, and reporting practices would ordinarily be required, for example, in cases where corporate reorganization or liquidation under bankruptcy is involved. The accountant operates on the going-concern assumption as long as there is no evidence to the contrary, as would be the case when a company is in bankruptcy.

The continuous operations of a business or other economic unit or entity over an extended period of time can be meaningfully segmented into equal time periods, such as a year, quarter, or month. The periodic and timely reporting assumption requires that accounting reporting should be done periodically and on a timely basis so that it is relevant and reliable.

The monetary unit assumption requires that financial information be measured and accounted for in the basic monetary unit of the country in which the enterprise is located (dollars for U.S. firms). The monetary value of an economic event or transaction, determined at the time it is recorded, is not adjusted for subsequent changes in the purchasing power of

A

the monetary unit (as occurs in periods of inflation or deflation).

See also Accounting theory; Conservatism; Materiality; Full disclosure; Accounting principles; Accounting period; Accounting policies; Accounting functions.

REFERENCE
Smith, Jay M., and Skousen, K. Fred, *Intermediate Accounting* (South-Western, Cincinnati, OH, 1984).

ACCOUNTING BASIS

Major bases of accounting include the accrual, cash, and modified cash basis of accounting. In accrual accounting, revenue and gains are recognized in the period when they are earned. Expenses and losses are recognized in the period they are incurred. Accrual accounting is concerned with the economic consequences of events and transactions instead of merely with cash receipts and cash payments. Under accrual accounting, net income does not necessarily reflect cash receipts and cash payments for a time period. Accrual accounting generally provides the best measure of earnings, earning power, managerial performance, and stewardship. SFAC No.1, Objectives of Financial Reporting by Business Enterprises, states that

> "...accrual accounting attempts to record the financial effects on an enterprise of transactions and other events, and circumstances for the enterprise in the periods in which those transactions, events, and circumstances occur rather than only in the periods in which cash is received or paid by the enterprise."

Cash-basis accounting recognizes only transactions involving actual cash receipts and disbursements occurring in a given period. Cash-basis accounting recognizes revenues and gains when cash is received and expenses and losses when cash is paid. No attempt is made to record unpaid bills or amounts owed to or by the entity. Cash-basis accounting is generally deficient as an accounting model that attempts to produce a statement of financial position and an income statement. However, cash-basis accounting is widely used for income tax purposes and by small businesses.

Under a modified cash basis of accounting, certain expenditures would be capitalized and amortized in the future. For example, under cash-basis accounting, the purchase of equipment for cash is expensed immediately; under a modified cash basis, the purchase is recorded as an asset. A portion of the acquisition cost is later recognized as an expense when the services of the asset are consumed.

To illustrate the difference between the accrual basis and the cash basis of accounting, assume the following data. A company is engaged in a service business. During 1990 the company billed its customers for $100,000 for services performed during 1990. These billings resulted in cash payments to the company of $80,000 in 1990 and $20,000 in 1991. The company incurred expenses of $70,000 while carrying out these services during 1990. The company paid out $40,000 in cash on these expenses during 1990 and $30,000 in 1991. No other revenue or expense transactions occurred during 1990 or 1991.

| | Accrual Basis | | Cash Basis | |
	1990	1991	1990	1991
Revenue	$100,000	– – –	$80,000	$ 20,000
Expenses	70,000	– – –	40,000	30,000
Net income (loss)	$ 30,000	– – –	$40,000	$(10,000)

Note that although the combined net income (loss) for the two years is the same, the amounts in the separate years differ. Accrual-basis accounting typically provides a better measure of net income than does cash-basis accounting.

To convert accrual-basis income to cash-basis income, certain adjustments must be made for all noncash charges and

A

credits contained in accrual-basis net income. Cash from operations can be conceptualized as follows:

> Cash from operations = Cash collected from customers − Cash paid for inventory purchases − Cash paid for expenses
>
> or
>
> Cash from operations = Net income on accrual basis + Accounting charges not requiring cash outlays − Accounting credits not providing cash

Net income from operations computed according to generally accepted accounting principles can be converted to cash flow from operations according to the following general procedures:

> Net income from operations
>
> Plus: Items reducing income but not using cash, such as depreciation, depletion, and amortization expenses
> Decreases in current assets other than cash
> Increases in current liabilities
>
> Less: Increases in current assets other than cash
> Decreases in current liabilities
>
> Equals: Cash flow from operations

See Exhibit A–2 for an illustration of how accrual-basis accounting statements can be adjusted to cash-basis statements.

See also Other comprehensive methods of accounting; Income tax accounting; Cash flow.

REFERENCE
Smith, Jay M., and Skousen, K. Fred, *Intermediate Accounting* (South-Western, Cincinnati, OH, 1984).

Exhibit A–2
Converting Net Income from Operations to Cash Flow from Operations

Net income from operations		$20,000
Add:		
Items reducing income but not using cash:		
Depreciation, building and equipment	$20,000	
Amortization, patent	10,000	30,000
Decreases in current assets other than cash:		
Accounts receivable	$15,000	
Prepaid expenses	5,000	20,000
Increases in current liabilities:		
Accounts payable	$10,000	
Accrued liabilities	5,000	15,000
Subtotal		85,000
Deduct:		
Increases in current assets other than cash:		
Inventories	$15,000	
Decreases in current liabilities:		
Wages payable	5,000	20,000
Cash flow from operations		$65,000

ACCOUNTING CHANGES

An accounting change may be a change in accounting principle, in accounting estimate, or in reporting entity. Accounting changes can significantly affect the financial statements for an accounting period, trends in comparative statements, and historical summaries as well as the confidence that financial statement users have in the statements. Consistency in the application of accounting principles and methods is assumed to enhance the usefulness and understandability of financial statements. Consistency does not imply uniformity or comparability among different independent entities (Company A and Company B) or even within a company (LIFO inventory for

Department A and FIFO for Department B). The professional judgment of the accountant or auditor must be relied on to deal with problems related to consistency and changes in accounting.

If a firm changes the way an item is measured or reported in its financial statements, the change situation should fit one of the three following types of accounting changes:

1. *Change in accounting principle.* A change from one generally accepted accounting principle to another generally accepted accounting principle: for example, a change in the method of depreciation from straight-line depreciation to double-declining method.

2. *Change in accounting estimate.* A change that results from new or additional information: for example, a change in the estimate of the useful lives of depreciable assets or a change in the estimate of uncollectible accounts receivable.

3. *Change in reporting entity.* A change from reporting as one type of entity to another type: for example, presenting consolidated or combined statements in place of statements of individual companies.

The income effect of accounting changes should generally be recognized by one of the following procedures:

1. *Retroactively.* Recognize the cumulative effect of the change in prior years' earnings as a prior-period adjustment (that is, as an adjustment of the beginning balance in retained earnings for the current year and restate prior years' financial statements accordingly). Retroactive treatment is required for several major types of accounting changes: (1) a change from LIFO inventory pricing to another method, (2) a change in the method of accounting for long-term

construction-type contracts, and (3) a change to or from the full-cost method of accounting in the extractive industries. A change in accounting entity (e.g., changing the companies included in financial statements) and the correction of errors require retroactive treatment.

2. *Currently.* Recognize the entire cumulative effect of the change in prior years' earnings as an element in calculating net income in the year of the change. Changes in accounting principles are generally treated currently (a catch-up approach).

3. *Prospectively.* Spread the cumulative effect of the change in prior years' earnings over the year of the change and a number of future years, where appropriate. Changes in accounting estimates are treated prospectively.

The *cumulative effect of an accounting change* refers to the effect of the change on assets or liabilities at the beginning of the period in which the change is made. The cumulative effect is the difference between the present carrying value of the asset or liability and what the carrying value would have been if the accounting change had been in effect in all previous periods of the asset's or liability's existence.

Errors are not accounting changes. Errors in financial statements are primarily the result of mathematical mistakes, misapplication of accounting principles, misuse or oversight of data that were available when the financial statements were prepared, and incorrect classification of accounting elements such as assets and liabilities. An error in a previously issued financial statement is treated as a prior-period adjustment. Retained earnings as of the beginning of the current period is charged or credited for the cumulative effect of the error on earnings of prior years. Financial statements of prior periods must be restated when presented in subsequent financial reports so as not to reproduce the errors that have been made.

See also Prior-period adjustments; Errors; Consistency.

REFERENCES
Nikolai, Loren A., et al., *Intermediate Accounting* (Kent, Boston, 1985).
ABB No. 20, Accounting Changes (APB, 1971).

ACCOUNTING CYCLE
The accounting cycle is a sequence of activities that records, summarizes, and reports economic events and transactions. The steps in the accounting cycle include journalizing transactions, posting to a ledger, taking a trial balance, adjusting the accounts, preparing financial statements, closing the accounts, and taking a postclosing trial balance. The accounting cycle is repeated each accounting period. The operations of the cycle can be conceptualized as shown in Exhibit A-3.

See also Accounting system; Journal; Ledger; Adjusting entries; Closing entries; Reversing entries; Financial statements; Operating cycle.

ACCOUNTING EQUATION
The accounting equation expresses the relationship that exists between assets, liabilities, and owners' equity. In its simplest form, the accounting equation can be represented as follows:

$$\text{ASSETS} - \text{LIABILITIES} = \text{OWNERS' EQUITY}$$

The accounting equation states an equality and establishes a relationship among the three major accounting elements. Owners' equity is shown as the residual of assets over liabilities. The accounting equation can be restated in this form:

$$\text{ASSETS} = \text{LIABILITIES} + \text{OWNERS' EQUITY}$$

When the accounting equation is expressed in this format, owners and creditors are shown as having claims against the

Exhibit A–3
The Accounting Process (or Cycle)

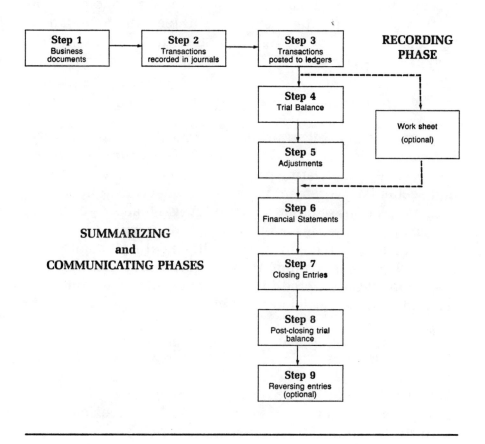

assets of the enterprise. The accounting equation can also be expressed in a format that combines liabilities and owners' equity into a single concept referred to as equities:

ASSETS = EQUITIES

See also Account; Net assets; Capital.

ACCOUNTING FUNCTIONS

Accounting deals with numbers and measurable quantities. The accounting system accumulates, measures, and communicates numbers and measurable quantities of economic information about an enterprise. These three functions can be represented as a flow of information from source to destination as follows:

Accumulation refers primarily to recording and classifying data in journals and ledgers. The accounting system accumulates data relating primarily to completed transactions and events. Measurement refers to the quantification of business transactions or other economic events that have occurred or that may occur. Measurement determines how to select the best amounts to recognize in the financial statements. The accounting system communicates relevant and reliable information to investors, creditors, managers, and others for internal and external decision making.

See also Accounting; Information; Measurement.

ACCOUNTING PERIODS

Custom as well as income tax and other legal considerations have focused on annual reporting periods and an annual accounting cycle. If the reporting period begins on January 1 and ends on December 31, this is referred to as a *calendar-year* accounting period. Any other beginning and ending period of one year is called a *fiscal-year*. The accounting period should be clearly identified on the financial statements.

In selecting an annual reporting period, some entities adopt a reporting period that ends when operations are at a low point in order to simplify year-end accounting procedures and permit more rapid preparation of financial statements. At such a date, inventories and accounts receivable will normally be at their lowest point. Such an accounting period is referred to as a *natural business year* since it conforms to the natural annual cycle of the entity.

Some firms use a 52-53-week accounting period for reporting purposes. The yearly reporting period varies from 52 to 53 weeks since it always ends on the same day of the week (e.g., the last Friday of the year), either the last one of such days in a calendar month or the closest one to the last day of a calendar month.

Financial reports for periods shorter than one year, such as quarterly reports, are referred to as *interim reports* or *interim statements*.

For income tax purposes, the accounting period is usually a year. Unless a fiscal year is chosen, taxpayers must determine their tax liability by using the calendar year as the period of measurement. A change in accounting period requires the approval of the IRS.

See also Accounting cycle; Accounting assumptions; Financial statements; Interim financial reports.

ACCOUNTING POLICIES
The accounting policies of a reporting entity are the specific accounting principles and the methods of applying those principles that are judged by the management of the enterprise to be the most appropriate in the circumstances to fairly present financial position, changes in financial position, and results of operations in accordance with generally accepted accounting principles, and that have been adopted for preparing the financial statements. Information about the accounting policies adopted by a reporting enterprise is essential for financial statement users and should be disclosed. Accounting principles and their methods of application in the following areas are considered particularly important:

1. A selection from existing alternatives.

2. Areas that are peculiar to a particular industry in which the company operates.

3. Unusual and innovative applications of generally accepted accounting principles.

Examples of disclosures by a business enterprise commonly required include those relating to depreciation methods, inventory pricing, basis of consolidations, and recognition of profit on long-term, construction-type contracts.

The preferable place to disclose accounting policies is under the caption Summary of Significant Accounting Policies or as the initial note to the financial statements.

See also Accounting principles; Accounting procedures; Notes to financial statements.

REFERENCES
Kelly-Newton, Lauren, *Accounting Policy Formulation* (Addison-Wesley, Reading, MA, 1980).
APB No. 22, Disclosure of Accounting Policies (APB, 1972).

ACCOUNTING PRINCIPLES
Accounting principles are the guidelines, laws, or rules which are adopted by the accounting profession and which serve as guides to accounting practice. Accounting principles include the accounting and reporting assumptions, standards, and practices that a company must use in preparing external financial statements. An objective of GAAP is to reduce the differences and inconsistencies in accounting practice, thereby improving the comparability and credibility of financial reports.

The phrase "generally accepted accounting principles," or GAAP, is a technical term that identifies the conventions, rules, and procedures that represent accepted accounting practice at a particular period of time. GAAP reflect a consensus of what the professional considers good accounting practices and procedures. GAAP are prescribed by authoritative bodies, such as the Financial Accounting Standards Board. The term "principle" does not imply a rule or law from which there can be no deviation or exception. The application of generally accepted accounting principles typically requires the professional judgment of the accountant. Accounting principles are understood to have application primarily to material and significant items. Items with little or no consequence can usually be dealt with on a basis of expediency or practicality. The Accounting Principles Board stated that

"Generally accepted accounting principles incorporate the consensus at a particular time as to which economic resources and obligations should be recorded as assets and liabilities... which changes in assets and liabilities should be recorded, when these changes should be recorded, how the recorded assets and liabilities and changes in them should be measured, what information should be disclosed, and which financial statements should be prepared."

Sources of generally accepted accounting principles include:

1. Pronouncements of the Financial Accounting Standards Board (FASB) and its predecessors, the Accounting Principles Board (APB) and the Committee on Accounting Procedures (CAP). These pronouncements include FASB statements of Standards and Interpretations, APB Opinions, and American Institute of Certified Public Accountants Accounting Research Bulletins (ARB).

2. FASB Technical Bulletins and AICPA's Interpretations, Audit Guides, Accounting Guides, and Statements of Position.

3. General accounting practice.

4. Securities and Exchange Commission regulations.

5. Internal Revenue Service regulations.

6. Accounting literature.

Levels of authority of sources of accounting principles are determined according to the following hierarchy:

1. Pronouncements of authoritative bodies specified by Rule 203 of the AICPA Code of Professional Ethics. These include FASB Standards and Interpretations, APB Opinions, and CAP Accounting Research Bulletins.

2. Pronouncements of bodies composed of expert accountants that follow a due process procedure. These include AICPA Industry Audit Guides and Accounting Guides and Statements of Position.

3. Pronouncements, or practices, that represent prevalent practice or application to specific circumstances of generally accepted pronouncements. These include FASB Technical Bulletins, AICPA Interpretations, and industry practices.

4. Other accounting literature. These include APB Statements, AICPA Issues Papers, FASB Concept Statements, pronouncements of other professional associations or regulatory agencies, and textbooks and journal articles.

When applying the scheme, work down from the top of the classification described in the preceding paragraph until an answer is found. Where an inconsistency between categories exists, it is recommended that the rule suggested by the higher level of authoritative literature shall prevail. In cases of a conflict between sources within a category, attempt to establish which treatment better presents the substance of the transaction given the specific circumstances.

See also Generally accepted accounting principles; Accounting theory; Accounting assumptions; Accounting functions; Financial reporting; Financial accounting; Accounting; Financial Accounting Standards Board; Statements of financial accounting standards; Conceptual framework of accounting; Statements of financial accounting concepts; Accounting policies; Accounting procedures; Accounting principles overload; Audit; Full disclosure; Materiality; Consistency; Substance over form; Personal financial statements; Development stage companies; Economic consequences of accounting; Economic environment of accounting.

REFERENCES
Committee to Prepare a Statement of Basic Accounting Theory, A Statement of Basic Accounting Theory (AAA, Evanston, IL, 1966).
Grady, Paul, *Inventory of Generally Accepted Accounting Principles for Business Enterprises* (AICPA, 1965).
Meddaugh, E. James, *Guide to Professional Accounting Standards* (Prentice-Hall, Englewood Cliffs, N.J., 1983).

ACCOUNTING PROCEDURES

Accounting procedures are those rules and practices that are associated with the operations of an accounting system and lead to the development of financial statements. Accounting procedures include the methods, practices, and techniques used to carry out accounting objectives and to implement accounting principles. For example, LIFO, FIFO, and other inventory methods are accounting procedures, as are various depreciation methods such as straight-line depreciation and accelerated depreciation. An accounting convention is an accounting procedure which does not have official approval by an authoritative body such as the Financial Accounting Standards Board.

Accounting procedures can vary from company to company and from industry to industry. An accounting procedure should be selected in a given circumstance if its use reflects generally accepted accounting principles and if it is appropriate to record, process, and report the event or transaction.

See also Accounting principles; Accounting theory; Accounting policies; Accounting system.

ACCOUNTING PROFESSION

A profession is an association of individuals engaged in a vocation or occupation that generally is expected to meet the following criteria:

1. It renders essential service to society.
2. It depends upon a body of specialized knowledge acquired through formal education.
3. It has developed a language of its own.
4. It has requirements for admission to the profession which are regulated by law.
5. Its members are governed by ethical principles which emphasize the virtues of honesty, probity, and devotion to the welfare of those served.
6. It has procedures for disciplining those whose conduct violates ethical standards.

The accounting profession is typically subdivided into public accountants who function as independent experts and perform services for clients and internal accountants who work for a particular entity. The profession can be further subdivided as follows:

Public Accountant	Internal Accounting
External auditor	Financial or general accountant
Tax specialist	Cost accountant
Management consultant	Internal auditor
	Tax accountant
	Systems analyst

A certified public accountant (CPA) is an accountant who has fulfilled certain requirements established by a state law for the practice of public accounting and becomes licensed to practice public accounting in that state. To become a CPA, an accountant must pass a comprehensive examination in accounting theory, practice, auditing, and law. In addition to the CPA examination, other professional examinations have been developed to test the competency level of practitioners. These examinations include the Certificate in Management Accounting (CMA) and the Certified Internal Auditor (CIA).

See also Certified public accountant; Accounting associations; Financial Accounting Standards Board; Audit; Controller; Peer Review.

REFERENCES
Most, Kenneth S., *Accounting Theory* (Grid, Columbus, OH, 1977).
Previts, Gary John, *The Scope of CPA Services* (John Wiley & Sons, N.Y., 1985).
Carey, John L., *Getting Acquainted with Accounting* (Houghton Mifflin, Boston, 1973).

ACCOUNTING STANDARDS OVERLOAD
Many accounting practitioners have criticized generally accepted accounting principles (GAAP) as being too detailed, complex, cumbersome, and impractical for small or closely held businesses. This is sometimes referred to as an "accounting standards overload." Specific criticisms related to the overload include:

1. The existence of too many accounting standards.

2. Accounting standards inundated with detail.

3. Failure of accounting standards to provide for differences in the needs of accountants, preparers, and users of financial information.

4. Failure to provide for differences between:
   — Public and nonpublic companies.
   — Annual and interim financial statements.
   — Large and small enterprises.
   — Audited and unaudited financial statements.

5. An excessive amount of disclosures required for financial statement presentations.

6. Complex measurement requirements of GAAP.

Accounting and disclosure requirements related to the following specific items are considered by many parties not to apply to private companies or do not sufficiently benefit the users of private companies' financial statements to justify their costs and are examples of accounting standards overload:

Deferred income taxes
Leases
Capitalization of interest
Imputed interest
Compensated absences
Troubled debt restructurings
Tax benefits of operating loss carryforward
Investment tax credit

Many recommendations have been forthcoming concerning how to deal with the overload problem. No major resolution of this issue is currently foreseeable.

See also Accounting principles; Generally accepted accounting principles; Financial Accounting Standards Board; Economic consequences of accounting; Materiality; Efficient market hypothesis.

REFERENCE
Accounting Standards Division, Generally Accepted Accounting Principles for Smaller and/or Closely Held Businesses (AICPA, 1976).

ACCOUNTING SYSTEM

An accounting system is a management information system within an organization which is responsible for the collection and processing of data to produce information which is useful to decision makers in planning and controlling the activities of the organization. The accounting system deals primarily with one category of information, that is, financial information which concerns the flow of financial resources through the organization.

The data processing cycle of an accounting system can be conceptualized as the total structure of records and procedures that are associated with five activities: collection or recording, classifying, processing, including calculating and summarizing, maintenance or storage, and output or reporting. The processing of data in a typical accounting system can be illustrated as follows:

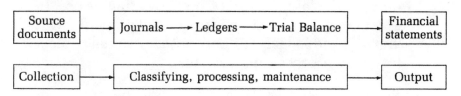

The development of an accounting information system includes these stages: analysis, design, implementation, and operation. During the system analysis stage, the analyst determines the information needs of the system, sources of information, and the strengths and deficiencies of the current system. The design stage typically involves an evaluation of different kinds of data processing equipment, processing methods, and procedures which are suitable to the proposed project. During this stage the detailed system design is completed. After the system is designed, the implemetation of the system can commence. During this stage, the system is installed and made ready to begin functioning. After the system has been implemented, it becomes operational. Modifications of the system may be required as problems arise or as new needs develop.

The essential functions of any information system include:

1. *Collection of data.* Data must be collected through a selection process involving observations, measurements, and recording. In an accounting information system, this is done primarily through the use of business documents, including sales invoices, purchase orders, payroll documents, and many other forms.

2. *Information representation.* The data being collected must be described and assigned a measurement number. In accounting, this is accomplished primarily in monetary units, e.g,. the U.S. dollar.

3. *Storage (memory).* The acquired data must be organized, classified, and stored awaiting its use. In accounting, this function is performed primarily with journals and ledgers utilizing either manual or electronic data processing systems.

4. *Search procedures.* Data stored must be capable of being retrieved through an organized search process. The search process produces an intermediate output for the system. In accounting, this is accomplished primarily with a trial balance and worksheet procedures.

5. *Dissemination (or transmission).* The final output selected by the search process must be transmitted, distributed, or displayed in an organized physical form so that it can be made available to decision makers. Much financial reporting is disseminated through financial statements and reports.

See also Accounting cycle; Accounting; Controller; Financial reporting; Electronic data processing; Voucher system.

REFERENCES
Cushing, Barry E., *Accounting Information Systems and Business Organizations* (Addison-Wesley, Reading, MA, 1978).
Moscove, Stephen A., and Simkin, Mark G., *Accounting Information Systems* (John Wiley & Sons, N.Y., 1984).

ACCOUNTING THEORY

Theory is a systematic statement of principles which serve as a foundation and explanation for underlying phenomena. In general, theory should provide an explanation, a basis for predicting outcomes or results, and guidance for practice. Accounting theory consists of a systematic statement of accounting principles and methodology. Accounting theory is both positive and normative. Positive theory explains what is (descriptive); normative theory describes what ought to be. Accounting theory has also been developed using either a deductive or an inductive approach. The deductive approach involves reasoning from the general to the particular; the inductive approach involves reasoning from the particular to the general. No generally recognized, comprehensive theory of accounting exists at the present time.

The objective of accounting theory is to establish a framework or reference point to guide and evaluate accounting practice. Accounting theory also provides a basis for inherent logic, consistency, and usefulness of accounting principles and procedures. Much of accounting theory has developed over the years through the process of general acceptance by accountants, regulatory agencies, and users of financial statements. Some accounting theories have gained acceptability based on their predictive qualities. The predictive approach to the development of accounting theory relies heavily on statistical procedures and analysis. Accounting theory plays a major role in the standard-setting process which develops generally accepted accounting principles.

A committee of the American Accounting Association defined "theory" in A Statement of Basic Accounting Theory (ASOBAT) as "...a cohesive set of hypothetical, conceptual and pragmatic principles forming a general frame of reference for a field of study." The committee applied this definition to accounting and assigned itself the following tasks:

1. To identify the field of accounting in order to develop a coherent theory of accounting.

2. To establish standards for accounting information.

3. To suggest ways to improve accounting practice.

4. To develop a framework for accounting research.

Accounting theory currently consists of assumptions, concepts or elements, principles, and modifying conventions used in the preparation of financial statements. Here is a general outline of these factors:

Basic assumptions:
    Economic (or accounting) entity
    Going concern
    Monetary measurement
    Periodicity
Basic concepts or elements:
    Assets, liabilities, equities
    Revenue, gain, expense, loss, comprehensive income
    Investment by owners, distribution to owners
Broad principles:
    Historical (or acquisition) cost
    Revenue realization
    Revenue recognition
    Matching costs and revenues
    Accrual accounting
    Consistency
    Adequate (or full) disclosure
    Objectivity
    Articulated (or interrelated) financial statements
Modifying conventions:
    Materiality
    Conservatism
    Industry practices

Accounting procedures refer to specific methods of applying accounting theory in practice. These include: first-in, first-out, last-in, first-out, and other cost flow assumptions for inventories; completed contract and percentage-of-completion methods of income recognition for long-term construction-type contracts; and purchase and pooling-of-interest methods of accounting for business combinations.

See also Accounting assumptions; Accounting principles; Generally accepted accounting principles; Financial Accounting Standards Board; Conceptual framework of accounting; Elements of financial statements of business enterprises; Realization; Recognition; Matching costs and revenues; Measurement; Full disclosure; Materiality; Conservatism; Accounting basis; Consistency; Objectivity; Agency theory.

REFERENCES
American Accounting Association, Statement on Accounting Theory and Theory Acceptance (AAA, 1977).
American Accounting Association, Accounting and Reporting Standards for Corporate Financial Statements and Preceding Statements and Supplements (AAA, 1957).
American Accounting Association, A Statement of Basic Accounting Theory (AAA, 1966).
American Institute of Certified Public Accountants, The Basic Postulates of Accounting, Accounting Research Study No. 1 (AICPA, 1961).
American Institute of Certified Public Accountants, Basic Concepts and Accounting Principles Underlying Financial Statements of Business Enterprises, APB Statement No. 4 (AICPA, 1970).
American Institute of Certified Public Accountants, A Tentative Set of Broad Accounting Principles for Business Enterprises, Accounting Research Study No. 3 (AICPA, 1962).
American Institute of Certified Public Accountants, Inventory of Generally Accepted Accounting Principles for Business Enterprises, Accounting Research Study No. 7 (AICPA, 1965).
Belkaoui, Ahmed, Accounting Theory (Harcourt Brace Jovanovich, San Diego, CA, 1985).
Bird, Francis A., Accounting Theory (Robert F. Dame, Houston, TX, 1981).
Most, Kenneth S., Accounting Theory (Grid, Columbus, OH, 1977).

A

Paton, W. A., *Accounting Theory* (Ronald Press, N.Y., 1922).
Wolk, Harry I.; Francis, Jere R.; Tearney, Michael G., *Accounting Theory: A Conceptual and Institutional Approach* (Kent, Boston, 1984).

ADJUSTING ENTRIES

Toward the close of an accounting period, after all external transactions and events have been recorded in the accounts, additional internal changes in assets and liabilities and the offsetting changes in revenue and expense items may have to be recorded so that the financial statements properly include the correct amounts for the current accounting period. These entries are called adjusting entries. Adjusting entries are usually required to adjust certain accounts so that all revenues/gains and expenses/losses and balance sheet items have correct ending balances. Adjusting entries fall into one of the following categories:

1. Apportionment of prepaid and unearned items.

    a. Prepaid expense. A prepaid expense is an expense paid in advance. A prepaid expense (or prepaid asset) represents goods or services purchased by the company for use in operations but which are not completely consumed or used as of the end of the accounting period. Prepaid expenses consist of such items as prepaid rent, insurance, and supplies. The portion of such expenditures that is not consumed in the current period, and hence will benefit a future period(s), is called a prepaid expense.

    b. Unearned revenue. Unearned revenue is revenue received from a customer prior to the delivery of a product or performance of a service. When such revenue is received in advance, the company has an obligation to deliver the product or perform the service. When the product or service has been provided, the unearned revenue is eliminated and revenue is recognized as being earned. Examples of unearned revenue include unearned rent and interest.

2. Recording accrued expenses (or liabilities) and accrued revenue (or receivables). An accrued expense is an expense that has been incurred during the accounting period but one which has not been paid or recognized in the accounts. Accrued expenses include such items as accrued salaries, interest, rent, and taxes. Accrued revenue is revenue for which the service has been performed but which has not been received or recorded in the accounts. Accrued revenues include such items as accrued interest, rent, royalties, and fees.

3. Items which must be estimated.

   a. Depreciation, amortization, and depletion. The cost of certain assets, such as machines, buildings, office fixtures, patents, goodwill, and natural resources (oil and gas reserves), must be systematically and rationally allocated as an expense to an appropriate accounting period. This cost allocation is referred to as depreciation, depletion, or amortization.

   b. Bad debt expense. When sales are made on credit, some of the accounts will undoubtedly turn out to be uncollectible. An adjustment is usually required to account for the fact that the accounts receivable are probably overstated and that a bad debt expense should be reported on the income statement to match revenue and expenses.

   c. Inventory adjustments. When the periodic inventory method is used, the inventory account at the end of the year contains the beginning-of-the-year inventory amount. The inventory account must be adjusted to show the cost of the merchandise on hand at the end of the period and to record the cost of goods sold during the period.

To summarize, unearned (or deferred) revenue involves the receipt of cash before the revenue is recognized; prepaid (or deferred) expense involves the payment of cash before the expense is recognized. An accrued revenue is a revenue recognized before related cash is received; an accrued expense is an expense recognized before it is paid.

See also Accounting cycle; Closing entries; Reversing entries; Allocation; Deferred charge (credit).

AGENCY THEORY
Agency theory is a branch of economics and law relating to the relationship of principals (such as owners) and their agents (such as managers, auditors), especially as it relates to the responsibilities and authority assigned by the principal to the agent. Agency theory is concerned with the contractual relationships that exist among parties such as management, owners, auditors, creditors, and government. Agency theory is used to predict and explain the behavior of persons or groups involved with the firm. The firm is viewed as the intersection of agency relationships. Organizational behavior can be understood and interpreted in terms of the effects of agents and principals relationships. One study of agency theory as it relates to accounting indicated that a company's management attempts to maximize its own welfare by minimizing agency costs. If managers' compensation is related to reported income, managers are inclined to select an accounting principle or method which maximizes net income, especially if they anticipate no negative political side effects such as antitrust action. Agency theory offers a promising research orientation for accounting theory and practice.

See also Accounting theory; Economic consequences of accounting.

REFERENCE
Wolk, Harry I. et al., *Accounting Theory* (Kent, Boston, 1984).

AGING SCHEDULE

An aging schedule includes a breakdown of each account receivable by the length of time passed between the date of sale and the balance sheet date. The schedule is prepared primarily for the purpose of estimating the amount of uncollectible accounts receivable as of a specific date and testing the validity of the receivables. Most audit tests of accounts receivable and the allowance for uncollectible accounts are based on the aging schedule (or the aged trial balance). The auditor needs to know whether the accounts receivable in the aging schedule agree with related subsidiary ledger accounts and whether the total is correctly added and agrees with the general ledger. The auditor would also want to determine whether the accounts receivable in the schedule are valid, owned by the company, properly valued, and properly classified in the financial statements. Exhibit A–4 shows a typical aging schedule for accounts receivable.

Exhibit A–4
Aging Schedule for Accounts Receivable

Customer	Balance	Amount Not Due	Number of Days Past Due			
			1–30	31–60	61–90	Over 90
X Co.	2,800	1,300			1,500	
Y Co.	1,800	1,800				
Z Co.	500	400	100			
Others	498,500	450,000	20,000	15,000	8,500	5,000
Totals Dec. 31, 1995	503,600	453,500	20,100	15,000	10,000	5,000

See also Receivables.

ALLOCATION

Allocation is generally considered to be the accounting process of assigning or distributing an amount according to a plan or a formula. Allocation problems arise in many situations which involve accounting, including:

1. reducing an amount by periodic payments or write-downs:

    a. reducing a liability which arose as a result of a cash receipt by recognizing revenue, e.g., unearned rent;

    b. reducing an asset, e.g., depreciation, depletion, amortization, including amortization of prepayments and deferrals;

2. assigning manufacturing costs to production departments or cost centers and subsequently to units of product to determine "product cost;" and

3. apportioning the cost of a "lump-sum" or "basket" purchase to individual assets on the basis of their relative market values.

Currently, accountants recognize that within the existing framework of conventional accounting principles and methods, allocations are generally arbitrary. Current allocation theory and practice attempt to allocate portions of the costs of non-monetary inputs in relation to benefits received from them by the enterprise. In this context, benefits involve an increase in the entity's income (or decrease in losses) or are related to cash flows. The generally recognized minimum criteria of any allocation method are:

1. The method should be unambiguous.

2. The method should be defendable, i.e., theoretically justifiable.

3. The method should divide up what is available to be allocated, i.e., the allocation should be additive.

The allocation problem in accounting is related to the matching process that assigns the costs of monetary and non-monetary inputs, such as plant assets and inventories, and revenues, to accounting periods for purposes of determining net income. The objective of this form of allocation is to systematically spread a cost or revenue over two or more time periods. For example, depreciation accounting is a system which allocates the cost of a tangible fixed asset over its estimated useful life.

The allocation of common costs to products or departments is another significant cost allocation problem. Common costs are those costs which are not directly identifiable with a product, process, or department but which result from the joint use of a facility. For example, the cafeteria of a manufacturing plant is used by employees from the manufacturing departments and office department. Some practical way must be found to allocate the cafeteria costs to the various departments (e.g., the number of employees in a department). Common cost allocations are made primarily for product-costing purposes (e.g., inventory valuation). Common cost allocations are frequently arbitrary in nature.

The common cost allocation process involves (1) accumulating costs, (2) identifying the department or process that is to be allocated the costs, and (3) selecting a basis for allocating the common costs to the recipients. Selecting a basis of allocation is often done by examining the past behavior of the cost to determine whether a relation between the costs and an allocation base (e.g., number of employees, square footage) can be identified. In some cases, it is possible to evaluate operations to find a logical relation between costs and an allocation base. If these attempts are not productive, then costs would be assigned on an arbitrary base. The following is a relatively simple illustration involving two service departments (cafeteria and personnel) and two manufacturing departments (Departments A and B).

Cost	Allocation Base	Service		Manufacturing		Total
		Cafeteria	Personnel	Dept A	Dept B	
Direct cost	Direct	$10,000	$5,000	$50,000	$75,000	$140,000
Indirect:						
Rent	Sq. foot	2,000	1,000	10,000	15,000	28,000
Utilities	Sq. foot	4,000	2,000	20,000	30.000	56,000
Totals		$16,000	$8,000	$80,000	$120,000	$224,000
Allocation of service depts.:						
Cafeteria	No. of employees	$(16,000)	$ 2,000	$ 7,000	$ 7,000	– – –
Personnel	No. of employees		(10,000)	5,000	5,000	– – –
Totals				$92,000	$132,000	$224,000

Note that costs that can be directly associated with departments are allocated first, e.g., the direct costs. Costs such as rent and utilities are allocated on a rational basis (for example, floor space). Next, service department costs are allocated to manufacturing departments. When service departments service other service departments as well as production departments, their costs are usually allocated first. In the illustration, it was decided to first allocate the cafeteria costs to the personnel department and the two manufacturing departments. After a service department's costs have been distributed, no additional costs are allocated to it. The company now knows the costs allocated to the two manufacturing departments. If more than one product comes from the production process, the costs incurred prior to the split-off point of separable products are referred to as *joint costs*. Joint costs are usually allocated to the separable products based on their relative sales value or some physical measure (for example, pounds of beef, board feet of lumber).

The allocation problem also arises when dissimilar assets are acquired for a single lump-sum price. The purchase price must be allocated to the individual assets purchased. The basis for the allocation of the purchase price in lump-sum or "basket" purchases is usually considered to be the relative fair market values of the individual assets. To illustrate a lump-sum acquisition, assume that land and building are acquired for $1,000,000. The fair market values of the land and building are $250,000 and $1,000,000, respectively. The lump-sum purchase price would be allocated to the two assets as follows:

	Appraisal value	Relative fair market value	× Total cost	=	Allocated cost
Land	$ 250,000	$250,000/$1,250,000 × $1,000,000	=		$ 200,000
Building	1,000,000	$1,000,000/$1,250,000 × $1,000,000	=		800,000
	$1,250,000				$1,000,000

See also Adjusting entries; Cost accounting; Depreciation; Amortization; Joint products; Income tax allocation.

REFERENCE
Thomas, Arthur L., *The Allocation Problem* (AAA, 1969).

AMORTIZATION
Amortization is the accounting or financial process of reducing an amount by periodic payments or write-downs. Amortization refers to the liquidation, writing off, or extinguishing of a debt over a period of time and to the write-off of a portion of the book value of an asset. The periodic retirement of a debt, such as a mortgage of serial bonds, and the periodic write-down of a bond premium are examples of amortization. The write-down of the book value of intangible assets, such as copyrights and patents, also is referred to as amortization.

See also Allocation; Depreciation; Bonds; Intangible assets.

ANNUITY
An annuity is a series of equal cash flows (payments or receipts) occurring at equal intervals over a period of time. The equal cash flows are called rents. Annuities can be classified as an ordinary annuity (or an annuity in arrears) or an annuity due

(or an annuity in advance). If the first payment occurs at the end of the first interest period, the annuity is called an ordinary annuity. If the first payment occurs at the beginning of the first period, the annuity is called an annuity due. The difference between an ordinary annuity and an annuity due of four rents (receipts or payments) is illustrated in Exhibit A–5, where 0 is the current date. Each cash flow or rent is indicated by an R.

Exhibit A–5
Ordinary Annuity and Annuity Due Illustrated

Ordinary Annuity

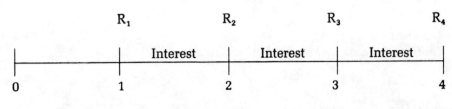

Periods

Annuity Due

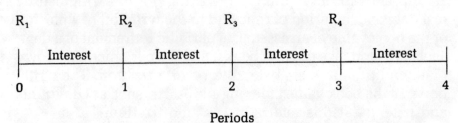

Periods

R = Periodic rents

The amount, or future value, of an ordinary annuity is the total amount on deposit immediately after the last rent in the series is made. The amount of an annuity due is determined one period after the last rent in the series. The present value of an annuity is the present value of a series of equal rents made in the future. If the present value of the series of cash flows or rents is determined one period before the receipt or payment of the first rent, the series of rents is known as the present value of an ordinary annuity. The present value of an annuity due is determined on the date of payment of the first rent. A deferred annuity is an annuity that does not start to produce rents until two or more periods have passed. A perpetuity is an annuity that continues indefinitely. Formulas for the future value and present value of an ordinary annuity are shown in Exhibit A–6. In the formulas, i = interest rate and n = number of rents. Examples of annuity tables for the future value and the present value of an ordinary annuity are shown in Exhibits A–7 and A–7a.

REFERENCE
Woelfel, Charles, J., *Financial Managers Desktop Reference to Money, Time, Interest and Yield* (Probus, Chicago, 1986).

ANTITRUST LEGISLATION
The Sherman Antitrust Act of 1890 was the first major legislation in the area of antitrust. This act was a response to firms that sought to lessen competition through such practices as price agreements, dividing up shares of the market, and the creation of trusts to dominate the market. The main provisions of the act were the following:

1. "Section 1. *Every contract, combination in the form of trust or otherwise, or conspiracy in restraint of trade or commerce among the several states, or with foreign nations is hereby declared to be illegal. . . .*"

2. "Section 2. *Every person who shall monopolize, or combine or conspire with any other person or persons, to monopolize any part of the trade or commerce among several states or with foreign nations shall be deemed guilty. . . .*"

A

Exhibit A–6
Future Value and Present Value of an Ordinary Annuity Illustrated

Future Value of an Ordinary Annuity

Formula:

$$FV = R \left[\frac{(1 + i)^n - 1}{i} \right]$$

Where FV = future value (or amount) of an ordinary annuity of a series of
          rents of any amount
      R = value of each rent
      n = number of rents
      i = compound interest rate

Example 1. Compute the future amount of 4 rents of $1,000 with interest compounded annually at 14%. The first rent occurs on December 31, 1996, and the last rent occurs on December 31, 1999.

$$FV = \$1,000 \left[\frac{(1.14)^4 - 1}{0.14} \right]$$

$$= \$1,000(4.92114)$$
$$= \$4,921.14$$

Present Value of an Ordinary Annuity

Formula:

$$PV = R \left[\frac{1 - \dfrac{1}{(1 + i)^n}}{i} \right]$$

Where PV = present value of an ordinary annuity of a series of rents
      R = value of each rent
      n = number of rents
      i = compound discount

Example 2. Use the same data in Example 1 to compute the present value of an ordinary annuity.

$$PV = \$1,000 \left[\frac{1 - \dfrac{1}{(1.14)^4}}{0.14} \right]$$

$$= \$1,000(2.91371)$$
$$= \$2,913.71$$

The Tables in Exhibit A–7 could be used to get the factors (4.92114 and 2.91371) used in Examples 1 and 2.

Exhibit A-7

Future Amount of an Ordinary Annuity of $1: F_0 = \dfrac{(1+i)^n - 1}{i}$

n	8.0%	9.0%	10.0%	12.0%	14.0%	16.0%	18.0%
1	1.000000	1.000000	1.000000	1.000000	1.000000	1.000000	1.000000
2	2.080000	2.090000	2.100000	2.120000	2.140000	2.160000	2.180000
3	3.246400	3.278100	3.310000	3.374400	3.439600	3.505600	3.572400
4	4.506112	4.573129	4.641000	4.779328	4.921144	5.066496	5.215432
5	5.866601	5.984711	6.105100	6.352847	6.610104	6.877135	7.154210
6	7.335929	7.523335	7.715610	8.115189	8.535519	8.977477	9.441968
7	8.922803	9.200435	9.487171	10.089012	10.730491	11.413873	12.141522
8	10.636628	11.028474	11.435888	12.299693	13.232760	14.240093	15.326996
9	12.487558	13.021036	13.579477	14.775656	16.085347	17.518508	19.085855
10	14.486562	15.192930	15.937425	17.548735	19.337295	21.321469	23.521309
11	16.645487	17.560293	18.531167	20.654583	23.044516	25.732904	28.755144
12	18.977126	20.140720	21.384284	24.133133	27.270749	30.850169	34.931070
13	21.495297	22.953385	24.522712	28.029109	32.088654	36.786196	42.218663
14	24.214920	26.019189	27.974983	32.392602	37.581065	43.671987	50.818022
15	27.152114	29.360916	31.772482	37.279715	43.842414	51.659505	60.965266
16	30.324283	33.003399	35.949730	42.753280	50.980352	60.925026	72.939014
17	33.750226	36.973705	40.544703	48.883674	59.117601	71.673030	87.068036
18	37.450244	41.301338	45.599173	55.749715	68.394066	84.140715	103.740283
19	41.446263	46.018458	51.159090	63.439681	78.969235	98.603230	123.413534
20	45.761964	51.160120	57.274999	72.052442	91.024928	115.379747	146.627970
21	50.422921	56.764530	64.002499	81.698736	104.768418	134.840506	174.021005
22	55.456755	62.873338	71.402749	92.502584	120.435996	157.414987	206.344785
23	60.893296	69.531939	79.543024	104.602894	138.297035	183.601385	244.486847
24	66.764759	76.789813	88.497327	118.155241	158.658620	213.977607	289.494479
25	73.105940	84.700896	98.347059	133.333870	181.870827	249.214024	342.603486
26	79.954415	93.323977	109.181765	150.333934	208.332743	290.088267	405.272113
27	87.350768	102.723135	121.099942	169.374007	238.499327	337.502390	479.221093
28	95.338830	112.968217	134.209936	190.698687	272.889233	392.502773	566.480890
29	103.965936	124.135356	148.630930	214.582754	312.093725	456.303216	669.447450
30	113.283211	136.307539	164.494023	241.332684	356.786847	530.311731	790.947991

Exhibit A-7a
Present Value of an Ordinary Annuity of 1: $P_0 = \dfrac{1 - \dfrac{1}{(1+i)^n}}{i}$

n	8.0%	9.0%	10.0%	12.0%	14.0%	16.0%	18.0%
1	0.925926	0.917431	0.909091	0.892857	0.877193	0.862069	0.847458
2	1.783265	1.759111	1.735537	1.690051	1.646661	1.605232	1.565642
3	2.577097	2.531295	2.486852	2.401831	2.321632	2.245890	2.174273
4	3.312127	3.239720	3.169865	3.037349	2.913712	2.798181	2.690062
5	3.992710	3.889651	3.790787	3.604776	3.433081	3.274294	3.127171
6	4.622880	4.485919	4.355261	4.111407	3.880668	3.684736	3.497603
7	5.206370	5.032953	4.868419	4.563757	4.288305	4.038565	3.811528
8	5.746639	5.534819	5.334926	4.967640	4.638864	4.343591	4.077566
9	6.246888	5.995247	5.759024	5.328250	4.946372	4.606544	4.303022
10	6.710081	6.417658	6.144567	5.650223	5.216116	4.833227	4.494086
11	7.138964	6.805191	6.495061	5.937699	5.452733	5.028644	4.656005
12	7.536078	7.160725	6.813692	6.194374	5.660292	5.197107	4.793225
13	7.903776	7.486904	7.103356	6.423548	5.842362	5.342334	4.909513
14	8.244237	7.786150	7.366687	6.628168	6.002072	5.467529	5.008062
15	8.559479	8.060688	7.606080	6.810864	6.142168	5.575456	5.091578
16	8.851369	8.312558	7.823709	6.973986	6.265060	5.668497	5.162354
17	9.121638	8.543631	8.021553	7.119630	6.372859	5.748704	5.222334
18	9.371887	8.755625	8.201412	7.249670	6.467420	5.817848	5.273164
19	9.603599	8.950115	8.364920	7.365777	6.550369	5.877455	5.316241
20	9.818147	9.128546	8.513564	7.469444	6.623131	5.928841	5.352746
21	10.016803	9.292244	8.648694	7.562003	6.686957	5.973139	5.383683
22	10.200744	9.442425	8.771540	7.644646	6.742944	6.011326	5.409901
23	10.371059	9.580207	8.883218	7.718434	6.792056	6.044247	5.432120
24	10.528758	9.706612	8.984744	7.784316	6.835137	6.072627	5.450949
25	10.674776	9.822580	9.077040	7.843139	6.872927	6.097092	5.466906
26	10.809978	9.928972	9.160945	7.895660	6.906077	6.118183	5.480429
27	10.935165	10.026580	9.237223	7.942554	6.935155	6.136364	5.491889
28	11.051078	10.116128	9.306567	7.984423	6.960662	6.152038	5.501601
29	11.158406	10.198283	9.369606	8.021806	6.983037	6.165550	5.509831
30	11.257783	10.2737	9.426914	8.055184	7.002664	6.177198	5.516806

The Federal Trade Commission Act (1914) declared that "unfair methods of competition" were unlawful. The FTC attempts to deal with unfair methods of competition and unfair or deceptive acts or practices, such as exclusive dealing, tie-in sales, reciprocity, and mergers. The FTC also serves as a consumer protection agency by preventing deceptive claims and other practices.

The Clayton Act (1914) was enacted to curb additional types of restraint in trade not covered by the Sherman Act. It prohibited such practices as price discriminating between different purchasers, the acquisition of stock of another corporation if the effect is to substantially lessen competition, and interlocking directorates.

The Robinson-Patman Act (1936) was passed for the purpose of expanding the original prohibition against price discrimination contained in the Clayton Act. This act makes it unlawful for any person engaged in interstate commerce to discriminate in price between purchasers of commodities of like grade, quality, and quantity. It also prohibits the paying or receiving of brokerage commissions, discounts, or rebates to customers which result in price discrimination.

The Consumer Credit Protection Act of 1968 (truth-in-lending act) was enacted to protect consumers by requiring full disclosure of the terms and conditions associated with finance charges in credit transactions and in offers to extend credit.

See also Free enterprise system.

REFERENCE
Hailstones, Thomas J., *Basic Economics* (Smith-Western, Cincinnati, OH, 1984).

ARM'S-LENGTH TRANSACTION
An arm's-length transaction is one in which buyer and seller both seek his/her own best interests and are free to act accordingly. Transactions between related parties and affiliated com-

panies are often not arm's-length transactions. In dealings between related parties, the question that should be asked is: Would unrelated parties have handled the transaction in the same way? When assets are acquired at a cost, it is assumed that each acquisition results from an arm's-length market transaction by two independent parties who are presumed to be acting rationally in their own self-interest. Arm's-length transactions are the basis for a fair market value determination used to record the acquisition or historical costs of assets. The arm's-length concept is also an important judicial concept relating to tax law.

See also Cost principle; Related party transactions.

ASSETS

Assets are probable future economic benefits obtained or controlled by a particular entity as a result of past transactions or events. *Future economic benefits* refers to the capacity of an asset to benefit the enterprise by being exchanged for something else of value to the enterprise, by being used to produce something of value to the enterprise, or by being used to settle its liabilities. The future economic benefits of assets usually results in net cash inflows to the enterprise.

To be an asset, a resource other than cash must have three essential characteristics:

1. The resource must, singly or in combination with other resources, contribute directly or indirectly to future net cash inflows.

2. The enterprise must be able to obtain the benefit and control others' access to it.

3. The transaction or other event giving rise to the enterprise's right to or control of the benefit must already have occurred.

Assets currently reported in the financial statements are measured by different attributes including historical or acquisition cost, current (replacement) cost, current market value, net realizable value (selling price of the item less direct costs necessary to convert the asset), and present value of future cash flows, depending on the nature of the item and the relevance and reliability of the attribute measured.

Assets are recognized in the financial statements when (1) the item meets the definition of an asset, (2) it can be measured with sufficient reliability, (3) the information about it is capable of making a difference in user decisions, and (4) the information about the item is reliable (verifiable, neutral or unbiased, and representationally faithful). Assets need not be recognized in a set of financial statements if the item is not large enough to be material and the aggregate of individual immaterial items is not large enough to be material to those financial statements.

Assets are usually classified on a balance sheet in the order of their liquidity (or nearness to cash) as follows:

Current assets
Long-term investments
Property, plant, and equipment
Intangible assets
Other assets (including deferred charges)

Current assets are cash and other assets which are reasonably expected to be converted into cash, sold, or consumed within the normal operating cycle of the business or one year, whichever is longer. An operating cycle is the average time required to expend cash for inventory, process and sell the inventory, collect the receivables, and convert them back into cash.

See also Elements of financial statements; Conceptual framework of accounting; Recognition; Cost principle; Deferred charge (credit); Working capital; Operating cycle; Current asset; Wealth; Property, plant, and equipment; Intangible assets; Contra account.

REFERENCE
SFAC No. 3, Elements of Financial Statements of Business Enterprises (FASB, 1980).

ASSET/LIABILITY ASSUMPTION AND REVENUE/EXPENSE ASSUMPTION

Two major views of financial accounting and financial statements have been proposed as the bases for defining the elements of financial statements: (1) the asset and liability view, and (2) the revenue and expense view. Under the asset/liability view, the main focus of financial reporting is on determining and defining an entity's assets and liabilities. The determination of net income is accomplished by comparing statements of financial position at two different points in time. Net income is defined primarily in terms of increases and decreases in assets and liabilities.

According to the asset/liability theory, net income for a period can be computed independently of revenue and expenses according to the following formula:

Net income = Ending net assets –
Beginning net assets +
Asset withdrawals –
Asset investments

According to the revenue/expense assumption, net income for a period would be computed by referring to revenues and expenses for the period:

Net income = Revenues – Expenses

The revenue/expense view of financial accounting and financial statements emphasizes the relative importance of earnings to investors and that the measurement of earnings is the fundamental measurement process in financial accounting. Revenues are realized and expenses are incurred and then matched to arrive at net income for the period. Assets and liabilities are the result of the realization of revenue and the incurring of expenses.

See also Elements of accounting; Measurement; Realization; Recognition; Income statement; Statement of financial position.

REFERENCE
SFAC No. 5, Recognition and Measurement in Financial Statements of Business Enterprises (FASB, 1984).

AUDIT
Auditing is defined as a systematic process of objectively obtaining and evaluating evidence about a specific entity by a competent independent person for purposes of determining and reporting on the correspondence between assertions about economic events, actions, and other information and established criteria for reporting these assertions. An audit and the auditor's report provide additional assurance to users of financial statements concerning the information presented in the statements.

Three major types of audits are the audit of financial statements, the operational audit, and the compliance audit. A financial statement audit (or attest audit) is a systematic examination of financial statements, records, and related operations to ascertain adherence to generally accepted accounting principles, management policies, and other considerations. Operational auditing is a systematic review of an organization's activities for the purposes of assessing performance, identifying opportunities for improvement, and developing recommendations for improvement or further action. A compliance audit has as its objective the determination of whether the entity being audited is following procedures or rules established by a higher authority.

The audit committee is a major committee of the board of directors of a corporation. The committee usually is composed of outside directors who nominate the independent auditors and react to the auditor's report and findings. Matters which the auditor believes should be brought to the attention of the shareholders are first brought before the audit committee.

In The Philosophy of Auditing, R. K. Mautz and Hussein A. Sharaf identify eight tentative postulates of auditing:

1. Financial statements and financial data are verifiable.

2. There is no necessary conflict of interest between the auditor and the management of the enterprise under audit.

3. The financial statements and other information submitted for verification are free from collusive and other unusual irregularities.

4. The existence of a satisfactory system of internal control eliminates the probability of irregularities.

5. Consistent application of generally accepted principles of accounting results in the fair presentation of financial position and the results of operations.

6. In the absence of clear evidence to the contrary, what has held true in the past for the enterprise under examination will hold true in the future.

7. When examining financial data for the purpose of expressing an independent opinion thereon, the auditor acts exclusively in the capacity of an auditor.

8. The professional status of the independent auditor imposes commensurate professional obligations.

An independent auditor performs an examination with the objective of issuing a report containing an opinion on a client's financial statements. The attest function of external auditing refers to the auditor's expressing an opinion on a company's financial statements. Generally, the criteria for judging an auditee's financial statement are generally accepted accounting principles. The typical audit leads to an attestation regarding the fairness and dependability of the financial statements which is communicated to the officials of the audited entity in the form of a written report which accompanies the financial statements. The auditing process is based on standards, concepts, procedures, and reporting practices. The auditing process relies on evidence, analysis, convention, and informed professional judgment. Auditing standards imposed by the American Institute of Certified Public Accountants are presented in Exhibit A–8. The standards for internal auditors are established by the Institute of Internal Auditors. The General Accounting Office establishes audit standards for governmental auditors.

The auditor generally proceeds with an audit according to the following process:

1. Plans the audit.

2. Gathers evidence:

    a. Studies, tests, and evaluates the firm's internal accounting control system.

    b. Performs and evaluates substantive tests including:

        (1) Independent tests of account balances and transactions. Such tests include compliance tests which answer the question: Were the accounting controls adequate and was the system operating as designed? Substantive testing answers the question: Were the dollar amounts of the transactions correctly recorded?

        (2) Other general procedures, including analytical tests (ratios and trends) and background

Exhibit A–8
AICPA Auditing Standards

General Standards
1. The examination is to be performed by a person or persons having adequate technical training and proficiency as an auditor.
2. In all matters relating to the assignment, an independence in mental attitude is to be maintained by the auditor or auditors.
3. Due professional care is to be exercised in the performance of the examination and the preparation of the report.

Standards of Field Work
1. The work is to be adequately planned and assistants, if any, are to be properly supervised.
2. There is to be a proper study and evaluation of the existing internal control as a basis for reliance thereon and for the determination of the resultant extent of tests to which auditing procedures are to be restricted.
3. Sufficient competent evidential matter is to be obtained through inspection, observation, inquiries, and confirmations to afford a reasonable basis for an opinion regarding the financial statements under examination.

Standards of Reporting
1. The report shall state whether the financial statements are presented in accordance with generally accepted accounting principles.
2. The report shall state whether such principles have been consistently observed in the current period in relation to the preceding period.
3. Informative disclosures in the financial statements are to be regarded as reasonably adequate unless otherwise stated in the report.
4. The report shall contain either an expression of opinion regarding the financial statements, taken as a whole, or an assertion to the effect that an opinion cannot be expressed. When an overall opinion cannot be expressed, the reasons therefor should be stated. In all cases where an auditor's name is associated with financial statements the report should contain a clear-cut indication of the character of the auditor's examination, if any, and the degree of responsibility he is taking.

information (to understand the client's business, operations, personnel).

3. Issues a report.

Exhibit A–9 shows a diagram of an audit.

In planning the audit, the auditor develops an audit program which identifies and schedules audit procedures that are to be performed to obtain the evidence supporting the auditor's report. Audit evidence is proof obtained to support the audit's conclusion. Audit procedures include those activities undertaken by the auditor to obtain the evidence. Evidence-gathering procedures include observation, confirmation, calculation, analysis, inquiry, inspection, and comparison. An audit trail is a chronological record of economic events or transactions that have been experienced by an organization. The audit trail enables an auditor to evaluate the strengths and weaknesses of internal control, system designs, company policies and procedures.

The independent audit report sets forth the independent auditor's opinion regarding the financial statements, that is, that they are fairly presented in conformity with generally accepted accounting principles applied on a basis consistent with that of the preceding year (or in conformity with some other comprehensive basis of accounting that is appropriate for the entity). A fair presentation of financial statements is generally understood by accountants to refer to whether

1. the accounting principles used in the statements have general acceptability;

2. the accounting principles are appropriate in the circumstances;

3. the financial statements are prepared so as to favorably affect their use, understanding, and interpretation;

Exhibit A–9
Diagram of an Audit

INTERNAL CONTROL REVIEW AND EVALUATION   **SUBSTANTIVE TESTS**

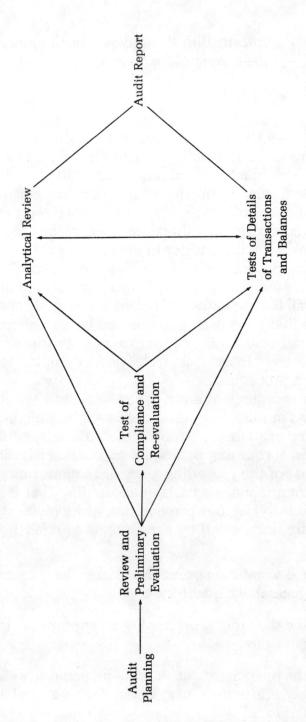

Kinney, William R., Jr., "Decision Theory Aspects of Internal Control System Design/Compliance, and Substantive Tests," *Journal of Accounting Research* (Supplement, 1975), p. 16 (adapted).

4. the information presented in the financial statements is classified and summarized in a reasonable manner; and

5. the financial statements reflect the underlying events and transactions in a way that presents the financial position, results of operations, and changes in financial position within reasonable and practical limits.

A typical short-form audit report format consists of two paragraphs. The first paragraph, or scope section, describes the nature and limits of the examination. The second paragraph is the opinion or judgment section. A typical short-form audit report is illustrated in Exhibit A–10.

Exhibit A–10
Short-form Audit Report

SHORT-FORM AUDIT REPORT RECOMMENDED BY AICPA

March 8, 1989

To the Stockholders of the ABC Company:

We have examined the balance sheet of the ABC Company as of December 31, 1989, and the related statements of income, retained earnings, and changes in financial position for the year then ended. Our examination was made in accordance with generally accepted auditing standards, and accordingly included such tests of the accounting records and such other auditing proceures as we considered necessary in the circumstances.

In our opinion, the financial statements referred to above present fairly the financial position of the ABC Company as of December 31, 1989, and the results of its operations and the changes in its financial position for the year then ended, in conformity with generally accepted accounting principles applied on a basis consistent with that of the preceding year.

A

An audit report will include an unqualified opinion if the auditor has no reservations concerning the financial statements. A qualified audit report is one in which the auditor takes exception to certain current-period accounting applications or is unable to establish the possible outcome of a material uncertainty. A disclaimer of opinion (no opinion) is included in an audit report if the auditor has been so restricted that an opinion cannot be rendered, if statements are issued without audit, or if there are major unauditable uncertainties. An adverse (unfavorable) opinion is issued when the financial statements are misleading or do not reflect the proper application of generally accepted accounting principles, and qualification is not considered appropriate. Exhibit A–11 identifies various types of audit opinions.

The fair presentation of financial statements does not mean that the statements are fraud-proof. The independent auditor has the responsibility to search for errors or irregularities within the recognized limitations of the auditing process. An auditor understands that his/her examination based on selective testing is subject to risks that material errors or irregularities, if they exist, will not be detected. The Institute of Internal Auditors (IIA) in its Standards for the Professional Practice of Internal Auditing states

> *"In exercising due professional care, internal auditors should be alert to the possibility of intentional wrongdoing, errors and omissions, inefficiency, waste, and conflicts of interest. They should also be alert to those conditions and activities where irregularities are most likely to occur.... Accordingly, the internal auditor cannot give absolute assurance that noncompliance or irregularities do not exist."*

Auditors sometimes perform social audits and statutory audits. A social audit is an examination of an accounting entity in areas of social and environmental concerns, such as minority relations, waste management, etc. A statutory audit is an audit

Exhibit A–11
Types of Audit Opinions

Types of Opinions	Types of Material Deficiencies in Financial Statements or Audits
UNQUALIFIED	No deficiencies in the financial statements or the audit
QUALIFIED (Financial statements taken as a whole present fairly but have a material deficiency)	
• "except for"	Accounting deficiency in financial statements or scope restriction in audit
• "subject to"	Uncertainty involving the financial statements
ADVERSE (Financial statements taken as a whole do not present fairly)	Accounting deficiency in financial statements
DISCLAIMER (No opinion is expressed on the financial statements)	Uncertainty involving the financial statements or scope restriction in audit
NO OPINION OR DISCLAIMER	Due to unusual circumstances, the auditor withdraws from the engagement

performed to comply with requirements of a governing body, such as a federal, state, or city government.

Internal auditing is an independent appraisal function established by an organization to examine and evaluate its activities as a service to the organization. Internal auditors are employees of the organizations whose activities they evaluate.

A

The primary focus of internal auditing is the determination of the extent to which the organization adheres to managerial policies, procedures, or requirements.

The legal responsibilities of the auditor are determined primarily by:

1. specific contractual obligations undertaken,

2. statutes and the common law governing the conduct and responsibilities of public accountants, and

3. rules and regulations of voluntary professional organizations.

See also Accounting profession; Certified Public Accountant; Opinion; Ethics; Privileged communications; Fraud; Compilation; Review; Accounting principles; Working papers; Related parties.

REFERENCES

Taylor, Donald H., and Glezen, G. William, *Auditing* (John Wiley & Sons, NY, 1982).

Bavishi, Vinod B., and Wyman, Harold E., *Who Audits the World?* (Center for Transnational Accounting and Financial Accounting, University of Connecticut, 1983).

Causey, Denzil Y., Jr., *Duties and Liabilities of the CPA* (Bureau of Business Research, The University of Texas at Austin, 1973).

AICPA, *Professional Standards* (Commerce Clearing House, Inc., Chicago, latest edition).

B

BALANCE SHEET
See Statement of Financial Position.

BANK RECONCILIATION
A bank reconciliation is a process of bringing into agreement the balance of a depositor's account in the bank's records and the balance of the cash account in the company's books. The objective of the bank reconciliation is to disclose any errors or irregularities in either the bank's or the company's records. For internal control purposes, the reconciliation should be made by a person who does not handle cash or have access to the books of the company. The bank reconciliation illustrated in Exhibit B–1 adjusts both the book balance and the bank balance to reflect the adjusted balance (the correct balances that should exist). The bank statement balance is adjusted for items not yet recorded by the bank and for errors made by the bank. The cash account balance is adjusted for items not yet recorded in the cash account and for any errors in the company's books. The adjusted balances should be equal.

Exhibit B–1
Bank Reconciliation in Form that Adjusts Bank and Book Balances

Bank Statement

Balance per bank statement	$15,000
Add: Deposit in transit	5,000
	20,000
Deduct: Outstanding checks	7,000
ADJUSTED BANK BALANCE	$13,000

Cash Account

Balance per cash account	$ 6,950
Add: Note collected by bank and interest	6,060
	13,010
Deduct: Bank service charge	10
ADJUSTED CASH ACCOUNT BALANCE	$13,000

Exhibit B–2
Proof of Cash

	Balance Nov. 30	December Deposits	December Withdrawals	Balance Dec. 31
Transactions per bank	$5,500	$12,300	$2,800	$15,000
Deposits in transit				
November 30	1,000	(1,000)		
December 31		5,000		5,000
Oustanding checks:				
November 30	(700)		(700)	
December 31			7,100	(7,100)
Bank service charge			10	10
Note/interest collected by bank		(6,060)		(6,060)
Customer's N.S.F. check			(50)	50
Transactions per books	$5,800	$10,240	$9,140	$ 6,900

A special four-column bank reconciliation, "proof of cash," or "block reconciliation," reconciles the bank and book balances at both the beginning and end of the period as well as cash receipts and disbursements during the period. Exhibit B–2 shows this form of a reconciliation.

See also Cash; Internal control.

BANKRUPTCY

Bankruptcy is a judicial procedure used to reconcile the conflicting interests that occur when a debtor has incurred too much debt. The Bankruptcy Reform Act of 1978 is the major federal law dealing with bankruptcy. The public policy goal of bankruptcy is to give the debtor a "fresh start' in financial dealings and to obtain a fair distribution of the debtor's assets among the creditors. A discharge in bankruptcy refers to the absolution of a bankrupt's debt, by court order, upon the liquidation or rehabilitation of the bankrupt.

A bankrupt is a person recognized by law as being unable to pay debts. A business is insolvent in the legal sense when the financial condition is such that the sum of the entity's debts is greater than the entity's property at fair valuation. All federal bankruptcy cases must be filed under a specific chapter of the Reform Act. In Chapter 7 of the Reform Act, the assets of the debtor are liquidated in an effort to satisfy creditors. Chapter 11 provides for the reorganization of the debtor's finances and operations so that it can continue operating. Chapter 13 provides for the adjustment of debts of an individual regular income to enable the person to work through financial problems while avoiding liquidation. Chapter 9 applies to municipalities and sets forth the procedures for the rehabilitation of a financially troubled municipality.

The Reform Act established a new bankruptcy court system. Special bankruptcy courts are located in each federal judicial district. These courts have judicial authority over all cases and proceedings brought under the act. The courts have exclusive authority over all property of the debtor.

Chapter 7 liquidation cases begin voluntarily when a debtor corporation files a petition with the bankruptcy court or involuntarily when three or more entities file the petition. In Chapter 7 cases, the estate of the debtor corporation is turned over to an interim trustee until a trustee is elected by unsecured creditors. A Chapter 11 reorganization case can be initiated either voluntarily by a debtor or involuntarily by creditors. In Chapter 11 cases, a trustee may be appointed for cause; otherwise, the debtor corporation continues in possession.

A statement of affairs is a report prepared to show the immediate liquidation amounts of assets, instead of historical costs, and the estimated amounts that would be received by each class of claim or party of interest in the event of the liquidation of an enterprise. The report is essentially a balance sheet prepared on the assumption that the enterprise is to be liquidated rather than on the going-concern assumption which normally applies to the preparation of financial statements. Emphasis is placed on the legal status of resources and claims against those resources. Creditors and owners can use the statement to estimate the amounts that could be realized on the disposition of the assets and the priority of claims as well as any estimated deficiency that would result if the enterprise were to be liquidated. A typical statement of affairs discloses the following information about assets and liabilities:

Assets
Assets pledged with fully secured creditors
Assets pledged with partially secured creditors
Free assets

Liabilities
Liabilities having priorities
Fully secured liabilities
Partially secured creditors
Unsecured creditors

A trustee or receiver is usually required to prepare a realization and liquidation account or report to summarize his/her activities during a reporting period. The report typically discloses the following information:

Realization and Liquidation Account

Assets to be realized	Assets realized
Assets acquired	Assets not realized
Liabilities liquidated	Liabilities to be liquidated
Liabilities not liquidated	Liabilities incurred
Supplementary charges (expenses)	Supplementary credits (revenues)

See also Solvency and insolvency; Reorganization; Liquidation; Quasi-reorganization.

REFERENCE
Ginsberg, Robert E., *Bankruptcy* (Prentice-Hall, Englewood Cliffs, NJ, 1985).

BETA COEFFICIENT

The beta coefficient can be used to assess market risks of stock. Assessing market risk involves the consideration of many factors including the nature of the business, the quality of assets and earnings, managerial capabilities, the track record of the company, and others. One particular measure that shows the volatility, or fluctuation, in the price of a stock in relation to that of the prices of all stocks in the market is called market risk beta. A beta of 1.0 means that a stock should move with the market. A beta above 1.0 indicates a stock is more volatile than the market, while a beta below 1.0 indicates less volatility.

The computation of market risk is complex, but a simple example illustrates the concept. Assume the following data about the changes in price of the stock of Company A and Company B and the average change in the prices of all stocks in the market:

Average Percent Change in Price of All Stock	Percent Change in Price of "A" Stock	Percent Change in Price of "B" Stock
+ 10	+ 15	+ 5
− 10	− 15	− 5

The beta coefficient for the two companies is computed as follows:

Company A $\quad \dfrac{\text{Specific change}}{\text{Average change}} \quad \dfrac{15}{10} = 1.5$

Company B $\quad \dfrac{\text{Specific change}}{\text{Average change}} \quad \dfrac{5}{10} = .5$

See also Ratios; Financial markets.

REFERENCE
Gitman, Lawrence J., and Joehnk, Michael D., *Fundamentals of Investing* (Harper & Row, New York, 1981).

BIG EIGHT

The Big Eight refers to the eight largest public accounting partnerships. Currently the Big Eight includes the following firms arranged in alphabetical order: Arthur Andersen & Co; Coopers & Lybrand; Deloitte Haskins & Sells; Ernst & Whinney; Peat, Marwick, Mitchell & Co.; Price Waterhouse & Co.; Touche Ross & Co.; and Arthur Young & Company. In addition to the Big Eight accounting firms, there are many excellent regional and local firms engaged in the practice of public accounting.

BONDS

A bond is a written, unconditional promise made under corporate seal in which the borrower promises to pay a specific sum at a determinable future date, together with interest at a fixed rate and at fixed dates. A bond issuer is a debtor. The bondholder is a creditor of the issuer and is not an owner as is a stockholder. Corporate bonds are usually issued in denominations of $1,000, although bonds issued in other amounts are sometimes used. The amount shown on the bond is the face value, maturity value, or principal of the bond. Bond prices are usually quoted as a percentage of face value. For example, a $1,000 bond priced to sell at $980 would be quoted at 98 which means that the bond is selling at 98 percent of $1,000. The nominal, or coupon, interest rate on a bond is the rate the issuer agrees to pay and is shown on the bond or in the bond agreement. Interest payments, usually made semiannually, are based on the face value of the bond and not on the issuance price. The effective, or market, interest rate is the nominal rate adjusted for the premium, or discount, on the purchase and indicates the actual yield on the bond. Bonds that have a single fixed maturity date are *term bonds*. *Serial bonds* provide for the repayment of principal in a series of periodic installments.

If bonds are sold above face value, they are sold at a premium. If bonds are sold at a premium, the effective interest rate is less than the nominal rate since the issuer received more than the face amount of the bond but is required to pay interest on only the face amount. If bonds are sold below face value, they are sold at a discount. If bonds are sold at a discount, the effective interest rate paid is more than the nominal rate since the issuer received less than the face amount of the bonds but is required to pay interest on the face amount.

Callable bonds are bonds which can be redeemed by the issuer at specific prices, usually at a premium, prior to their maturity. *Convertible bonds* are bonds which at the option of the bondholder can be exchanged for other securities, usually equity securities, of the corporation issuing the bonds during a specific period of time at a determined or determinable conversion rate. The conversion price is the price at which convertible securities can be converted into common stock. The conversion ratio is the number of shares of common stock that may be obtained by converting one convertible bond or share of convertible preferred stock. *Secured bonds* are bonds that have a specific claim against assets of the corporation. If the corporation fails to make interest payments or the maturity payment, the pledged assets can be seized by the bondholder or their representative. *Real estate mortgage bonds* have a specific claim against certain real property of the issuer, such as land and building. A *chattel mortgage bond* has a claim against personal property such as equipment or livestock. *Collateral trust bonds* are secured by negotiable securities owned by the bond issuer, such as stocks or bonds. *Guaranteed bonds* are bonds on which the payment of interest and/or principal is guaranteed by another party. *Income bonds* are bonds on which interest payments are made only from operating income of the issuing entity. *Unsecured bonds*, or *debentures*, are bonds under which the holder has no claim against any specific assets of the issuer or others but relies on the general creditworthiness of the issuer for security.

Senior securities are securities that have claims that must be satisfied before payments can be made to more junior securities. *Junior securities* have a lower-priority claim to assets and income of the issuer than senior securities.

Zero-coupon (or compound discount) *bonds* are non-interest-bearing bonds issued by many companies at a substantial discount. Zero-coupon bonds sell for much less than their maturity value. The discount on the bonds represents the interest earned over the life of the bonds. For example, if an investor purchased a $1,000 ten-year maturity zero-coupon bond for $300, he would be receiving a compound interest yield of approximately 12.79% annually. At the end of the ten years, he would redeem the bond for $1,000 from the issuing company.

Registered bonds are issued in the name of the owner and are recorded in the owner's name on the records of the issuer. *Coupon bonds* are bearer bonds which can be transferred from one investor to another by delivery. Interest coupons are attached to the bonds. On interest payment dates, the coupons are detached and submitted for payment to the issuer or an agent. *Sinking fund bonds* are bonds for which a fund is established into which periodic cash deposits are made for the purpose of redeeming outstanding bonds.

Bonds may be sold by the issuing company directly to investors or to an investment banker who markets the bonds. The investment banker might underwrite the issue which guarantees the issuer a specific amount or sell the bonds on a commission (best efforts) basis for the issuer.

The price of bonds can be determined by mathematical computation or from bond tables. A bond table shows the current price of a bond as a function of the coupon rate, years to maturity, and the effective yield to maturity (or effective rate). An excerpt from a bond table is presented in Exhibit B-3. When mathematics is used, the price of a bond can be computed using present value tables. The price of a bond is

1. the present value at the effective rate of a series of interest payments, i.e., an annuity, and

2. the present value of the maturity value of the bonds.

To determine the price of a $1,000 four-year bond having a 7 percent nominal interest rate with interest payable semiannually purchased to yield 6 percent, use the following procedure:

1. Present value of maturity value at effective rate (3%) for eight periods:

   $1,000 × .789409   (= present value of 1 at 3% when the number of periods is 8) $ 789.41

2. Present value of an annuity of eight interest receipts of $35 each at effective interest rate of 3%:

   $35 × 7.01969   (= present value of an annuity of 1 at 3% for eight periods)   245.69

   Price of the bond $1,035.10

Exhibit B–3
Excerpts from Bond Table

Four Years Interest Payable Semiannually

Per Cent	Nominal Rate						
Per Annum	3%	3½%	4%	4½%	5%	6%	7%
4.00	96.31	98.17	100.00	101.83	103.66	107.33	110.99
4.10	95.98	97.81	99.63	101.46	103.29	106.94	110.60
4.125	95.89	97.72	99.54	101.37	103.20	105.85	110.50
4.20	95.62	97.45	99.27	101.09	102.92	106.56	110.21
4.25	95.45	97.27	99.00	100.91	102.73	106.38	110.02
4.30	95.27	97.09	98.91	100.73	102.55	106.19	109.83
4.375	95.00	96.82	98.64	100.45	102.27	105.90	109.54
4.40	94.92	96.73	98.55	100.36	102.18	105.81	100.44
4.50	94.56	96.38	98.19	100.00	101.81	105.44	109.06
4.60	94.21	96.02	97.83	99.64	101.45	105.06	108.68
4.625	94.13	95.93	97.74	99.55	101.36	104.97	108.58
4.70	93.87	95.67	97.47	99.28	101.08	104.69	108.30
4.75	93.69	95.49	97.30	99.10	100.90	104.51	108.11
4.80	93.52	95.32	97.12	98.92	100.72	104.32	107.92
4.875	93.26	95.06	96.85	98.65	100.45	104.04	107.64
4.90	93.17	94.97	96.77	98.56	100.36	103.95	107.54
5.00	92.83	94.62	96.41	98.21	100.00	103.59	107.17
5.10	92.49	94.28	96.06	97.85	99.64	103.22	106.80
5.125	92.40	94.19	95.98	97.77	99.55	103.13	106.70
5.20	92.15	93.93	95.72	97.50	99.29	102.86	106.43
5.25	91.98	93.76	95.54	97.33	99.11	102.67	106.24
5.30	91.81	93.59	93.37	97.15	98.93	102.49	106.06
5.375	91.55	93.33	95.11	96.89	98.67	102.22	105.78
5.40	91.47	93.25	95.02	96.80	98.58	102.13	105.69
5.50	91.13	92.91	94.68	96.45	98.23	101.77	105.32
5.625	90.71	92.48	94.25	96.02	97.79	101.33	104.86
5.75	90.30	92.06	93.83	95.59	97.35	100.38	104.41
5.875	89.88	91.64	93.40	95.16	96.92	100.44	103.96
6.00	89.47	91.23	92.98	94.74	96.49	100.00	103.51

Effective Rate

Example: A $1,000 4-year, 6% bond purchased at 104.69 (= $1,046.90) yields 4.70% effective interest. Interest is payable semiannually. To purchase this bond to yield 4.70% effective interest, an investor should pay $1,046.90.

The carrying value (or book value) of the bond issue at any time is the face value plus any unamortized premium or minus any unamortized discount. The periodic write-off of a bond discount or bond premium adjusts the carrying value of the bond toward the bond's face value. Amortization of the discount increases the amount of interest expense while the amortization of a premium decreases the amount of interest expense reported. Exhibit B–4 illustrates the amortization of a bond premium using the effective interest method. The total interest expense each year is computed by multiplying the carrying value of the bond at the beginning of the period. The difference between the interest paid or payable during the period and the total interest expense represents the discount or premium amortized for the period. The carrying value of the bond increases (decreases) each year as the discount (premium) is amortized to interest expense until maturity. At maturity, the carrying value of the bonds is their face amount. The use of the effective rate method recognizes a constant rate of interest on the bonds over the life of the bonds. The straight-line method of amortization is sometimes used to amortize bond premiums and discounts. This method amortizes an equal amount of premium or discount each period. When this method is used, the interest expense for the periods remains constant over the life of the bonds.

In reporting long-term debt on the balance sheet, the nature of the liability, maturity date, interest rate, conversion privileges, borrowing restrictions, and other significant matters should be disclosed.

Credit rating agencies, such as Standard and Poor, Moody, and others, report on the quality of corporate and municipal bond issues. The reports of these agencies serve as a basis for evaluating the risks, profitability, and probability of default on bond issues. Bond ratings are based on various factors, including: issuer's existing debt level; issuer's previous record of payment; and the safety of the assets or revenues committed to paying off principal and interest. Symbols such as AAA or Aaa (triple a) refer to the highest-quality rating. Other

Exhibit B–4
Schedule of Bond Premium Amortization—Effective Interest Method

Schedule of Bond Premium Amortization
Effective Interest Method—Semiannual Interest Payments
$100,000 8% Bonds Sold to Yield 6%

Date	Cash	Interest Expense	Amortization of Bond Discount	Carrying Value of Bonds
1/1/90				$108,530
7/1/90	$ 4,000[a]	$3,256[b]	$ 744[c]	107.786[d]
1/1/91	4,000	3,234	766	107,020
7/1/91	4,000	3,211	789	106,231
1/1/92	4,000	3,187	813	105.418
7/1/92	4,000	3,162	838	104,580
1/1/93	4,000	3,137	863	103.717
7/1/93	4,000	3,112	888	102,829
1/1/94	4,000	3,085	915	101,914
7/1/94	4,000	3,057	943	100,971
1/1/95	4,000	3,029	971	100,000
	$40,000	$31,470	$8,530	

[a]$4,000 = $100,000 × .08 × 6/12

[b]$3,256 = $108,530 × .06 × 6/12

[c]$744 = $4,000 − $3,256

[d]$107,786 = $108,530 − $744

symbols are used to refer to high-quality bonds, investment grade bonds, substandard bonds, and speculative bonds.

See also Convertible securities; Financial markets; Leverage; Liabilities; Book value.

REFERENCE
Darst, David M., *The Handbook of the Bond and Money Markets* (McGraw-Hill, N.Y., 1981).

BOOK VALUE

Book value is a term that refers to the carrying value of an item in the financial statements, accounts, or books. The book value of plant assets is the difference between cost and accumulated depreciation. The book value of intangible assets is cost less amortization taken to date. The book value of an enterprise is the excess of total assets over total liabilities (or net assets). The book value per share of stock is the total stockholders' equity divided by the total number of shares outstanding. The book value per share is the dollar amount per share a shareholder would receive if assets were liquidated and liabilities settled at the amounts reported on the financial statements. If preferred stock is outstanding, the book value per share of common stock is computed after deducting from total stockholders' equity the equity assigned to the preferred stock. To determine the book value of preferred stock, it is customary to begin with the liquidating value to which any dividends in arrears are added. This total is divided by the number of preferred shares outstanding.

The book value of bonds payable is affected by any premium or discount related to the bond issue. The book (or carrying) value of the bonds changes each period by the amount of amortized discount or premium. The book value of the bonds equals the face amount minus any unamortized discount or plus any unamortized premium.

Caution should be exercised in interpreting the meaning of book value. It should be understood that market value per share is usually different from book value per share. Market value is influenced by a variety of factors that may not be reflected in book value. Book value reflects the accounting principles and methods used in preparing the financial statements.

See also Contra account; Bonds; Depreciation; Amortization.

BOOKKEEPING

A distinction is made between accounting and bookkeeping. Bookkeeping is usually associated with the mechanical, routine, and repetitive aspects of the accounting process, such as journalizing, posting, and taking a trial balance. Accounting relates to the theoretical, conceptual, and logical relationships of the entire information system as well as to the practical operations of the system. Accounting is concerned with such matters as the preparation of financial statements, compliance with generally accepted accounting principles, the fairness of the financial statements, system design, transaction analysis, budgeting, income taxes, and cost reports. Accounting includes bookkeeping.

See also Accounting; Certified Public Accountant.

BRANCH AND AGENCY
A business may expand its operations by establishing ancillary operating units physically away from the home or central office of the enterprise. These units are often referred to as branches or agencies. A branch or agency is not organized as a separate legal entity or subsidiary. Branches and agencies are usually established to enable a firm to be close to customers, suppliers, or a labor market. Branches and agencies are separate accounting entities, but they are not separate legal entities. An agency typically is established to take sales orders. An agency usually carries no inventory or a very limited amount. Credit, shipping, and collection functions are usually performed by the home office. A branch usually carries considerable inventory and performs many of the basic functions of any business.

The accounting function for branches and agencies can be either centralized at the home office or decentralized at the branch or agency. Combined financial statements are prepared for the home office and the branch or agency. Branch or agency assets, liabilities, revenues, and expenses are combined with those of the home office. The combined statements report on the entire economic entity in a manner somewhat similar to consolidated financial statements prepared for a parent-subsidiary relationship. This form of reporting is required for external purposes. Separate statements for internal managerial use would normally be prepared for each branch or agency.

See also Combined statements; Consolidated financial statements.

REFERENCE
Beams, Floyd A., *Advanced Accounting* (Prentice-Hall, Englewood Cliffs, NJ, 1985).

BREAK-EVEN POINT

The break-even point is the volume of sales at which total costs equal total revenues. Profits equal zero at the break-even point. A sales volume below the break-even point results in a loss; a volume above the break-even point results in a profit. Break-even analysis is a technique for studying the relationship between profits and sales volume.

The formula used to compute the break-even point is as follows:

Sales at break-even point = Variable expenses + Fixed expenses

Fixed expenses are those expenses that tend to remain constant in total within a given period of time and over a wide range of activity (the relevant range) regardless of sales volume. Variable expenses are expenses that tend to remain uniform per unit but which vary in total in direct proportion to changes in the level of activity. Mixed expenses (semivariable) represent a combination of fixed and variable expenses. Mixed expenses increase with volume but not in the same proportion.

To illustrate the computation of the break-even formula, assume the following data:

Sales (60,000 units @ $20 per unit)	$1,200,000
Less: Variable expenses (60,000 units @ $12 per unit)	720,000
Contribution margin	480,000
Less: Fixed expenses	400,000
Net income	$ 80,000

The computation of the break-even point follows where S equals sales at the break-even point; variable expenses are expressed as a percentage of sales:

$$S = (\$720,000/\$1,200,000)(S) + \$400,000$$
$$S = (.60)(S) + \$400,000$$
$$.40S = \$400,000$$
$$S = \$1,000,000$$

To verify this computation, consider the following:

Sales at the break-even point	$1,000,000
Less: Variable expenses (60% of sales)	600,000
Contribution margin	400,000
Less: Fixed expenses	400,000
Net income	–0–

Note that variable expenses are 60 percent of sales ($720,000/$1,200,000). With a sales price of $20 per unit, it will take sales of 50,000 units ($1,000,000/$20) to break even. A break-even chart for this problem is shown in Exhibit B–5.

The basic relationship contained in the break-even model can also be used to make additional analyses. For example, these relationships should be recognized:

Net income = Sales – Variable expenses – Fixed expenses

or

Sales = Variable expenses + Fixed expenses + Net Income

Using the data in the problem, what sales are required to make a profit of $100,000?

Exhibit B-5
Conventional Break-Even Chart

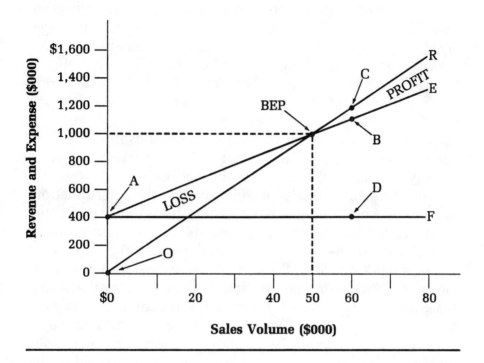

Sales to make
$100,000 profit = ($720,000/$1,200,000)(S) + $400,000 + $100,000

= $1,250,000

See also Contribution margin analysis.

REFERENCE
Horngren, Charles T., *Introduction to Management Accounting* (Prentice-Hall, Englewood Cliffs, NJ, 1984).

BUDGET
A budget is an orderly and coordinated plan of financial planning and management. It is a major tool for planning, motivat-

ing, and controlling business operations. The budgeting process forces management to determine its goals and objectives and to develop a coordinated plan for achieving these ends.

The master, or comprehensive, budget is a relatively complete blueprint of the future operations of the firm. The budget period is usually short enough to permit reasonably accurate predictions and long enough to allow time for implementation. The budget period usually coincides with the fiscal period of the business so that actual results of operations can be compared with budgetary estimates. An operating budget is usually prepared for a year, with supporting schedules in monthly or quarterly terms. A capital expenditure or project budget is usually developed for a longer time period.

The budgeting process usually involves the determination, by a budget committee, of basic assumptions under which the details of the budget are to be prepared. The board of directors (or other high-level, decision-making group) approves the assumptions set forth by the budget committee. A budget director then begins to prepare the detailed budget. Detailed budgeting usually begins with a forecast of revenue from sales of products or services. After revenue has been estimated, estimates are made of expenses, costs, collections, and payments. Budgeted financial statements are then compiled and examined to determine how the budgeted activities will affect the company, stockholders, creditors, and other external parties. After this phase of the budgeting process is completed, the budget is implemented.

The second phase of the budgetary control process involves monitoring operations so that operating plans and targets can be attained. Budgetary control relies primarily on analyses of differences (1) between actual costs/revenues and budgeted costs/revenues, and (2) between actual costs and standard costs. Aspects of the control process involve (1) establishing lines of responsibility for performance, (2) communicating plans to those assigned performance responsibilities, (3) evaluating variances between actual results and budgeted estimates, and (4) taking appropriate action thereon.

The master budget which has been discussed here is primarily a planning tool. It is often a static or inflexible budget and is usually prepared for one level of activities—the anticipated or normal level of output. A flexible or variable budget is usually used as the tool for controlling costs and evaluating performance. A flexible budget is prepared for a range of activity because costs are affected by changes in level of activity. Flexible budgets are often expressed in terms of units of output or in standard direct-labor hours allowed for that output. A simplified flexible budget prepared in terms of product output for three activity levels is shown here:

| | Levels of Output Activity | | |
	10,000	15,000	20,000
Direct materials	$100,000	$150,000	$200,000
Direct labor	50,000	75,000	100,000
Variable factory overhead	20,000	30,000	40,000
Fixed factory overhead	30,000	30,000	30,000
Total costs	$200,000	$285,000	$370,000

If the actual level of output for the period was 15,000 units, actual costs would be compared with the flexible budget prepared at the 15,000 unit level. Any cost variances between actual and budgeted should be explained and corrected, if necessary. Performance reports for cost control purposes could be prepared using the following format:

Cost	Actual Costs	Flexible Budget	Variance	Explanation

A capital budget is a plan for acquiring and maintaining long-term assets and providing the means of financing these activities. Financial theory strongly supports the separation of the investment decision from the financing decision. A capital budget typically includes one or more of the following:

1. New facilities and major additions.
2. Major renovations and repairs to existing facilities.

B

A variety of methods are currently used for making investment decisions associated with capital budgeting. The net present value method or some modification thereof is considered the preferred method. The application of the net present value method of capital budgeting involves the following process:

1. Estimate the future cash inflows and outflows for each alternative project under consideration.

2. Discount the future cash flows to the present using the firm's cost of capital.

3. Accept or reject the proposed project according to a decision rule that will maximize the firm's wealth.

Budgeting is considered especially important in governmental accounting. Governmental accounting requires that an annual budget(s) be adopted by every governmental unit. The accounting system should provide the basis for appropriate budgetary control. Budgetary comparisons should be included in the appropriate financial statements and schedules for governmental funds for which an annual budget has been adopted.

See also Planning and control; Forecast; Governmental accounting.

REFERENCE
Horngren, Charles T., *Introduction to Management Accounting* (Prentice-Hall, Englewood Cliffs, NJ, 1984).

BUSINESS COMBINATIONS
A business combination occurs when a corporation and one or more incorporated or unincorporated businesses are brought together into one accounting entity. The single entity carries on the activities of the previously separate, independent enterprises. Business combinations can be classified structurally into

three types: horizontal, vertical, and conglomerate. A horizontal combination is one that involves companies within the same industry that have previously been competitors; a vertical combination involves a company and its suppliers or customers; and a combination resulting in a conglomerate is one involving companies in unrelated industries having few, if any, production or market similarities.

Business combinations can be classified by method of combination as statutory mergers, statutory consolidations, and stock acquisitions. A statutory merger occurs when one company acquires all of the net assets of one or more other companies. The acquiring company survives; the acquired company or companies cease to exist as a separate legal entity. For example, a merger occurs between constituent corporations A and B if A remains the same legal entity (essentially with the combined assets and liabilities of A and B) and B goes out of existence.

A statutory consolidation requires the formation of a new corporation which acquires two or more other corporations; the acquired corporations then cease to exist as separate legal entities. For example, Corporations A and B agree to transfer their assets and liabilities to a new corporation C and then go out of existence, leaving C as the corporation to carry on the activities of A and B.

A stock acquisition occurs when one corporation pays cash or issues stock or debt for more than 50 percent of the voting stock of another company and the acquired company remains intact as a separate legal entity. The relationship of the acquiring company to the acquired company in a stock acquisition is described as a parent-subsidiary relationship. The acquiring company is referred to as the parent (investor) and the acquired company as a subsidiary. The related companies are called affiliated companies. Each of the affiliated companies continues as a separate legal entity. The parent company carries its interest in a subsidiary as an investment in its accounts. Consolidated financial statements are prepared only when the business combination was carried out as a stock acquisition.

B

The parent-subsidiary relationship can be visualized as follows:

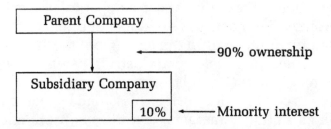

In the above illustration of a parent-subsidiary relationship, the Parent Company owns 90 percent of the Subsidiary. A 10 percent interest in the subsidiary is owned by someone other than the parent. This interest is referred to as a minority interest.

The relationship between mergers, consolidations, and stock acquisitions can be summarized as follows:

	Prior to Combination	Survivors
Merger	A and B	A or B
Statutory consolidation	A and B	C
Acquisition	A and B	A and B

Two methods of accounting are available for recording a business combination—purchase and pooling of interest. These methods are discussed separately under Purchase Accounting and Pooling of Interests.

See also Consolidated financial statements; Purchase accounting; Pooling of interests; Goodwill; Substance over form.

REFERENCES
Haried, Andrew A., et al., *Advanced Accounting* (John Wiley & Sons, N.Y., 1985).
APB No. 16, Business Combinations (APB, 1970).
Hartz, Peter F., *Merger* (William Morrow, N.Y., 1985).

C

C

CAPITAL

Capital has many different meanings in accounting and finance. In this section of the book, capital is the residual interest in the assets of an entity that remains after deducting its liabilities. Hence, capital is the ownership interest, or equity. Capital is the cumulative result of investments by owners, earnings, and distribution to owners. Typically, liabilities have priority over ownership interest as claims against enterprise assets. In a corporation, capital is referred to as stockholders' equity, or shareholders' equity. In accounting for stockholders' equity, the basic purposes are:

1. To identify the source of corporate capital.
2. To identify legal capital.
3. To indicate the dividends that could be distributed to the stockholders.

A distinction is often made between capital originating from stockholders' investments, referred to as contributed capital or paid-in capital, and the equity originating from earnings, referred to as retained earnings. Contributed, or paid-in, capital is usually reported as (1) capital stock representing that portion of capital contributed by stockholders and assignable to the shares of stock issued and (2) additional paid-in capital representing investments by stockholders in excess of the amounts assignable to capital stock as well as invested capital from other sources. The capital stock balance is generally considered legal capital, or permanent capital, of the corporation. Retained earnings is the amount of undistributed earnings of past periods. An excess of dividends and losses over earnings results in a deficit. Portions of retained earnings are sometimes restricted and unavailable as a basis for dividends.

The stockholders' equity section of a balance sheet is illustrated in Exhibit C-1.

Note that the stockholders' equity is reported by sources. The classes of capital stock are reported separately and are

Exhibit C-1
Stockholders' Equity Section of a Balance Sheet

Capital stock:		
Preferred stock, $100 par value, 8% cumulative, 200,000 shares authorized, 30,000 shares issued and outstanding		$3,000,000
Common stock, $10 par value, 500,000 shares authorized, 400,000 shares issued		4,000,000
		7,000,000
Additional paid-in capital:		
Excess over par—preferred stock	$ 150,000	
Excess over par value—common stock	50,000	150,000
Total paid-in capital		7,150,000
Donated capital		50,000
Retained earnings:		
Appropriated for plant expansion	500,000	
Unappropriated	1,500,000	2,000,000
Total paid-in capital and retained earnings		9,200,000
Less cost of treasury stock (2,000 shares, common)		(100,000)
Total stockholders' equity		$9,100,000

described in considerable detail. A portion of the retained earnings has been restricted for contingencies. The cost of treasury stock is deducted in determining total stockholders' equity. Treasury stock is a company's own stock, previously paid for and issued, reacquired, and held in the name of the company rather than formally retired.

The term *capital* is used in many different ways, including the following: in economics, a factor of production; capital goods; legal capital; stated capital; circulating capital; working capital; capital assets; assets invested in the business; liabilities and stockholders' equity; capital surplus; financial capital; physical capital; capital budgeting; capital leases; capital maintenance; capital markets; capital projects; capital stock; contributed capital; simple capital structure; complex capital structure; capital expenditure; return on capital. The term *capitalization of a corporation* is frequently used by investment analysts to refer to shareholders' equity plus bonds outstanding.

See also Capital stock; Corporation; Net assets; Income; Capital maintenance theories; Preferred stock; Treasury stock.

REFERENCE
Kieso, Donald E., and Weygandt, Jerry J., *Intermediate Accounting* (John Wiley, N.Y., 1986).

CAPITAL AND REVENUE EXPENDITURES
A capital expenditure is an expenditure that is expected to benefit future periods. Capital expenditures are recorded as assets and are normally depreciated. Revenue expenditures are normal, recurring expenditures that benefit only the current accounting period and are expensed when they occur.

Capital expenditures either increase the quantity of services received from an asset (longer useful life or more output) or increase the quality of the service of the asset. Some firms establish a minimum amount for capital expenditures, which represents a materiality, or expediency, threshold.

Expenditures related to plant and equipment include additions, replacements and betterments (improvements), rearrangements and relocations, and repair and maintenance. An addition is a major expenditure that increases the service potential of the related asset. For example, a company may add a new wing to its plant. Additions are usually capitalized. Replacements and betterments are essentially substitutions of a new part of an asset for an existing part. Replacements involve substituting a similar asset for the existing asset. A betterment involves substituting an asset that reflects an improvement in quality for the existing asset. Replacements and substitutions are usually considered capital expenditures. Rearrangements and relocations of existing assets are capitalized if they are expected to benefit future periods. Repairs and maintenance are those expenditures that are required to maintain the current operating capabilities of the existing asset. Repair and maintenance expenditures are usually expensed unless they are considered major, in which case they could be capitalized.

In tax law, a capital expenditure is an expenditure which must be added to the basis of the property improved. Generally, any cost recovery in the form of a tax deduction has to come in the form of depreciation.

See also Property, plant, and equipment; Depreciation.

REFERENCE
Smith, Jay M., and Skousen, K. Fred, *Intermediate Accounting* (South-Western, Cincinnati, OH, 1984).

CAPITAL MAINTENANCE THEORIES

Accountants generally recognize that earnings result only after capital has been maintained or costs recovered. In this context, capital ordinarily refers to owners' equity or net assets of a business enterprise. Capital at the beginning of a period is maintained during the period if earnings for the period equal or exceed dividends (withdrawals) for the period. Earnings in excess of dividends for a period become part of investment capital or net assets to be maintained in the following period. There are two major views concerning the kind of capital to be maintained:

1. Financial capital maintenance (e.g., dollars invested directly by owners or through nondistribution of earnings in the past). Financial capital maintenance can compute income measurement in terms of (1) historical cost or (2) current cost. Under financial capital maintenance, earnings occur if a company recovers more from revenues than the nominal dollars invested in the asset sold. This concept is associated with the conventional accounting and reporting system.

2. Physical capital maintenance (e.g., physical properties of assets required to produce goods or services or productive capacity). Income arises only if an enterprise recovers in revenues more than the replacement cost of items sold.

The major difference between these two concepts involves certain changes in prices of assets during accounting periods that result in "holding gains and losses." Holding gains and losses are amounts that arise solely because of price or value changes in assets. For example, assume that an item of inventory is purchased on January 1 for $10,000 and its price at December 31 is $12,000. The asset is unsold at the end of the year. A holding gain of $2,000 resulted from holding the asset. The decision paths that result from the different views of capital can be diagrammed as follows:

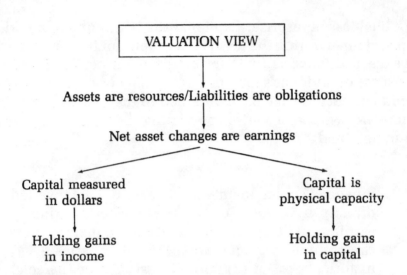

The two capital maintenance concepts can be illustrated by a simple example. Assume the following:

Initial capital of $15,000 cash is invested in inventory and a machine priced at $8,000 and $7,000, respectively. The machine has a 10-year life that will be depreciated using straight-line depreciation.

Inventory transactions during the year are as follows:

Inventory purchased as described above	$8,000
Inventory sold for $9,000; replacement cost at time of sale (inventory not replaced at this time)	8,300
Actual cost to replenish stock	8,500
Year-end inventory replacement cost	8,700

Exhibit C–2 shows an income statement and a balance sheet assuming financial capital maintenance (at historical cost and current value) and physical capital maintenance.

Under the financial capital maintenance approach (historical cost), the company maintained its beginning of the year $15,000 capital and earned $300 in income during the year. Accountants have generally used the concept of maintenance of financial capital based on historical cost because investors

Exhibit C-2
Theories of Capital Maintenance—Financial Capital and Physical Capital

	Financial Capital		Current Value/
	Historical Cost	Current Value	Physical Capital
INCOME STATEMENT			
Sales	$ 9,000	$ 9,000	$ 9,000
Cost of Sales	8,000	8,300	8,300
Depreciation	700	790	790
	8,700	9,090	9,090
	300	(90)	(90)
Holding gains (inv. sold $300; inv. held $200; lathe $900)	—	1,400	—
Income (loss)	$ 300	$ 1,310	$ (90)
BALANCE SHEET			
Cash	$ 500	$ 500	$ 500
Inventory	8,500	8,700	8,700
Lathe-net	6,300	7,110	7,110
Total	$ 15,300	$ 16,310	$ 16,310
Capital	$ 15,000	$ 15,000	$ 15,000
Undistributed income (loss)	300	1,310	(90)
Capital Maintenance	—	—	1,400
Total	$ 15,300	$ 16,310	$ 16,310

are assumed to be interested primarily in the monetary (dollar) return on their investment. Holding gains are not recognized until assets are sold. When holding gains are realized, they are not identified separately on the income statement. Under the current value concept of financial capital maintenance, inventory and depreciable assets are revalued every year at current cost, usually replacement cost. Holding gains are considered to be income but are separately identified in the income statement. Under the financial capital maintenance approach, holding gains and losses are included in income (or loss).

Under the physical capital maintenance concept, the cost of capital consumed (inventories sold and depreciation of assets) exceeded revenues by $90. Physical capital was not maintained. Notice that an additional charge must be made against income for the additional cost of sales and depreciation necessary to reflect those higher replacement costs. In the illustration, physical capital was eroded. Holding gains or losses are not reported on the income statement but are shown as a separate component of capital on the balance sheet.

It is also possible to adjust capital to reflect changes in the purchasing power of the dollar resulting from inflation or deflation. Income is then shown after maintenance of the purchasing power of the investors' capital. Income results only if the company can recover from revenues more than the general purchasing power equivalent of its investment. The basic concept of capital maintenance is not changed as a result of this additional consideration.

See also Capital; Current value accounting; Constant dollar accounting.

REFERENCE
FASB, SFAC No. 5, Recognition and Measurement in Financial Statements of Business Enterprises (FASB, 1984).

CAPITAL STOCK

Ownership in a corporation is divided into shares of capital stock with the physical evidence of ownership being a stock certificate. The following terms are associated with capital stock:

1. *Authorized capital stock*—shares that can be legally issued as specified by the corporate charter.
2. *Issued capital stock*—authorized shares that have been issued by the corporation.
3. *Unissued capital stock*—shares of authorized capital stock that have never been issued.
4. *Outstanding capital stock*—shares of authorized stock held by shareholders at a specific time.
5. *Subscribed capital stock*—stock for which a purchase agreement has been entered into but the agreed amount has not yet been paid. Subscribed stock is normally issued when the subscriber pays the full agreed price of the stock.

Par value stock are shares of corporate stock having a specified dollar amount per share assigned to each share by the articles of incorporation and designated on the face of the stock certificate. Stock issued at a price above par is issued at a premium, while stock issued below par value is issued at a discount. The original purchases of stock at a price below par are usually liable to creditors for the discount. Par value should not be taken as an indicator of the market value or book value of the stock. No-par value stock is stock that has not been assigned a par value in the articles of incorporation. The board of directors is generally given the power to determine whether no-par value stock is to have a stated value. True no-par value stock has neither a par nor stated value assigned to it.

Common stock is the basic capital stock of a corporation and carries with it major rights, including:

1. A share in the management of the corporation by voting, especially as reflected in the election of the board of directors and by participation at stockholders' meetings.

2. Participation in the earnings of the corporation through dividends when declared by the board of directors.

3. A share in the assets of the corporation if the corporation is dissolved.

4. A pro rata participation in the acquisition of additional shares of capital stock issued by the corporation. This right is referred to as the preemptive right; its purpose is to protect the proportionate interests of shareholders. Currently many shares are issued without this right.

Common stock may be classified into Class A and Class B stock. One class usually has the basic features of common stock while the other has restrictions, such as the denial or deferment of voting rights.

Common stockholders are referred to as the residual owners of the business since their interest in liquidation is subordinate to the claims of all other stockholders, such as preferred stockholders, and creditors.

Preferred stock is a form of capital stock that possesses certain preferences or priorities over common stock. The preferences are usually associated with a prior claim to dividends and the distribution of assets upon the liquidation of the corporation.

See also Preferred stock; Corporation; Capital; Legal capital; Financial markets.

REFERENCE
Davidson, Sidney, et al., *Intermediate Accounting* (The Dryden Press, Chicago, 1985).

CAPITALIZATION OF INTEREST
Companies frequently borrow to finance the construction of an asset. The question arises as to whether interest charged on such borrowings should be considered as a cost of the asset constructed. Interest has usually been considered a financing charge and not a part of the cost of an asset. Currently, generally accepted accounting principles require the capitalization of interest cost incurred in financing certain assets that take a period of time to prepare for their intended use, if its effect is material. In effect, interest should be capitalized as a part of the historical cost of acquiring certain assets. The historical cost of acquiring an asset includes the costs necessarily incurred to bring it to the condition and location required for its intended use. Qualifying assets include assets that an enterprise constructs for its own use, such as new facilities, and assets intended for sale or lease that are constructed as separate projects, such as ships or real estate developments.

The objectives of capitalizing interest are (a) to obtain a measure of acquisition cost that more clearly reflects the enterprise's total investment in the asset and (b) to charge a cost that relates to the acquisition of a resource that will benefit future periods against the revenues of the periods benefited (FASB Statement No. 34).

The amount of interest cost to be capitalized for qualifying assets is that portion of the interest costs incurred during the asset's acquisition period that theoretically could have been avoided if expenditures for the asset had not been made. The amount capitalized in an accounting period is computed by applying an interest rate to the average amount of accumulated expenditures for the asset during the period. The interest rate used is usually the rate charged on funds actually borrowed to finance the construction of the asset, the rate on other recent borrowings, or a weighted-average interest rate on old borrowings. The amount of interest capitalized cannot exceed the total interest costs incurred during the period.

See also Capital and revenue expenditures.

C

REFERENCE
SFAS No. 34, Capitalizaton of Interest Cost (FASB, 1979).

CASH

For accounting purposes, cash consists of any item that would be accepted for deposit in a checking account in a commercial bank. Cash includes coins, paper currency, checks, money orders, bank drafts, certified checks, cashiers' checks, and demand deposits in banks. Savings accounts are often classified as cash even though the bank retains the legal right to require notice before a withdrawal can be made. Items such as postage stamps, postdated checks, IOUs, dishonored checks, and deposits in closed banks are excluded from cash. When the use of cash is restricted for a particular purpose, such as for the retirement of bonds, it would be excluded from cash and classified under either investments or other asset categories on a balance sheet.

To provide for cash disbursements involving small amounts, many firms establish a petty cash fund to handle such payments. Under an imprest petty cash fund, a fund is established for a specific amount. When the fund is to be replenished, a check equal to the payments made from the fund is cashed and deposited in the fund to bring the fund balance up to the original amount established in the fund.

Two major issues are paramount when managing cash: (1) how much cash should be maintained to carry out the operations of the business, and (2) how cash can be safeguarded against theft, misappropriation, and similar irregularities. Safeguarding cash is usually accomplished by establishing control procedures for cash receipts and disbursements, using an imprest petty cash system, reconciling bank accounts periodically, utilizing cash forecasts, and using a voucher system for cash payments.

See also Internal control; Voucher system; Bank reconciliation; Checks.

REFERENCE
Garbutt, Douglas, *How to Budget and Control Cash* (Gower, Brookfield, VT, 1985).

CASH FLOW
Cash flow refers to the total cash receipts from sales less actual cash expenditures required to obtain those sales. The term *cash flow* can also be used in a broader sense to indicate a company's sources and uses of cash during an accounting period. Cash flow can be presented in a cash flow statement that shows a listing of cash receipts (sources) and disbursements (uses), with the difference between the receipts and disbursements disclosed as the increase or decrease in cash for the period. A condensed cash flow statement is presented here:

XYZ Corporation
Cash Flow Statement
For the Year Ended December 3, 19X7

Sources of cash		
Operations	$ 50,000	
Sales of equipment	10,000	
Issuance of common stock	100,000	
Total sources of cash		$160,000
Uses of cash		
Purchase of equipment	$110,000	
Cash dividend paid	30,000	
Total uses of cash		140,000
Increase in cash		$ 20,000

The cash flow statement can help users of financial statements understand the effects of cash flows, especially as they relate to income-generating, investing, and financing activities of an enterprise. Such statements also provide insights into the liquidity, financial flexibility and risk, and operating capability of an enterprise.

See also Statement of changes in financial position; Accounting basis.

CASH SURRENDER VALUE

The cash surrender value of life insurance is that portion of the annual life insurance premium which will be returned to the policyholder in the event the policy is cancelled. The cash surrender value of the policy increases each year as long as the policy is in force. Part of each annual premium represents an investment and part represents insurance expense. The portion of the yearly premium that does not increase the cash surrender value of the policy represents insurance expense. The amount of the cash surrender value of the policy is reported on the balance sheet as an asset under the investment classification. At death, the difference between the proceeds from the policy and the cash surrender value is reported on the income statement as an extraordinary gain or as income before extraordinary items.

See also Insurance.

CERTIFIED PUBLIC ACCOUNTANT (CPA)

A certified public accountant is an accountant who has fulfilled certain requirements established by a state law for the practice of public accounting in that state. The intent of legislation governing public accounting is to regulate the practice of the profession so as to ensure that certain basic standards of practice and professional conduct are maintained because of the public interest that is directly involved.

To become a CPA, an accountant must pass a comprehensive examination that is divided into four areas: accounting practice, accounting theory, auditing, and business law. Some states also require that an examination on professional ethics be passed before the CPA certificate is issued. The CPA examination is designed to measure the competence of candidates, including technical knowledge of accounting, the ability to apply this knowledge to practical problems, and the candidate's understanding of professional responsibilities. Membership in the major professional association (AICPA) is over 200,000.

In 1984, Chief Justice Warren Burger, U.S. Supreme Court, was quoted as saying: "By certifying the reports that . . . depict a corporation's financial status, the independent auditor assumes a public responsibility transcending away any employment relationship with [the] client." This statement asserts the social justification for the audit and for the practice of public accounting. The professional conduct of accountants has changed in recent decades. Advertising, fee quotations, and solicitation of new clients are no longer banned. Competition among accounting firms is strong. Specialization in practice is common, especially as it is reflected in technical functions and by industry. The internationalization of accounting practice is already underway. Major concerns of the profession include expansion of services, self-regulation, competition, computerization, specialization, quality control, CPA qualifications, and continuing professional education. In addition to accountants, many accounting firms employ engineers, lawyers, economists, actuaries, information technologists, and other professionals which enable the firms to offer a full range of advisory services. Competence, integrity, and independence are still considered the cornerstones of the profession. In 1944, Victor Stempf, then president of the AICPA, wrote: "Statesmanship in the profession looks beyond immediate selfish interest or expediency toward the long range development of the influence, recognition, and prestige of the profession through unmistakable service in the public interest. Statesmanship demands constant vigilance and vigorous action. . . . As a profession we have an inalienable right to set for ourselves objective standards of independence, integrity, and competence."

C

See also Accounting associations; Accounting profession; Accounting; Audit.

REFERENCE
Previts, Gary John, *The Scope of CPA Services* (John Wiley & Sons, N.Y., 1985).

CHART OF ACCOUNTS

A chart of accounts is a list of a firm's general and subsidiary ledger accounts and numbers systematically organized. An account-numbering system is usually designed as a code that indicates classifications and relationships of accounts. For example, each asset account might be assigned a number between 101 and 199. General ledger accounts are usually arranged in the order in which they appear on the financial statements. First, assets, liabilities, and permanent owners' equity accounts appear in the order of their listing on the statement of financial position. Then revenue and expense accounts appear in the order of their listing on the income statement. This arrangement facilitates the preparation of financial statements.

See also Account; Ledger.

CHECKS

A *check* is a written instrument which by its terms directs a bank at which the drawer of the check (the person making out the check) has a deposit to pay on demand a certain sum of money to a payee (the party to whom the check is to be paid). The Federal Reserve Board defines a check as "a draft or order upon a bank or banking house purporting to be drawn upon a deposit of funds for the payment at all events of a certain sum of money to a certain person therein named or to him or his order or to bearer and payable instantly on demand." The balance in the cash account is reduced when a check is issued, not when it clears the bank.

A *certified check* is a check drawn by a depositor and taken by the depositor to his/her bank for certification. When a check is certified by the bank at the request of the holder, the bank becomes primarily responsible. It is almost the same as the holder's obtaining the cash and redepositing it. If a bank certifies a check at the request of the drawer, the drawer's liability continues. A *cashier's check* is a check drawn by an officer of a bank on that bank and payable to some other persons. A *traveler's check* is a credit instrument or draft drawn upon a company (such as American Express) or a bank by one of its officers. Traveler's checks are frequently used as substitutes for cash when traveling or making payment where the risks of losing cash are to be avoided.

A *letter of credit* is a written promise by a bank to accept and pay orders for money drawn upon it up to the amount stated and for the party named in the letter of credit. A *certificate of deposit* is a written instrument in the form of a receipt given by a bank or other type of financial institution for a sum of money it has received on deposit. A *trade acceptance* is a draft drawn by a seller of goods and services on the buyer of those goods or services that is payable either to the seller or to the seller's bank. Trade acceptances are usually drawn to require payment at a future date which allows the buyer to receive the goods or services and possibly sell them before payment is required.

See also Cash.

CLASSIFIED FINANCIAL STATEMENTS

A classified balance sheet arranges the major categories of assets, liabilities, and owners' equity into significant groups and subgroups. Classifying items on the balance sheet provides information concerning the liquidity of the assets and the maturity dates of liabilities. For example, assets, liabilities, and shareholders' equity are usually classified on a classified balance sheet as follows:

Assets

Current assets
Long-term investments (or Investments)
Property, plant, and equipment
Intangible assets
Deferred charges

Liabilities

Current liabilities
Long-term liabilities
Shareholders' equity
Capital stock
Additional paid-in capital
Retained earnings

See also Statement of Financial Position.

CLOSING ENTRIES

Closing entries are general journal entries made at the end of an accounting period to reduce the balance in revenue and expense accounts to zero and to transfer the balances to related balance sheet accounts. Revenue and expense accounts are temporary accounts and are used during an accounting period to accumulate and summarize information relating to net income for the period. The balances in these accounts are no longer required once the accounting period is over. By reducing these account balances to zero, the accounts are ready to begin accumulating and summarizing data for the following period. The dividends account is also closed out for the same reason.

See also Accounting cycle; Adjusting entries; Reversing entries.

COMBINED STATEMENTS

When used in governmental accounting, a combined statement is one in which separate columns present the data for each governmental fund, the data in each column being the total data for all funds which can be included in a total column. Interfund transactions are not eliminated in a combined statement as intercompany transactions are eliminated in consolidated financial statements. Combined statements are also used in agency and branch accounting as well as in personal financial statements.

See also Agency and branch; Personal financial statements; Consolidated financial statements.

COMMITMENT

Unconditional purchase commitments are obligations to transfer funds, products, or services in fixed or minimum amounts. Special financial statement disclosure requirements are specified for such commitments which meet and do not meet criteria established by generally accepted accounting principles. Criteria for determining when accounting recognition is required are not specified.

REFERENCE
FASB No. 47, Disclosure of Long-term Obligations (FASB, 1981).

COMMON STOCK
See Capital stock.

COMPILATION
A compilation is the presentation in the form of financial statements information that is the representation of management (owners) without the expression of any assurance on the statements. A compilation requires that the accountant understand the industry and nature of the business in which the client is engaged, including the accounting records, qualifications of personnel, and the accounting basis on which the financial statements are presented. The accountant is not required to

make inquiries or perform other procedures to verify, corroborate, or review information supplied by his client. A compilation report states that a compilation has been performed, describes a compilation, and states that no opinion or other form of assurance is expressed on the statements.

See also Audit; Review.

REFERENCE
Burton, John C., et al., *Handbook of Accounting and Auditing* (Warren, Gorham & Lamont, Boston, 1981).

COMPREHENSIVE INCOME

"Comprehensive income is the change in equity (net assets) of an entity during a period from transactions and other events and circumstances from nonowner sources. It includes all changes in equity during a period except those resulting from investments by owners and distributions to owners" (FASB). "Comprehensive income arises from (a) exchange transactions and other transfers between the enterprise and other entities that are not its owners, (b) the enterprise's productive efforts, and (c) price changes, casualties, and other effects of interactions between the enterprise and the economic, legal, social, political, and physical environment of which it is part" (FASB).

Comprehensive income includes not only revenues, expenses, gains, and losses but also various intermediate components, measures, or subtotals, including gross margin, contribution margin, income from continuing operations before taxes, income from continuing operations, and operating income. Comprehensive income has significance for those attempting to use financial statements, as it relates to investment, credit, and similar decisions, especially as it refers to evaluating stability, risk, and predictability.

See also Elements of financial statements; Income; Statement of earnings and comprehensive income.

REFERENCE
SFAC No. 3, Elements of Financial Statements of Business Enterprises
(FASB, 1981).

CONCEPTUAL FRAMEWORK OF ACCOUNTING

The Financial Accounting Standards Board has undertaken a major project involving the development of a conceptual framework for financial accounting and reporting. A conceptual framework has been viewed as a constitution or a coherent system of interrelated objectives and fundamentals that can lead to consistent standards for accounting. The fundamentals are the underlying concepts of financial accounting—concepts that guide the selection of transactions, events, and circumstances to be accounted for; their recognition and measurement; and the means of summarizing and communicating them to interested parties (FASB). The framework would also prescribe the nature, function, and limits of financial accounting and financial statements.

As currently conceived, the FASB Conceptual Framework has eight major components, as shown in Exhibit C–3.

The FASB acknowledges that the conceptual framework will not directly solve financial accounting and reporting problems. Instead, the framework provides direction and tools for solving problems. The Board considers that it will be the most direct beneficiary of the guidance provided by the conceptual framework in that it will guide the Board in developing accounting and reporting standards by providing the Board with a common foundation and basic reasoning on which to consider merits of alternatives. Statements of Financial Accounting Concepts, which are the product of the FASB project, do not establish standards prescribing accounting procedures or disclosure practices.

To date, Statements of Financial Accounting Concepts issued include:

Objectives of Financial Reporting by Business Enterprises (No. 1)
Qualitative Characteristics of Accounting Information (No. 2)

Exhibit C–3
Conceptual Framework for Financial Accounting and Reporting

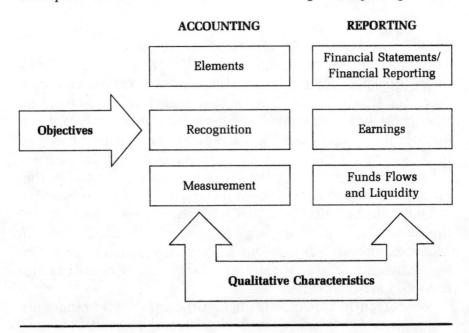

Elements of Financial Statements of Business Enterprises (No. 3)
Objectives of Financial Reporting by Nonbusiness Organizations
(No. 4)
Recognition and Measurement in Financial Statements of Business
Enterprises (No. 5)
Elements of Financial Statements (No. 6)

Statement No. 1 focuses on establishing goals for financial reporting that will enable financial reports to assist investors, creditors, and others in making economic decisions. The objectives of financial reporting are not intended to directly determine the resolution of those decisions.

Statement No. 2 describes the characteristics that make accounting information useful for decision making, such as relevance and reliability.

Statement No. 3 defines the basic elements, or "building blocks," of financial statements. This statement identifies ten elements of financial reporting: assets, liabilities, equity, revenues, expenses, gains, losses, investments by owners, distributions to owners, and comprehensive income.

Statement No. 4 establishes the objectives of general purpose external financial reporting by nonbusiness organizations.

Statement No. 5 sets forth fundamental recognition criteria and guidance on what information should be formally incorporated into financial statements and when. The statement also discusses what financial statements should be presented and how those statements contribute to the objectives of financial reporting.

Statement No. 6 defines three classes of new assets for not-for-profit organizations: permanently restricted, temporarily restricted, and unrestricted. Statements No. 2 and No. 3 now encompass not-for-profit organizations.

See also Objectives of financial reporting of business enterprises; Qualitative characteristics of accounting information; Elements of financial statements; Objectives of financial reporting by nonbusiness organizations; Recognition and measurement; Financial Accounting Standards Board; Accounting principles.

REFERENCE
FASB, Accounting Standards: Statements of Financial Accounting Concepts 1-5 (McGraw-Hill, 1985).

CONSERVATISM
Conservatism is a basic accounting convention that requires the reasonable anticipation of potential losses in recorded assets or in the settlement of liabilities at the time when financial statements are prepared. The principle of conservatism is sometimes expressed as follows: "Recognize all losses and anticipate no profit," or "Recognize the lowest of possible values

C

for assets and the highest of possible values for liabilities." The application of the principle does not require the deliberate understatement of assets or overstatement of liabilities. The application of the principle requires astute professional judgment by the accountant or auditor. Application of conservatism typically requires that (1) sales and other revenues are not to be anticipated, and (2) all liabilities or losses should be properly recorded and recognized in the reporting process.

Conservatism is sometimes justified on the grounds that it compensates for the overoptimism of managers and owners. Another view is that it is preferable to understate net income and net assets rather than overstate them since the consequences of loss or bankruptcy are more serious than those associated with profitable operations. It should be remembered, however, that accounting reports should provide users with sufficient information to allow them to make their own evaluation of risks and opportunities.

See also Accounting assumptions; Accounting principles; Qualitative characteristics of accounting.

REFERENCES

Grady, Paul, *Inventory of Generally Accepted Accounting Principles for Business Enterprises* (AICPA, 1965).

SFAC No. 2, Qualitative Characteristics of Accounting Information (FASB, 1980).

CONSIGNMENT

A consignment is an arrangement whereby one party transfers goods to another for purposes of sale without the ownership of the goods changing hands. The company delivering the goods (the consignor) retains ownership while the company (the consignee) attempts to sell them. If the merchandise is sold, the consignee returns the sales price to the consignor minus a commission and related expenses. Since the consignor has title to the goods, the goods are included in the consignor's inventory until they are sold.

See also Inventory.

CONSOLIDATED FINANCIAL STATEMENTS

A stock acquisition is one form of business combination. In a stock acquisition, one corporation acquires all or part of the voting stock of another company, and the acquired company remains intact as a separate legal entity. The relationship of the acquiring company to the acquired firm is described as a parent-subsidiary relationship. The acquiring company is referred to as the parent (investor) and the acquired company as a subsidiary. The related companies are called affiliated companies. Consolidated financial statements are generally prepared for affiliated companies.

There are certain advantages to acquiring the majority of the voting stock of another company rather than purchasing its resources. For example:

1. Stock acquisition is relatively simple by open market purchases or by cash tender offers to the subsidiary's stockholders.

2. A smaller investment is typically required to obtain control of the subsidiary since only a majority of the stock must be purchased.

3. The separate legal existence of the affiliated companies provides a degree of protection of the parent's assets from creditors of the subsidiaries.

Consolidated financial statements include a complete set of statements prepared for the consolidated entity and include the sum of the assets, liabilities, revenue, and expenses of the affiliated companies after eliminating the effect of any transactions among the affiliated companies. The consolidated statements present the financial position and results of operations of the economic unit controlled by the parent company as a single accounting entity. Emphasis is placed on the economic unit under control of one management rather than upon the legal form of the separate entities. The consolidated financial statements are prepared primarily for the benefit of the shareholders and creditors of the parent company. There is a presumption that consolidated statements are more meaningful than the separate statements of members of the affiliation. However, subsidiary creditors, minority shareholders, and regulatory agencies must rely on the statements of the subsidiary to assess their claims.

The usual condition for controlling financial interest is ownership of a majority voting interest in common stock. As a general rule, ownership by one company, directly or indirectly, of over 50 percent of the outstanding voting shares of another company is required for consolidation. A subsidiary would ordinarily not be consolidated:

1. Where control is likely to be temporary.

2. Where the subsidiary is in legal reorganization or in bankruptcy.

3. Where a subsidiary is a bank or an insurance company and the parent and other subsidiaries are engaged in manufacturing operations.

4. Where the subsidiary is a foreign company in a country that has expropriated the company or has imposed currency restrictions that prohibit cash remittances to the parent company.

To illustrate basic concepts associated with the preparation of consolidated financial statements, assume that the Parent Company purchased 90 percent of the Subsidiary Company's common stock in the open market for $160,000. A work sheet for the preparation of a consolidated balance sheet at the date of acquisition is presented in Exhibit C–4.

Things to note about the work sheet in Exhibit C–4 that produces the consolidated sheet in the last column include:

Exhibit C-4
Consolidated Financial Statement Work Sheet

PARENT COMPANY AND SUBSIDIARY COMPANY
Consolidated Balance Sheet Working Paper
December 31, 1986

	Parent Company	Subsidiary Company	Eliminations Debit	Eliminations Credit	Minority	Consolidated Balance Sheet
Assets						
Investment in Subsidiary	$160,000			160,000		- -
Goodwill			25,000			$ 25,000
Other assets	140,000	$250,000				390,000
	$300,000	$250,000				$415,000
Liabilities and Stockholders' Equity						
Liabilities	$ 50,000	$100,000				$150,000
Common Stock:						
Parent Company	175,000					175,000
Subsidiary Company		100,000	90,000		10,000	- -
Retained earnings:						
Parent Company	75,000					75,000
Subsidiary Company		50,000	45,000		5,000	*15,000
	$300,000	$250,000	160,000	160,000	15,000	$415,000

*Minority interest.

1. The separate balance sheets of the Parent Company and Subsidiary Company are presented in the first two money columns. The consolidated balance sheet is shown in the last column.

2. The Parent Company paid $160,000 for 90 percent of the net assets of the Subsidiary Company. The net assets of the Subsidiary Company totaled $150,000 (= total assets minus total liabilities; or common stock and retained earnings of the Subsidiary Company). In this case, it is assumed that the fair value of the Subsidiary Company's net assets is equal to

their book value. Since the Parent Company paid more than fair market value for 90 percent of the net assets of the Subsidiary ($135,000 = 90% × $150,000), the excess $25,000 (= $160,000 − $135,000) represents purchased goodwill and is reported as such on the consolidated balance sheet.

3. A minority interest of 10 percent in the Subsidiary's net assets equals $15,000 (10% × $150,000) and is reported on the consolidated balance sheet.

4. The assets and liabilities of the Subsidiary Company and goodwill are substituted in the consolidated balance sheet for the Investment in Subsidiary account which is eliminated on the work sheet.

5. On the consolidated balance sheet, the Parent Company's common stock and retained earnings are reported. The Subsidiary's equity accounts do not appear on the consolidated balance sheet. The Investment in Subsidiary account on the parent company's statement and the stockholders' equity accounts of the subsidiary are essentially intercompany accounts which from a consolidated viewpoint must be eliminated.

A consolidated balance sheet can be prepared for the affiliated companies from the last column of the work sheet. As can be noted, the consolidated balance sheet reports the sum of the assets, liabilities, and equities of the parent and its subsidiaries as they constitute a single company. Consolidated financial statements emphasize the economic substance of the parent-subsidiary relationship (one economic entity) rather than the legal form (separate legal entities).

When a parent company owns at least an 80 percent interest in a domestic subsidiary, the companies may elect to file a consolidated income tax return. When consolidated income tax returns are filed, intercompany transactions are eliminated. Consolidated net income usually approximates taxable income.

If separate income tax returns are filed, consolidated net income will usually differ from taxable income because intercompany transactions would not be eliminated. These timing differences usually require special accounting recognition.

Push-down accounting is an approach to accounting for an acquisition which involves establishing a new basis of accounting and reporting for a subsidiary in its separate financial statements. According to this method, the parent company's cost of acquiring a subsidiary is "pushed down" and used to establish a new accounting basis for the assets and liabilities of the subsidiary. The assets and liabilities of the subsidiary would be updated to report the amounts at which they are shown on the parent's consolidated statements. The SEC has required push-down accounting under special circumstances since 1983.

When an enterprise owns a substantial but not controlling interest in another company, some accountants prefer to use "proportionate consolidation" for the arrangement. For example, if a company has a one-third interest in a noncorporate joint venture, the investor company would include in the consolidated financial statements one-third of each of the assets, liabilities, revenues, and expenses of the venture. Proportionate consolidation of joint ventures is used primarily in the real estate and construction, oil and gas, and utilities industries.

In some situations, enterprises are affiliated as a result of common management or common control instead of as a result of a majority voting interest held by a parent in its subsidiaries. Combined statements are sometimes prepared for some arrangements. The procedures used to prepare combined statements are similar to those used when preparing consolidated statements. Any intercompany investment is eliminated against the related equity of the other enterprise. Where there is no intercompany investment but merely common management, the individual company equities are combined.

One-line consolidation occurs when an investment in another company is accounted for by the equity method of accounting. The effect of using the equity method on reported

C

income and the total balance sheet assets of the investee are identical to those that would be reported if the investee were consolidated. The difference would be that income and total assets of the investee would be reported on a single line in the income statement and balance sheet of the investor.

See also Business Combinations; Substance over form; Branch and agency; Purchase accounting; Pooling of interest; Goodwill; Combined statements.

REFERENCES
Burton, John C., Palmer, Russel E., & Kay, Robert S., eds. *Handbook of Accounting and Auditing* (Warren, Gorham & Lamont, Inc., Boston, 1981).
Haried, Andrew A., et al., *Advanced Accounting* (John Wiley & Sons, N.Y., 1985).
ARB 51, Consolidated Financial Statements (AICPA, Committee on Accounting Procedures, 1959).

CONSISTENCY
Consistency means conformity from period to period by a firm, with accounting policies and procedure remaining unchanged. Consistency is essential to improving comparability across accounting periods. Should change be required because of a more relevant or objective accounting policy or procedure, full disclosure must be made so that users of financial statements are aware of the change. Auditors are required to qualify their opinions for changes in accounting methods so that users of the financial statements are informed that a firm has not used the same methods of accounting consistently over time.

See also Accounting changes; Audit; Qualitative characteristics of accounting information; Accounting principles.

CONSTANT DOLLAR ACCOUNTING
Constant dollar accounting is a method of reporting financial statement elements in dollars which have the same (i.e., con-

stant) general purchasing power. Constant dollar accounting is also referred to as general price-level accounting. In constant dollar accounting, the dollars (not the principles and methods) used in historical cost financial statements are adjusted for changes in the purchasing power of the dollar. These adjustments make it possible to compare dollar amounts from different accounting periods in dollars of equal purchasing power. Constant dollar accounting eliminates the impact of general inflation from the financial statements. The statements are restated using an index of the general price level such as the Consumer Price Index for all Urban Consumers (CPI-U). A price index is a weighted-average relation between money and a given set of goods and services.

The restatement of the financial statements amounts is done according to the following formula:

$$
\begin{array}{c}
\text{Historical cost of nonmonetary} \\
\text{assets or nominal amount} \\
\text{of liability}
\end{array}
\times
\dfrac{\text{Index at end of current period}}{\begin{array}{c}\text{Index at date of nonmonetary} \\ \text{transaction}\end{array}}
$$

or

$$
\$100{,}000 \ \times \ \frac{1986 \text{ index}}{1979 \text{ index}} = \text{Cost of item in terms of 1986 dollars}
$$

where the cost of an asset acquired in 1979 is restated in terms of 1986 dollars.

In constant dollar accounting, an important distinction is made between monetary items and nonmonetary items. Monetary items are assets, liabilities, and equities whose balances are fixed in terms of numbers of dollars regardless of changes in the general price level, such as cash, receivables, and payables. All other items are nonmonetary items, such as inventory, property, plant, and equipment. In periods of changing prices, purchasing power gains or losses result from holding monetary items. For example, if one holds $1,000 in cash for a year during a period of inflation, purchasing power of the cash is reduced at the end of the year. The difference between a company's monetary assets and its monetary liabilities and equities is referred to as the net monetary position. The relationship between a net monetary position and rising/declining prices is illustrated here:

	Rising prices	Falling prices
Monetary assets exceed monetary liabilities	Loss	Gain
Monetary liabilities exceed monetary assets	Gain	Loss

The computation of the purchasing power gain or loss on net monetary items is illustrated in Exhibit C–5.

Constant dollar accounting provides for the meaningful comparisons of accounting data with measuring units that are comparable. Constant dollar accounting takes into consideration changes in the general price level. The recognition of the purchasing power gains and losses provides significant infor-

---

Exhibit C–5
Computing Purchasing Power Gain and Loss on Net Monetary Assets

		(000s)	
	Nominal Dollars	Conversion Factor	Average 19X9 Dollars
Balance, January 1, 19X9	$55,000 ×	$\dfrac{220.9 \text{ (avg. 19X9)}}{212.9 \text{ (Dec. 19X8)}}$	C$57,067
Increase in net monetary liabilities during the year	6,000		6,000
			63,067
Balance, December 31, 19X9	$61,000 ×	$\dfrac{220.9 \text{ (avg. 19X9)}}{243.5 \text{ (Dec. 19X9)}}$	55,338
Purchasing power gain on net monetary items			C$ 7,729

*Assumed to be in average 19X9 dollars. (FAS33, §232)

Source: FASB, Statement No. 33.

---

mation concerning the impact of inflation regarding monetary items. For these and other reasons, proponents of constant dollar accounting maintain that constant dollar information is relevant to decision makers.

On the other hand, constant dollar accounting does not take into consideration changes in specific prices of goods, such as inventories, plant, and equipment. Furthermore, constant dollar accounting requires the use of price indexes which can have statistical weaknesses which could impact on the reliability of the output of constant dollar adjustments.

See also Current value accounting; Capital maintenance theories; Monetary assets and liabilities; Accounting.

REFERENCE
SFAC No. 33, Financial Reporting and Changing Prices (FASB, 1979).

CONSTRUCTION-TYPE CONTRACTS
A construction-type contract is one which involves a construction project and extends over more than one accounting period. Two methods are currently used to account for such contracts:

1. Completed contract method. When this method is used, all of the profit from the contract is recognized in the accounting period the contract is completed. An expected loss on such a contract is recognized in the period when the loss is first forecast.

2. Percentage-of-completion method. When this method is used, profit is allocated to each of the construction periods ordinarily based on estimates of cost incurred during the period to total costs of the project or on an efforts-expended method. When the efforts-expended method is used, the percentage of completion is measured by comparing the work performed to date with the total estimated work for the project. The work performed can be considered labor

hours, labor dollars, machine hours, materials used, and other input measures. Progress towards completion can also be measured in other ways, such as the passage of time, units produced, units delivered, value added, the collection of billings, and appraisal. When the percentage of completion is determined, this percentage is multiplied by the total revenue on the contract to compute the revenue to be recognized to date. The revenue to be recognized to date minus any revenue recognized in previous years represents the revenue to recognize in the current year. The costs to be recognized are determined in a similar manner. Inventory is valued at the costs incurred plus the profit recognized to date, less any partial billings.

The completed contract method would be used only when the seller is unable to determine reliably either the amount of progress made in each year or the amount of costs needed to complete the entire project. The percentage-of-completion method would be used when the following conditions are met:

1. Reasonably dependable estimates can be made of the extent of progress towards completion, revenues, and costs.

2. The contract contains enforceable rights pertaining to the goods or services to be provided, the consideration involved, and the terms of settlement.

3. The buyer is able to satisfy the obligations under the contract.

4. The contractor is expected to be able to perform its obligations under the contract.

The major advantage of the completed-contract method is that gross profit is objectively determined when the project is completed rather than on estimates. The disadvantages of this method are that income does not reflect current performance and that any income recognition is deferred until complete performance under the contract. The percentage-of-completion method recognizes income currently and does not wait until final performance under the contract. The percentage-of-completion method reflects the application of accrual accounting, and usually produces a better measure of periodic income. This method also emphasizes the economic substance of the contract rather than the legal form of the contract. The major disadvantage of this method is that it relies on estimates for measuring income and inventory.

See also Revenue; Recognition; Realization; Accrual basis; Substance over form.

REFERENCE
AICPA, Statement of Position 81-1, Accounting for Performance of Construction-Type Contracts (AICPA, 1981).

CONTINGENCIES
A contingency is an existing condition, situation, or set of circumstances involving uncertainty as to possible gain or loss to an enterprise that will ultimately be resolved when one or more future events occurs or fails to occur (FASB Statement No. 5). The resulting gain or loss is referred to as a ''gain contingency'' or a ''loss contingency.'' Gain contingencies do not receive accounting recognition. Loss contingencies are related to the possible incurrence of liabilities or the impairment of assets. Examples of certain loss contingencies include collectibility of receivables, obligations related to product warranties, product defects and customers' premiums, threat of expropriation, litigation, claims and assessments, and guarantees of indebtedness of others. Three terms are used to describe the range of possibilities of an event occurring: probable, reasonably possible, and remote. Different accounting is prescribed for contingencies which fall within these ranges. These situations are outlined in Exhibit C–6.

Exhibit C-6
Ranges for Contingencies

Term	Definition	Accounting Action
Probable	The future event(s) is likely to occur.	Record the probable event in the accounts if the amount can be reasonably estimated. If not estimable, disclose facts in note.
Reasonably possible	The chance of the future event(s) occurring is more than remote but less than likely.	Report the contingency in a note.
Remote	The chance of the future event(s) occurring is slight.	No recording or reporting unless contingency represents a guarantee. Then note disclosure is required.

Loss contingencies related to general or unspecified business risks, such as losses related to a strike or recession, are not disclosed in financial statements.

See also Liabilities.

REFERENCE
SFAS No. 5, Accounting for Contingencies (FASB, 1975).

CONTRA ACCOUNT
Special accounts are frequently used to recognize the fact that the balance in a related account is not a complete description of the account. If the account is a deduction from the regular account, the account is referred to as a contra account. Contra accounts are also referred to as offset, valuation, and negative-asset accounts. The accumulated depreciation account is a *contra account* to the plant or equipment account. The

C

allowance for uncollectible receivables account is a contra account to the accounts receivable account. On the income statement, the sales returns and allowance account is a contra account to the sales account. A contra account would be reported as follows on the balance sheet:

Accounts receivable	$100,000	
Less: Allowance for uncollectible receivables	5,000	$95,000

The difference between the asset account and its related contra account ($95,000) is referred to as the book value, or carrying value, of the asset.

If the special account is an addition to the regular account, it is referred to as an adjunct account. A premium on bonds payable account is an adjunct account to the bonds payable account. The liability is the sum of the two account balances at a specific date.

Contra and adjunct accounts are neither assets nor liabilities in their own right.

See also Assets.

CONTRIBUTION MARGIN ANALYSIS
Contribution margin is defined as sales less variable expenses and can be illustrated as follows:

Sales (50,000 units)	$100,000
Less: Variable expenses	60,000
CONTRIBUTION MARGIN	40,000
Less: Fixed expenses	10,000
Net income	$ 30,000
Contribution margin per unit (50,000 units)	$0.80
Contribution margin rate (on sales)	40%

Variable expenses are those expenses that change in direct proportion to the change in volume of sales over the relevant range of business activity. The total variable expense fluctuates as sales volume fluctuates. The variable expense per unit remains constant. Fixed expenses are those expenses that remain constant at any relevant range of volume within the operating capacity of the firm. The total fixed expenses remain constant; the per unit fixed expense varies with change in volume. Contribution is that portion of revenue that is available to cover fixed expenses and produce a profit.

The contribution margin can be used in a variety of ways. For example, the break-even point of a business can be computed using the contribution-margin approach. The break-even point in units can be computed using the following formula:

$$\text{Sales at break-even point} = \frac{\text{Fixed expense}}{\text{Contribution margin per unit}}$$

$$= \frac{\$10,000}{\$0.80\ (=\$40,000/50,000\ \text{units})}$$

$$= 12,500\ \text{units}$$

The contribution margin rate is computed as follows: contribution margin divided by sales. Sales at the break-even point in dollars can be computed using the contribution-margin rate as follows:

$$\begin{array}{c}\text{Sales at break-even point} \\ \text{in dollars}\end{array} = \frac{\text{Fixed expense}}{\text{Contribution rate}}$$

$$= \frac{\$10,000}{.40\ (=\$40,000/\$100,000)}$$

$$= \$25,000$$

Using data on contribution margin per unit, management can make quick estimates of the impact on net income resulting from changes in sales:

C

Change in net income = Change in volume × Contribution margin per unit

Change in net income = Change in sales revenue × Contribution-margin rate

Change in selling price or unit cost required to achieve a desired contribution margin = Desired change in total contribution margin / Number of units to be sold

Sales required for desired net income = (Fixed expenses + Desired net income) / Contribution margin rate

A cost-volume-profit chart (Exhibit C–7) shows the profit or loss potential for an extensive range of volume. At any level of output, the profit or loss is the vertical difference between the sales line and the total cost line. The break-even point is the intersection of sales and total costs. The contribution margin at any level of output is the vertical difference between the sales line and the variable expenses line. The total expenses and variable expenses lines are parallel; the difference between them equals fixed expense.

Contribution margin analysis facilitates other decisions such as the utilization of scarce resources, make-or-buy equipment, sell now or process further, and plant acquisition decisions. To illustrate several applications, assume the following data about a company that can produce and sell three products or any combination thereof. However, the company's production capacity is limited by the number of machine hours available to produce the products.

	Product A	Product B	Product C
Sales price per unit	$12	$15	$18
Variable expense per unit	7	9	10
Contribution margin per unit	5	6	8
Machine hours to produce one unit	5	3	16
Contribution margin per machine hour	$ 1	$ 2	0.80

129

Exhibit C–7
Contribution Margin Analysis—Cost-Volume-Profit Chart

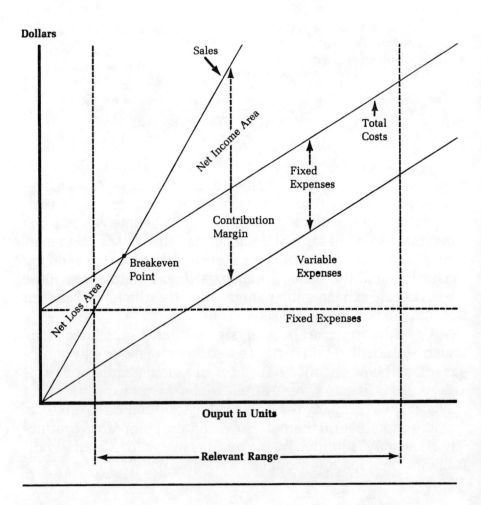

Although Product C has the largest contribution margin per unit, Product B should be produced since it has the largest contribution per the constraining factor (machine hours).

The following illustration shows the income statement for a company that has revenue but is operating at a $20,000 loss. This is considered to be a temporary situation. Should the com-

	Continue operations	Shut down
Sales	$1,000,000	– – –
Less: Variable expenses	900,000	– – –
Contribution margin	100,000	– – –
Less: Fixed expenses	120,000	$120,000
Net loss	$ 20,000	$120,000

pany continue operations or shut down? If the company closes down, the fixed expenses will continue.

The firm should continue to operate because the contribution margin is larger than zero. The contribution margin from continued operations helps pay some of the fixed expenses.

See also Break-even point; Gross margin analysis; Planning and control.

REFERENCE
Liao, Woody M., and Boockholdt, James L., *Cost Accounting for Managerial Planning, Decision Making and Control* (Dame, Houston, TX, 1985).

CONTROLLER

The controller (or comptroller) is the chief accounting executive in most business organizations. Major functions performed by the controller include internal auditing, general accounting, tax planning, cost accounting, and budgeting. The treasurer is responsible for assuring that the firm has the financial resources required to conduct its activities. In addition, the treasurer usually has responsibilities relating to the custody of cash, banking, investments, and insurance. The treasurer's function is basically custodial; the controller's function is basically an information and reporting function. The following functions are usually assigned to controllers and treasurers:

C

Controller:

1. Planning for control
2. Reporting and interpreting reports and statements
3. Evaluating and consulting on financial matters
4. Tax administration
5. Government reporting
6. Protection of assets
7. Economic appraisal

Treasurer:

1. Provision of capital
2. Investor relations
3. Short-term financing
4. Banking and custody
5. Credit and collections
6. Investments
7. Insurance

See also Certified Public Accountant; Accounting system; Accounting profession; Accounting.

CONVERTIBLE SECURITIES

Convertible securities are bonds or preferred stocks that can be exchanged for common stock at the option of the holder. Deferred securities are often used as a form of deferred common stock financing, as a device to assist debt or preferred financing, and for raising relatively less expensive financing.

Convertible securities are usually convertible only within or after a certain time period. Time limits are imposed primarily to meet the issuer's long-term financial needs. The conversion ratio is the ratio in which the convertible security can be exchanged for common stock or preferred stock. If the conversion ratio is known, the conversion price can be computed by dividing the face value (not the market value) of the converti ble security by the conversion ratio. For example, a $1,000 face value bond convertible into 25 shares of common stock has a conversion ratio of 25 and a conversion price of $40 ($1,000 divided by 25). The issuer of convertible securities usually establishes a conversion price or ratio so as to make the conversion price at the time of issuance of the security somewhere between 10 and 20 percent above the current market price of the firm's stock. A predictable opportunity to convert must be available in order to improve the marketability of a convertible security. The conversion value of a convertible security is the value of the security measured in relation to the market value of the security into which it can be converted. The conversion value can usually be determined by multiplying the conversion ratio by the current market price of the firm's common stock (if convertible into common stock). If the conversion ratio of a bond is 20 and the market price of the common is $60, the conversion value is $1,200. A conversion premium is the percentage difference between the conversion price and the issuance price of a security.

See also Bonds; Preferred stock; Liability.

CORPORATION
A corporation is an entity created by law, capable of owning assets, incurring liabilities, and engaging in specified activities. The corporation is a legal entity separate from its owners (shareholders). Ownership in a corporation is evidenced by a stock certificate, a serially numbered document that shows the number of shares owned and the par value, if any. Ownership in a corporation is readily transferable and shareholders have no personal liability for the corporate debts and frequently have little active role in its management.

To form a corporation, three or more individuals, called incorporators, must file an application (articles of incorporation) with the proper state official. Articles of incorporation are the legal documents that specify a corporation's name,

C

period of existence, purpose and powers, authorized number of shares, classes of stock, and other information related to the corporation's existence and operations. When approved, this becomes the corporate charter which authorizes the company to do business. Incorporators next hold a stockholders' meeting to elect a board of directors and to pass bylaws to guide the operations of the corporation. The directors then hold a meeting to elect officers of the corporation, who manage the enterprise. The "cumulative method" of voting is sometimes used when electing a board of directors. When the cumulative method of voting is used, the owner of any one share is allowed as many votes for one or more candidates as there are directors to be elected. The activities of the board are recorded in a minutes book that becomes the official record of policy decisions. A typical corporate structure is shown here:

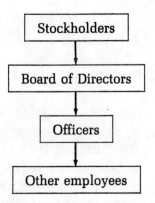

When a corporation issues stock, it gives the stockholders a stock certificate for the number of shares acquired, as evidence of ownership. The corporation maintains a shareowners' ledger that contains an account for each stockholder, showing the number of shares held by each owner of shares. When stock that has been issued is transferred from one owner to another, the transfer is recorded in a stock transfer book. Larger corporations often arrange for a transfer agent to maintain their stock transfer books and shareowners' ledgers. To ensure independent control over the process of issuing stock, many corporations engage a stock registrar to countersign stock certificates and to insure that each certificate is properly issued. Banks and trust companies in financial centers often serve as stock registrars and transfer agents.

A *de jure* corporation is a corporation formed in compliance with the provisions of an incorporation statute. A *de facto* corporation is a corporation formed without full compliance with all material, mandatory provisions of an incorporation statute. Acts beyond the scope of corporate powers are referred to as "ultra vires" acts. Directors are personally liable for such acts which they approve.

Corporations are classified as public or private corporations. Private corporations may be stock or nonstock corporations. Stock companies normally operate for profit, while nonstock corporations such as certain hospitals and churches usually are not-for-profit organizations. Corporations can also be classified as follows:

1. Public corporations are government-owned entities, such as the Federal Deposit Insurance Corporation.

2. Open corporations are private stock corporations whose stock is available to the public and is usually traded on a stock exchange (a listed corporation) or in the over-the-counter market (unlisted).

3. Closed corporations are private corporations whose stock is not offered for sale to the general public but rather is usually held by a few individuals.

4. Domestic corporations are corporations incorporated in a particular state.

5. Foreign corporations are companies that operate in a state other than the one in which they are incorporated.

C

The major advantages associated with the corporate form of business organization include limited liability to stockholders, ease of capital formation, ease of transfer of ownership, lack of mutual agency relationships, continuous existence, and centralized authority and responsibility. The major disadvantages of the corporate form include government regulation and taxation. A corporation, unlike a partnership or single proprietorship, is subject to taxation on income. Individual stockholders are subject to taxation on the dividend distributions of net income which results in a form of double taxation.

The comparative advantages and disadvantages of the corporate, partnership, and sole proprietorship types of business are presented in Exhibit C-8.

Professional corporations are closely held corporations established by members of a legally recognized profession, such as accountancy, law, and medicine. Membership in professional corporations is limited to members of the profession to ensure the integrity of the profession and to minimize professional compromises. Subchapter S corporations are also closely held corporations and are created through income tax legislation. Such corporations have the usual advantages of the corporate form of business organization but do not have the disadvantage of double taxation.

See also Capital; Capital stock.

REFERENCE
Kieso, Donald E., and Weygandt, Jerry J., *Intermediate Accounting* (John Wiley & Sons, N.Y., 1986).

COST

A cost is an expenditure (a decrease in assets or an increase in liabilities) made to obtain an economic benefit, usually resources that can produce revenue. A cost can also be defined as the sacrifice to acquire a good or service. Used in this sense, a cost represents an asset. An expense is a cost that has been

Exhibit C-8
Comparison of Legal Forms of Business Organization

FEATURE	PROPRIETORSHIP	PARTNERSHIP	CORPORATION
Number of owners	One.	Two or more.	Usually three or more.
Assets owned by	Proprietor.	Partners as co-owners.	Corporation.
Liability	Sole proprietor is personally liable for all business debts. *Unlimited liability.*	Each partner is personally liable for all business debts. *Unlimited liability.*	Stockholder's liability is usually limited to his own investment. *Limited liability.*
Legal existence	Extension of proprietor.	Extension of partners.	Separate entity, distinct from stockholders.
Life	Ends with change in ownership—for example, death or insolvency of proprietor.	Ends with change in ownership—for example, death or insolvency of a partner, withdrawal of a partner.	Perpetual unless limited by charter.
Organization agreement	Unnecessary.	Should have formal Articles of Copartnership setting forth agreement among partners.	Must be chartered by state.
Ownership powers	Complete.	Complete; any partner binds all other partners unless a partner is restricted.	Certain rights given by stock agreement to stockholders—for example, the right to vote, to receive declared dividends, to buy additional issues of stock.
Federal income tax	Proprietor reports income statement data on his personal tax return and is taxed on profit of the business; the business pays no income tax.	Partners report income statement data of partnership and show income distribution among partners on their personal tax returns; each partner is taxed on his share of the business' net income; the partnership pays no income tax.	Corporation pays income tax; shareholders report dividends as income on their personal tax returns (double taxation of corporate income).
Owners' salary	Personal withdrawal from owner's equity.	Division of net income among partners.	Salaries paid as operating expense; net income may be paid out as dividends.
Advantages	a. Relatively easy to start. b. Relatively free from government regulation. c. Profits taxed once to owner.	Approximately the same as those for proprietorship.	a. Ability to raise large sums of money. b. Ownership shares are relatively easy to transfer. c. Limited liability of shareholders. d. Life of corporations can be perpetual.
Disadvantages	a. Unlimited liability of owner. b. Difficulties of raising large amounts of money. c. Lack of permanency as a form of organization.	Approximately the same as those for proprietorship.	a. Double taxation of income distributed to shareholders. b. Subject to government regulation not required of other forms of business organization.

utilized by the company in the process of obtaining revenues; i.e., the benefits associated with the good or service have expired. Costs can be classified in many ways including:

1. Direct and indirect costs:

   a. Direct costs are outlays that can be identified with a specific product, department, or activity. For example, the costs of material and labor that are identifiable with a particular physical product are direct costs for the product.

   b. Indirect costs are those outlays that cannot be identified with a specific product, department, or activity. Taxes, insurance, and telephone expense are common examples of indirect costs.

2. Product and period costs:

   a. Product costs are outlays that can be associated with production. For example, the direct costs of materials and labor used in the production of an item are product costs.

   b. Period costs are expenditures that are not directly associated with production, but are associated with the passage of a time period. The president's salary, advertising expense, interest, and rent expenses are examples of period costs.

3. Fixed, variable, and mixed costs:

   a. Fixed costs are costs that remain constant in total (not per unit) regardless of the volume of production or sales, over a relevant range of production or sales. Rent and depreciation are typically fixed costs. Total depreciation remains constant; depreciation per unit of output changes with changes in volume or activity.

   b. Variable costs are costs that fluctuate in total (not per unit) as the volume of production or sales fluctuates. Direct labor and direct material costs used in production and sales commissions are examples of variable costs. Total commission expense varies with changes in sales volume; commission expense per unit of sales remains constant as sales volume changes.

c. Mixed costs are costs that fluctuate with production or sales, but not in direct proportion to production or sales. Mixed costs contain elements of fixed and variable costs. Costs of supervision and inspections are often mixed costs.

4. Controllable and uncontrollable costs:

a. Controllable costs are costs that are identified as a responsibility of an individual or department, and that can be regulated within a given period of time. Office supplies would ordinarily be considered a controllable cost for an office manager.

b. Uncontrollable costs are those costs that cannot be regulated by an individual or department within a given period of time. For example, rent expense is uncontrollable by the factory foreman.

5. Out-of-pocket costs and sunk costs:

a. Out-of-pocket costs are costs that require the use of current economic resources. Taxes and insurance are generally out-of-pocket costs.

b. Sunk costs are outlays or commitments that have already been incurred. The cost of equipment already purchased is a sunk cost.

6. Incremental, opportunity, and imputed costs:

a. Incremental (or differential) cost is the difference in total costs between alternatives. Incremental costs can also be considered as the total cost added or subtracted by switching from one level or plan of activity to another.

b. Opportunity cost is the maximum alternative benefit that could be obtained if economic resources were applied to an alternative use.

c. Imputed costs are costs that can be associated with an economic event when no exchange transaction has occurred. For example, if a company "rents to itself" a building that it might otherwise have rented to an outside party, the rent for the building is an imputed cost.

7. Relevant cost. A relevant cost is an expected future cost and a cost that represents difference in costs among alternatives. Assume you purchased an airline ticket from New York to London at a cost of $300 and that you have made an unrefundable $75 downpayment on the ticket. The remaining $225 will be paid when you pick up the ticket. The ticket is nontransferable. You later discover that you can purchase a ticket to London on another airline for $200. Everything related to the two tickets is equal. The $75 downpayment is not relevant to this decision since it is not a future cost that differs among alternatives. You should buy the new ticket for $200.

See also Expenses; Losses; Elements of financial statements; Break-even analysis; Contribution margin analysis; Cost accounting.

REFERENCE
Moscove, Stephen A., et al., *Cost Accounting* (Houghton Mifflin, Inc., Boston, 1985).

COST ACCOUNTING
Cost accounting is a subset of accounting that develops detailed information about costs as they relate to units of output and

to departments, primarily for purposes of providing inventory valuations (product costing) for financial statements, control, and decision making.

Manufacturing costs flow through three basic responsibility centers: raw materials storeroom, the factory, and the finished goods storeroom. Three inventory accounts are usually provided to accumulate costs as they relate to the three responsibility centers: raw material inventory, work-in-process inventory, and finished goods inventory. When goods are sold, costs are transferred from the finished goods inventory account to the cost of goods sold account. The flow of costs through the manufacturing process can be illustrated as follows:

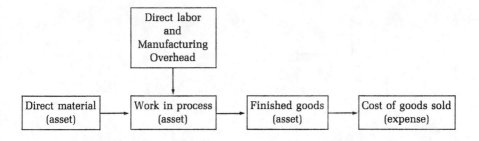

A job-order cost system or a process cost system is used to assign costs to manufactured products for purposes of controlling costs and costing products:

1. A job-order (or production order) cost system (Exhibit C–9) accumulates costs of material, labor, and manufacturing overhead by specific orders, jobs, batches, or lots. Job-order cost systems are widely used in the construction, furniture, aircraft, printing, and similar industries where the costs of a specific job depend on the particular order specifications.

2. A process cost system (Exhibit C–10) accumulates costs by processes or departments over a period of time. Product cost systems are used by firms that manufacture products through continuous-flow sys-

Exhibit C–9
Flow of Costs in Job-order Cost System

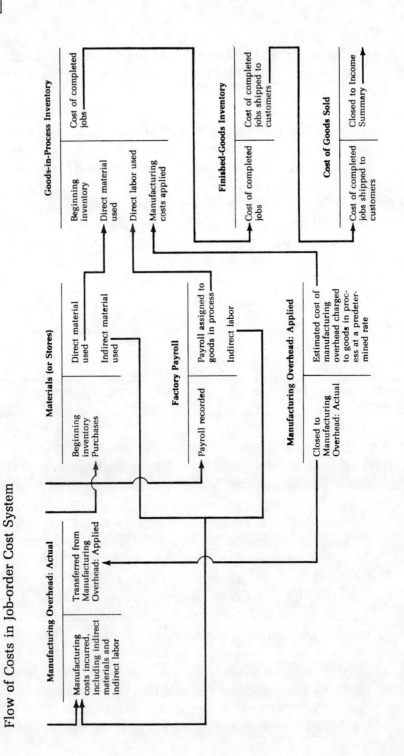

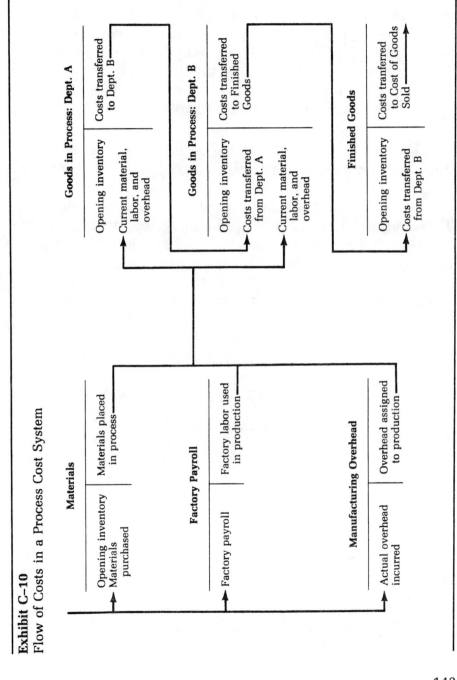

Exhibit C–10
Flow of Costs in a Process Cost System

Materials

| Opening inventory Materials purchased | Materials placed in process |

Factory Payroll

| Factory payroll | Factory labor used in production |

Manufacturing Overhead

| Actual overhead incurred | Overhead assigned to production |

Goods in Process: Dept. A

| Opening inventory | Costs transferred to Dept. B |
| Current material, labor, and overhead | |

Goods in Process: Dept. B

Opening inventory	Costs transferred to Finished Goods
Costs transferred from Dept. A	
Current material, labor, and overhead	

Finished Goods

| Opening inventory | Costs tranferred to Cost of Goods Sold |
| Costs transferred from Dept. B | |

tems or on a mass-production basis. Industries that use process cost systems include chemical, petroleum products, textiles, cement, glass, mining, and others. In a process cost system, costs for a department or process are accumulated. Per-unit costs are obtained by dividing the total departmental costs by the quantity produced during a given period in the department or process.

Direct material and direct labor costs can usually be traced directly to particular units manufactured. Manufacturing overhead costs incurred during a period are usually allocated to units manufactured based on a predetermined overhead rate. This overhead rate is based on the budgeted overhead costs for the period and the estimated level of activity (for example, units produced, direct labor hours, direct labor costs). The predetermined factory overhead rate per direct labor hour would be computed as follows using assumed data:

$$\text{Predetermined overhead rate} = \frac{\text{Estimated overhead costs for the year}}{\text{Estimated direct labor hours for the year}}$$

$$= \frac{\$500,000}{100,000}$$

$$= \$5 \text{ per direct labor hour}$$

If 400 direct labor hours were worked on a particular job, $2,000 overhead costs would be assigned to that job. Any difference between the total overhead costs actually incurred during a year and the total amount assigned to units in production can be charged to cost of goods sold for the year if the amount is not material. If material, the variance can be distributed among the work in process inventory, finished goods inventory, and cost of goods sold.

Standard cost systems are widely used for budgeting and performance evaluation purposes. Standard costs can be used in both job-order and process cost systems. In a standard cost system, product costing is achieved by using predetermined standard costs for material, direct labor, and overhead. Standard costs are developed on the basis of historical cost data adjusted for expected changes in the product, production technology, engineering estimates, and other procedures. Standards may be established at any one of the following levels:

1. Ideal standards are set for the level of maximum efficiency.

2. Normal standards are set to reflect the conditions that are expected to exist over a period of time sufficient to take into consideration seasonal and cyclical fluctuations.

3. Currently attainable standards are set at a level which represents anticipated conditions assuming efficient operations.

Because predetermined standards usually differ from actual costs incurred, a variance typically exists. An unfavorable variance results when actual cost exceeds standard cost; a favorable variance results when standard cost exceeds actual cost. The usual approach followed in standard cost analysis is to separate price factors from efficiency factors. When the actual amount paid differs from the standard amount, the variance is referred to as a price, rate, or spending variance. When the actual input quantity (e.g., ton, labor hours) differs from the standard input quantity, the variance is referred to as a quantity, volume, or yield variance. The relationships between actual and standard price/quantity are illustrated in the following diagram. The diagram shows two types of prices and quantities: actual and standard. A price variance is conceptualized as the difference between quadrants 1 and 2. A quantity variance is reflected in the difference between quadrants 2 and 4.

C

	Actual Price	**Standard Price**
Actual Quantity	Actual quantity at actual price *Quadrant 1*	Actual quantity at standard price *Quadrant 2*
Standard Quantity	Standard quantity at actual price *Quadrant 3*	Standard quantity at standard price *Quadrant 4*

The formulas for typical direct material and direct labor variances include:

1. Direct material price variance = Actual quantities purchased × (Actual price − Standard price).

2. Material quantity (usage, efficiency) variance = (Actual quantity used − Standard quantity allowed) × Standard price.

3. Direct labor rate variance = Actual hours used × (Actual labor rate − Standard labor rate).

4. Direct labor efficiency variance = (Actual hours used − Standard hours allowed) × Standard labor rate.

The following data will be used to illustrate the computation of the direct material and direct labor variances:

Direct material:
    Purchased   10,000 pounds @ $10 per pound
    Standard price $9 per pound

Direct labor:
    Purchased   12,000 hours @ $6 per hour
    Standard rate $7

The computations are as follows:

1. Direct materials price variance = 10,000 × ($10 − $9)
                                = $10,000 unfavorable price variance

2. Direct materials quantity variance = $9 × (10,000 pounds – 12,000)
   = $18,000 favorable quantity variance

3. Direct labor rate variance = 12,000 × ($6 – $7)
   = $12,000 favorable rate variance

4. Direct labor efficiency variance = $7 × (12,000 – 14,000 hours)
   = $14,000 favorable efficiency variance

Controlling overhead costs is usually more difficult than controlling direct material and direct labor costs because it is difficult to assign responsibility for overhead costs incurred. A general approach to controlling overhead costs involves computing two variances: the controllable overhead variance and the overhead volume variance. The controllable overhead variance is the difference between the actual overhead costs incurred and the factory overhead budgeted for the level of production achieved. This variance measures the difference between the overhead costs actually incurred and the costs that should have been incurred at the level of output attained. The overhead volume (or usage) variance is the difference between the factory overhead budgeted for the level of production achieved and the overhead applied to production using the standard overhead rate. A volume variance arises if more or less plant capacity than normal is actually utilized. When the expected capacity usage is exceeded, the overhead volume variance is favorable.

Variances should be analyzed if the cost of doing so does not exceed the benefits that can be expected from the analysis. If the variances are to be analyzed, they should be examined to find their causes. At this point, it should be determined what action should be taken, if any.

See also Planning and control; Budget.

C

REFERENCE
Horngren, Charles T., *Cost Accounting: A Managerial Emphasis* (Prentice-Hall, Inc., Englewood Cliffs, NJ, 1981).

COST-BENEFIT ANALYSIS

Cost-benefit analysis is a procedure or system for evaluating a course of action or program by comparing the costs to the expected benefits from the action or program. If benefits exceed costs, the action or program is considered desirable.

The typical cost-benefit evaluation examines the benefits and costs of programs being created or of an existing program. A standard classification for such evaluations is (1) summative evaluations and (2) formative evaluations. Summative evaluations typically seek an answer concerning whether the program works or doesn't work. Answers to such questions as the following are sought: Does the value of the benefits exceed the costs? For alternative programs that accomplish a given task, which is less costly? Such evaluations involving comparative analysis are sometimes referred to as "cost-effectiveness" evaluations. Formative evaluations typically inquire as to whether the program can be improved.

Cost-benefit analysis usually involves the following activities: alternatives are compared; benefits and costs are specified and measured for the current and future periods; and the cost-benefit approach is applied using common techniques throughout the entity. Cost-benefit analysis is widely used by governmental entities at all levels of operations.

Cost-benefit analysis has occasionally been applied to the auditing and the accounting standard-setting processes. As applied to auditing, costs often include audit fees and other costs incurred by the entity being audited. Benefits often relate to the reliability of the financial statements being audited and to the discovery or prevention of fraud. It should be kept in mind that many of the benefits associated with an audit accrue to the general public and often are not measurable, while costs of an audit are usually paid for by a particular entity.

See also Qualitative characteristics of accounting.

REFERENCE
Gramlich, Edward M., *Benefit-Cost Analysis of Government Programs* (Prentice-Hall, Englewood Cliffs, NJ, 1981).

COST METHOD
The cost method of accounting for investments in common stock records the investment at cost. Dividends received from the investment are recognized as income. However, dividends received in excess of the investor's share of earnings after the investment is acquired are considered a return of capital and are recorded as a reduction in the investment account. If the securities are considered marketable equity securities, the lower-of-cost-or-market procedure is usually applied. The cost method contrasts with the equity method of accounting for stock investments. When the equity method is used, the investment is recorded at cost and is adjusted for earnings, losses, and dividends. Other major applications of the cost method are discussed in the entry Cost Principle.

See also Equity method of accounting; Cost principle.

REFERENCE
Beams, Floyd A., *Advanced Accounting* (Prentice-Hall, Inc., Englewood Cliffs, NJ, 1985).

COST OF CAPITAL
The cost of capital usually refers to the cost of funds invested in an enterprise. In this sense, the cost of capital is the weighted average of the cost of each type of debt and equity capital. The weight for each type of capital is the ratio of the market value of the securities representing that particular source of capital to the market value of all securities issued by the company. To illustrate, assume that the market value of a company's com-

mon stock is $600,000 and the dividend yield is 10 percent. The market value of the company's interest-bearing debt is $400,000 with an average after-tax yield of 8 percent. The average cost of capital for the company can be estimated as follows:

Source	Proportion of total capital	Cost	
Common stock	0.60	0.10	0.06
Debt	0.40	0.08	0.032
Average cost of capital			0.092

Cost of capital also refers to the discount rate that equates the expected present value of future cash flows to common shareholders with the market value of the common stock at a specific time.

See also Discounted cash flow.

REFERENCE
Bierman, Harold, Jr., and Smidt, Seymour, *The Capital Budgeting Decision* (Macmillan, N.Y., 1966).

COST OF GOODS SOLD
Cost of goods sold is the expense that was incurred for the merchandise (or goods) that was sold during the period. Cost of goods sold can be computed as follows:

Beginning inventory, January 1, 1985	$100,000
Add: Purchases (net) during the year	700,000
Goods available for sale during the year	800,000
Less: Ending inventory, December 31, 1985	60,000
Cost of goods sold	$740,000

Gross margin is the excess of sales over cost of goods sold:

Sales (net)	$950,000
Less: Cost of goods sold	740,000
Gross margin	$210,000

Gross margin is available for other expenses and net income.

See also Income statement; Gross margin analysis.

COST PRINCIPLE

The cost (or initial recording) principle requires that assets, liabilities, owners' equity, revenue, expenses, and other elements of accounting be initially recorded in the accounting system at the time of exchange and at the prices agreed upon by the parties to the exchange. The cost principle is also referred to as the historical (or acquisition) cost principle. Acquisition cost is equal to the amount of cash given or the cash equivalent value of other consideration exchanged. When an asset is acquired from a donation, its "cost" is assumed to be its fair market value. When an asset is acquired in an exchange, the accounting required to record the acquisition depends on (1) whether the two assets exchanged are similar or dissimilar, and (2) whether a cash difference (boot) is paid or received. The general rule for recording an exchange of assets is as follows: If the assets exchanged are similar, the exchange should be recorded on a "book value" basis because the earning process on the old asset is not completed. The book value of the old asset is assigned to the asset acquired in the exchange. If the assets exchanged are dissimilar (equipment for land), the exchange should be recorded on a "fair market value" basis because the earning process on the old asset has been completed.

The cost principle is based on the assumption that cost represents the fair market value at the date of acquisition. Those who advocate historical cost measurement emphasize that such costs are objective and reliable. Opponents of the historical cost principle argue that historical costs lack relevance because they do not reflect current market values or the effects of inflation when included in financial statements subsequent to the time the assets are acquired. Nevertheless, the cost principle is one of the most basic concepts in accounting theory.

See also Measurement; Nonmonetary exchanges; Property, plant, and equipment; Arm's-length transaction.

REFERENCE
Grady, Paul, *Inventory of Generally Accepted Accounting Principles for Business Enterprises* (AICPA, 1965).

CREDIT CARDS

Credit card companies such as Diners Club, Visa, American Express, and banks issue cards to members after a credit check. The credit cards entitle cardholders to purchase merchandise or services from businesses which participate in the program. After a sale is made to a customer or client with a credit card, the business forwards the charge slip to the credit card company, which remits the amount of the sale less a fee to the business. The customer is sent periodic statements, usually monthly, indicating the credit charges, the amount due, and the minimum payment required.

A major advantage to a business of participating in a credit card plan is the potential increase in business from customers who have preestablished credit. Also, less bookkeeping is required for accounts receivable, fewer credit losses are experienced, and quicker realization on receivables is customary. Fees charged by credit card companies range from 3 percent to 18 percent or more of the sales price.

CURRENT ASSETS

Current assets include those economic resources of the entity that are in the form of cash and those that are reasonably expected to be sold, consumed, or converted into cash during the normal operating cycle of the business or within one year if the operating cycle is shorter than one year. The normal operating cycle of a business is the average time it takes to convert cash into inventory, sell the inventory, and collect the amount due that results from the sale. Typical items included among current assets include cash, temporary investments, accounts receivable, notes receivable, inventory, and prepaid expenses. In the balance sheet, current assets are usually listed in the order of their liquidity—that is, the ease and speed with which they could be converted into cash.

See also Working capital; Operating cycle; Asset; Current liability.

CURRENT LIABILITY

A current liability is an obligation that must be discharged within the normal operating cycle of the business or within one year, whichever is longer. Current liabilities are normally expected to be paid using existing resources properly classified as current assets or by creating other current liabilities. Items commonly included in current liabilities include accounts payable, collections received in advance of delivery of goods or services, and other debts resulting from the normal operations of the enterprise. Current liabilities are usually listed on the balance sheet in the order of their liquidation date and are usually reported as the amount to be paid. Current liabilities are important in computing working capital, which is the excess of current assets over current liabilities.

Current liabilities are commonly classified as either (1) definitely determinable liabilities or (2) estimated liabilities. Current liabilities that can be measured precisely are referred to as definitely determinable liabilities and include obligations that are established by contract or by statute. Estimated liabilities are definite obligations of the enterprise the exact amount of which cannot be determined until a later date. Examples of estimated liabilities include product warranties, vacation pay, income taxes, and property taxes.

See also Liability; Current asset; Working capital; Operating cycle.

CURRENT VALUE ACCOUNTING

Current value (or cost) accounting is a procedure that attempts to measure the current values of assets, liabilities, and equities. The objective of current value accounting is to report the effects of specific price changes on the operating performance and financial position of the firm. It provides a measurement of current value as distinguished from historical acquisition cost. Current values can be measured in nominal dollars or in constant dollars (dollars adjusted for changes in the general purchasing power of the dollar).

Current costs can be expressed as follows:

1. Current cost. The current cost of an item is the amount of cash or equivalent that would be required on the date of the balance sheet to obtain the same items (an identical asset or one with equivalent productive capacity).

2. Current exit value. The current exit value of an item is the amount of cash which could be obtained on the date of the balance sheet by selling the asset, in its present condition, in an orderly liquidation.

3. Expected exit value. The expected exit value of an asset is the amount of cash or equivalent into which the asset is expected to be converted in the ordinary operations of the entity, less any expected costs related to completion and disposal. Expected exit value is also referred to as net realizable value.

4. Present value. The present value of an asset is the amount of discounted expected cash inflows less the discounted expected cash outflows relating to the item.

Current cost accounting is a method of measuring and reporting assets and expenses associated with the use or sale of assets at their current cost or lower recoverable amount at the balance sheet date or at the date of use or sale. Current cost/constant dollar accounting is a method of accounting based on measures of current cost or lower recoverable amount in terms of dollars, each of which has the same general purchasing power. Current cost/nominal dollar accounting is a method of accounting based on measures of current cost or lower recoverable amount without restatement into units, each of which has the same general purchasing power.

See also Measurement; Capital maintenance theories; Constant dollar accounting.

REFERENCE
Kieso, Donald E., and Weygandt, Jerry J., *Intermediate Accounting* (John Wiley & Sons, N.Y., 1986).

D

DEFEASANCE

In addition to retirement at maturity or prior to maturity, debt can be extinguished by defeasance or by in-substance defeasance. Defeasance of debt refers to a release from the legal liability related to the debt. The debtor is legally released from being the primary obligor for the debt either by law or by the creditor. The debtor eliminates the liability from its statements and can recognize an extraordinary gain. For example, a parent company in an affiliation might agree to become the primary obligor for a debt of a subsidiary company.

In-substance defeasance is an arrangement whereby a company provides for the future repayment of one or more issues of its long-term debt by irrevocably placing with an independent trustee essentially risk-free securities to be used solely for satisfying the debt service requirements. The assets held in the trust must provide cash flows from interest and principal that are similar as to timing and amount to the scheduled interest and principal payments on the debt being extinguished. In most cases, the debtor is not legally released from being the primary obligor under the debt obligation. In periods when interest rates are relatively high, a company can service its debt profitably by purchasing and placing in an irrevocable trust U.S. Government securities at a cost less than the carrying amount of the debt. This procedure can result in an immediate gain for accounting purposes. For financial reporting purposes, the debt is removed from the balance sheet and an extraordinary gain is usually recognized in the income statement. For tax purposes, no gain or loss is currently recognized because no cancellation of debt occurs.

See also Off-balance sheet items; Liabilities.

REFERENCE
FASB, SFAS No. 76, Early Extinguishment of Debt (FASB, 1983).

DEFERRED CHARGE (CREDIT)

Deferred charges are long-term prepayment of expenses and include prepaid income taxes, bond issue costs, and organization costs. They represent prepaid costs which have a future benefit in the form of reduced future cash outflows for services. Deferred charges (delayed debits) are amortized over their expected economic lives but not to exceed forty years, usually by the straight-line method. Certain deferred charges represent a cost which is deferred from expense recognition because of income measurement rules, such as situations where the income tax liability exceeds accounting-based tax expense. Deferred credits refer to certain long-term liabilities (delayed credits) which will increase income in future accounting periods. Deferred credits include deferred income taxes resulting from the application of income measurement rules and collections received in advance of performing services on a long-term basis (prepaid revenue).

See also Assets; Liabilities; Deferred tax credits (debits); Income tax allocation; Adjusting entries.

DEFERRED TAX CREDITS (DEBITS)

Deferred tax credits arise as a result of the timing difference between pretax accounting income and taxable income that originated in one accounting period and reverses in a future accounting period(s).

Timing differences arise when different methods of reporting revenues and expenses are used in determining pretax-accounting income and taxable income. Timing differences exist because revenues and expenses are recognized in different accounting periods for purposes of pretax-accounting income and taxable income. The matching principle of accounting requires that income tax expense for a period be based on the revenues and expenses included in the pretax-accounting income that is subject to income tax. Timing differences can be classified as follows:

1. Revenues and gains recognized in pretax-accounting income earlier than in taxable income.

2. Expenses and losses recognized in pretax-accounting income earlier than in taxable income.

3. Revenues and gains included in taxable income earlier than in pretax-accounting income.

4. Expenses included in taxable income earlier than in pretax-accounting income.

The following list shows some possible alternatives:

	Financial Reporting	Tax Reporting
Sales (No. 1 above)	Point of sale	Installment method
Estimated costs of product warranties (No. 2 above)	Period of sale	Deferred until paid
Rents and royalties (No. 3 above)	Delayed until earned	When received
Depreciation (No. 4 above)	Straight-line	Accelerated
Inventories	FIFO	LIFO

The deferred income tax liability (or credit) arises when the pretax income shown on the tax return is less than what is reported as income before taxes for financial reporting. The deferred income tax credit represents the amount of taxes delayed as a result of using different accounting principles or methods for tax purposes and for financial reporting. An obligation to pay the taxes does not exist when it is recorded. If cumulative taxable income exceeds cumulative reported income before taxes because of timing differences, a deferred charge (or debit) will be reported. The following equations are used to conceptualize deferred income tax debits and credits:

Income tax expense = Pretax accounting income × Income tax rate
Income tax liability = Taxable income × Income tax rate
Deferred income taxes = Timing difference × Income tax rate

To illustrate this concept, assume that a company has pretax accounting income of $100,000 and taxable income of $90,000. The difference between the accounting and taxable income is attributable to the use of different depreciation methods. The tax rate is 50 percent. The entry to record the tax expense, taxes payable, and the deferred tax credit is as follows:

Income Tax Expense ($100,000 × 50%)	50,000	
Income Tax Payable ($90,000 × 50%)		45,000
Deferred Income Taxes ($10,000 × 50%)		5,000

Note that the deferred income taxes account is credited because pretax accounting income exceeded taxable income. The deferred income taxes credit is reported on the balance sheet as a liability. It will reverse when taxable income exceeds accounting income as a result of more depreciation being reported on the books than on the tax return. The deferred income tax liability does not represent an obligation of the enterprise to transfer assets in the future. The deferred credit merely reflects a past transaction which resulted in income taxes saved currently because book income exceeds taxable income.

In the illustration shown above, if taxable income had exceeded pretax accounting income (e.g., taxable income of $100,000 and pretax accounting income of $90,000), a deferred charge would have resulted. The entry would have been as follows:

```
Income Tax Expense ($90,000 × 50%)             45,000
Deferred Income Taxes Charge ($10,000 × 50%)    5,000
    Income Taxes Payable ($100,000 × 50%)              50,000
```

The deferred income taxes charge would be reported as a long-term asset in the deferred charge section of the balance sheet. It also would reverse in a subsequent period(s).

Observe that the total income tax expense reported during the period is the tax expense associated with accounting income (and not taxable income) to provide a proper matching of accounting revenue for the period with the related tax expense. It is not clear whether income tax credits actually represent liabilities for future income taxes or income tax debits represent assets in the form of reduced future income taxes. This would be correct if the timing differences that give rise to the deferred tax accounts actually reverse in the future. In certain cases, some deferred taxes resulting from recurring timing differences tend to increase over time rather than decrease as timing differences reverse; for example, those resulting from the use of different depreciation methods for tax purposes and accounting purposes.

See also Income tax allocation; Deferred charges (credits).

REFERENCE
APB No. 11, Accounting for Income Taxes (APB, 1967).

D

DEFICIT

Retained earnings is the amount of undistributed earnings of a past period. An excess of dividends and losses over earnings results in a negative retained earned balance which is referred to as a deficit. The retained earnings account has a debit balance when a deficit exists.

See also Retained earnings; Quasi-reorganization.

DEFINED BENEFIT PENSION PLANS

A defined benefit pension plan is one in which the benefits payable to the employee are determinable at any time. The plan specifies the benefits employees will receive upon retirement. The amounts usually depend on a formula that includes employee's earnings, years of employment, age, and other variables. The determination of periodic contributions to the plan is made by actuaries based on estimates of the variables.

A defined contribution plan is essentially a money purchase (pension) plan or arrangement, usually based on a formula, where the employer makes a cash contribution to eligible individual employee accounts according to the terms of the plan. Benefits received by an employee are dependent on the rate of return on the assets invested in the plan. The amount to be contributed annually by the employer is specified rather than the benefits to be paid.

The primary purpose of a pension plan's financial statements is to provide financial information that is useful in assessing the plan's present and future ability to pay benefits when due. The primary users of these statements are the plan's participants. The reporting focuses on th needs of plan participants, especially their need to evaluate the fund's ability to provide current and future benefits to employees. Information relating to the following matters is ordinarily considered necessary: (1) fair value of plan investments; (2) present value of estimated future pension benefits; and (3) changes in asset values and the present value of future benefits during the year.

See also Pensions.

DEPRECIATION
Depreciation is the accounting process of allocating the cost
or other basic value of a tangible, long-lived asset or group of
assets less salvage value, if any, over the estimated useful life
of the asset(s) in a systematic and rational manner. Systematic
means methodical or with design and regularity. Rational
means that the depreciation method used should relate to the
expected benefits to be obtained from the asset being
depreciated. Depreciation can also be conceptualized as the
expiration of service potential of an asset. Depreciation is a
process of allocation, not of valuation. Recording depreciation
is not an attempt to determine the market value of an asset at
a balance sheet date.

Depreciation expense for an accounting period is the portion of the total cost of an asset that is allocated to that period.
Depreciation charges are noncash expenses that reduce net
income. The depreciation allowance is not a cash fund accumulated to cover the replacement cost of an asset. The accounting entry that records depreciation does not of itself accumulate
any cash. A typical accounting entry made at the end of an
accounting period to record depreciation expense for the period
is shown here:

| Depreciation Expense | 50,000 | |
| Accumulated Depreciation—Equipment | | 50,000 |

Depreciation expense is reported on the income statement.
The accumulated depreciation account is a contra asset account
and is deducted from the related asset—equipment—in the
illustration.

In making a determination of the amount of depreciation
to be taken in an accounting period, three factors are considered: acquisition cost, salvage value, and useful life. The esti-

mated useful life of an asset is related to both physical and functional factors:

1. Physical factors: decay and deterioration from wear and tear of use, passage of time, and other factors which affect the physical life of the asset.

2. Functional (or economic) factors: obsolescence arising from technological improvements, inadequacy of the asset for its intended purpose(s), or ecological and energy-saving considerations.

The useful life of an asset may be expressed in terms of

1. time (for example, a certain number of years);

2. operating periods (for example, a certain number of working hours); or

3. units of output (for example, a certain number of items).

Various methods of computing depreciation are available. Major methods of depreciation currently in use include:

1. Straight-line depreciation. Under straight-line depreciation, the cost, less salvage value, of the asset is spread in equal periodic amounts over its estimated useful life.

2. Accelerated depreciation. Accelerated depreciation methods recognize relatively larger amounts of depreciation in the earlier years of the asset's useful life and smaller amounts in later years. Two such methods are the declining-balance method and the sum-of-the-years' digits method. Declining-balance depreciation is computed by applying a constant rate (generally a rate double the straight-line rate) to the remaining undepreciated balance. When the sum-of-

the-years' depreciation method is used, the sum of the total years of life of the asset is used as a denominator of a fraction of the depreciable base (cost of the asset less estimated salvage value). The numerator is always the remaining years of life. For example, assume that an asset acquired for $900 has a three-year life and no salvage value. Depreciation would be computed as follows for the three years:

Year 1:	3/6 × $900 =	$450
Year 2:	2/6 × $900 =	300
Year 3:	1/6 × $900 =	150
Total		$900

3. Unit-of-production method. The useful life of certain assets, such as machinery, can be estimated in terms of units produced or hours of operations rather than years. Depreciation would be computed as the ratio of the actual number of units produced or hours operated during the period to the total number of units or hours in the estimated useful life of the asset.

The various depreciation methods are illustrated in Exhibit D–1 using the following information concerning a machine acquired at the beginning of the company's fiscal year:

Cost of equipment	$1,100
Years	5
Working hours	500
Units of production	1,000
Hours worked this period	75
Units of production this period	300

The inventory (or appraisal) method of depreciation is sometimes used. Under this method, the company takes a physical inventory of its tangible, long-lived assets at the end of the period and assigns a value to them. The difference between the book value of the assets at the beginning of the year and

Exhibit D-1
Depreciation Methods Illustrated

1. *Straight-line depreciation:*

$$\text{Depreciation} = \frac{\text{Cost} - \text{Salvage value}}{\text{Estimated number of years of service life}}$$

$$= \frac{\$1,100 - 100}{5}$$

$$= \$200$$

2. *Rate per working hour:*

$$\text{Depreciation rate} = \frac{\text{Cost} - \text{Salvage value}}{\text{Estimated life of asset in working hours}}$$

$$= \frac{\$1,100 - \$100}{500 \text{ working hours}}$$

$$= \$2 \text{ per hour}$$

$$\text{Depreciation expense} = 75 \text{ hours} \times \$2$$

$$= \$150$$

3. *Unit-of-production method (activity-based method)*

$$\text{Depreciation rate} = \frac{\text{Cost} - \text{Salvage value}}{\text{Estimated units of production during life}}$$

$$= \frac{\$1,100 - \$100}{1,000 \text{ widgets produced}}$$

$$= \$1 \text{ per widget produced.}$$

$$\text{Depreciation expense} = 300 \text{ widgets produced} \times \$1$$

$$= \$300$$

4. *Double-declining-balance method (An accelerated method):*

$$\text{Depreciation rate} = (\text{Straight-line rate}) \times 2$$

$$= (100\%/\text{life in year}) \times 2$$

$$= (1/5 = 20\%) \times 2$$

$$= 40\% \text{ per year of carrying value}$$

Year	Computation	Annual Depreciation	Accumulated Depreciation	Carrying Value
1	40% × $1,000	$400	$400	$600
2	40% × 600	240	640	360
3	40% × 360	144	784	216
4	40% × 216	86*	870	130
5	40% × 130 = $52	80†	950	50

*Rounded to nearest dollar.
†In the last year of the estimated life of the asset, the annual depreciation charge is adjusted to the amount needed to bring the carrying value of the asset to its salvage value.

the assigned value at the end of the year represents depreciation expense for the period, after allowing for acquisitions and disposals during the period.

Retirement and replacement depreciation methods are also sometimes use to record depreciation. Under the retirement method, the company records depreciation expense only when the asset is retired from use; the cost of the retired asset is recognized as depreciation expense for the year that the asset is retired. Under the replacement method, the acquisition cost of the replacement asset, net of any salvage proceeds from the asset being replaced, represents depreciation expense in the year of replacement.

Companies frequently account for depreciation on a composite or group basis. The composite method of depreciation applies depreciation to a collection of dissimilar assets; the group method applies depreciation to a collection of similar assets. These two methods are illustrated in Exhibit D–2. Procedures for applying the two methods are identical, with depreciation expense being computed by applying the average depreciation rate times the balance in the group asset account at the beginning of the year.

The Economic Recovery Tax Act (ERTA) of 1981 provided for the use of a new method of computing depreciation for tax purposes called the accelerated cost recovery system (ACRS). The new depreciation rules were developed to simplify the computation of depreciation and to provide for a more rapid recovery of asset costs to offset depreciation and stimulate investment in the economy. ACRS requires that certain property provided after December 31, 1980, be depreciated over three, five, ten, or fifteen years, depending on the type of property. Cost recovery tables for each class of property specify the percentage of cost recovery for each year.

See also Property, plant, and equipment; Depletion; Amortization; Allocation.

D

Exhibit D–2
Group Depreciation Illustrated

Asset	Cost	Estimated Salvage Value	Depreciable Cost	Estimated Useful Life (in years)	Annual Straight-Line Depreciation
1	$10,000	$ 0	$10,000	10	$1,000
2	5,500	500	5,000	2½	2,000
3	2,200	200	2,000	5	400
	$17,700	$700	$17,000		$3,400

$$\text{Average life} = \frac{\text{Depreciable cost}}{\text{Annual depreciation}} = \frac{\$17,000}{\$3,400/\text{year}} = 5 \text{ years.}$$

The annual rate of depreciation (rounded value) is computed as follows:

$$\text{Annual rate} = \frac{\text{Annual depreciation}}{\text{Total cost}} = \frac{\$3,400/\text{year}}{\$17,700/\text{year}} = 19.21\% \text{ per year.}$$

Depreciation per year at the average rate of 19.21% (rounded) applied to total cost of $17,700 is $3,400 (rounded).

REFERENCE
Lamden, Charles W., et al., *Accounting for Depreciable Assets* (AICPA, 1975).

DEVELOPMENT STAGE COMPANIES
An enterprise is a development stage company if substantially all of its efforts are devoted to establishing a new business and either of the following is present:

a. principal operations have not begun, or

b. principal operations have begun but revenue produced is insignificant.

Activities of a development stage enterprise frequently include financial planning, raising capital, research and development, personnel recruiting and training, and market development.

A development stage enterprise must follow generally accepted accounting principles applicable to operating enterprises in the preparation of its financial statements. In its balance sheet, the company must report cumulative net losses separately in the equity section. In it income statement it must report cumulative revenues and expenses from the inception of the enterprise. In its statement of changes in financial position, it must report cumulative sources and uses of funds from the inception of the enterprise. Its statement of stockholders' equity should include the number of shares issued and the date of their issuance as well as the dollar amounts received for its shares from the date of inception. Notes to the financial statements should identify the entity as a development stage enterprise and describe the nature of development stage activities. During the first period of normal operations, the enterprise must disclose in notes to the financial statements that the enterprise was but is no longer in the development stage.

See also Accounting principles.

REFERENCE
SFAS No. 7, Accounting and Reporting by Development Stage Companies (FASB, 1975).

DIRECT COSTING AND ABSORPTION COSTING
Direct (or variable) costing and absorption costing are two approaches to product costing. With direct costing, ending inventory includes only variable production costs, such as direct materials, direct labor, and variable manufacturing overhead. Fixed overhead costs, which do not change with changes in production levels (such as rent, insurance), are expensed when incurred. With absorption costing, the cost of inventory

includes both variable and fixed factory overhead costs. Variable costing is frequently used for decision-making purposes but is not generally accepted for external financial reporting. The differences between the two methods are due entirely to the treatment of fixed factory overhead. To illustrate the difference between direct and absorption costing, assume the following data. A company that manufactures radios incurred the following costs for the year: raw material costs, $100,000; direct labor costs, $200,000; variable factory overhead, $50,000; fixed factory overhead, $25,000. There was no beginning or ending work in process inventories.

	Direct Costing	Absorption Costing
Direct materials	$100,000	$100,000
Direct labor	200,000	200,000
Variable factory overhead	50,000	50,000
Fixed factory overhead		25,000
Ending finished goods inventory	$350,000	$375,000

When production exceeds sales, absorption costing will cause net income to exceed net income under direct costing because some fixed overhead costs are deferred in inventory rather than being written off as a period cost. When sales exceed production, the opposite effects on net income occur because some previously deferred fixed factory costs are included with current fixed overhead costs in cost of goods sold.

Direct costing is useful for controlling current costs, and profit planning (sales promotions; special pricing; make or buy decisions). When direct costing is used, periodic net income varies directly with sales volume since variable costs are proportional to sales. When absorption costing is used, the volume/profit relationship becomes more difficult to estimate since fixed costs are a component of inventory.

See also Inventory; Cost.

REFERENCE
Morse, Wayne J., *Cost Accounting* (Addison-Wesley, Reading, MA, 1978).

DISCONTINUED OPERATIONS

Discontinued operations are those operations of an enterprise that have been sold, abandoned, or otherwise disposed of. The results of continued operations must be reported separately in the income statement from discontinued operations and any gain or loss from disposal of a segment must be reported along with the operating results of the discontinued segment. A segment of a business is a component of an entity whose activities represent a separate major line of business or class of customer. A segment may be a subsidiary, a division, or a department if its assets, results of operations, and activities can be distinguished physically and operationally and for financial reporting purposes from those of the entity.

The presentation of discontinued operations should be reported as follows:

Income from continuing operations before taxes		$500,000
Provision for income taxes		150,000
Income from continuing operations		350,000
Discontinued operations:		
Income from operations of discontinued division (less applicable income taxes of $50,000)	$200,000	
Loss on disposal of division	(350,000)	150,000
Net income		$200,000

See also Income statement.

REFERENCE
APB No. 30, Reporting the Results of Operations (APB, 1973).

DISCOUNT

Discounts from the list price of goods can be classified as trade discounts and cash discounts. A cash discount is the amount allowed as a deduction from the selling price if payment is made within a specific time period. Cash discounts are used as incentives for prompt payment. Credit terms of 2/10, n/30, means that a 2 percent discount is allowed on the invoice price if the account is paid within 10 days. In any event, the account is due within 30 days. Failure to take advantage of the discount means that the customer is paying approximately 36 percent interest for the extra 20 days available under the credit terms.

A trade discount is a reduction from list price that is offered to purchasers who fit into certain categories—for example, wholesalers and retailers. The gross purchase price is the price after any applicable trade discount but before any cash discount. For example, suppose that merchandise with a list price of $1,000 is purchased at $1,000 less trade discounts of 30% and 10% and a cash discount of 2%. In this case, the gross and net purchase prices are computed as follows:

```
$1,000 less 30%  =  $700
  $700 less 10%  =  $630, the gross purchase price
  $630 less  2%  =  $617.40, the net purchase price
```

DISCOUNTED CASH FLOW

The discounted cash flow technique is a tool used in evaluating investment decisions. When this method is used, expected future cash inflows and outflows associated with the investment are discounted to the present time, using a minimum discounting rate acceptable to management. The net present value is the difference between the present value of the cost of the investment and the present value of the cash inflow expected from the investment. If the net present value of the cash flows is positive (cash inflows exceed cash outflows), the investment is acceptable. To illustrate the discounted cash flow method, assume that management is considering the purchase of a new machine for $11,000. The machine has an expected life of five years and a scrap value of $1,000 at the end of its life. Management assumes a minimum desired rate of return of 10 percent on the investment. The new machine will create cost savings of $4,000 per year for the next five years; the cost savings are realized at the end of each year. Exhibit D–3 shows a work sheet used to solve this problem. Dollar amounts of cash inflows and outflows are recorded in the columns for the appropriate period. Cash outflows are recorded as negative amounts. Cash savings are considered cash inflows. Present-value discounting factors are determined from present-value tables and entered in the appropriate column. Note that the cash operating savings can be treated as an annuity. Present values of each item are computed and entered in the last column. These values are totaled to determine the net present value of the investment.

The initial cash outflow for purchase of the machine is not discounted because it is made at the beginning of the first period. The cash inflows due to operating savings are discounted as a $4,000 annuity for five years at a 10 percent discount rate. The disposal value is discounted as a sum of $1,000 to be received five years in the future at a 10 percent discount rate. Because the net present value of the investment is positive (cash inflows exceed cash outflows), the investment is considered desirable.

See also Annuity; Present value; Cost of capital.

REFERENCE
Moscove, Stephen A., et al., *Cost Accounting* (Houghton Mifflin, Boston, 1985).

Exhibit D–3
Discounted Cash Flow Procedures

	Cash flows at end of period						Discount factor	Total present value
	0	1	2	3	4	5		
Initial cost	$(11,000)						1.0000	$(11,000)
Cash operating savings		$4,000	$4,000	$4,000	$4,000	$4,000	3.2741	13,096
Disposal value						1,000	.4761	476
Net present value								$ 2,572

D

DIVIDENDS

A dividend is a distribution of cash, other assets, liabilities, or a company's own stock to stockholders in proportion to the number of shares owned. The distribution is usually generated from earnings of the corporation. The board of directors of a corporation is responsible for determining dividend policy including the amount, timing, and type of dividends to be declared. The dividend policy usually takes into consideration applicable state legislation concerning dividends, the impact on legal capital, contractual restrictions, the financial feasibility of the dividends, and the needs of shareholders.

The types of dividends can be classified as follows:

1. Dividends that decrease total stockholders' equity:

   a. Cash dividends

   b. Property dividends

   c. Script dividends

2. Dividends not affecting total stockholders' equity:

   a. Dividends decreasing retained earnings and increasing contributed capital (stock dividends)

   b. "Dividends" not affecting any stockholders' equity account (stock splits in the form of a dividend)

A cash dividend is one in which cash is used as the method of paying the dividend. A property dividend is a dividend that is paid in noncash assets of the corporation. Such dividends could include distributions of stocks, bonds, inventory, or other assets. A liability dividend is a dividend in which the corporation distributes promissory notes to its stockholders. The notes are to be redeemed at a future date and generally pay interest. A stock dividend is the issuance by a corporation of its own shares of common stock to its common stockholders without consideration.

Corporations sometimes issue stock dividends when they want to make a distribution to their stockholders but either do not want to distribute assets or do not have enough assets to distribute. Stock dividends have also been used to reduce the market value of a corporation's stock, thereby making it available to a larger number of potential investors and hopefully increasing the demand for the stock. In other cases, tax considerations have prompted the issuance of stock dividends. When a corporation distributes a stock dividend, each stockholder receives additional whole shares, fractional shares, or fractional share warrants of a corporations's stock in proportion to the stockholder's holding of that stock. The net assets of the corporation are not affected by a stock dividend, and each stockholder's total interest in the corporation is unchanged. Each stockholder owns a larger number of shares, but the total book value of the shares remains the same after the dividend as before the dividend.

Occasionally, corporate dividends reflect a distribution from capital rather than retained earnings. Such dividends are commonly referred to as liquidating dividends if they represent a return of contributed capital to investors. In the extractive industries, some firms distribute regular dividends equal to accumulated income and liquidating dividends equal to the depletion allowance. This practice is used when there are no plans to replace the natural resource and operations will cease upon their exhaustion.

Constructive dividends are a taxable benefit derived by a shareholder from a corporation although such benefit was not designated as a dividend. Constructive dividends could include unreasonable compensation, excessive rent payments, shareholder use of corporate property, and bargain purchases of corporate property.

Except for stock dividends, dividends become a liability of the corporation when they are declared by the board of directors. Most state laws specify that dividends can be distributed only to the extent of a credit balance in the retained earnings account. A few states permit dividends up to the amount of

D

net income for previous years even though the retained earnings account may have a deficit. Some states permit dividends from retained earnings and contributed capital to the extent that it does not impair legal capital (which is often the par or stated value of the issued stock). Undeclared dividends on cumulative preferred stock are not recognized as liabilities since there is no legal obligation on the part of the corporation to pay such dividends. Undeclared dividends are referred to as dividends in arrears.

The date of declaration is the date the directors declare a dividend. The date of record is a date the board establishes to whom the dividend will be paid on the payment date. Stockholders who purchased shares in the market before the ex-dividend date (usually four trading days before the date of record) receive the dividend regardless of whether they own the shares at the declaration or payment dates. Generally, the market price of the shares traded between the declaration date and the ex-dividend date will increase by the amount of the dividend. From the declaration date to the ex-dividend date, the shares trade "dividends on." After the ex-dividend date, the shares sell "ex-dividends" and the person who purchases the shares after this date will not receive the dividend.

The dividend yield is a ratio of dividends declared for the year divided by market price of the stock as of a specific time.

See also Stock dividends; Stock split; Corporation; Capital stock; Preferred stock.

REFERENCE
Kieso, Donald E., and Weygandt, Jerry J., *Intermediate Accounting* (John Wiley & Sons, N.Y., 1986).

DOUBLE-ENTRY SYSTEM
The double-entry system of accounting requires that for each transaction or event recorded, the total dollar amount of the debits entered in all the related accounts must be equal to the

total dollar amount of the credits. For example, a journal entry recorded in a double-entry system would take the following form:

Equipment	10,000	
Cash		8,000
Notes Payable		2,000
To record the acquisition of equipment		
with cash and a note payable.		

Note the dollar equality of debits and credits. Double-entry accounting also maintains the following equality:

Total dollar amount assigned to assets	=	Total dollar amount assigned to liabilities and equities

A single-entry accounting system makes only a record or memorandum entry of a transaction and does not record the double entry or dual effect of each transaction. Single-entry accounting does not involve equal debits and credits. On the balance sheet, owners' equity is calculated as the excess of total assets over total liabilities. The single-entry system does not provide for the simultaneous determination of net income and the ending balances of assets and liabilities. In order to get the customary financial statements, single-entry transactions have to be analyzed as to their dual effects on other accounts. A single-entry accounting entry to record the purchase of the equipment illustrated above could assume this form:

Equipment was purchased for $8,000 cash and a $2,000 note payable.

See also Accounting equation; Account; Journal.

REFERENCE
Sterling, Robert R., *An Explication and Analysis of the Structure of Accounting—Part One* (School of Business, The University of Kansas, Lawrence, Kansas, 1971).

E

EARNINGS PER SHARE

Earnings per share of stock is one of the most significant ratios in financial management and investment analysis. If the capital structure of a corporation contains only common stock, earnings per share is computed as follows:

$$\text{Earnings per common share} = \frac{\text{Net income}}{\text{Weighted number of common shares outstanding}}$$

If the capital structure contains common stock and nonconvertible, cumulative preferred stock or noncumulative preferred stock on which the dividends have been paid, the earnings per share is computed as follows:

$$\text{Earnings per common share} = \frac{\text{Net income} - \text{Preferred stock dividends}}{\text{Weighted number of common shares outstanding}}$$

The weighted average number of shares outstanding in the denominator is equal to the number of common shares outstanding at the end of the accounting period if no shares have been issued or reacquired during the year. If shares have been issued or reacquired, a weighted average of these shares must be calculated. For example, If 10,000 shares were issued on July 1, these shares would be included in the denominator as 5,000 shares.

Corporations issue a variety of securities that can be converted into common stock—for example, convertible bonds and convertible preferred stock. Stock options and warrants are other securities that can be converted into common stock under specified conditions. If these common stock equivalents were converted, they would increase the number of shares of common stock outstanding and could decrease (dilute) earnings per share. If such securities exist, generally accepted accounting principles require a disclosure of the dilution that would develop if all possible contingencies occurred. In such cases, a dual presentation of earnings per share would usually be required:

1. Primary earnings per share. This presentation is based on the outstanding common shares and those securities that are in substance equivalent to common shares and have a dilutive effect.

2. Fully diluted earnings per share. This is a proforma presentation which affects the dilution of earnings per share that would have occurred if all contingent issuances of common stock that would individually reduce earnings per share had taken place at the beginning of the period.

The details of earnings-per-share computations are highly technical and are not the proper subject of this book. The basic factors entering into the computations of primary and fully diluted earnings per share are summarized here:

$$\text{Primary earnings per share} = \frac{\begin{array}{c}\text{Net income after taxes} - \\ \text{preferred dividends on noncom-} \\ \text{mon stock equivalents} + \text{interest and} \\ \text{dividends (net of tax effect) on securities} \\ \text{considered to be common stock equivalents}\end{array}}{\begin{array}{c}\text{Weighted average of common shares out-} \\ \text{standing} + \text{shares issuable from} \\ \text{common stock equivalents}\end{array}}$$

$$\text{Fully diluted earnings per share} = \frac{\begin{array}{c}\text{The numerator for primary} \\ \text{EPS} + \text{interest and dividends (net} \\ \text{of tax effect) on securities assumed} \\ \text{converted for fully diluted purposes}\end{array}}{\begin{array}{c}\text{The denominator for primary EPS} + \text{all} \\ \text{other contingently issuable shares}\end{array}}$$

In the formulas, common stock equivalents are securities that, in substance, can be considered common stock. These include convertible debt and preferred stock, stock options and warrants, and contingent shares. Securities which have an antidilutive (increase earnings or reduce loss) effect on primary earnings per share are excluded from the computations. In the numerator of the formula, the addition to net income for "adjustments for common stock equivalents" could include such items as the after-tax effect of interest on convertible bonds and dividends on preferred stock that were subtracted in determining net income available to common stock which must be added back. The special treatment given to stock options could also result in increasing the numerator of the formula.

Earnings per share data are widely used in judging the operating performance of a business. This ratio appears frequently in financial statements and business publications. It is perhaps the one most significant figure appearing on the income statement because it condenses into a single figure the data reflecting the current net income of the period in relation to the number of shares of stock outstanding. Separate earnings per share data must be shown for income from continuing operations and net income. Earnings per share may be reported for the results from discontinued operations, extraordinary items, or cumulative effects of changes in accounting principles if they are reported on the income statement. Current accounting practice requires that earnings per share be disclosed prominently on the face of the income statement.

See also Income statement; Retained earnings.

REFERENCE
APB No. 15, Earnings per share (APB, 1969).

ECONOMIC CONSEQUENCES OF ACCOUNTING
Accounting reports and financial statements can have economic consequences for decision makers, especially creditors and investors. Economic consequences refer primarily to the costs and benefits resulting from compliance with financial reporting requirements. Accountants are not held accountable for the effects that accounting might have on the decisions of users of accounting information. However, accounting principles, methods, and their application can have a significant impact on the decision-making process. For example, the failure of accounting to take current costs and changes in the general price level into consideration when preparing basic financial statements frequently overstates reported profits of companies. These illusory profits are subsequently taxed as if they were real, thus depriving companies of working capital to replace assets at current prices. In accounting for research and development expenditures, accounting standards require that such costs be expensed and reported on the income statement. In certain cases, this practice results in lower reported earnings and lower stockholders' equity which impact adversely on the markets for securities of research-intensive companies.

Most accountants take the position that accounting policies and standards should not be developed to encourage or discourage economic transactions. This does not imply that standard setters should not be aware of the economic consequences of their actions.

See also Economics; Economic environment of accounting; Accounting principles; Accounting standards overload; Financial Accounting Standards Board; Efficient market hypothesis.

REFERENCE
Wolk, Harry I., et al., Accounting Theory (Kent, Boston, 1984).

ECONOMIC ENVIRONMENT OF ACCOUNTING

The economic environment of accounting places constraints upon the practice of accounting. To a great extent, the ecomomic environment determines what accounting can do and what it must do. The economic environment identifies persons and institutions for whom an accounting is to be made and determines what is to be accounted for.

Economics is a science that is concerned with the production, distribution, exchange, and consumption of goods and services. Every economic system exists within an environment. The issues raised by any economic system which affect accounting include:

1. What kinds and amounts of goods and services shall be produced? In economics, this question deals with the production process.

2. For whom are goods and services to be produced? This question deals with the distribution of income. Distribution is the process of assigning the outputs of the production process among the four factors of production:

   a. land with its return called rents;

   b. labor with its remuneration called wages;

    c. capital with its payment called interest;

    d. ownership with its reward for innovating and risk-taking called profit.

3. How are goods and services traded for other economic resources? This process of transforming one good into another through a price and market system is called the exchange process.

4. How is the output of the production process to be used? As the goods and services are used, their utility is lessened. This process is called consumption.

Accounting operates within an economic environment. A business enterprise is an economic organization. Economic events and transactions are accumulated, processed, and communicated by the accounting system. Objectives of accounting relate to the making of economic decisions concerning the use of limited economic resources. Accounting and economics deal with many of the same elements: economic resources (assets), economic obligations (liabilities), stores of wealth, flows of wealth, income, prices, costs, cash flows, savings, investments, and the allocation of scarce resources. This linkage reflects the economic environment in which accounting functions.

Accountants have largely focused their attention on accumulating, measuring, and reporting historical financial information. Economists have utilized this information to examine the relationship of the firm or other economic entity to its external environment and to search out underlying trends and directions. The closeness of the two disciplines is often misunderstood since terminology used in each discipline for similar items is often different.

See also Accounting; Economics; Economic consequences of accounting; Financial Accounting Standards Board.

ECONOMICS

Economics is a science that is concerned with the production, distribution, and consumption of goods and services. Economizing refers to the process of applying scarce economic goods and services to satisfy the unlimited wants of individuals or the total economy.

Economic theory is essentially a theory of choice, production, distribution, and value. In addition to financial matters, economic theory deals with the following:

1. activities that involve exchanges, for money or barter;

2. economic issues associated with government policies and their impact on economic activity in general and price levels in particular;

3. the utilization or underutilization of economic resources;

4. wealth and its distribution;

5. economic growth and development: domestic, foreign, and international;

6. the economic welfare of nations and people.

Economic goods and services are capable of satisfying wants. They may be in the form of wealth or income. Economic goods are material, useful, scarce, and transferable. Economic goods can be classified as consumer goods and capital goods. Consumer goods are directly used by a consumer, e.g., food, clothing, tires, shelter. Capital (producer) goods are used to produce other goods, e.g., buildings, machinery, and equipment. Wealth is things of value owned and is generally considered to be the total of economic goods at any given time (a stock concept). Income is the total value of the goods and services produced over a period of time (a flow concept). Economic services are useful, scarce, and transferable.

Economics can be divided into two major categories: microeconomics and macroeconomics. Microeconomics deals with the economic problems and concerns of the individual, firm, and industry. Macroeconomics deals with the aggregates of economics, e.g., total investment and savings, the general price level, full employment.

In the United States, a market economy or free enterprise capitalistic system is in operation. Under this system, most capital goods are owned and used by individuals and firms rather than by governmental agencies. Private property is a major feature of a capitalistic economic system. In a capitalistic system, profit is the incentive, or motive, for obtaining and using capital goods to produce goods and services that satisfy consumer needs and wants. The free enterprise system is regulated primarily by competition, although extensive governmental regulation exists. In a free enterprise system, the forces of supply and demand generally determine price. The goals of the national economy include full employment, stable prices, economic growth, and equilibrium in the international balance of payments.

See also Finance; Accounting; Free enterprise system; Federal Reserve System; Financial markets; Wealth; Economic environment of accounting; Economic consequences of accounting.

REFERENCE
Baumol, W. J., and Blinder, Alan S., Economics: Principles and Policy (Harcourt Brace Jovanovich, San Diego, CA, 1986).

EFFICIENT MARKET HYPOTHESIS
An efficient market is one which processes information immediately and reflects this information in security prices. Since information is assumed to be available to the market, an investor should not be able to adopt a trading strategy that produces returns above the average. Since all current facts and expectations about a security are assumed known by the investing public, the security is fairly priced.

However, there is much information that is not available to many security analysts and traders, especially "insiders' information" which is not generally available to the market. Furthermore, financial accounting and reporting practices tend to summarize complex data in an effort to make it more understandable. Through the summarization process, some information is lost to both the sophisticated and average investor. The full disclosure assumption of accounting theoretically should support the efficient market hypothesis. Recent disclosure requirements in financial reports imposed by standard setters and government regulators have increased both in detail and complexity. Research in accounting has been unable to identify or isolate the economic consequences of these reporting requirements.

See also Economic consequences of accounting; Full disclosure; Accounting standards overload.

REFERENCE
Dyckman, Thomas; Downes, David; and Magee, Robert, Efficient Capital Markets and Accounting: A Critical Analysis (Prentice-Hall, Englewood Cliffs, NJ, 1975).

ELECTRONIC DATA PROCESSING
An electronic data processing system is a network of machine and software components. The system accepts data, processes it according to instructions provided by programmers and operators, and prints out or displays the results for those who use the system. Available computer facilities have a wide range of capabilities including speed, storage capacity, and other features.

The central processor in a computer data processing system has three major components: (1) the control unit, which directs and coordinates various parts of the computer; (2) the arithmetic/logic unit, which performs the computations and other functions; and (3) the storage (or memory) unit, which retains instructions and other data for later use. Common output devices include printers, card punches, and cathode ray tubes. Exhibit E–1 illustrates the data processing cycle in accounting.

Computer software includes programs, instructions, and routines for using computer hardware.

System analysts usually design the data processing system. Programmers develop and write instructions for the computer. Computer operators run the computer system.

See also Accounting system.

ELEMENTS OF FINANCIAL STATEMENTS

Elements of financial statements are described as the building blocks with which financial statements are constructed, that is, the classes of items that financial statements comprise. There are currently ten interrelated elements that are directly related to measuring performance and status of an enterprise as defined in the FASB's Statement of Financial Accounting Concepts No. 3, Elements of Financial Statements of Business Enterprises:

ASSETS are probable future economic benefits obtained or controlled by a particular entity as a result of past transactions or events.

LIABILITIES are probable future sacrifices of economic benefits arising from present obligations of a particular entity to transfer assets or provide services to other entities in the future as a result of past transactions or events.

EQUITY is the residual interest in the assets of an entity that remains after deducting its liabilities. In a business entity, the equity is the ownership interest.

INVESTMENTS BY OWNERS are increases in net assets of a particular enterprise resulting from transfers to it from other entities of something of value to obtain or increase ownership interests (or equity) in it.

Exhibit E–1
Basic Components of an Electronic Data Processing System

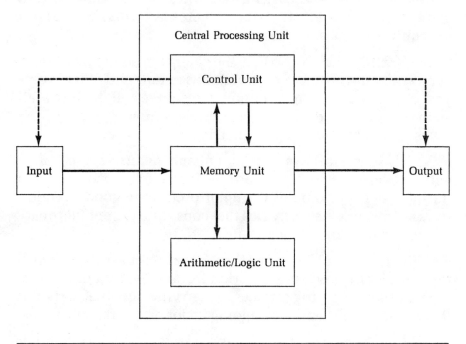

The Data Processing Cycle in Accounting

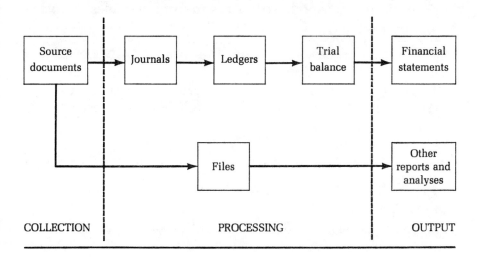

DISTRIBUTIONS TO OWNERS are decreases in net assets of a particular enterprise resulting from transferring assets, rendering services, or incurring liabilities by the enterprise to owners. Distributions to owners decrease ownership interest (or equity) in an enterprise.

COMPREHENSIVE INCOME is the change in equity (net assets) of an entity during a period from transactions and other events and circumstances from nonowner sources. It includes all changes in equity during a period except those resulting from investments by owners and distributions to owners.

REVENUES are inflows or other enhancements of assets of an entity or settlement of its liabilities (or a combination of both) during a period from delivering or producing goods, rendering services, or other activities that constitute the entity's ongoing major or central operations.

EXPENSES are outflows or other using up of assets or incurrence of liabilities during a period from delivering or producing goods or rendering services, or carrying out other activities that constitute the entity's ongoing major or central operations.

GAINS are increases in equity (net assets) from peripheral or incidental transactions of an entity and from all other transactions and other events and circumstances affecting the entity during a period except those that result from revenues or investments by owners.

LOSSES are decreases in equity (net assets) from peripheral or incidental transactions of an entity and from all other transactions and other events and circumstances affecting the entity during a period except those that result from expenses or distributions to owners.

See also each of the elements; Conceptual framework of accounting.

REFERENCE
SFAC No. 3, Elements of Financial Statements of Business Enterprises (FASB, 1978).

EQUITY METHOD OF ACCOUNTING

When an investor corporation can exercise significant influence over the operations and financial policies of an investee corporation, generally accepted accounting principles require that the investment in the investee be reported using the equity method. Significant influence can be determined by such factors as representation on the board of directors, participation in policy making processes, material intercompany transactions, interchange of managerial personnel, and technological dependency. It is presumed that an investor can exercise significant influence if it owns 20-50 percent of the outstanding common stock of the investee, unless evidence to the contrary is available.

The equity method of accounting for common stock investments reflects the economic substance rather than the legal form that underlies the investment in common stock of another company. When the equity method of accounting is used, the investor initially records the investment in the stock of an investee at cost. The investment account is then adjusted to recognize the investor's share of the income or losses of the investee after the date of acquisition when it is earned by the investee. Such amounts are included in determining the net income of the investor in the period they are reported by the investee. This procedure reflects accrual-basis accounting in that revenue is recognized when earned and losses when incurred. Dividends received from an investee reduce the carrying amount of the investment and are not reported as dividend income. As a result of applying the equity method, the investment account reflects the investor's equity in the underlying net assets of the investee. As an exception to the general rule of revenue recognition, revenue is recognized without a change in working capital.

In the investor's income statement, the proportionate share of the investee's net income is reported as a single-line item, except where the investee has extraordinary items that would be material in the investor's income statement. In such a case, the extraordinary item would be reported in the investor's income statement as extraordinary. Intercompany profits and losses are eliminated. Any excess of price paid for the shares over the underlying book value of the net assets of the subsidiary purchased must be identified (e.g., purchased goodwill) and, where appropriate, amortized or depreciated.

When an investor owns over 50 percent of the outstanding common stock of an investee and so can exercise control over the investee's operations, consolidated financial statements for the affiliated group are normally presented.

Investments in unconsolidated subsidiaries are reported in consolidated financial statements by the equity method. In unconsolidated financial statements of a parent company, investments in subsidiaries are reported by the equity method.

The relationship of ownership and the proper accounting method to use for investments in common stock can be illustrated as follows:

Percentage of Ownership

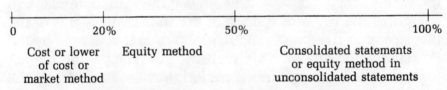

See also Cost method; Cost principle; Lower of cost or market; Consolidated financial statements; Joint venture.

REFERENCE
APB No. 18, The Equity Method of Accounting for Investments in Common Stock (APB, 1971).

ERISA

The Employee Retirement Income Security Act of 1974 (ERISA) established procedures for protecting employee pension rights. The act established strict minimum funding, vesting, benefit requirements, and employees' participation. In addition, certain types and amounts of transactions are prohibited, for example, not more than 10 percent of a plan's assets can be represented by securities of the sponsoring enterprise. The law requires that the financial statements of all employee benefit plans with more than 100 participants that are not fully insured must be examined and reported on by an independent, qualified public accountant.

ERISA created the Pension Benefit Guaranty Corporation (PBGC) to insure pension plans and administer terminated plans. In situations where a plan is unfunded or terminates, the PBGC can establish a lien on the employer's assets that takes precedence over almost all other creditor claims.

See also Pensions.

ERRORS

Accounting errors result from mistakes or omissions in the financial accounting process. Typical errors include mathematical mistakes, mistakes in the application of accounting principles, or oversight or misuse of facts. A change from an accounting principle that is unacceptable to a generally acceptable accounting principle is considered a correction of an error (and not a change in accounting principle). The information required for the correction of an error was available during a prior period. The use of newly acquired information or new facts resulting in a change of estimate is not an error. For example, a building was originally estimated to have a 20-year life and was being depreciated over that period. Several years later an engineering review of the building lowered the estimate to 15 years. Subsequent charges for annual depreciation would take this new information into consideration. Depreciation already recorded in prior years would not be adjusted. This situation is considered a change in estimate and is not an accounting error. The information required to revise the accounting estimate was not available in a prior period when the financial statements were issued.

Correction of an error should be reported as a prior-period adjustment which requires an adjustment to the beginning retained earnings on the Statement of Retained Earnings (and is not reported on the income statement). Disclosure would include the nature of the error, the effect of correcting it on the income before extraordinary items, net income, and related per share amounts.

See also Accounting Change; Prior period adjustment; Consistency.

REFERENCE
APB No. 20, Accounting change (APB, 1971).

ESTATES AND TRUSTS

An estate is comprised of the real and personal property owned by a person at the time of death. Real property is land or anything permanently attached to it. Personal property is all property that is not classified as real property. An estate ceases to exist when the property has been distributed according to a will or the law.

A decedent who leaves a valid will is referred to as the testator or testatrix and is said to have died testate. If a person dies without leaving a will, he or she is said to have died intestate. A will is a written instrument, legally executed, by which a person disposes of his or her estate after death. A will is usually executed by the signature of the testator and witnesses. Probate (to prove) refers to the judicial proof of a will. Generally, the validity of a will is determined by an examination of the document and the testimony of the witnesses. Various state courts (probate, surrogate, or orphan's courts) exercise authority over the probate of wills and the administration of estates. Probate is the first step in the orderly passing of assets of a decedent in accordance with a will. If a person dies without leaving a will or without leaving a valid will, his or her estate is nevertheless probated. Court-supervised probate should accomplish the following objectives:

1. Establish ownership of or benefits from property.
2. Provide for the transfer of property to the person(s) entitled to receive the property.
3. Assure that debts and taxes are paid.

The probate process requires that a petition for probate be filed with the appropriate court. Notice of the probate is forwarded to interested parties, especially to persons named in the will. An interested party may challenge or contest the probate of the document that the court is being asked to certify. If the will is certified as being valid, the court issues letters testamentary which establish the executor's legal authority to act for the estate.

The executor of a will is the person designated by the will to serve as the decedent's personal representative for purposes of carrying out the terms of the will. The executor collects the assets of the estate, manages the property with reasonable care, invests estate resources prudently, pays creditors, and distributes the remaining property as prescribed by the will. An administrator is a person appointed by the court to administer an intestate estate, a will that fails to name an executor, or a will whose named executor is unable to perform. The court issues letters of administration to an administrator which give the legal power to act on behalf of the estate. Executors and administrators are referred to as fiduciaries because of their function as stewards of the estate.

A distributee is a person entitled to a decedent's real or personal property by the will or by the statutes of intestate succession (generally referred to as probate codes). A legacy (or bequest) is a testamentary disposition of personal property. A legatee is a person entitled to receive personal property under a will. A devise is a distribution of real property. Real property usually passes directly to devisees identified in the will. Legacies can be classified as follows:

1. A general legacy is a gift of a designated amount or quantity of an asset payable from the general assets of the estate: $11,000 or 50 cases of beer.

2. A specific legacy is a gift of a particular, identifiable asset: $10,000 in a savings account in the First National bank.

3. A demonstrative legacy is a gift from a specific source, with the will stipulating that if the amount cannot be satisfied from that source, it shall be satisfied from the general estate: $100,000 from various insurance policies.

4. A residual legacy is a gift composed of all estate property remaining after distribution of general, specific, and demonstrative legacies.

When a person dies intestate, real property is distributed according to the laws of descent of the state where the property is located, and personal property is distributed according to the laws of distribution of the decedent's state of domicile. As a general rule, only a spouse or blood relative can receive an intestate distribution. Spouse or blood relative is described as an heir or as next of kin depending on the kind of property distributed. The laws of intestate succession generally favor the surviving spouse, children, and grandchildren and then move to the parents and grandparents and to brothers and sisters. Testate and intestate distributions are illustrated in Exhibit E–2.

When income from estate assets are granted to a person for life (a life tenant) or for a specific period of time after which the assets are to be distributed to another party (the remainderman), a distinction must be made between the principal and the income of the estate for accounting purposes. Principal (or

Exhibit E–2
Testate and Intestate Distributions of a Decedent

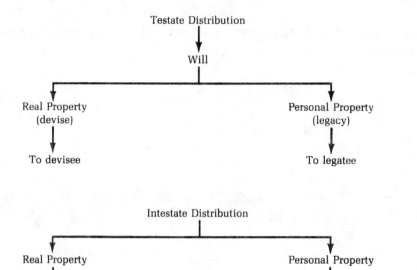

corpus) is the principal sum, property, or capital of an estate or trust that is to be eventually delivered to a remainderman. Principal includes partnership income allocatable to the decedent to date of death, proceeds of insurance on principal assets, stock and liquidating dividends, and accrued rent, interest, and other revenue at the date of death of the testator. Income (or interest) is the return in money or property derived from the use of principal, including rent, interest, cash dividends, and other revenue received during administration of a decedent's estate. The Revised Uniform Principal and Income Act provides for charges against and credits to principal and income. Generally, all expenses related to the settlement of a decedent's estate are charged to principal; costs of operating, preserving, and managing income producing property are charged against income.

The form of reporting by a fiduciary to the court is specified by state statutes or established by the court of jurisdiction. Two basic statements generally give an adequate accounting by the fiduciary:

1. Charge-and-discharge statement as to principal. This statement discloses the fiduciary's activities for a period of time as they relate to principal.

2. Charge-and-discharge statement as to income. This statement discloses the fiduciary's activities for a period of time as they relate to income.

A charge-and-discharge statement as to principal is illustrated in Exhibit E–3. Such statements generally have an "I charge myself with" section, which discloses the assets for which the fiduciary was responsible, and an "I credit myself with" section, which discloses how the fiduciary carried out his or her responsibilitles.

A trust is a fiduciary relationship under which property is held by one person (a trustee) for the benefit of another (the beneficiary). The income beneficiary is called a *cestui que trust*; he or she is also a life tenant if he or she is to receive income for life. The eventual recipient of the principal is a remainderman. The trust agreement provides for the distribution of trust principal and the income earned thereon. A trust is usually created by the owner of property (the trustor or grantor) who transfers property to the trustee. A trust established while the grantor is alive is referred to as an *inter vivos or living trust*. A trust established by will is a testamentary trust. The administration of trusts usually proceeds without any involvement of the courts. Trust administration involves primarily the prudent management of funds to provide continuing benefits to an income beneficiary and then to a re-

Exhibit E-3
Charge and Discharge Statement as to the Principal of an Estate

Dee Rose, Executor for the Estate of Charles Smith
Charge-and-Discharge Statement as to Principal
June 1, 19x1, to November 30, 19x1

I Charge Myself With:		
Assets per inventory (Schedule A)	$300,000	
Assets Discovered (Schedule B)	15,000	
Total Charges		$315,000
I Credit Myself With:		
Loss on Realization of Principal		
Assets (Schedule C)	500	
Funeral Expenses	5,000	
Administrative Expenses (Schedule D)	30,950	
Debts of Decendent Paid (Schedule E)	52,725	
Legacies Paid or Delivered (Schedule F)	80,550	
Devise Distributed,	50,000	
Total Credits		219,725
Balance as to Principal		$ 95,275
Consisting of:		
Principal Cash		$ 10,275
Savings Accounts		20,000
Common Stock		65,000
Total		$95,275

mainderman. Estate administration is primarily a liquidating process.

Estate planning is the process of providing for the proper disposition of a person's assets after death. Its objectives are usually related to the reduction of estate taxes, settlement costs, and other expenses so as to provide a maximum distribution to those for whom the estate exists. The federal estate tax is imposed on the right to transfer property by death and is assessed against the net assets of an estate and not on the parties receiving the property. State inheritance taxes are imposed on the right to receive property from a decedent and are assessed against devisees and heirs of a decedent.

See also Prudent man rule; Fiduciary.

REFERENCES
Bernstein, Leopold A., and Engler, Calvin, *Advanced Accounting* (Richard D. Irwin, Homewood, IL, 1982).
AICPA, Professional Standards (Commerce Clearing House, Inc., Chicago, latest edition).

ETHICS

The Code of Professional Ethics of the American Institute of Certified Public Accountants is designed to promote higher standards of professional conduct among its members. The Code provides guidelines for accounting practitioners. The Code also deals with such matters as the independence required of accountants, technical standards, relationships with clients and colleagues, and a variety of other expectations. For example, independence in auditing means that the auditor has an unbiased viewpoint in the performance of the audit both in fact and in appearance. Auditors are also expected to comply with the technical standards of the profession as they relate to generally accepted accounting principles and auditing standards.

A code of ethics for management accountants was prepared by the National Association of Accountants. This statement is referred to as Statement on Management Accounting No. 1C: Standards of Ethical Conduct for Management Accountants. The statement identifies four major elements of professional conduct for management accountants: competence, confidentiality, integrity, and objectivity. The statement also describes a procedure for resolving conflicts when situations involving ethics arise.

A distinction can be made between ethical, professional, and legal conduct. Ethical conduct implies voluntary behavior or intentional dispositions to act for which the individual can be held responsible to a recognized standard of right and wrong. Professional conduct refers to standards of conduct that are normal, expected, or precedented in a particular profession, such as law or accounting. Professional standards prescribe the basis upon which professionals ought to conduct their activities. In addition, professional standards establish the basis by which a profession can be explained, interpreted, and judged. Professional and ethical standards can be distinguished from legal standards which are established by the rules, laws, and conventions imposed by legislative and administrative authorities. There are areas of conduct where ethical, professional, and legal standards overlap.

See also Accounting profession; Audit.

REFERENCE
AICPA, AICPA Professional Standards, Vol. B (Commerce Clearing House, Inc., Chicago, latest edition).

EVENTS, TRANSACTIONS, EXCHANGES, AND CIRCUMSTANCES

Events, transactions, exchanges, and circumstances affecting an entity describe the sources or causes of revenue, expense, gains, and losses as well as changes in assets, liabilities, and equity. An understanding of events, exchanges, transactions, and circumstances is important because they change or affect in some manner the underlying assets, liabilities, and equity of an enterprise. They consequently determine the contents of an enterprise's financial statements and have economic consequences. Events, transactions, and exchanges can be outlined as follows:

1. *Event* — An event is a happening or occurrence that has economic consequences for an entity. Economic events may be external or internal to the entity.

   a. *Internal event* — An internal event occurs within an entity, such as the use of raw material in the production process.

   b. *External event* — An external event is an event that requires an interaction between an entity and its environment, such as the sale or purchase of a product.

2. *Transaction* — A transaction is a particular kind of external event that requires accounting recognition. A transaction involves the transfer of something of value between two or more entities. An investment purchased from a stockbroker is a transaction. Transactions are classified as either an exchange for a nonreciprocal transfer.

   a. *Exchange* — In an exchange, each participant receives and sacrifices something of value, such as the acquisition of inventory for cash.

   b. *Nonreciprocal transfer* — A nonreciprocal transfer involves the transfer of assets in one direction. Transfers can occur between the enterprise and its owners and between the enterprise and entities other than its owners. The acquisition and disposition of assets by donation or gifts and property dividends are examples of nonreciprocal transfers.

Exhibit E–4 illustrates the relationship between comprehensive income and other transactions, events, and circumstances. An outline of events and transactions is given in Exhibit E–5.

See also Accounting; Double-entry system.

Exhibit E-4
Relationship of Comprehensive Income and Other Transactions, Events, and Circumstances

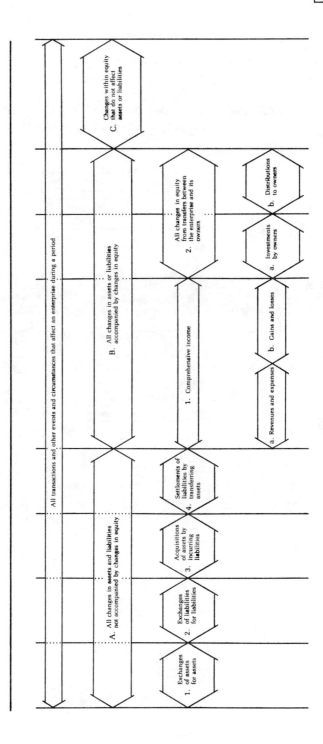

Exhibit E–5
Outline of Events and Transactions

Source: FASB Research Report: Recognition in Financial Statements:
          Underlying Concepts and Practical Conventions

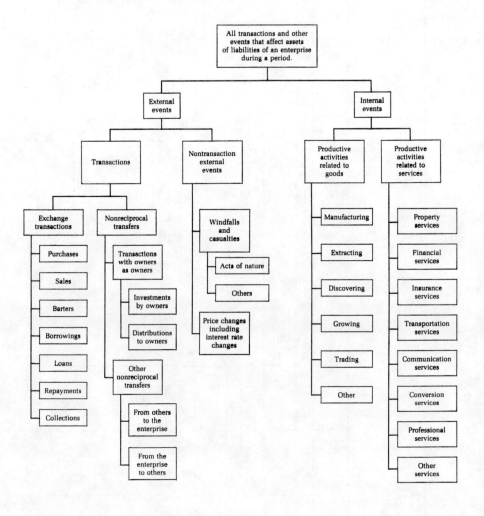

EXPENSES

Expenses are outflows or other using up of assets or incurrence of liabilities (or a combination of both) during a period from delivering or producing goods, rendering services, or carrying out other activities that constitute the entity's ongoing major or central operations.

Expenses represent actual or expected cash outflows that have occurred or will eventually occur as a result of the enterprise's ongoing major or central operations during a period. The matching principle of accounting requires that expenses be matched with revenues whenever it is reasonable and practicable. Three major expense recognition principles have been established for determining the accounting period in which expenses are recognized and reported:

1. Associating cause and effect. Some costs are recognized as expenses on the basis of a presumed direct association with specific revenues. For example, a sale of a product involves both sales revenue and cost of goods sold. The cost of the goods sold would be recognized in the accounting period that the sales revenue was recognized.

2. Systematic and rational allocation. Where there is no cause and effect relationship, an attempt is made to associate costs in a systematic and rational manner with the products of the periods affected. Costs that are associated with periods in a systematic way include depreciation and amortization expenses.

3. Immediate recognition. Costs that cannot be related to revenues either by associating cause and effect or by systematic and rational allocation are recognized as expenses of the current period. Such costs could include auditor's fees, research and development costs, and officers' salaries.

Expenses are classified on a multi-step income statement in various categories. Operating expenses are usually reported in two categories: (1) selling expenses and (2) general and administrative expenses. Selling expenses include expenses associated with the sales function, such as sales salaries, advertising, store supplies used, and delivery expenses. General and administrative expenses are those expenses generally associated with the general operations of the enterprise. General and administrative expenses include officers' and office salaries, office supplies used, depreciation of office furniture, telephone, postage, legal and accounting services, and contributions. Other expenses include those identified with financial management and miscellaneous activities. Such expenses include interest expense and the write-down of obsolete inventory.

Expenses never include such items as dividend payments, repayment of loan principal, and expenditures to acquire items having future value (assets) to an enterprise.

The term *cost* should not be used to refer to expense. An expense is an expired cost. A cost can refer to an item that has service potential (an asset). An expense would arise when the cost no longer has service potential.

See also Matching principle; Losses; Cost; Income; Income statement; Materiality.

REFERENCE
SFAC No. 3, Elements of Financial Statements of Business Enterprises (FASB, 1981).

EXTRAORDINARY ITEM

Extraordinary items are material events and transactions that are both unusual in nature and infrequent of occurrence. To be unusual in nature, the underlying event or transaction must have a high degree of abnormality and be of a type clearly unrelated to, or only incidentally related to, the ordinary and typical activities of the entity, taking into account the environment in which the entity operates. Infrequency of occurrence relates to the requirement that the underlying event or transaction should be of a type that would not reasonably be expected to recur in the foreseeable future, taking into account the environment in which the entity operates. The materiality effect of individual events or transactions is considered separately and not aggregated unless the effects result from a single identifiable transaction or event that meets the definition of an extraordinary item.

Extraordinary items could result if gains or losses were the direct result of any of the following events or circumstances:

1. a major casualty, such as an earthquake,

2. an expropriation of property by a foreign government, or

3. a prohibition under a newly enacted law or regulation.

The income statement should disclose captions and amounts for individual extraordinary events or transactions on the face of the statement. Income taxes applicable to the extraordinary item should be disclosed. Extraordinary items can be reported as follows:

Income before extraordinary items	$XXX
Extraordinary items (less applicable income taxes of $XXX)	XXX
Net income	$XXX

A material event or transaction that is unusual in nature or occurs infrequently is reported as a separate element of income from continuing operations and is not classified as an extraordinary item.

See also Income statement.

REFERENCE
APB No. 30, Reporting the Results of Operations (APB, 1973).

F

FACTORING

Factoring is a method of financing where a firm sells its accounts receivable to another party, called a factor, for cash. Receivables can be assigned to a factor in a variety of ways:

1. Selling with recourse (seller collects);
2. Selling with recourse (factor collects);
3. Selling without recourse.

Exhibit F-1 describes a typical factoring relationship.

When receivables are sold with recourse, the seller guarantees the receivables; the seller has an obligation to the buying firm if the collections of receivables are less than anticipated. In factoring arrangements, the accounts receivable are physically transferred to the factor, and the selling firm gives up all rights to future collections. The factor does not pay face value for the receivables purchased.

Accounts receivable are sometimes pledged as collateral for a loan. The borrower agrees to collect the receivables and to use the proceeds to repay the loan.

In an assignment of accounts receivable, a borrower (the assignor) transfers its rights in certain receivables to a lender

Exhibit F–1
Typical Factoring Arrangement

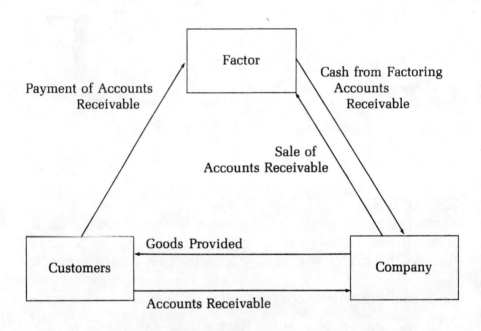

(the assignee) in exchange for a loan. When the receivables are collected, the proceeds are used to repay the loan. The assignment is on either a notification or a nonnotification basis. When the assignment is on a notification basis, customers are informed that their accounts have been assigned and that they are to make payments directly to the assignee.

See also Receivables.

REFERENCE
Smith, Jay M., and Skousen, K. Fred, *Intermediate Accounting* (South-Western, Cincinnati, OH, 1985).

FEDERAL RESERVE SYSTEM

The administration of monetary policy in the United States is carried out through the Federal Reserve System. The System includes twelve Federal Reserve Banks, the Board of Governors in Washington, and the Federal Open Market Committee. All national banks and many state banks are members of the System.

A primary function of the Federal Reserve System is to promote a flow of credit and money that will facilitate economic growth, a stable dollar, and long-run balance in international payments. The principal means available to the System to influence monetary policy include open market purchases and sales, primarily of U.S. Government securities but also of foreign currencies, discount operations (lending to commercial banks), and changes in bank reserve requirements. The System also influences the availability of stock market credit by setting limits on the amount that brokers and dealers in securities, banks, and others may lend on securities, real estate, or commodities. Bank reserves constitute the legally required basis of bank deposits. Changes in the reserve position of banks can directly affect the flow of bank credit and money throughout the economy. The System can directly affect bank reserves through its ability to increase or decrease the volume and cost of bank reserves. The System also supervises reporting banks to ensure the maintenance of an adequate and responsive banking system. The System is responsive to the supply and demand for currency in the United States and pays out currency in response to the public's demand and absorbs excessive currency.

Interest rates are the prices paid for borrowed money. Interest rates are established primarily in credit markets as supplies of and demands for loanable funds seek equilibrium. The Federal Reserve System can influence interest rates by exerting pressure on the nation's saving and investment, market expectations, and the flow of bank credit and money as they affect decisions to lend, spend, and save. Operations by the System in foreign exchange markets have an impact on the

F

international balance of payments.

The Federal Reserve System's relationship to national credit policy is illustrated in Exhibit F–2.

See also Economics; Finance; Financial markets; Money market; Interest.

REFERENCE
Board of Governors, *The Federal Reserve System: Purposes and Functions* (Federal Reserve System, Washington, DC).

FIDUCIARY

A fiduciary is a person who holds something in trust for another. Executors and administrators of estates and trusts are often referred to as fiduciaries. The term can also be applied to agencies, guardianships, directors of corporations, trustees of not-for-profit organizations, and others.

Financial reporting places considerable emphasis on the stewardship function of the management of an enterprise. Managers are accountable not only for the custody and safekeeping of an enterprise's resources but also for the efficient and effective use of those resources, including protecting the enterprise from the unfavorable impact of inflation, deflations, technological and social change, and similar environmental factors. In a larger sense, society may impose stewardship functions on enterprises and their managements. Statements of financial position and income statements are basic references for evaluating how managers have performed their stewardship function, especially to owners.

Assessing management's stewardship function for nonbusiness organizations is especially important. Information about such organizations' performance should ordinarily be the focus for assessing the stewardship or accountability of managers. Uses of financial statements of nonbusiness organizations require assurance that managers have utilized available resources in a manner that corresponds to those specified by resource providers.

Exhibit F-2
The Federal Reserve System: Relationship to Credit Policy Instruments

THE FEDERAL RESERVE SYSTEM: RELATION TO INSTRUMENTS OF CREDIT POLICY

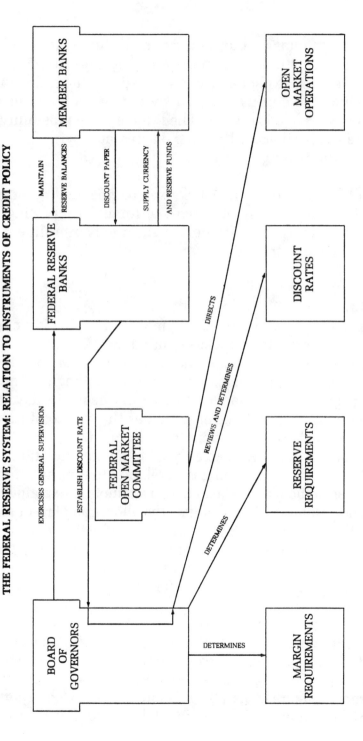

Source: Board of Governors, The Federal Reserve System: Purposes and Functions.

F

In governmental accounting, fiduciary funds are used to account for assets held in a trust or agency capacity. Fiduciary funds include expendable and nonexpendable trust funds (funds where the corpus may or may not be spent), pension trust funds, and agency funds. The fiduciary responsibility is to operate the fund according to the agreement with the contributor of the principal or corpus.

See also Estates and trusts; Objectives of financial reporting by business enterprises; Objectives of financial reporting by nonbusiness enterprises; Prudent man rule; Nonprofit enterprises; Governmental accounting.

FINANCE

Finance is the science of managing money. Finance is closely related to both economics and accounting. Economics provides an understanding of the institutional structures in which money and credit flow (macroeconomics) and the profit maximization guidelines associated with the theory of the firm (microeconomics). Accounting provides the source of financial and other data for financial management.

Financial theory deals primarily with the accumulation and allocation of economic resources in relation to time and under varied states of the world. Finance also attempts to explain how money and capital markets facilitate the allocation of resources. Finance is concerned with the valuation of the firm as a going concern and investment opportunities and with factors that can change these values. It deals with the acquisition and use of funds, including their impact on the profitability and growth of the firm. Financial theory is applicable to nonprofit entities as well as for-profit enterprises.

The functions of a financial manager are (1) financial analysis and planning, (2) the management of the firm's asset structure, and (3) the management of its financial structure. A firm's asset structure refers to both the mix and type of assets reported on the firm's balance sheet. Financial structure refers to the appropriate mix of short-term and long-term financing, including both debt and equity financing. The goal of financial management is to achieve the objectives of the firm's owners, which is sometimes considered to be the maximization of profit or wealth. The maximization of profit and wealth requires financial managers to consider the owner's realizable return on the investment, a short-run and a long-run viewpoint, the timing of benefits, risks, and the distribution of returns.

See also Accounting; Economics.

REFERENCE
Pringle, John and Harris, Robert J., *Essentials of Managerial Finance* (Scott, Foresman & Co., Glenview, IL, 1984).

FINANCIAL ACCOUNTING
Financial accounting is a subset of financial reporting that is primarily concerned with measuring and reporting financial information in a set of basic general purpose financial statements. Financial accounting is designed primarily to meet the needs of external users of the financial statements of an enterprise. General purpose financial statements are statements designed to reasonably meet the needs of most users, primarily investors and creditors. Managerial accounting is concerned primarily with internal reporting. It relates essentially to planning, controlling, evaluating performance, and product costing for income valuation and income determination. There is some overlap between financial accounting and managerial accounting.

See also Financial reporting; Conceptual framework of accounting; Financial Accounting Standards Board; Statements of Financial Accounting Concepts; Statements of Financial Accounting Standards.

FINANCIAL ACCOUNTING STANDARDS BOARD

The Financial Accounting Standards Board (FASB) is the authoritative standard setter for generally accepted accounting principles in the United States. The FASB succeeded the Accounting Principles Board in 1973.

Since 1973 the Financial Accounting Standards Board has been the designated organization in the private sector for establishing standards of financial accounting and reporting. These standards are essentially rules governing the preparation of financial reports. The FASB standards are officially recognized as authoritative by the Securities and Exchange Commission and the American Institute of Certified Public Accountants.

When the Accounting Principles Board came under increasing criticism, the AICPA established a Study Group on Establishment of Accounting Principles (commonly called the Wheat Committee after its chairman) to examine the organization and operation of the APB. The Study Group recommended the creation of the FASB. This recommendation was implemented by early 1973. The organizational structure of this standard-setting body is shown in Exhibit F-3.

The Financial Accounting Foundation is the independent entity whose board of trustees oversees the basic structure of the standard-setting process. The trustees are appointed by representatives of the following organizations: the American Accounting Association, AICPA, National Association of Accountants, Financial Executives Institute, Financial Analysts Federation, and Securities Industry Association. The trustees appoint members to the FASB and to the FASB's advisory council and seek funds for the FASB's operations.

The Financial Accounting Standards Board is an independent body consisting of seven members appointed by the Financial Accounting Foundation's trustees. The FASB is composed of accountants and nonaccountants. FASB members serve full-time and are fully remunerated. Members are not required to be CPAs. An affirmative vote of four of the seven FASB members is needed to approve a pronouncement. The Board's deliberations are open to the public.

Exhibit F–3
Organizational Structure for Establishing Accounting Standards

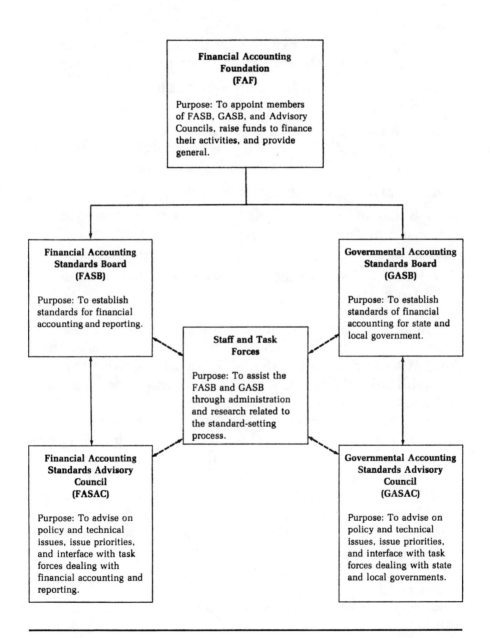

Financial Accounting Foundation (FAF)

Purpose: To appoint members of FASB, GASB, and Advisory Councils, raise funds to finance their activities, and provide general.

Financial Accounting Standards Board (FASB)

Purpose: To establish standards for financial accounting and reporting.

Governmental Accounting Standards Board (GASB)

Purpose: To establish standards of financial accounting for state and local government.

Staff and Task Forces

Purpose: To assist the FASB and GASB through administration and research related to the standard-setting process.

Financial Accounting Standards Advisory Council (FASAC)

Purpose: To advise on policy and technical issues, issue priorities, and interface with task forces dealing with financial accounting and reporting.

Governmental Accounting Standards Advisory Council (GASAC)

Purpose: To advise on policy and technical issues, issue priorities, and interface with task forces dealing with state and local governments.

F

Before it issues a Statement, the Board is required to follow extensive "due process" procedures. In connection with each of its major, standard-setting projects, the Board takes the following steps:

1. Appoints a task force of technical experts representing a broad spectrum of advisors on the project.
2. Studies existing literature on the subject and conducts such additional research as may be necessary.
3. Publishes a comprehensive discussion of issues and possible solutions as the basis for public comment, referred to as Discussion Memorandum.
4. Conducts a public hearing on the project.
5. Issues an Exposure Draft, which is a preliminary version of a pronouncement for public comment.
6. Issues a Statement of Financial Accounting Standard after it has analyzed the response to the Exposure Draft.

The Financial Accounting Standards Advisory Council is a diversified group of individuals from various areas of business. The Council assists the FASB in setting priorities and in establishing ad hoc task forces. It also provides feedback to the FASB on proposed pronouncements.

The FASB has established an Emerging Issues Task Force (EITF) to identify and solve emerging accounting and reporting issues in the profession, especially those arising from new and different types of transactions. The establishment of the Task Force was a response to the demands of the profession and business to deal expeditiously with reporting issues. If members of the EITF reach a consensus that there is a single preferred treatment, the Chief Accountant of the SEC will accept this type of consensus as authoritative support for practices to be used in financial reports filed with the SEC. Currently, no other group has declared that the EITF is authoritative.

In 1984 a Governmental Accounting Standards Board (GASB) was established to deal with state and local governmental reporting issues. The GASB has an advisory council, technical staff, and task forces.

See also Financial reporting; Conceptual framework of accounting; Accounting profession; Generally accepted accounting principles; Accounting principles; Statements of Financial Accounting Standards; Statements of Financial Accounting Concepts.

REFERENCES
Practer, Paul A., "The FASB After Ten Years: History and Emerging Trends," *Financial Accounting Theory*, Zeff, Stephen A., and Keller, Thomas F., Editors (McGraw-Hill, N.Y., 1985).
Miller, Paul B.W., and Redding, Rodney, *The FASB: The People, the Process, & the Politics*, (Richard D. Irwin, Chicago, 1986).

FINANCIAL MARKETS

A financial market brings together borrowers and lenders or investors and establishes and communicates the prices at which they are willing to make transactions. Financial markets assume many shapes and forms.

Credit markets, or "money markets," include financial markets in which instruments of short-term maturity (up to one year or slightly longer) as well as bank loans, trade credit, and other forms of indebtedness of short duration are involved. Capital markets, or "bond markets," usually include notes, bonds, and most other forms of intermediate and longer-term indebtedness. Capital markets exist for new issues of stocks and bonds and secondary capital markets include the stock exchanges and brokers and dealers in securities. Money markets and bond markets identify separate maturity subdivisions of the fixed-income securities markets. Other markets include (1) the foreign exchange market, which involves international financial transactions between the United States and other countries and agencies, (2) the commodity markets, such as the cotton, grain, and sugar exchanges, and (3) the insurance, shipping, and other markets requiring short-term credit accommodations in their operations. The open market for credit instruments is subdivided as follows: (1) short-term government securities including Treasury bills and certificates, (2) the commercial paper market, (3) the bankers' acceptance market, (4) negotiable certificates of time deposits issued by commercial banks, and (5) Federal Funds Market.

Exhibit F–4 describes in general terms the American financial system as it relates to the credit and capital markets.

Exhibit F–4
Diagram of Flows in U.S. Financial System

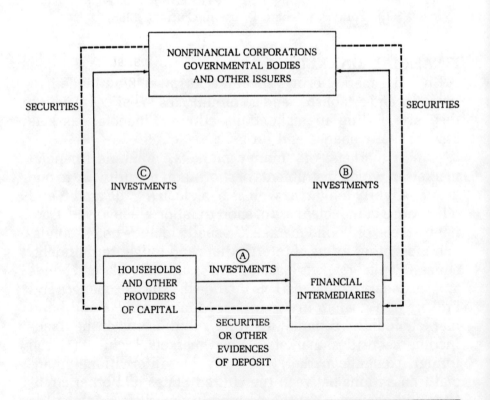

Commercial paper is unsecured, short-term notes issued by large firms to meet seasonal financing requirements and also serve as a tool for investing short-term corporate funds. Bankers' acceptances are bills for goods shipped for which a commercial bank accepts the obligation to pay the amount stated on the face of the bill on the date specified. Certificates of deposit (CD) are evidence of short-term debt issued by a commercial bank, with a specified rate of interest and maturity date, to a depositor of funds. Banks are required to maintain a certain amount of reserves against deposits at Federal Reserve Banks. At times, banks may be deficient in reserves or have a surplus. Commercial banks can adjust their reserve positions by borrowing from other banks in a well-organized market known as the Federal Funds Market. Banks, U.S. government security dealers, and others borrow and lend federal funds in this market from time to time.

Credit and capital market instruments are sometimes classified as follows: U.S. government securities, state and local government obligations, corporate and foreign bonds, mortgages, consumer credit, bank loans, and other loans (open-market paper, commercial paper, bankers' acceptances, Federal funds and security repurchase agreements, finance company loans to business, U.S. government loans, sponsored credit agency loans, and loans on insurance policies).

A stock exchange is an auction market in which securities are sold to the highest bidder and bought from the lowest seller. In the United States, the New York Stock Exchange (the Big Board) and the American Stock Exchange are the two national marketplaces for transactions in stocks and bonds. In addition to these national exchanges, there are regional exchanges located in principal cities throughout the country.

A listed security is one that has been accepted by an exchange as being qualified for trading on the exchange. Basic standards for listing on the New York Stock Exchange include: a going concern, national investors' interest in the firm, good standing in the industry, net assets and earnings above a specified amount, and a minimum number of shares outstanding.

Trading on the exchange is done in standard numbers of shares, called round lots, usually 100 shares or a multiple thereof. For bonds, the standard unit is one $1,000 bond. Lots smaller than round lots are called odd lots. In an odd-lot transaction, one-eighth of a point is added to (or deducted from) the price of each share purchased (or sold). Market prices are listed in points; a point is equal to a market price of $1 per share. Listings normally are given to the nearest one-eighth of a point. The execution price for an odd lot includes the price differential charged for handling the odd lot. The delivery and settlement of securities traded on the exchanges are closely regulated. In most cases, a transaction is settled "regular way"—that is, payment for and delivery of the securities on the fifth full business day following the transaction. A commission is imposed on both buyers and sellers of stock on an exchange.

The over-the-counter, or unlisted, market consists of a network of dealers in cities throughout the country, linked together by telephone and teletype. In this market, securities not listed on the exchanges are bought and sold. Transactions are arranged by "negotiation" rather than by auction.

Exhibit F-5 summarizes typical investment characteristics of bonds, preferred stock, and common stock.

Exhibit F-5
Investment Characteristics of Stocks and Bonds

Type of Security	Safety of Principal	Income	Growth
Bonds	Best	Very stable	Very limited
Preferred stock	Good	Stable	Variable
Common stock	Least	Variable	Considerable

The securities markets involve many complex trading practices and procedures. Such arrangements include market orders, limited orders, stop-loss orders, buy-stop orders, quotations, time limits, bonds sold flat, call and put options, long holdings, selling against the box, short sales, trading on margin, and others.

When an investor sells short, the investor sells a security that he/she does not own, intending to purchase the security before the time when the security must be delivered. A short sale is practically the reverse of a normal securities transaction. The major reason for an investor to sell short is that he/she expects the price of the security to decline.

In a margin transaction, the investor purchases securities and pays only a percentage of their cost; the balance is paid by the broker and is treated as a loan to the investor. The Federal Reserve System sets margin requirements. The investor who buys on margin expects the price of the stock to rise. If the price of the stock declines, the investor could sell the stock at a loss. If the investor does not sell the stock and the price declines significantly, the buyer will receive a margin call from his broker, asking that the investor put up additional cash or collateral to keep the investor's equity up to a required level. If the additional resources are not forthcoming, the broker sells the stock to recover the amount of the loan and any interest due.

A mutual fund combines the investment resources of many investors who purchase shares in a large investment pool. This pool is managed by the directors or trustees of the funds, who use the available resources to acquire stocks or bonds of other companies or of governments. Mutual funds provide investors an opportunity to diversify their investments and to obtain some benefit from professional management and supervision of their investments. The price of mutual fund shares is usually calculated daily by taking the net value of securities and cash owned by the fund and dividing by the number of fund shares outstanding. This calculation yields a "net asset value," which is the "bid" price used in the negotiation process to arrive at an "asked" price. A money market fund is a mutual fund whose investments are in short-term, high-yield money market instruments such as commercial paper, certificates of deposit, or government securities. A unit investment trust is a fixed portfolio of securities designed to achieve specific investment objectives, usually monthly income and preservation of capital through diversification. Such trusts are held in trust on behalf of investors by a bank trustee. They are called "unit" investment trusts because ownership interests in them can be purchased in one or more units valued in most circumstances at about $1,000 each.

GNMA (Mortgage-backed Government Securities, or Ginnie Maes) investments are made up of pools of FHA and VA residential mortgages. A mortgage banker assembles a pool of mortgages guaranteed by either the Federal Housing Administration or Veterans Administration. The Government National Mortgage Association issues securities against these mortgages, which can be sold to investors. As homeowners pay down their mortgages each month, principal and interest are passed through the pool to holders of Ginnie Mae securities.

A stock option is a right to buy or sell a given number of shares of a specific stock, usually 100 shares, within a certain time. A call option ("call") gives a person the right to buy and a put option ("put") the right to sell. The advantages of option buying are usually related to leverage, reduced cost, and limited risk. The risk in buying an option is that the option may expire prior to its exercise or sale and so become worthless. Covered writing refers to selling call options on stocks owned.

A futures position is a commitment to buy or sell a specified quantity and quality of a futures product at a designated time in the future at a price which is agreed upon when the commitment is made. The person taking a futures position, as with commodity futures, will either fulfill the agreement to buy or sell when it matures, or liquidate it prior to the position's maturity date.

Underwriters play a major role in advising companies on opportunities for financing and in structuring securities issuances as well as assisting companies in selling the securities to the public. In underwriting an offering, the underwriter usually operates under one of the following arrangements:

1. Best efforts. The underwriter agrees to his or her best efforts to sell the issue but assumes no obligation to purchase unsold securities.

2. Best efforts, all or none. Under this arrangement, the offering is cancelled if the underwriter is unable to sell the entire issue.

3. Firm commitment. Under this arrangement, the underwriter agrees to purchase all of the offering and assumes the risk for any unsold securities.

Comfort letters usually are supplied by accountants and others prior to the offering of the securities to the public. These letters usually provide the following assurances: (1) that the accountant is independent and that the financial statements covered in the auditor's report comply with the requirements of securities legislation; and (2) that nothing came to the attention of the party supplying the comfort letter indicating that discrepancies were found (negative assurance).

Federal and state governments and the securities industry attempt to protect investors through detailed regulations and supervision. Every state has "blue sky" laws that set forth requirements relating to licensing of securities representatives as well as registration and disclosure procedures for products offered for sale.

See also Bonds; Convertible securities; Capital stock; Preferred stock; Securities and Exchange Commission; Federal Reserve System; Finance; Economics.

REFERENCE
Darst, David M., *The Handbook of the Bond and Money Markets* (McGraw-Hill, N.Y., 1981).

F

FINANCIAL PLANNING
Personal financial planning involves the evaluation of a person's current financial position and financial goals leading to a presentation of a plan to achieve those goals. A typical financial plan includes:

1. A balance sheet analysis
2. Projection of cash flow
3. Long-term accumulation plans for retirement, education, etc.
4. Statement of individual's goals
5. Insurance analysis
6. Estate and tax planning
7. Projection of income taxes
8. Overview of weaknesses and strengths in the individual's financial outlook
9. Recommendations for implementing the plan

Financial planners charge clients in one of three major ways: a fee-only basis, a fee-and-commission basis, or a commission basis.

Currently two professional organizations accredit planners after they have completed certain educational and professional requirements: The College for Financial Planning confers the Certified Financial Planner (CFP) and the American College confers the Chartered Financial Consultant (ChFC) designation. Two major professional organizations are associated with financial planning: the International Association for Financial Planning and the Institute of Certified Financial Planners.

See also Management advisory services.

REFERENCE
Bailard, Thomas E., et al., *Personal Money Management* (Science Research Associates, Chicago, 1986).

FINANCIAL REPORTING

Financial reporting includes not only financial statements but also other means of communicating information that relates, directly or indirectly, to the information provided by the accounting system. Financial reporting is intended primarily to provide information that is useful in making business and economic decisions.

Financial reporting is a broad concept encompassing financial statements, notes to financial statements (and parenthetical disclosures), supplementary information (such as changing prices disclosures and oil and gas reserves information), and other means of financial reporting (such as management discussion and analysis, and letters to stockholders). Financial reporting is but one source of information needed by those who make economic decisions about business enterprises. Exhibit F-6 shows the relationship of financial reporting to other information useful for investment, credit, and similar decisions.

The primary focus of financial reporting is information about earnings and its components. Information about earnings based on accrual accounting usually provides a better indication of an enterprise's present and continuing ability to generate positive cash flows than that provided by cash receipts and payments.

See also Objectives of financial reporting; Financial accounting; Financial statements; Financial Accounting Standards Board; Accounting basis.

REFERENCE
FAC No. 1, Objectives of Financial Reporting by Business Enterprises (FASB, 1978).

FINANCIAL STATEMENT ANALYSIS

The purpose of financial statement analysis is to examine past and current financial data so that a company's performance and financial position can be evaluated and future risks and

F

Exhibit F-6
Relationship of Financial Reporting to Other Information Sources

All Information Useful for Investment, Credit, and Similar Decisions
(Concepts Statement 1. paragraph 22: partly quoted in footnote 6)

Financial Reporting
(Concepts Statement 1. paragraphs 5‒8)

Area Directly Affected by Existing FASB Standards

Basic Financial Statements
(in AICPA Auditing Standards Literature)

Scope of Recognition and Measurement Concepts Statement

Financial Statements	Notes to Financial Statements (& parenthetical disclosures)	Supplementary Information	Other Means of Financial Reporting	Other Information
Examples: • Statement of Financial Position • Statements of Earnings and Comprehensive Income • Statement of Cash Flows • Statement of Investments by and Distributions to Owners	Examples: • Accounting Policies • Contingencies • Inventory Methods • Number of Shares of Stock Outstanding • Alternative Measures (market values of items carried at historical cost)	Examples: • Changing Prices Disclosures (FASB Statement 33 as amended) • Oil and Gas Reserves Information (FASB Statement 69)	Examples: • Management Discussion and Analysis • Letters to Stockholders	Examples: • Discussion of Competition and Order Backlog in SEC Form 10-K (under SEC Reg. S-K) • Analysts' Reports • Economic Statistics • News Articles about Company

potential estimated. Financial statement analysis can yield valuable information about trends and relationships, the quality of a company's earnings, and the strengths and weaknesses of its financial position.

Creditors, investors, potential investors, and others are interested in evaluating a company's financial statements. Creditors are usually interested in knowing whether a company has the ability to meet its obligations as they mature and the long-term solvency of the company. They are also interested in knowing the sources of a debtor's capital, how it has been invested, and how it is being employed. Investors and potential investors are primarily interested in evaluating the investment characteristics of a company, including the relationship of the current value of a company's stock to expectations of its future value, the safety of their investment, the dividend policy of the company, the company's growth potential, and how the managers have carried out their stewardship function.

Financial statement analysis begins with establishing the objective(s) of the analysis. For example, is the analysis undertaken to provide a basis for granting credit or making an investment? After the objective of the analysis is established, the data is accumulated from the financial statements and from other sources. The results of the analysis are summarized and interpreted. Conclusions are reached and a report is made to the person(s) for whom the analysis was undertaken.

To evaluate financial statements, a person must

1. be acquainted with business practices,

2. understand the purpose, nature, and limitations of accounting,

3. be familiar with the terminology of business and accounting, and

4. be acquainted with the tools of financial statement analysis.

Financial analysis of a company should include an examination of the financial statements of the company, including notes to the financial statements, and the auditor's report. The auditor's report will state whether the financial statements have been audited in accordance with generally accepted auditing standards. The report also indicates whether the statements fairly present the company's financial position, results of operations, and changes in financial position in accordance with generally accepted accounting principles. Notes to the financial statement are often more meaningful than the data found within the body of the statements. The notes explain the accounting policies of the company and usually provide detailed explanations of how those policies were applied along with supporting details. Analysts often compare the financial statements of one company with other companies in the same industry and with the industry in which the company operates as well as with prior year statements of the company being analyzed.

Comparative financial statements provide analysts with significant information about trends and relationships over two or more years. Comparative statements are considerably more significant for evaluating a company than are single-year statements. Financial statement ratios are additional tools for analyzing financial statements. Financial ratios establish relationships between varius items appearing on financial statements. Ratios can be classified as follows:

1. Liquidity ratios measure the ability of the enterprise to pay its debts as they mature.

2. Activity (or turnover) ratios measure how effectively the enterprise is using its assets.

3. Profitability ratios measure management's success in generating returns for those who provide capital to the enterprise.

4. Coverage ratios measure the protection for long-term creditors and investors.

The entry "Ratios" in this book provides a detailed overview of financial ratios.

Horizontal analysis and vertical analysis of financial statements are additional techniques that can be used effectively when evaluating a company. Horizontal analysis and vertical analysis are forms of percentage analysis. Horizontal analysis spotlights trends and establishes relationships between items that appear on the same row of a comparative statement. Horizontal analysis discloses changes on items in financial statements over time. Each item (such as sales) on a row for one fiscal period is compared with the same item in a different period. Horizontal analysis can be carried out in terms of changes in dollar amounts, percentages of change, or in a ratio format. Exhibit F-7 illustrates horizontal analysis on an income

Exhibit F-7
Horizontal Analysis of a Statement of Financial Position

HORIZONTAL COMPANY
Statement of Financial Position
December 31, 19X3 to 19X2

	19X3	19X2	Amount of Change	Percentage of Change	Ratio 19X3 to 19X2
Assets					
Cash	$ 15,000	$ 10,000	$ 5,000	50.0%	1.50
Accounts receivable	5,000	10,000	(5,000)	(50.0)	0.50
Inventory	30,000	—	30,000	—	—
Property, plant, and equipment	125,000	150,000	(25,000)	(16.7)	0.83
Total assets	$175,000	$170,000	$ 5,000	2.9	1.03
Liabilities					
Accounts payable	$ 15,000	—	$ 15,000	—	—
Bonds payable	—	$100,000	(100,000)	(100.0)	0.00
Owner's Equity					
Common Stock	155,000	80,000	75,000	93.8	1.94
Retained earnings	5,000	(10,000)	15,000	—	—
Total liabilities and owner's equity	$175,000	$170,000	$ 5,000	2.9	1.03

statement. Vertical analysis involves the conversion of items appearing in statement columns into terms of percentages of a base figure to show the relative significance of the items and to facilitate comparisons. For example, individual items appearing on the income statement can be expressed as percentages of sales. On the balance sheet, individual assets can be expressed as a percentage of total assets. Liabilities and owners' equity accounts can be expressed in terms of their relationship to total liabilities and owners' equity. Exhibit F–8 illustrates vertical analysis of a balance sheet. Statements omitting dollar amounts and showing only percentages can be prepared. Such statements are referred to as "common size statements" because each item in the statement has a common basis for comparison, for example, total assets and net sales.

Investors and creditors should be interested not only in the quantity of an enterprise's assets and earnings but in their quality as well. The quality of assets refers to whether a company has a well-balanced composition of assets, their condition, liquidity, and profitability. How well are the plant and equipment maintained? How saleable is the inventory? What is the

---

Exhibit F–8
Vertical Analysis of an Income Statement

VERTICAL COMPANY
Income Statement
For the Year Ended December 31, 19X1

		Percentage of Net Sales
Sales (net)	$200,000	100.0%
Cost of goods sold	50,000	25.0
Gross margin on sales	150,000	75.0
Operating expenses	100,000	50.0
Net operating income	50,000	25.0
Federal income tax	25,000	12.5
Net Income	$25,000	12.5%

---

relationship between debt and stockholders' equity? The quality of earnings is related to the amount and stability of earnings, the security of the source(s) of earnings, the rate of earnings on sales, total assets, owners' equity, and the accounting methods used to measure income (conservative or otherwise).

Financial statement analysis has its limitations. Statements represent the past and do not necessarily predict the future. However, financial statement analysis can provide clues or suggest a need for further investigation. What is found on financial statements is the product of accounting conventions and procedures (LIFO or FIFO inventory; straight-line or accelerated depreciation) that sometimes distort the economic reality or substance of the underlying situation. Financial statements say little directly about changes in markets, the business cycle, technological developments, laws and regulations, management personnel, price-level changes, and other critical analytical concerns.

See also Ratios; Financial statements; Notes to financial statements; Opinion; Return on investment; Leverage.

REFERENCE
Bernstein, Leopold A., *Financial Statement Analysis: Theory, Application, and Interpretation* (Richard D. Irwin, Homewood, IL, 1983).

FINANCIAL STATEMENTS
Financial statements are the most widely used and the most comprehensive way of communicating financial information to users of the information provided on the reports. Different users of financial statements have different informational needs. General purpose financial statements have been developed to meet the needs of the users of financial statements, primarily the needs of investors and creditors.

F

The basic output of the financial accounting process is presented in the following interrelated general purpose financial statements:

1. A balance sheet (or statement of financial position) summarizes the financial position of an accounting entity at a particular point in time.

2. An income statement summarizes the results of operations for a given period of time.

3. A statement of changes in financial position summarizes an enterprise's financing and investing activities over a given period of time.

4. A statement of retained earnings shows the increases and decreases in earnings retained by the company over a given period of time. This statement is sometimes combined with the income statement. The statement of retained earnings is sometimes expanded into a statement of stockholders' equity that discloses changes in other stockholders' equity accounts in addition to retained earnings.

Notes to financial statements are considered an integral part of a complete set of financial statements.

The major financial statements are interrelated (or articulate) with each other. The income statement and the statement of changes in financial position can be viewed as connecting links between the beginning and ending statements of financial position. The income statement basically describes the changes in the statement of financial position accounts that result from operations. The statement of changes in financial position explains changes in the balance sheet of cash or working capital between two points in time. Exhibit F-9 shows graphically the interrelationship of the financial statements.

Financial statements can be presented in various ways including general-purpose financial statements, classified, comparative, annual, interim, consolidated, combined, con-

Exhibit F-9
Articulation of Financial Statements

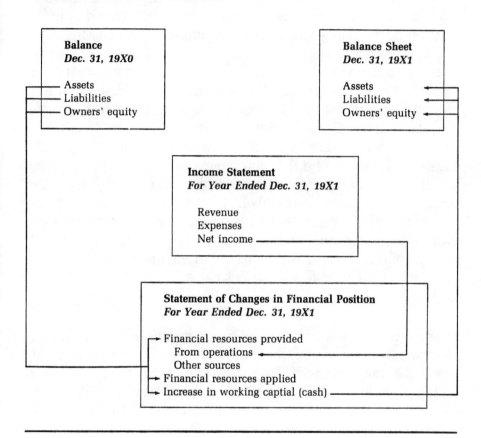

stant dollar, and common size. General purpose financial statements are reports published by a company for use by persons who do not have the ability to obtain specialized financial reports designed to meet their interests. Such statements include the balance sheet, income statement, statement of retained earnings, and the statement of changes in financial position. Classified financial statements separate the major items appearing on financial statements into subcategories. For example, a classified balance sheet divides assets, liabilities, and owners' equity into subclassifications. Comparative statements present data for two or more successive accounting periods placed in columns side by side to disclose trends and relationships. Annual statements are statements showing information for a fiscal year; interim statements disclose information for a period less than a year, such as quarterly or monthly statements. Consolidated statements are statements that present information about legally separate companies as though they were a single entity, for example, a parent company and its subsidiaries. Combined statements are similar to consolidated statments except that intercompany transactions are not eliminated. Constant dollar statements are financial statements in which the monetary units are restated so as to represent the same general purchasing power. Common size statements are prepared using percentages instead of dollars; for example, individual items on a balance sheet could be shown as a percentage of total assets, and items on an income statement could be shown as a percentage of net sales.

See also Objectives of financial reporting; Qualitative characteristics of accounting information; Audit; Financial accounting; Financial reporting; Interim financial reports; Notes to financial statements; Statement of financial position; Statement of changes in financial position; Statement of investment by and distribution to owners; Income statement; Personal financial statements; Special reports; Other comprehensive methods of accounting; Segments; Subsequent events; Foreign operations and exchanges; Constant dollar accounting; Current value accounting.

REFERENCE
SFAC No. 1, Objectives of Financial Reporting by Business Enterprises (FASB, 1978).

FORECAST

A financial forecast for an enterprise is an estimate of the most probable financial position, results of operations, and changes in financial position for one or more future periods. "Most probable" means that the forecast is based on management's judgment of the most likely set of conditions and its most likely course of action. A financial projection is an estimate of financial results based on assumptions which are not necessarily the most likely (SOP 75-4). A financial projection is sometimes used to present hypothetical courses of action for evaluation. A feasibility study is an analysis of a proposed investment or course of action (SOP 75-4).

See also Budget.

REFERENCES
Burton, John C., et al., eds. *Handbook of Accounting and Auditing* (Warren, Gorham & Lamont, Boston, 1981).
Auditing Standards Board, Statement on Standards for Accountants' Services on Prospective Financial Information—Financial Forecasts and Projections (AICPA, 1986).

FOREIGN CORRUPT PRACTICES ACT (FCPA)

Congress passed the Foreign Corrupt Practices Act in 1977. The FCPA established a legal requirement that publicly held companies must maintain internal accounting controls sufficient to provide reasonable assurances as to the achievement of the accuracy of accounting records. Two major provisions of the act are:

1. It is a criminal offense to offer a bribe to a foreign official, foreign political party, party official, or candidate for foreign political office for the purpose of obtaining, retaining, or directing business to any person.

2. Every public company must devise, document, and maintain a system of internal accounting records to ascertain that the objectives of internal control are attained.

See also Foreign operations and exchanges; Internal control; Fraud.

REFERENCE
Burton, John C., et al., eds., *Handbook of Accounting and Auditing* (Warren, Gorham & Lamont, Boston, 1981).

FOREIGN EXCHANGE RATES

An exchange rate is the ratio between a unit of one currency and the amount of another currency for which that unit can be exchanged at a particular time. A direct exchange quotation is the rate quoted in terms of how many units of the domestic currency can be converted into one unit of foreign currency. For example, a direct quotation of U.S. dollars for one British pound is 1.102, meaning that $1.102 can be exchanged for one British pound. An indirect quotation is the rate expressed in terms of converting one unit of the domestic currency into units of a foreign currency. An increase (decrease) in the direct exchange rate will increase (decrease) the number of dollars required to purchase a foreign currency. A spot exchange rate is a rate quoted for immediate delivery of currencies. A forward or future rate is a rate for the future delivery of currencies. Free rates are exchange rates which reflect the supply and demand for a currency as determined by market forces. Official rates are exchange rates established by governments rather than by market forces.

In accounting, the current rate of exchange refers to a rate existing at the balance-sheet date. An historic rate is a rate that existed at the time a particular transaction occurred.

See also Foreign operations and exchanges.

REFERENCE
Haried, Andrew A., et al., *Advanced Accounting* (John Wiley & Sons, N.Y., NY, 1985).

FOREIGN OPERATIONS AND EXCHANGES

Many U.S. companies do business with foreign firms and engage in operations outside the United States. When business transactions are undertaken abroad, accounting for these transactions by a U.S. company is done in U.S. dollars—the unit of measurement in the United States. The accountant normally becomes involved in foreign operations in one of two ways:

1. Foreign currency transactions. A foreign currency transaction is one that requires settlement in a foreign currency. Foreign currency transactions include buying and selling, borrowing or lending, or investing in a foreign enterprise in which foreign currencies are received or paid. Transactions are normally measured and recorded in the currency of the reporting entity. A transaction is denominated in a currency if the amount is fixed in terms of that currency. For example, if a transaction is to be settled by the payment of foreign currency, the U.S. firm measures and records the transaction in dollars, but the transaction is said to be denominated in the foreign currency.

2. Translation of financial statements denominated in a foreign currency. Translation is the process of expressing functional currency measurements in the reporting currency. The reporting currency is the currency in which an enterprise prepares its financial statements. Functional currency is the currency of the primary economic environment in which an entity operates. Normally, the functional currency is the currency of the environment in which an entity

generates and expends cash. Translation usually becomes necessary when a U.S. company owns a branch, division, or subsidiary in a foreign country. The unit keeps its accounting records and financial statements in the foreign country's currency. The statements must be translated before the U.S. company can include the foreign operations in combined or consolidated statements.

Foreign currency transactions are accounted for as follows:

1. Receivables, payables, revenues, and expenses are translated and recorded in dollars at the spot rate existing on the transaction date. An exchange rate that indicates the price of foreign currencies on a particular date for immediate delivery is called a spot rate.

2. At the balance-sheet date, receivables and payables are adjusted to the spot rate.

3. Exchange gains and losses resulting from changes in the spot rate from one point in time to another are usually recognized in the current income statement.

The accounting required for forward exchange contracts depends upon management's intent when entering into the transaction. A forward exchange contract is an agreement to exchange different currencies at a specified future date and at a specified forward rate. A forward margin is the difference between today's price of a currency (the spot rate) and the price at some date in the future (the forward rate). The margin may be either a premium or a discount. A premium or discount on an identifiable hedge or on the hedge of a net investment in a foreign country is either amortized to net income over the life of the contract or recognized as part of the total gain or loss on the identifiable transaction. All other hedges are amortized to net income over the life of the forward exchange contract. A hedge is an arrangement entered into to try to avoid or lessen a loss by making a counterbalancing investment or commitment. The recognition of exchange gains and losses on forward contracts depends upon the classification of the forward contract: speculation, hedge of a net asset or liability position, hedge of an identifiable commitment (for example, the purchase or sale of equipment), or hedge of a net investment in a foreign entity. In hedging contracts, gain or loss is the difference between the balance sheet date spot exchange rate and the spot exchange rate at the inception of the contract, multiplied by the amount of foreign currency involved in the transaction. In speculative contracts, gain or loss is the difference between the agreed upon forward exchange rate and the forward exchange rate relating to the remaining maturity of the contract, multiplied by the amount of foreign currency involved in the transaction. FASB Statement No. 52 requires that gains and losses on foreign currency transactions be generally included in determining net income for the period in which exchange rates change unless the transaction hedges a foreign currency commitment or a net investment in a foreign entity.

Accounting principles for purposes of consolidation, combination, or reporting on the equity method for foreign operations can be summarized in broad terms as follows:

1. Foreign currency financial statements must be in conformity with generally accepted accounting principles before they are translated.

2. The functional currency of an entity is the currency of the primary economic environment in which the foreign entity operates. The functional currency may be the currency of the country in which the foreign entity is located (the local currency), the U.S. dollar, or the currency of another foreign country. If the foreign entity's operations are self-contained and integrated in a particular country and are not depend-

ent on the economic environment of the parent company, the functional currency is the foreign currency. This type of foreign operation typically generates and spends foreign currency; the net cash flow can be reinvested, converted, or distributed to the parent company. For example, if a London subsidiary of a U.S. company purchases merchandise from a London supplier on credit, the payable will be settled with pounds sterling generated by the self-contained London subsidiary. Changes in the foreign exchange rate between dollars and pounds will have little economic significance since dollars were not used to retire the debt. On the other hand, the functional currency of a foreign company would be the U.S. dollar if the foreign operation is an integral component or extension of the parent company's operation. The daily operations and cash flows of the foreign operation of the foreign entity are dependent on the economic environment of the parent company.

3. The functional currency statements of the foreign entity are translated into the functional currency of the reporting entity (the U.S. company) using the current rate of exchange method. No actual conversion of assets or liabilities from one currency to another occurs. The current rate method requires that the current rate of exchange be used to translate the assets and liabilities of a foreign entity from its functional currency into the reporting currency. The weighted-average exchange rate for the period is used to translate revenue and expenses. Gain or loss resulting from the translation of foreign currency financial statements is not recognized in current net income. Such gains or losses are reported as a separate component of stockholders' equity.

4. If a foreign entity's records are not kept in the functional currency, they must be remeasured into the

functional currency prior to translation, using what is referred to as the temporal method of translation. Remeasurement is the process of measuring in the functional currency those financial statements amounts that are denominated in another currency. The temporal method requires that account balances be translated in a manner that retains their measurement basis. Under the temporal method, monetary assets and liabilities (such as cash, receivables, and most liabilities) expressed in the balance sheet of the foreign entity at current values are translated using the current exchange rate. Accounts that are carried at past exchange prices (historical cost) are translated at historical rates (rates that existed when the transaction occurred). This results in translating these amounts into dollars as of the date the transaction took place. Gains and losses resulting from the remeasurement are included in current income. The temporal method is also used when the entity operates in a highly inflationary economy.

The distinction between remeasurement required when the functional currency is the U.S. dollar and translation when the function currency is the local currency (foreign currency) can be illustrated as follows:

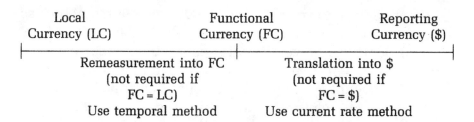

Local Currency (LC)	Functional Currency (FC)	Reporting Currency ($)
Remeasurement into FC (not required if FC = LC) Use temporal method	Translation into $ (not required if FC = $) Use current rate method	

Only when the entity's functional currency is another foreign currency (neither its local currency nor the U.S. dollar) are remeasurement and translation required (i.e., two separate numerical calculations).

Exhibit F–10 illustrates the temporal method, which assumes that the functional currency of a Canadian subsidiary is the U.S. dollar. The subsidiary was established at the beginning of the year. The current rate of exchange is $.80; the historical rate used for the building and common stock is $.90; the average rate for the year is $.85. The computation of the exchange loss for the year, the first year of operations, is also shown and results from the impact of rate changes on the net monetary position (monetary assets minus monetary liabilities) during the year. The $10,406 exchange loss occurred because the subsidiary held net monetary assets denominated in Canadian dollars when the Canadian dollar decreased in value relative to the U.S. dollar.

Exhibit F–11 reworks the problem and assumes that the foreign currency is the functional currency. For this reason, the current rate method of translation is used. The exhibit also shows the computation of the translation adjustment for the year which results from the impact of rate changes on the net monetary position (total assets minus total liabilities) during the year. The translation adjustment arises because assets and liabilities are translated at the current rate while stockholders' equity accounts (net assets) are translated at the historical rate and income statement accounts at an average rate. The net assets (equity) of the investor in the foreign subsidiary are at risk to exchange rate fluctuations and not merely the net monetary assets.

Proponents of the current rate method maintain that the use of this method will reflect most clearly the true economic facts since presenting all revenue and expense items at current rates reflects the actual earnings (those that can be remitted to the home country) of a foreign operation at that time. Also, stating all items at the current rate retains the operating relationships after the translation intact with those that existed before the translation; e.g., the current ratio would be the same after translation as before translation. Critics of the current rate method claim that since fixed assets are translated at the current rate and not at the rate that existed when they were

Exhibit F–10
Temporal Method—Remeasurement under FASB Statement No. 52

	Canadian Dollars	Exchange Rate	U.S. Dollars
Balance Sheet:			
Assets			
Cash	C$ 77,555	.80	US$ 62,044
Rent Receivable	25,00	.80	20,000
Building (net)	475,000	.90	427,500
	C$ 577,555		US$ 509,544
Liabilities and Equity			
Accounts Payable	6,000	.80	4,800
Salaries Payable	4,000	.80	3,200
Common Stock	555,555	.90	500,000
Retained Earnings	12,000	See below.	1,544
	C$ 577,555		US$ 509,544
Income Statement:			
Rent Revenue	C$ 125,000	.85	US$ 106,250
Operating Expenses	(28,000)	.85	(23,800)
Depreciation Expense	(25,000)	.90	(22,500)
Translation Exchange Loss	—		(10,406)
Net Income	C$ 72,000		US$ 49,544
Retained Earnings Statement:			
Balance, January 1, Year 1	C$ —		US$ —
Net Income	72,000	See above.	49,544
Dividends	(60,000)	.80	(48,000)
Balance, December 31, Year 1	C$ 12,000		US$ 1,544

continued on next page

F

Exhibit F–10 - Continued

Temporal Method — Remeasurement under FASB Statement No. 52

Computation of Translation Exchange Loss for S for Year 1

	Canadian Dollars	Exchange Rate	U.S. Dollars
Net Monetary Position January 1, Year 1	C$ —		US$ —
Plus:			
Cash Invested by P	555,555	.90	500,000
Cash and Receivable from Rents	125,000	.85	106,250
Less:			
Cash Disbursed for Building .	(500,000)	.90	(450,000)
Cash Disbursed and Liabilities Incurred for Operating Expenses . . .	(28,000)	.85	(23,800)
Cash Disbursed for Dividends	(60,000)	.80	(48,000)
Subtotal			84,450
Net Monetary Position, December 31, Year 1	C$ 92,555	.80	74,044
Translation Exchange Loss			US$ 10,406

Source: Belcher, Finley E., and Stickney, Clyde P., Business Combinations and Consolidated Financial Statements (Richard D. Irwin, Homewood, Ill.).

Exhibit F-11
Translation of Foreign Financial Statements—All-Current Methodology

	Canadian Dollars	Exchange Rate	U.S. Dollars
Balance Sheet:			
Assets			
Cash	C$ 77,555	.80	US$ 62,044
Rent Receivable	25,000	.80	20,000
Building (net)..............	475,000	.80	380,000
	C$ 577,555		US$ 462,044
Liabilities and Equity			
Accounts Payable............	6,000	.80	4,800
Salaries Payable	4,000	.80	3,200
Common Stock..............	555,555	.90	500,000
Translation Adjustment.......			(59,156)
Retained Earnings	12,000	See below.	13,200
	C$ 577,555		US$ 462,044
Income Statement:			
Rent Revenue	C$ 125,000	.85	US$ 106,250
Operating Expenses	(28,000)	.85	(23,800)
Depreciation Expense	(25,000)	.90	(21,500)
Net Income	C$ 72,000		US$ 61,200
Retained Earnings Statement:			
Balance, January 1, Year 1	C$ —		—
Net Income	72,000	See above.	US$ 61,200
Dividends	(60,000)	.80	(48,000)
Balance, December 31, Year 1 .	C$ 12,000		US$ 13,200

continued on next page

F

Exhibit F–11 — Continued
Translation of Foreign Financial Statements—All-Current Methodology

Computation of Translation Adjustment for S for Year 1

	Canadian Dollars	Exchange Rate	U.S. Dollars
Net Asset Position			
January 1, Year 1	C$ —		US$ —
Plus:			
Cash Invested by P	555,555	.90	500,000
Net Income	72,000	.85	61,200
Less:			
Dividends	(60,000)	.80	(48,000)
Subtotal			513,200
Net Asset Position,			
December 31, Year 1	C$ 567,555	.80	454,044
Translation Adjustment			US$ 59,156

Source: Belcher, Finley, E., and Stickney, Clyde P., *Business Combinations and Consolidated Financial Statements* (Richard D. Irwin, Homewood, Ill.).

acquired, the translated amounts do not represent historical (acquisition) costs and therefore are not consistent with generally accepted accounting principles which are based to a great extent upon the application of the historical cost principle.

Since the temporal method states monetary assets at the current rate, proponents of this method claim that this reflects the foreign currency's ability to obtain U.S. dollars. Since historical rates are used for long-term assets and liabilities, the historical cost principle is maintained for balance sheet accounts. This reflects generally accepted accounting principles; generally accepted accounting principles are not changed by the translation process. However, the use of the temporal method distorts financial statement relationships that exist before remeasurement and after remeasurement.

See also Foreign exchange rate; Monetary assets and liabilities.

REFERENCE
Beams, Floyd A., Advanced Accounting (Prentice-Hall, Englewood Cliffs, NJ, 1985).

FRAUD

Fraud is a legal concept that requires a conscious knowledge of the falsity with deliberate intent to deceive. Fraud includes intentional deception, misappropriation of an enterprise's assets, and the manipulation of financial data to benefit the perpetrator (management or employee). Constructive fraud is a deceit that involves a false representation of a material fact without reasonable ground for belief that is relied on by another and results in his damage.

The adequacy of performance by an auditor relates primarily to the professional skill, judgment, and knowledge generally required of professional auditors. Ranges of misrepresentation include negligence (belief without adequate basis), constructively fraudulent (without belief in a position taken), and fraudulent (known to be false). The auditor's reliance on a company's internal control procedures makes the discovery of certain types of fraud more difficult. Furthermore, the concept of materiality can also effect fraud detection because items that are not material to the financial statements are not always examined or are merely sampled.

The Commission on Auditors' Responsibilities addressed the question of an auditor's responsibility to a client for fraud of client personnel as follows:

> "Under generally accepted auditing standards the indepentent auditor has the responsibility, within the inherent limitations of the auditing process... to plan his examination... to search for errors or irregularities that would have a material effect on the financial statements, and to exercise due skill and care in the conduct of the examination. The auditor's search for material errors or irregularities ordinarily is accomplished by the performance of those auditing procedures that in his judgment are appropriate in the circumstances to form an opinion on the financial statements; extended auditing procedures are required if the auditor's examination indicates that material errors or irregularities may exist....An independent auditor's standard report implicitly indicates his belief that the financial statements taken as a whole are not materially misstated as a result of errors or irregularities."

Kiting is a form of fraud that has been used to conceal weak cash positions and to increase the current ratio (current assets divided by current liabilities). For example, if an interbank transfer is added to one cash account on December 31 and subtracted from another account an January 2, the cash balance as of December 31 would be overstated as would be a liability account which made the fraud possible. Lapping is another form of fraud which involves misappropriating a customer's remittance. The customer's account is credited when cash is collected from another customer at a later date. Lapping requires continued misspropriations and delays in posting to customer's accounts.

In tax law, tax fraud falls into two categories: civil and criminal. Under civil fraud, the IRS can impose as a penalty an amount equal to 50 percent of the underpayment. Under criminal tax fraud, fines and/or imprisonment are prescribed for conviction of various types of fraud. Conviction under civil and criminal fraud require a specific intent on the part of the taxpayer to evade the tax. Negligence alone is not sufficient. Criminal fraud also requires willfulness (deliberately and with evil purpose). The IRS has the burden of proving fraud.

See also Audit; Foreign Corrupt Practices Act; Related Parties.

REFERENCE
Burton, John C., et al., eds. *Handbook of Accounting and Auditing* (Warren, Gorman & Lamont, Inc., Boston, 1981).

FREE ENTERPRISE SYSTEM
In the United States, the free (or private) enterprise system is the basic economic system. In a free enterprise system,

1. private citizens are free to own and operate a business,
2. the means of production (land, factories, equipment) are privately owned, although government does own and operate some enterprises such as the postal system,
3. incentive for investors and business is the profit motive, and
4. competition is a characteristic of the marketplace.

The terms *capitalism* and *free enterprise* are often used interchangeably. Accounting serves the free enterprise economic system by providing financial data that can be used to

F

make the economic choices that an enterprise or person must make, especially as these choices relate to the allocation of an enterprise's or investor's economic resources. Accounting also serves other economic systems.

See also Economics; Wealth; Antitrust legislation.

REFERENCE
Baumol, W.J., and Blinder, Alan S., *Economics: Principles and Policy* (Harcourt Brace Jovanovich, San Diego, CA, 1986).

FULL DISCLOSURE
Full (or adequate) disclosure is an accounting concept which requires that information provided in financial accounting reports be sufficiently complete to avoid misleading users of the reports by omitting significant facts or information. The disclosure concept also refers to revealing information that would be useful in the decision-making processes of informed users. Full disclosure is required for the fair presentation of financial statements. Examples of items usually included in financial statements include accounting policies, depreciation and inventory methods, contingencies, related-party transactions, and lease and pension details.

The Accounting Principles Board in APB Statement No. 4 stated that fair presentation is met when

". . .a proper balance has been achieved between the conflicting needs to disclose important aspects of financial positions and results of operations in accordance with conventional aspects and to summarize the voluminous underlying data into a limited number of financial statement captions and supporting notes."

Many disclosures are made in the body of the financial statements and in notes (footnotes), schedules, and supplementary statements. Significant accounting policies are usually disclosed in the first note to the financial statements or in a summary of significant policies preceding the first note.

See also Accounting assumptions; Accounting principles; Materiality; Off-balance sheet items; Subsequent events; Efficient market hypothesis.

FUTURE VALUE

The future value (or amount) of a single sum at compound interest is the orginal amount plus the compound interest thereon, stated as of a specific future date. For example, what will be the amount in a savings account on December 31, 1990, if $10,000 is invested at 14 percent interest on December 31, 1986? Using a Future Amount of 1 table (See Exhibit F–12) where i = 14 percent and n = 4, the future amount can be computed as follows:

$10,000 × 1.68896 = $16,889.60.

See also Annuity; Present value; Interest.

REFERENCE
Woelfel, Charles J., *Financial Managers Desktop Reference to Money, Time, Interest and Yield* (Probus, Chicago, 1986).

F

Exhibit F-12
Future Value (Amount) of 1 Table

FUTURE AMOUNT OF 1: $f = (1 + i)^n$

n	1.5%	4.0%	4.5%	5.0%	5.5%	6.0%	7.0%
1	1.015000	1.040000	1.045000	1.050000	1.055000	1.060000	1.070000
2	1.030225	1.081600	1.092025	1.102500	1.113025	1.123600	1.144900
3	1.045678	1.124864	1.141166	1.157625	1.174241	1.191016	1.225043
4	1.061364	1.169859	1.192519	1.215506	1.238825	1.262477	1.310796
5	1.077284	1.216653	1.246182	1.276282	1.306960	1.338226	1.402552
6	1.093443	1.265319	1.302260	1.340096	1.378843	1.418519	1.500730
7	1.109845	1.315932	1.360862	1.407100	1.454679	1.503630	1.605781
8	1.126493	1.368569	1.422101	1.477455	1.534687	1.593848	1.718186
9	1.143390	1.423312	1.486095	1.551328	1.619094	1.689479	1.838459
10	1.160541	1.480244	1.552969	1.628895	1.708144	1.790848	1.967151
11	1.177949	1.539454	1.622853	1.710339	1.802092	1.898299	2.104852
12	1.195618	1.601032	1.695881	1.795856	1.901207	2.012196	2.252192
13	1.213552	1.665074	1.772196	1.835649	2.005774	2.132928	2.409845
14	1.231756	1.731676	1.851945	1.979932	2.116091	2.260904	2.578534
15	1.250232	1.800944	1.935282	2.078928	2.232476	2.396558	2.759032
16	1.268986	1.872981	2.022370	2.182875	2.355263	2.540352	2.952164
17	1.288020	1.947900	2.113377	2.292018	2.484802	2.692773	3.1588.5
18	1.307341	2.025817	2.208479	2.406619	2.621466	2.854339	3.379932
19	1.326951	2.106849	2.307860	2.526950	2.765647	3.025600	3.616528
20	1.346855	2.191123	2.411714	2.653298	2.917757	3.207135	3.869684
21	1.367053	2.278768	2.520241	2.785963	3.078234	3.399564	4.140562
22	1.387564	2.369919	2.633652	2.925261	3.247537	3.603537	4.430402
23	1.408377	2.464716	2.752166	3.071524	3.426152	3.819750	4.740530
24	1.429503	2.563304	2.876014	3.225100	3.614590	4.048935	5.072367
25	1.450945	2.665836	3.005434	3.386355	3.813392	4.291871	5.427433
26	1.472710	2.772470	3.140679	3.555673	4.023129	4.549383	5.807353
27	1.494800	2.883369	3.282010	3.733456	4.244401	4.822346	6.213868
28	1.517222	2.998703	3.429700	3.920129	4.477843	5.111687	6.648838
29	1.539981	3.118651	3.584036	4.116136	4.724124	5.413388	7.114257
30	1.563080	3.243398	3.745318	4.321942	4.983951	5.743491	7.612255

Exhibit F-12 — Continued
Future Value (Amount) of 1 Table

n	8.0%	9.0%	10.0%	12.0%	14.0%	16.0%	18.0%
1	1.080000	1.090000	1.100000	1.120000	1.140000	1.160000	1.180000
2	1.166400	1.188100	1.210000	1.254400	1.299600	1.345600	1.392400
3	1.259712	1.295029	1.331000	1.404928	1.481544	1.560896	1.643032
4	1.360489	1.411582	1.464100	1.573519	1.688960	1.810639	1.938778
5	1.469328	1.538624	1.610510	1.762342	1.925415	2.100342	2.287758
6	1.586874	1.677100	1.771561	1.973823	2.194973	2.436396	2.699554
7	1.713824	1.828039	1.948717	2.210681	2.502269	2.826220	3.185474
8	1.850930	1.992563	2.143589	2.475963	2.852586	3.278415	3.758859
9	1.999005	2.171893	2.357948	2.773079	3.251949	3.802961	4.435454
10	2.158925	2.367364	2.593742	3.105848	3.707221	4.411435	5.233336
11	2.331639	2.580426	2.853117	3.478550	4.226232	5.117265	6.175926
12	2.518170	2.812665	3.138428	3.895976	4.817905	5.936027	7.287593
13	2.719624	3.065805	3.452271	4.363493	5.492411	6.885791	8.599359
14	2.937194	3.341727	3.797498	4.887112	6.261349	7.987518	10.147244
15	3.172169	3.642482	4.177248	5.473566	7.137938	9.265521	11.973748
16	3.425943	3.970306	4.594973	6.130394	8.137249	10.748004	14.129023
17	3.700018	4.327633	5.054470	6.866041	9.276464	12.467685	16.672247
18	3.996019	4.717120	5.559917	7.689966	10.575169	14.462514	19.673251
19	4.315701	5.141661	6.115909	8.612762	12.055693	16.776517	23.214436
20	4.660957	5.604411	6.727500	9.646293	13.743490	19.460759	27.393035
21	5.033834	6.108808	7.400250	10.803848	15.667578	22.574481	32.323781
22	5.436540	6.658600	8.140275	12.100310	17.861039	26.186398	38.142061
23	5.871464	7.257874	8.954302	13.552347	20.361585	30.376222	45.007632
24	6.341181	7.911083	9.849733	15.178629	23.212207	35.236417	53.109006
25	6.848475	8.623081	10.834706	17.000064	26.461916	40.874244	62.668627
26	7.396353	9.399158	11.918177	19.040072	30.166584	47.414123	73.948980
27	7.988061	10.245032	13.109994	21.324881	34.389906	55.000382	87.259797
28	8.627106	11.167140	14.420994	23.883866	39.204493	63.800444	102.966560
29	9.317275	12.172182	15.863093	26.749930	44.693122	74.008515	121.500541
30	10.062657	13.267678	17.449402	29.959922	50.950159	85.849977	143.370638

G

G

GAINS

Gains are increases in equity (net assets) from peripheral or incidental transactions of an entity and from all other transactions and other events and circumstances affecting the entity during a period except those that result from revenues or investments by owners. Gains often arise from events and circumstances that may be beyond the control of an enterprise or its managements. Gains result from such activities as sales of investments in marketable securities, dispositions of used equipment, the settlement of liabilities at other than their carrying amounts, or winning a lawsuit.

See also Elements of financial statements; Revenues; Income; Extraordinary item; Income statement.

REFERENCE
SFAC No. 3, Elements of Financial Statements of Business Enterprises (FASB, 1981).

GENERALLY ACCEPTED ACCOUNTING PRINCIPLES

Generally accepted accounting principles (GAAP) encompass the conventions, rules, and procedures necessary to define accepted accounting practice at a particular time. The responsibility for developing generally accepted accounting principles in the United States prior to 1973 rested to a great degree with the American Institute of Certified Public Accountants (AICPA). In 1938 the AICPA began issuing authoritative statements through its Committee on Accounting Procedure (CAP). This committee was authorized to issue pronouncements on accounting procedures and practices. It published a series of Accounting Research Bulletins.

CAP was replaced in 1959 by another committee of the AICPA called the Accounting Principles Board (APB). The APB was formed to counteract criticism of CAP and to create a policy-making body whose rules would be binding rather than optional. The APB issued a series of Statements and Opinions. The APB was replaced in 1973 by a new entity—the Financial Accounting Standards Board (FASB).

The FASB currently has the responsibility for setting accounting standards. The FASB is a separate entity from the AICPA. The FASB's authoritative pronouncements are issued in the form of Statements of Financial Accounting Standards and Interpretations. The FASB also issues Statements of Financial Accounting Concepts. Concept Statements do not create generally accepted accounting principles. They establish a theoretical foundation upon which to base financial accounting and reporting standards. The conceptual framework project is discussed elsewhere in this book. The FASB also publishes Technical Bulletins which provide guidance on accounting and reporting problems related to Statements of Standards or Interpretations. The FASB established the Emerging Issues Task Force in 1984 to identify new accounting and reporting issues that arise from new and different types of transactions. If members of the EITF reach a consensus that there is a single preferred treatment, the Chief Accountant of the SEC will accept the consensus as authoritative support for practices to be used for SEC reporting. The FASB has not sanctioned the EITF as an authoritative standard-setting body.

The AICPA issues Industry Accounting Guides and Industry Accounting Guides and Industry Audit Guides. These pronouncements constitute GAAP on the topics covered in the guides. Rule 203 of the Code of Professional Ethics of the AICPA provides that: "A member shall not express an opinion that financial statements are presented in conformity with generally accepted accounting principles if such statements contain any departure from accounting principle promulgated by the body designated by Council to establish such principles...." The Council of the AICPA has designated the FASB, and its predecessor bodies (CAP and APB), as the body to promulgate principles.

In 1968 the National Committee on Governmental Accounting of the Municipal Finance Officers Association published Governmental Accounting, Auditing, and Financial Reporting (GAAFR). This document was the primary source of accounting principles for governmental accounting. In 1979 the National Council on Government Accounting issued Statement 1, Governmental Accounting and Financial Reporting Principles, which superseded GAAFR and represents the primary authoritative pronouncement on governmental accounting. In 1984 the Governmental Accounting Standards Board (GASB) was established to determine generally accepted accounting principles for governmental entities. GASB sanctioned NCGA pronouncements and the AICPA Industry Audit Guide: Audits of State and Local Governmental Units, as authoritative.

Authoritative accounting principles for nonbusiness organizations such as colleges and universities, hospitals, voluntary health and welfare organizations, and other nonprofit organizations are contained in the following AICPA documents:

1. Audits of Colleges and Universities (1975)
2. Hospital Audit Guide (1982)
3. Audits of Voluntary Health and Welfare Organizations (1974)
4. Statement of Position 78-10, "Accounting Principles and Reporting Practices for Certain Nonprofit Organizations" (1979)

G

In addition to the policy-making bodies discussed above, other organizations have influenced the development of GAAP, including the following: the Securities and Exchange Commission (SEC), the Cost Accounting Standards Board (CASB), the Internal Revenue Service (IRS), the Governmental Accounting Standards Board (GASB), and various professional accounting associations. The SEC has statutory authority to establish financial accounting and reporting standards under the Securities Exchange Act of 1934. The Commission's policy has been to rely on the private sector for this function and has done so with only a very few exceptions.

Standard setting for hospitals, colleges and universities, voluntary health and welfare organizations, and other nonprofit organizations is discussed in the entry Nonprofit Enterprises. Standard setting for governmental entities is discussed in the entry Governmental Accounting.

See also Accounting principles; Financial Accounting Standards Board; Nonprofit Enterprises; Governmental accounting; Statements of Financial Accounting Standards; Other comprehensive methods of accounting.

REFERENCES
Grady, Paul, *Inventory of Generally Accepted Accounting Principles for Business Enterprises* (AICPA, 1965).
Financial Accounting Standards Board, *Accounting Standards* (McGraw-Hill, New York, latest edition).

GOODWILL
Goodwill is an unidentifiable intangible asset that represents the superior earning power of a business over the normal rate of return on net assets for the industry. Goodwill can also be conceptualized as the excess of the cost of a business over the value assigned to the tangible and other identifiable intangible assets of the firm.

Accounting principles require that goodwill not be recorded unless it is acquired in an arm's-length transaction when the net assets of a business, or a substantial portion thereof, are purchased. Goodwill cannot be acquired separately from a related enterprise or group of assets. Any goodwill recorded on the accounting records should be amortized over a period of years not to exceed forty years.

Various methods are available for estimating the amount of goodwill. One method involves capitalizing average net earnings. Capitalizing earnings means computing the principal value that will yield the stated earnings at a specified rate indefinitely. The difference between the amount to be paid for the business and the appraised values of the individual net assets can be considered the price paid for goodwill. For example, assume that an 8 percent return is required on an investment in a business. Earnings of the business are estimated at $100,000 per year. The net assets are currently appraised at $1,000,000. The entire business including goodwill would be capitalized at $1,250,000 ($100,000 divided by 8 percent). Goodwill would be valued at $250,000, the difference between the $1,250,000 capitalized value of the business and the $1,000,000 appraised value of the net assets.

If the price paid for the net assets of a business is less than the sum of the values of the individual net assets, negative goodwill may exist. Accounting principles require that the difference should be allocated as a reduction of the recorded cost of the identifiable noncurrent assets of the business. If this allocation reduced the noncurrent assets to zero, the remaining difference would be recorded as a deferred credit (negative goodwill) and amortized as an addition to income over a period of years not to exceed forty. For negative goodwill to exist, a business must be acquired in a bargain purchase where an enterprise is acquired for less than the fair market value of net current assets and marketable securities. For this reason, negative good will seldom is found on financial statements, except where there are significant unrecorded liabilities, such as for pensions.

See also Intangible assets; Business combinations; Consolidated financial statements.

REFERENCE
Wyatt, Arthur R., *A Critical Study of Accounting for Business Combinations* (AICPA, 1963).

GOVERNMENTAL ACCOUNTING

Governmental entities are established primarily to provide services to citizens. Governmental entities differ from profit-oriented entities in a number of significant ways: lack of profit motive; dependence on legislative authorities; responsibilities to citizens; taxes as a major source of revenue; restrictions and controls.

In 1984 the Governmental Accounting Standards Board (GASB) was established as the authoritative body that sets governmental accounting standards. From the 1930s through 1983, governmental accounting standards were established by the National Council on Governmental Accounting (NCGA). The NCGA's official governmental accounting standards pronouncement was Governmental Accounting, Auditing, and Financial Reporting (GAAFR). This document was revised in 1979 with the publication of NCGA Statement 1, Governmental Financial Accounting and Reporting Principles. The GASB specifies that all NCGA Statements and Interpretations remain in effect until modified by the GASB.

In governmental accounting, funds are established for major activities. Accounting and reporting for these self-balancing sets of accounts are the primary activity of governmental accounting. A fund is defined as "a fiscal and accounting entity with a self-balancing set of accounts recording cash and other financial resources, together with all related liabilities and residual equities and balances, and changes therein, which are segregated for the purpose of carrying on specific activities or attaining certain objectives in accordance with special regulations, restrictions, or limitations' (National Council on Governmental Accounting).

There are three broad categories of funds. Each category has subcategories. These include:

1. Governmental funds which account for all activities except those belonging to proprietary funds or fiduciary funds:

   a. The General Fund

   b. Special Revenue Funds

   c. Capital Projects Funds

   d. Debt Service Funds

   e. Special Assessment Funds

2. Proprietary funds which account for the sale of goods or services for which a fee is charged, e.g., a publicly owned utility:

   a. Enterprise Funds

   b. Internal Service Funds

3. Fiduciary funds which account for resources for which the governmental unit acts as a trustee or agent:

   a. Nonexpendable Trust Funds

   b. Expendable Trust Funds

   c. Pension Trust Funds

   d. Agency Funds

G

Two account groups provide a record of general government fixed assets and long-term liabilities which are not recorded in the government fund:

1. The General Fixed Assets Account Group

2. The General Long-Term Debt Account Group

Special governmental fund account terminology includes:

1. Estimated revenue: forecasts of asset inflows.

2. Appropriations: forecasts of and authorizations of asset outflows; budgetary expenditures enacted into law.

3. Revenue: additions to fund assets or decreases in fund liabilities other than those resulting from debt issue proceeds or transfers of financial resources from another fund.

4. Expenditures: increases in fund liabilities or decreases in fund assets which increase the residual equity of the fund other than a decrease resulting from a transfer of financial resources to another fund. They represent resources expended during the period to carry out the activities of the fund.

5. Fund balance: the residual equity account which balances the fund.

6. Encumbrances: an obligation in the form of purchase orders, contracts, or salary commitments chargeable to an appropriation, and for which a part of the appropriation is reserved. They cease to be encumbrances when the commitment is paid or recorded. The Reserve for Encumbrances account represents an earmarked reservation of the Fund Balance to liquidate the contingent obligations of goods ordered but not yet received.

7. Transfers: transfers of resources to other fund entities within an organization which do not represent decreases in the expendable resources of the entity as a whole.

Governmental entities use the accrual, cash, and modified accrual basis of accounting. They also use both budgetary accounts and proprietary accounts. Budgetary accounts are nominal accounts used to record budgetary estimates of revenues and expenditures. Proprietary accounts are used to record actual revenues, expenditures, and other transactions affecting the fund.

Financial statements necessary to fairly present financial position and operating results in conformity with generally accepted accounting principles are referred to as basic statements. It is acceptable for governmental units to present combined financial statements which consist of a balance sheet and a statement of revenues and expenditures, with a separate column for each of the eight fund types and two account groups.

See also Objectives of financial reporting by nonbusiness organizations; Financial Accounting Standards Board; Generally accepted accounting principles; Fiduciary.

REFERENCE
Henke, Emerson O., *Introduction to Nonprofit Organization Accounting* (Kent, Boston, 1985).

GROSS MARGIN ANALYSIS
Gross margin (or gross profit) is the excess of sales over cost of goods sold. Gross margin represents the dollar amount of financial resources produced by the basic selling activity of the firm. On an income statement, gross margin appears as follows:

	1991	1990	Change
Sales	$225,000	$100,000	$125,000
Cost of goods sold	90,000	50,000	40,000
GROSS MARGIN	135,000	50,000	85,000
Operating expenses	90,000	35,000	55,000
Net income	$ 45,000	15,000	$ 30,000

Changes in gross margin from period to period may be due to one or any combination of the following variables:

1. Change in sales caused by:
   a. change in selling price (sales-price variance);
   b. change in volume of goods sold (sales-volume variance).
2. Change in cost of goods sold caused by:
   a. change in unit cost (cost-price variance);
   b. change in volume of goods sold (cost-volume variance).

The four gross-margin variances can be computed for year-to-year data using the following formulas and the following data which relate to the income statement shown earlier. The analysis which results from interpreting these variances is referred to as gross-margin analysis.

	1991	1990
Number of units sold	150,000	100,000
Sales price per unit	$1.50	$1.00
Cost per unit	$0.60	$0.50

1. Sales-price variance
   = Current year's units sold × Change in sales price per unit
   = 150,000 × $0.50
   = $75,000 favorable variance
2. Sales-volume variance
   = Change in units sold × Last year's prices
   = 50,000 units × $1.00
   = $50,000 favorable variance

3. Cost-price variance
   = Current year's units sold × Change in cost
   per unit
   =   150,000   × $0.10
   = $15,000 unfavorable variance

4. Cost-volume variance
   = Change in units sold × Last year's cost
   =   50,000 units   × $0.50
   = $25,000 unfavorable variance

When the four variances are combined, the $85,000 change in gross profit from 1990 to 1991 is identified:

Sales-price variance	$75,000
Sales-volume variance	50,000
Cost-price variance	(15,000)
Cost-volume variance	(25,000)
Change in gross margin	$85,000

For a multiproduct firm, a sales-mix variance is usually computed. This variance identifies the change in gross margin attributable to shifts in the sales mix for the company. This approximates the effect of changing the sales mix at a constant volume. This variance can be computed using the following formula:

Sales-mix variance
   = Current year's sales × Change in gross margin rate
   = $225,000   × (.60—.50)
   = $22,500 favorable variance

See also Contribution margin analysis.

H

HUMAN RESOURCE ACCOUNTING

Human resource accounting refers to accounting for the cost of recruiting, familiarizing, and developing personnel in a manner somewhat similar to procedures relating to manufacturing inventories or acquiring plant and equipment. Human resource accounting makes an effort to measure more accurately the cost of employee-personnel practices, turnover, and similar matters. Human resource accounting attempts to report the importance of human resources (knowledge, skill, training, loyalty, etc.) in relation to the enterprise's earning process. Treating the costs normally associated with human resource accounting as assets and subsequently depreciating them does not currently represent generally accepted accounting principles.

See also Social Accounting.

REFERENCE
Flamholtz, Eric, *Human Resource Accounting* (Dickerson, Encinco, CA, 1974).

I

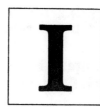

IMPLICIT INTEREST

Implicit interest (versus imputed interest) is interest implied in a contract. Implicit interest is interest that is neither paid nor received. The implicit interest rate is the interest rate that equates the present value of payments on a note with the face of the note. The implicit rate is determined by factors directly related to the note transaction. For example, assume that a dealer offers to sell a machine for $100,000 cash or $16,275 per year for ten years. By dividing the cash price by the annual payments (an annuity), a factor of 6.144 is computed ($100,000/ $16,275). By referring to a Present Value of an Annuity of 1 in Arrears table, 6.144 appears in the 10 percent interest column when ten payments are involved. Therefore, the implicit interest rate in this offer is 10 percent.

See also Imputed interest; Annuity; Present value.

REFERENCE
APB Opinion No. 21, Interest on Receivables and Payables (1971).

IMPUTED INTEREST

Interest imputation is the process that estimates the interest rate to be used in finding the cash price of an asset. An imputed interest rate is similar to an implicit interest rate in that it equates the present value of payments on a note with the face of the note, but it can also be established by factors not associated with the note transaction or underlying contract. The imputed rate approximates a negotiated rate (a fair market interest rate) between independent borrowers and lenders. The imputed rate takes into consideration the term of the note, the credit standing of the issuer, collateral, and other factors. For example, an investor is considering the purchase of a large tract of undeveloped land. The offering price is $450,000 in the form of a noninterest-bearing note that is to be paid in three yearly installments of $150,000. There is no market for the note or the property. When the investor considered the current prime rate, his credit standing, the collateral, other terms of the note, and rates available for similar borrowings, a 12 percent interest rate is imputed.

See also Implicit interest; Interest on receivables and payables.

REFERENCE
APB Opinion No. 21, Interest on Receivables and Payables (1971).

INCOME
Income has been defined in various ways according to authoritative sources:

1. "Income and profit . . . refer to amounts resulting from the deduction from revenues, or from operating revenues, of cost of goods sold, other expenses, and losses. . . " (Committee on Terminology, 1955).

2. "Net income (net loss)—the excess (deficit) of revenue over expenses for an accounting period. . . " (Accounting Principles Board, 1970).

3. "Comprehensive income is the change in equity (net assets) of an entity during a period of transactions and other events and circumstances from nonowner sources" (Financial Accounting Standards Board, 1980).

The measuring and reporting of income and its components are among the most significant accounting problems. Income as reported on the income statement can be conceptualized as follows:

Revenues – Expenses + Gains – Losses = Net income.

Income determination is based upon the matching of efforts (expenses and losses) and accomplishments (revenues and gains). Two approaches are available to compute net income: the net assets approach and the transaction approach. Under the net assets approach, the net assets (total assets-total liabilities) of an enterprise are compared at the beginning and ending of a period. If there have been no investments or withdrawals of assets by owners during the period, the increase in net assets represents net income. A decrease represents a net loss. The net assets approach to computing net income can be conceptualized as follows:

Net income = Ending net assets – Beginning net assets + Asset withdrawals – Asset investments.

For example, assume that a company's net assets at the beginning of a period were $100,000 and at the ending, $150,000. Owners invested $10,000 and withdrew $5,000 during the period. Net income is computed as follows:

Ending net assets	$150,000
Deduct: Beginning net assets	100,000
Change in net assets during the period	50,000
Add: Asset withdrawals	5,000
	55,000
Deduct: Asset investments	10,000
Net income for the period	$45,000

I

The transaction approach to measuring income measures and reports revenues and expenses relating to the enterprise that result in net income. This information is especially useful for decision making. For example, the accounting records could provide the following information:

Revenues	$150,000
Deduct: Expenses	105,000
Net income	$45,000

The term *profit* is generally used to refer to an enterprise's successful performance during a period. Profit has no technical meaning in accounting and is not displayed in financial statements. The term has no significant relationship to income or comprehensive income. The term *gross profit* is sometimes used to indicate the excess of sales over cost of goods sold.

See also Income statement; Wealth; Asset/liability assumption and Revenue/expense assumption; Capital; Retained earnings; Comprehensive income; Earnings per share; Expenses; Revenue; Matching principle; Gains.

REFERENCES

SFAC No. 3, Elements of Financial Statements of Business Enterprises (FASB, 1981).

SFAC No. 5, Recognition and Measurement in Financial Statements of Business Enterprises (FASB, 1984).

INCOME STATEMENT

An income statement presents the results of operations for a reporting period. The income statement provides information concerning return on investment, risk, financial flexibility, and operating capabilities. Return on investment is a measure of a firm's overall performance. Risk is the uncertainty associated with the future of the enterprise. Financial flexibility is the firm's ability to adapt to problems and opportunities. Operating capability relates to the firm's ability to maintain a given level of operations.

The question of how income should be reported on an income statement is an important accounting issue. Various theories have been used to suggest answers to this question. The current operating theory of net income emphasizes ordinary, normal, and recurring operations of the entity during the current period. Unusual or nonrecurring items (extraordinary items) and prior period adjustments (mainly accounting errors of prior periods) are excluded from the income statement and reported directly in the statement of retained earnings. Proponents of this theory maintain that the normal earnings represent what the enterprise is able to earn under current year's operating conditions and is the most useful figure for predicting future earnings. Excluding certain items from the income statement makes year-to-year comparisons more relevant.

The all-inclusive theory of income determination includes all revenues, gains, expenses, and losses affecting owners' equity during the period. According to this theory, extraordinary items and prior period adjustments are part of income. Proponents of this theory maintain that the annual income statements of the enterprise when added together should equal total net income for the firm during its existence. Such reporting provides a complete history of the earnings of the entity. Also, by excluding extraordinary items and prior period adjustments, management can manipulate annual earnings by choosing what to include or exclude from the statements.

The current official view expressed by the Accounting Principles Board is that income "should reflect all items of profit and loss recognized during the period," except for a few items that would go directly to retained earnings, notably prior period adjustments. The following summary illustrates the income statement currently considered to represent generally accepted accounting principles:

Revenues	$XXX
Deduct: Expenses	XXX

Gains and losses that are not extraordinary	XXX
Income from continuing operations	XXX
Discontinued operations	XXX
Extraordinary gains and losses	XXX
Cumulative effect of change in accounting principle	XXX
Net income	$XXX

Generally accepted accounting principles require disclosing earnings per share amounts on the income statement of all publicly reporting entities. Earnings per share data provides a measure of the enterprise's management and past performance and enables users of financial statements to evaluate future prospects of the enterprise and assess dividend distributions to shareholders. Disclosure of earnings per share effects of discontinued operations and extraordinary items is optional but is required for income from continuing operations, income before extraordinary items, the cumulative effect of a change in accounting principle, and net income.

Exhibit I-1 provides a comparative outline of the three income theories and also shows how they relate to a statement of retained earnings.

The income statement can be presented in one of two general forms: the single-step form or the multiple-step form. Neither form is presumed to be better than the other for all purposes. The single-step form shows all revenues and gains as a group and then deducts all expenses and losses as a group to obtain the income for the period. The multiple-step income statement is constructed with several intermediate calculations, such as net sales, cost of goods sold, gross margin, total operating expenses, and operating income. Examples of these two formats are illustrated in Exhibit I-2 and I-3.

On a multiple-step income statement, operating expenses include selling, general, and administrative expenses and exclude cost of goods sold, interest, and income tax expenses.

Exhibit I–1
Three Accounting Theories of Financial Income

	Current Operating Performance Theory	All-Inclusive Theory	APB-FASB Theory
Income statement:			
Revenues	$500,000	$500,000	$500,000
Expenses	(200,000)	(200,000)	(200,000)
Extraordinary item:			
Loss—earthquake damage		(50,000)	(50,000)
Prior period adjustment:			
Correction of errors		(75,000)	
Net income (now comprehensive income in the case of the last two theories)	$300,000	$175,000	$250,000
Statement of retained earnings:			
Beginning balance	$100,000	$100,000	$100,000
Less correction of error of prior period	75,000		75,000
Beginning balance restated	25,000		25,000
Add net income	300,000	175,000	250,000
Total	325,000	275,000	275,000
Less extraordinary items—			
Earthquake loss	50,000		
Balance	275,000		
Deduct dividends	25,000	25,000	25,000
Ending balance	$250,000	$250,000	$250,000

Exhibit I–2
Single-step Income Statement

THE EXAMPLE COMPANY
Income Statement
For the Year Ended December 31, 19X[1]

Revenues:
Net sales (Gross sales $1,000,000 less sales adjustments)		$980,000
Interest income		10,000
Dividend income		8,000
Total revenue		998,000
Cost and expenses:		
Cost of goods sold	$500,000	
Selling expenses	100,000	
General and administrative expenses	110,000	
Other expenses	4,000	
Income taxes	102,400	
Total cost and expenses		816,400
Income before extraordinary item		181,600
Extraordinary item:		
Earthquake loss, less applicable income taxes		46,600
Net income		$135,000
Earnings per common share (90,000 shares outstanding) (after deducting $6,400 for preferred dividends):		
Income before extraordinary item		$1.95
Extraordinary item (loss)		(.52)
Net income		$1.43

Exhibit I–3
Multi-step Income Statement

STYLE COMPANY
Income Statement
For the Year Ended December 31, 19☐[1]

Sales			$1,000,000
Less: Sales discounts		$ 10,000	
Sales returns and allowances		10,000	20,000
Net sales			$ 980,000
Cost of goods sold			500,000
Gross margin			$ 480,000
Operating expenses:			
Selling expenses:			
Sales salaries:	$50,000		
Advertising	10,000		
Depreciation of store equipment	40,000	$100,000	
General and administrative expenses:			
Officers and office salaries	$50,000		
Depreciation of office equipment	10,000		
Property taxes	30,000		
Insurance	20,000	110,000	210,000
Operating income			$ 270,000
Other revenue and expense:			
Interest income		$ 10,000	
Dividend income		8,000	
Total other revenue		$ 18,000	
Interest expense		4,000	14,000
Income before income taxes and extraordinary item			$ 284,000
Income taxes			102,400
Income before extraordinary item			$ 181,600
Extraordinary item:			
Fire loss		$ 4,800	
Less: Applicable income taxes		1,200	3,600
Net income			$ 178,000
Earnings per common share (10,000 shares outstanding):			
Income before extraordinary item			$18.16
Extraordinary item (loss)			(0.36)
Net income			$17.80

I

See also Income; Revenue; Expenses; Gains; Losses; Discontinued operations; Extraordinary item; Accounting changes; Prior-period adjustments; Income taxes; Earnings per share; Statement of earnings and comprehensive income; Objectives of financial reporting by business enterprises; Recognition; Measurement; Statement of retained earnings.

REFERENCE
APB No. 30, Reporting the Results of Operations (APB, 1973).

INCOME TAX ACCOUNTING
Congress has the power to levy and collect taxes on incomes. Because the purposes and policies of tax accounting (e.g., related to revenue-producing activities) and financial accounting (e.g., related to investment and credit needs) frequently differ, accounting practices also differ. As a general rule, the Internal Revenue Service accepts any accounting method that clearly reflects income as long as the tax statutes and regulations are followed.

Sole proprietors are not separate taxable entities. The owner of the business reports business transactions on his/her individual income tax return. Partnerships are not subject to the income tax. The results of partnership operations flow through to the individual partners. Estates and trusts have similarities to the partnership in that income is taxed only once. However, the tax may be imposed on the estate or trust. Whether the income of an estate or trust is taxed to the estate or trust or to the beneficiary generally depends on whether the income is retained by the entity or distributed to the beneficicary. The corporation is taxed as a separate taxpaying entity. Corporate income is taxed again to the shareholder when distributed as dividends, subject to certain limitations. Subchapter S corporations are usually treated as partnerships and so frequently can avoid taxes at the corporate level.

Corporations can choose a calendar year or a fiscal year for reporting purposes, as can individuals. A change in accounting period generally requires the approval of the IRS. Corporations can use a variety of accounting methods depending upon the surrounding circumstances: the cash or accrual method, the installment method, or the percentage of completion and the completed contract method when long-term contracts are involved. Corporations that are members of a parent-subsidiary group can file a consolidated income tax return for a taxable year. The affiliated group is considered to constitute a single taxable entity, although the members of the group are legally separate entities.

See also Income tax allocation; Accounting methods; Other comprehensive methods of accounting.

INCOME TAX ALLOCATION

Federal, state, and local governments impose taxes against individuals, businesses, and other entities. Taxable income is determined by applying the tax rules and regulations. Since tax rules and regulations are used to compute taxable income while accounting principles are used to compute income reported on financial statements, taxes payable can differ from the provision for income taxes (income tax expense) reported on the income statement. This difference can result in a special liability or deferred charge item being reported on the balance sheet. Accounting for these differences is generally accomplished by a process referred to as income tax allocation.

It is possible for some revenue and expense items to be included in accounting and taxable income in different accounting periods. Some items may be recognized earlier or later for accounting purposes than for tax purposes. These differences are called timing differences, and result in establishing deferred credits or deferred charges in the financial statements. When the item reverses in subsequent periods, the deferred balance is eliminated. For example, a company may use straight-line depreciation for accounting purposes and use accelerated depreciation when preparing its income tax return. The accounting procedure developed to deal with these timing differences is called interperiod tax allocation. Comprehensive income tax allocation requires allocation for all timing differences, including those not expected to recur in the future.

Permanent differences are distinguished from timing differences. A permanent difference is one that enters into accounting income but never into taxable income or vice versa. For example, interest received on state and municipal obligations is never a part of taxable income but is included in accounting income. Income tax allocation procedures relate only to timing differences and not to permanent differences.

The existence of a timing difference requires that income tax expense be based on pretax accounting income and not on taxable income.

Pretax book income	$100,000	$100,00
Excess of tax depreciation over book depreciation		10,000
Income subject to income tax	$100.000	$90,000
Income tax at 50%	$ 50,000	$45,000

The $5,000 difference between tax currently payable of $45,000 and the reported tax expense of $50,000 is due to the timing difference ($10,000 × 50%). This amount would be reported on the balance sheet as Deferred Income Tax in the long-term liability section. On the income statement, income tax expense would be reported at $50,000. In later years, the use of accelerated depreciation for tax purposes would decrease relative to depreciation for accounting purposes. When this occurred, the timing difference would reverse, and the deferred tax credit would be eliminated. On the income statement, income tax expense would be smaller than taxes payable. If taxable income had exceeded pretax accounting income because the company used straight-line depreciation for tax purposes and an accelerated depreciation method for accounting purposes, a Deferred Income Taxes charge (versus a liability) would have resulted. In later years when the effect of the different depreciation methods reversed, the Deferred Income Taxes charge would be eliminated, and income taxes expense on the income statement would exceed income taxes payable.

Deferred taxes are tax effects which are postponed for allocation to income taxes expense in future accounting periods. They are the result of an accounting procedure which has as its purpose the matching of income tax expense reported on the income statement with pretax accounting income. Classifying deferred income tax credits as a liability on the balance sheet can be questioned because there is no existing debt to be paid. The use of the term *deferred* is also questioned since deferred income tax credits have the characteristics of accruals rather than deferrals. An accrued liability is one that has been incurred during the period but which has not yet been recorded or paid. A deferred liability would refer to a debt or obligation to perform a service in the future, which obviously is not the case with deferred income tax credits.

Some revenue and expense items used in determining taxable income can be reported in accounting statements in different locations. The tax effect of such items is usually associated with the revenue or expense item. This practice is referred to as "net of tax reporting" or "intraperiod tax allocation." This practice requires that certain amounts reported in financial statements be adjusted for all income tax effects. As a result, all income taxes may not be reported on one line of the income statement. Income taxes would ordinarily be allocated to the following financial statement items: income from continuing operations, income from discontinued operations, extraordinary items, cumulative effects of accounting changes, and prior-period adjustments. For example, the tax on an extraordinary gain item is deducted in the extraordinary item section of the income statement. The tax on income from continuing operations is deducted from income from continuing operations in the income statement.

See also Deferred tax credits (debits); Deferred charge (credit); Allocation; Income tax accounting.

REFERENCE
APB No. 11, Accounting for Income Taxes (APB, 1967).

INFORMATION

Data are facts and figures that are accepted as input to an information system for storage and processing. Data are usually compiled from historical records, such as sales invoices, purchase orders, and payroll records. Information relates to the output of data processing that is useful to the person receiving it. Financial statements of a company represent significant financial information about a company. Information is useful if it provides a basis for action, especially for predicting and evaluating. An information system is a network of interacting and interrelated elements that accumulates, processes, and communicates information for users in decision-making situations. These operations can be visualized as a data processing cycle involving inputs, processing, storage, and outputs as follows:

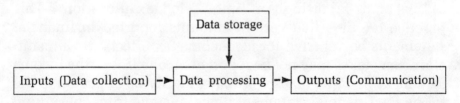

See also Accounting system; Electronic data processing; Accounting functions.

REFERENCE
Moscove, Stephen A., and Simkin, Mark G., *Accounting Information Systems* (John Wiley & Sons, N.Y., 1984).

INFORMATION SYSTEMS

The term *system* refers to the components or subsystems that interact and interrelate to accomplish a goal or objective. The activities of an information system include collection, processing, and communication of information. A management information system (MIS) includes the means by which information is provided to decision makers so that they may effectively attain the organization's goals and objectives. The major attributes of an MIS include relevance, accuracy, timeliness, completeness, conciseness, economy, and flexibility. Subsystems of a typical business organization include personnel subsystems, purchasing subsystems, production subsystems, marketing subsystems, order-processing subsystems, and financial subsystems. A primary subsystem is one that impacts the entire structure of an organization. A secondary subsystem is one that is limited to a single functional part of an organization.

Developing an MIS involves the following steps:

1. Establish the goals of the system.
2. Identify the information needed to attain the goal.
3. Design the system.
4. Test the system.
5. Implement the system.
6. Monitor and control the system.

See also Information; Electronic data processing; Accounting system.

REFERENCES

Wu, Frederick H., *Accounting Information System: Theory and Practice* (McGraw-Hill, N.Y., 1983).
Maciariello, Joseph A., *Management Control Systems* (Prentice-Hall, Englewood Cliffs, NJ, 1984).

I

INSTALLMENT SALES METHOD

The installment sales method of accounting recognizes revenue as cash is collected when receivables are collectible over an extended period of time, rather than at the time of sale. The installment sales method of recognizing revenue is a modification of the cash collection method.

The installment sales method should be used only when there is a significant uncertainty concerning the ultimate collection of the sales proceeds. In such situations, revenue recognition is postponed. For example, a company sold for $100,000 land which cost $60,000. The rate of gross profit on this transaction is 40 percent ($40,000/$100,000). It is assumed that there is considerable uncertainty concerning the collectibility of the receivable resulting from the transaction. During the first year, the company collected $20,000. Income (gross profit) in the amount of $8,000 ($20,000 × 40%) is recognized. As can be noted, payments are prorated between recovery of the cost of the property and profit to be recognized on the sale.

The cost recovery method is similar to the installment sales method of recognizing revenue. This method is more conservative than the installment sales method and is used when collection of the receivable is extremely uncertain and there is no way of estimating collectibility. Under this method, no income is recognized until all the cost has been recovered.

The deposit method is used in situations where cash is received prior to the delivery of goods (the point of sale). The cash is recorded as an advance (a liability) and not as a sale until the seller performs.

See also Revenue; Recognition; Realization.

INSURANCE

Insurance is a contract between an insurer and the insured whereby the insurer indemnifies the insured against loss due to specific risks, such as from fire, storm, death, etc. Insurance is an integral part of most enterprises' risk management.

Insurance contracts require an agreement, consideration, capacity, legality, compliance with the Statute of Frauds, and delivery. Liability insurance protects the insured from claims by third parties for damages resulting from actions or events that are the responsibility of the insured. Casualty insurance protects the insured from a variety of insurable events such as fire, storm, theft, explosion, and other casualties.

Insurance policies usually contain a deductible clause that excludes a fixed amount of the loss from recovery. Casualty insurance policies frequently contain a coinsurance clause in the contract. A coinsurance clause provides that the insurance company shall be liable for only a portion of any loss sustained by the insured unless the insured carries insurance which totals a certain percent, frequently 80-90 percent of the fair value of the asset. In the event of a loss, the insured recovers from the insurance company that portion of the loss which the face of the insurance policy bears to the amount of insurance that should be carried as required by the coinsurance clause.

The coinsurance indemnity is expressed as follows:

$$\frac{\text{Face amount of policy}}{\text{Coinsurance percentage} \times \text{Fair value of property at date of loss}} \times \text{Fair value}$$

To illustrate, assume a company purchases a $20,000 insurance policy on some equipment; the policy has an 80 percent coinsurance clause. A fire loss occurs at a time when the fair value of the equipment was $30,000. The amount of the loss was $6,000:

$$\frac{\$20,000}{(80\%)(\$30,000)} \times \$6,000 = \$5,000 \text{ recoverable from insurer}$$

The insured can recover the lowest of the face of the policy, the fair value of the loss, or the coinsurance indemnity.

I

See also Cash surrender value.

REFERENCE
Huebner, S. S., et al., *Property and Liability Insurance* (Prentice Hall, Inc., Englewood Cliffs, NJ, 1982).

INTANGIBLE ASSETS

Intangible assets are special rights, grants, privileges, and advantages possessed by a business which can benefit future operations by contributing to the enterprise's earning power. Intangible assets do not possess physical substance. Intangible assets include patents, copyrights, trademarks, trade names, franchises, licenses and royalties, formulas and processes, organization costs, leasehold and leasehold improvements, and goodwill.

Intangible assets may be acquired from other enterprises or individuals or developed by the company. Intangible assets can be classified as unidentifiable and identifiable intangible assets. An unidentifiable intangible is one that cannot exist independent of the business as a whole. Goodwill and organization costs are unidentifiable intangible assets. Identifiable intangible assets have a separate identity and existence of their own independent of the business as a whole. Patents and copyrights are examples of identifiable intangible assets. If acquired by purchase, the intangible item is recognized as an asset. If developed by the enterprise, the research and development costs are expenses when incurred.

The life of an intangible asset may be determinable if fixed by law, regulation, agreement, contract, or by the nature of the asset. The cost of an intangible asset having a determinable life should be amortized in a rational and systematic manner over the term of its existence, but not to exceed 40 years. If the life of the intangible asset is indeterminate, as might be the case for goodwill and trade names, the cost of the assets should be written off over a period of years established by management, but not to exceed 40 years. The straight-line method of amortization should be used to write off the cost of intangible assets over future periods to be benefited by the assets unless another systematic method is considered more relevant and reliable.

A patent has a legal life of 17 years. Copyrights are granted for a period of years covering the life of the creator of the copyright plus an additional 50 years. Franchises may be granted for a limited time or for an unlimited period. Organization costs are incurred during the formation of a corporation and prior to income-producing operations. Such costs include expenditures incurred relating to promoters, attorneys, accountants, underwriters' charges, as well as registration and listing fees and printing costs associated with the issuance of securities. Such costs should be written off over a period of time not to exceed 40 years. Leasehold improvements should be written off over the term of the lease or the service life of the improvement, whichever is shorter.

See also Assets; Organization costs; Research and development costs; Amortization.

REFERENCE
APB No. 17, Intangible Assets (APB, 1970).

INTEREST
Interest is the cost of using money over time. From a lender's viewpoint, interest is the excess money that is received over the amount that was loaned. From the borrower's viewpoint, interest is the excess money that is paid over the amount that was borrowed. Simple interest is interest on the original principal (funds originally received or paid). Simple interest is computed according to the following formula:

Interest = Principal × Rate × Time

where time is either a year, a fraction of a year, or a multiple of years. For example, if you borrow $100 for one year at 10%, the interest for the year is $10 ($100 x .10% × 1).

Compound interest is the interest that accrued on both the principal and the past unpaid accrued interest. When interest is compounded, interest is earned each period on the original principal and on the interest accumulated for the preceding periods. The difference between simple interest and compound interest is illustrated in Exhibit I-4.

See also Annuity; Future value; Present value; Interest on long-term receivables and payables; Capitalization of interest; U.S rule and merchants' rule; Rule of 72; Federal Reserve System. Reserve System.

REFERENCE
Woelfel, Charles J., *Financial Managers' Desktop Reference to Money, Time, Interest and Yield* (Probus, Chicago, 1986).

Exhibit I-4
Simple Interest and Compound Interest Compared

End of year	Interest Earned	Cumulative Interest	Balance
	SIMPLE INTEREST		
1	$1,000(.10) = $100	$100	$1,100
2	$1,000(.10) = 100	200	1,200
3	$1,000.(10) = 100	300	1,300
4	$1,000(.10) = 100	400	1,400
	COMPOUND INTEREST		
1	$1,000(.10) = $100.00	$100.00	$1,100.00
2	$1,100(.10) = 110.00	210.00	1,210.00
3	$1,210(.10) = 121.00	331.00	1,331.00
4	$1,331(.10) = 133.10	464.10	1,464.10

INTEREST ON LONG-TERM RECEIVABLES AND PAYABLES
Receivables and payables which are contractual rights to receive or pay money at a fixed or determinable date must be recorded at their present value, if (1) the interest rate is not stated, (2) the stated interest rate is unreasonable, or (3) the stated face amount of the note is materially different from the current cash sales price for the same or similar items or from current market value of the note. In such circumstances, the present value of the note is measured by the fair value of the property, goods, or services associated with the note transaction or by an amount that reasonably approximates the market value of the note, whichever is more clearly determinable. Any difference between the face amount of the note and its present value is a discount or premium that must be amortized over the life of the note.

A note received or issued solely for cash equal to its face amount is assumed to earn the interest stated on the note. The note is recorded at its face amount and any difference between the face amount and the cash proceeds should be recorded as a premium or discount on the note.

If rights or privileges are attached to the note, they must be evaluated separately and recognized in the accounts separate from the note. For example, a business may lend a supplier cash that is receivable ten years later with no stated interest in exchange for which the supplier agrees to sell products to the lender at bargain prices. In this case, the difference between the present value of the note and the amount of cash received should be recorded by the issuer of the note (borrower/supplier) both as a discount on the note (debit) and as unearned revenue (credit) on the future sales. The discount would be amortized to interest expense over the life of the note. The unearned revenue would be recognized as sales when sales to the lender occur.

See also Implicit interest; Imputed interest.

REFERENCE
Miller, Martin A., *GAAP Guide* (Harcourt Brace Jovanovich, Publishers, San Diego, CA., latest edition).

INTERIM FINANCIAL REPORTS

Interim reports are reports that cover periods of less than one year, such as months or a quarter of a year. In general, the results for each interim period should be based on the generally accepted accounting principles and reporting practices used in the last annual reporting period although certain modifications of accounting principles and practices are allowed when applied to interim reports. Interim reports are considered an integral part of the annual reporting period and are not viewed as a discrete (independent) time period. Interim reports are essential in providing investors, creditors, and others with more timely information as to the financial position and operating results of an enterprise. The usefulness of interim reports depends to a great extent upon how they relate to the annual reports. Major uses and objectives of interim reporting include:

1. To estimate annual earnings.

2. To make projections and predictions.

3. To identify turning points in operations and financial position.

4. To evaluate management performance.

5. To supplement information presented in the annual report.

Accounting principles do not require as much information in interim reports as would be required in annual financial statements, although companies are encouraged to publish complete interim financial statements. Interim information is usually reported for the current interim period (e.g., the third quarter) and current year-to-date (e.g., January 1 to September 30 for a company reporting on a calendar year basis) with comparative data for the preceding fiscal year. Publicly traded companies usually report the following summarized financial information at interim dates:

1. Gross revenues, provision for income taxes, extraordinary items, effects of accounting changes, and net income.

2. Primary and fully diluted earnings-per-share data.

3. Material seasonal variations of revenues, costs, and expenses.

4. Contingent items and effects of the disposal of a segment of a business.

5. Material changes in financial position.

Exhibit I-5 illustrates interim reporting practices.

Revenues are recognized on the same basis as that for fiscal periods. Product costs and other expenses are determined in a manner similar to the procedures used for the fiscal period, with some exceptions for inventory valuation, income taxes, and other items.

See also Financial statements; Accounting periods.

REFERENCE
APB No. 28, Interim Financial Reporting (APB, 1973).

INTERNAL CONTROL
Internal control refers to the systems, procedures, and policies employed by an enterprise to help assure that transactions are properly authorized and are appropriately executed and recorded. Internal control applies to both administrative controls and accounting controls. Administrative (operating) controls include a plan of organization, procedures, and records

I

Exhibit I–5
Interim Report

Adams-Millis Corporation
Summary of Quarterly Earnings (Unaudited)

For the year ended January 2, 1983
(52 weeks)

	First Quarter	Second Quarter	Third Quarter	Fourth Quarter
Net sales	$12,837,000	$16,394,000	$17,888,000	$14,970,000
Gross profit	1,054,000	2,716,000	3,076,000	2,053,000
Earnings (loss) from continuing operations	(125,000)	579,000	896,000	458,000
Earnings (loss) from discontinued operations	(26,000)	(33,000)	(33,000)	13,000
Net earnings (loss)	(151,000)	546,000	863,000	471,000
Earnings (loss) per share:				
Earnings (loss) from continuing operations	$(.05)	$.24	$.38	$.20
Earnings (loss) from discontinued operations	(.01)	(.01)	(.01)	—
Net earnings (loss)	(.06)	.23	.37	.20

For the year ended January 31, 1982
(53 Weeks)

	First Quarter	Second Quarter	Third Quarter	Fourth Quarter
Net sales	$13,585,000	$16,713,000	$17,771,000	$15,076,000
Gross profit	1,467,000	2,227,000	1,774,000	1,772,000
Earnings from continuing operations	228,000	654,000	570,000	—
Earnings (loss) from discontinued operations	281,000	(11,000)	15,000	31,000
Earnings before extraordinary gain	509,000	643,000	585,000	31,000
Extraordinary gain	—	—	1,834,000	1,655,000
Net earnings	509,000	643,000	2,419,000	1,686,000
Earnings per share:				
Earnings from continuing operations	$.10	$.29	$.24	$—
Earnings (loss) from discontinued operations	.12	(.01)	—	.02
Earnings before extraordinary gain	.22	.28	.24	.02
Extraordinary gain	—	—	.79	.71
Net earnings	.22	.28	1.03	.73

Source: Reprinted from Accounting Trends & Techniques, Copyright © 1983 by the American Institute of Certified Public Accountants Inc., p.3.

that lead up to management's authorization of transactions. Accounting (financial) controls deal with the plans, procedures, and records required for safeguarding assets and producing reliable financial records.

Auditing standards require that accounting controls be designed to provide reasonable assurance that:

1. Transactions are executed in accordance with management's general or specific authorization.

2. Transactions are recorded as necessary (1) to permit preparation of financial statements in conformity with generally accepted accounting principles or any other criteria applicable to such statements and (2) to maintain accountability for assets.

3. Access to assets is permitted only in accordance with management's authorization.

4. The recorded accountability for assets is compared with the existing assets at reasonable intervals and appropriate action is taken with respect to any difference.

The major objectives of internal auditing control are to ensure the following broad administrative objectives:

1. The reliability and integrity of information.

2. Compliance with policies, plans, procedures, laws, and regulations.

3. The efficient and economical use of resources.

4. The safeguarding of assets.

5. The accomplishment of objectives and goals for programs and operations.

Administrative controls includes most accounting controls but also extends to organizational plans, procedures, and records required to promote operational efficiency and adherence to management policies.

The system of internal control adopted by a company takes into consideration the size and nature of the enterprise. The establishment and maintenance of a system of internal control are the primary responsibility of management (and not of the auditor). The auditor evaluates control. The effectiveness of accounting controls depends to a great extent on the competence and integrity of an enterprise's personnel, their understanding of procedures, and the separation of assigned functions (e.g., no one person should handle all aspects of a transaction). To be effective, internal control procedures should assure that transactions are carried out with proper authorization and are recorded at the amounts intended in the accounting periods in which they occur and are properly classified.

Broad categories of control procedures that apply to both financial and administrative controls include:

1. Organizational:
   a. Separation of duties.
   b. Clear lines of authority and responsibility.
   c. Formal policies.
2. Procedures:
   a. Accounting checks.
   b. Proper documents and records.
   c. Error detection and correction procedures.
   d. Physical control over assets and records.
3. Competent, trustworthy personnel (bonded where appropriate).
4. Performance goals and objectives:
   a. Periodic reviews of performance.
   b. Comparisons of recorded accountability with assets.
5. Independent review of the system.

The Foreign Corrupt Practices Act passed in 1977 had a major impact on internal control applications in that it requires public companies to maintain reasonably complete and accurate financial records and a sufficient system of internal accounting controls. A major reason for this legislation was that Congress believed that public companies had inadequate controls to detect bribes and improper payments.

A review of internal accounting controls is essential to an audit of financial statements. A study of internal accounting controls enables the auditor to make a judgment concerning the reliance that can be placed on the records and to determine the nature, extent, and timing of various tests of the accounting data that the system has produced.

See also Audit; Foreign Corrupt Practices Act; Voucher system; Bank reconciliation.

REFERENCE
Burton, John C., et al., eds. *Handbook of Accounting and Auditing* (Warren, Gorham & Lamont, Boston, 1981).

INVENTORY
Inventory is a term used to identify material or merchandise owned by the enterprise that eventually will be sold to customers or used in the process of production. Merchandise inventory is a term used for goods held for sale by retail or wholesale firms. Goods held for resale by manufacturing firms are referred to as finished goods. Manufacturing firms may also have work-in-process inventories which represent partially completed products still in the production process. Manufacturing firms may also have raw materials inventories which consist of materials which will become part of goods to be manufactured. The inventory equation is expressed to show certain relationships affecting inventory:

Beginning inventory + Net additions (= net purchases)
 − Withdrawals = Ending inventory

The relationship of inventory to sales, cost of sales, and gross margin on an income statement is illustrated here:

Sales (net)		$500,000
Deduct: Cost of goods sold		
Beginning inventory	$100,000	
Purchases (net) during the period	300,000	
Goods available for sale	400,000	
Deduct: Ending inventory	75,000	
Cost of goods sold		325,000
Gross margin		$175,000

Note that the cost of goods available for sale during an accounting period is determined by adding the cost of the beginning inventory to the net cost of goods purchased during the period. The cost of the ending inventory is then subtracted to determine the cost of goods sold.

A company includes in its inventory all merchandise or material intended for sale in the normal course of business and to which it has legal title at the time the inventory is measured. As a general rule, title to inventory passes from seller to buyer when the goods are delivered to the buyer or his agent. Goods delivered on consignment are included in the consignor's inventory because title is retained until the goods are sold by the consignee.

Inventory valuation is a major accounting problem. Generally, inventory includes the invoice cost of the item (less any purchase discounts), transportation charges, insurance charges, import duties, and other expenditures needed to bring the inventory to its present location and condition. The cost of finished goods for a manufacturing company includes raw materials, direct factory labor, and factory overhead costs such as utilities, factory rent, depreciation, and factory supplies used.

There are two generally accepted methods of accounting for and controlling the quantities of inventory on hand:

1. The periodic inventory method, which requires a count of all the inventory on hand at specific times. This method is also called the physical inventory method because it is based on a physical count.

2. The perpetual inventory method, which requires a continuous record keeping of all inflows and out-flows of inventory items. Under this method, the inventory account is continuously updated with each purchase or sale transaction. This method is also called the continuous inventory, or book inventory, method.

Another major accounting problem is assigning cost to inventory. The American Institute of Certified Public Accountants stated: "A major objective of accounting for inventories is the proper determination of income through the process of matching appropriate costs against revenues." The matching process involves determining how much of the cost of the goods that were available for sale during a period should be deducted from (matched against) the period's sales and how much should be carried forward as inventory to be matched against sales of subsequent periods. A choice is usually made depending upon how "costs flow," for example, first-in, first-out or last-in, first-out. Whatever choice is made, the attribute being measured is historical cost in all methods. The process of assigning a cost to the ending inventory consists of two steps: (1) determining the quantity of each product on hand at the end of a period and (2) pricing the product using a cost flow assumption. The more common methods of assigning cost to inventory include:

1. Specific identification method. Each item in inventory is individually identified, and a record is kept

of its actual cost. The actual flow of goods is monitored and recorded exactly. Each item in the ending inventory can be identified, and its cost is assigned to the item.

2. First-in, first-out method (FIFO). The flow of goods is assumed to be such that the oldest items in the inventory are sold or used first. Inventory items on hand at the end of the period are assumed to have been acquired in the most recent purchases.

3. Last-in, first-out method (LIFO). The flow of goods is assumed to be such that the items most recently purchased are sold or used first. The ending inventory is assumed to have come from the earliest purchases.

4. Weighted average method. The flow of goods is assumed to be such that all items available for sale during the period are intermingled randomly, and items sold or used are picked randomly from this intermingled inventory. The weighted average cost per unit is computed according to this formula:

$$\frac{\text{Beginning inventory} + \text{Purchases}}{\text{Units in beginning inventory} + \text{Units purchased}} = \text{Average cost per unit}$$

5. Moving average method. The flow of goods is assumed to be such that the items in the inventory are intermingled randomly after each addition to the inventory; items sold or used are picked randomly from those items in the inventory at the time. Under this method, an average cost per unit for the items in the inventory is computed after each purchase according to this formula:

$$\frac{\text{Total cost of inventory on hand after each purchase}}{\substack{\text{Total number of units in the inventory on hand} \\ \text{after each purchase}}} = \text{Average cost per unit}$$

A short illustration of these inventory methods is presented in Exhibit I-6. The illustration uses the following data for transactions during 19X1:

Jan. 1   Inventory on hand of 1,000 units at $1 per unit
Mar. 7   Purchase of 6,000 units at $1.50 per unit
Apr. 2   Sale of 2,000 units
July 4   Purchase of 3,500 units at $2 per unit
Oct. 8   Sale of 500 units
Dec. 31   Ending inventory on hand 8,000 units

Exhibit I-6 shows a schedule summarizing the effects of these transactions on inventory. The problem is to assign the $17,000 cost of the units available for sale between the 8,000 units on hand in the ending inventory and the 2,500 units sold during the year. Computations for the five inventory methods are shown in the exhibit. For the specific identification method, assume that the items in the ending inventory are identified as follows:

500 units on hand at beginning of the year
4,000 units from March 7 purchase
3,500 units from July 4 purchase

When prices remain unchanged, all methods give the identical cost figures for the ending inventory. When prices are rising as in periods of inflation, LIFO and FIFO inventory procedures can produce significantly different financial statements. FIFo assigns the most recently incurred cost to inventory which is reported on the balance sheet (desirable); the older, lower costs are deducted on the income statement as cost of goods sold (not so desirable because it matches current sales dollars against not so current cost-of-goods-sold dollars). LIFO procedures have the opposite effect: inventory is reported on balance sheet at older dollars (not desirable) and cost of goods sold at current dollars (desirable). The understatement of inventories resulting from LIFO has a negative effect on working capital, current ratio, and inventories turnover rate. Major impacts of FIFO and LIFO inventory costing methods on financial statement items in times of rising prices are shown here:

	FIFO	LIFO
Ending inventory	Higher	Lower
Current assets	Higher	Lower
Working capital	Higher	Lower
Total assets	Higher	Lower
Cost of goods sold	Lower	Higher
Gross margin	Higher	Lower
Net income	Higher	Lower
Taxable income	Higher	Lower
Income taxes	Higher	Lower

The average method of costing inventory usually produces results similar to those experienced when FIFO is used since purchases during a period usually exceed opening inventory many times over. The specific identification method can produce a wide variety of results.

The major objective in selecting an inventory method should be to choose the one which, under the conditions and circumstances in practice, most clearly reflects periodic income. This criteria leaves the selection of the appropriate inventory method(s) up to the professional judgment of the responsible accountant.

Dollar-value LIFO is an inventory method that combines a variety of goods into one inventory pool. The inventory is viewed as a quantity (layers) of dollars instead of a physical quantity of goods. A LIFO inventory pool is viewed as being composed of layers of dollar values from different years. Adjustments to account for changing prices are made by using a specific price index appropriate for the items in the inventory.

An inventory pool would normally consist of inventory items that had economic similarities, such as being subject to similar price changes, rather than to physical characteristics. Under dollar-value LIFO, the ending inventory is priced at cur-

Exhibit I-6
Inventory Methods

Schedule of Merchandising Company's inventory transactions

Opening inventory	1,000 units @ $1 per unit	$ 1,000
March 7 purchase	6,000 units @ $1.50 per unit	9,000
July 4 purchase	3,500 units @ $2 per unit	7,000
Units available for sale	10,500 units	$17,000

Units sold:		
April 2 sale	2,000 units	
October 8 sale	500 units	
Units sold	2,500 units	

Units available for sale	10,500 units
Less: Units sold	2,500 units
Ending inventory	8,000 units

1. Specific Identification Method.

500 units on hand from beginning inventory @ cost of $1/unit	$ 500
4,000 units on hand from March 7 purchase @ cost of $1.50/unit	6,000
3,500 units on hand from July 4 purchase @ cost of $2/unit	7,000
8,000 units on hand at cost of	$13,500

2. FIFO Periodic Method.

3,500 units from purchase of July 4 @ cost of $2/unit	$ 7,000
4,500 units from purchase of March 7 @ cost of $1.50/unit	6,750
8,000 units on hand at cost of	$13,750

3. LIFO Periodic Method.

1,000 units from opening inventory @ $1/unit	$ 1,0500
6,000 units from purchase of March 7 @ $1.50/unit	9,000
1,000 units from purchase of July 4 @ $2/unit	2,000
8,000 units on hand at cost of	$12,000

4. Weighted Average Method.

Average cost per unit $= \dfrac{\$1,000 + \$16,000}{1,000 + 9,500} = \dfrac{\$17,000}{10,500} = \$1,619.$

Ending inventory = 8,000 units × $1.619/unit = $12,952.

5. Moving Average Perpetual Inventory Method.

$10,000/7,000 units = $1.4287/unit on March 2.

When the sale is made on April 2, the cost of the goods sold is computed from this average unit cost:

2,000 units × $1.4287/unit = $2,857.40.

A new moving average would be computed after each additional purchase.

rent cost. The total cost of the inventory is then restated to the cost existing when LIFO was adopted by means of a specific cost index. This restated ending inventory is compared with the beginning inventory which also is restated at base-year dollars to determine the change in the inventory on hand. Increases or decreases in the inventory are then assigned costs existing at the end of the accounting period in which the item was acquired. To illustrate dollar-value LIFO, assume that the ending inventories of a company in 1986 and 1987 were $10,000 and $22,000, respectively. Price indexes for the two years were 100 and 110, respectively. The base year is assumed to be 1986. The inventory at the end of 1987 would be determined as follows using dollar-value LIFO procedures:

1. Restate 1987 ending inventory at base-year costs:

   22,000 x 100 base-year index/110 current index = $20,000

   The 1987 inventory is now restated in terms of 1986 base-year costs.

2. The increase in inventory is $10,000 ($20,000 – $10,000). Restate this increase in terms of current-year cost:

   $10,000 x 110 current-year index/100 base-year index = 11,000

   The $11,000 assigned to the increase in inventory now is stated in 1987 cost. (If there is a decrease in the inventory level at base-year costs, each of the most recently added LIFO layers, or parts of layers, must be converted to cost. The ending inventory is the dollar-value LIFO cost at the beginning of the period minus the decrease at the cost of the most recently added layer.)

3. The ending inventory in 1987 can now be computed using dollar-value LIFO procedures as follows: Layers in LIFO ending inventory:

   $10,000 at 100 since it represents 1986 inventory still on hand
    11,000 increase in inventory at 1987 costs
   $21,000 dollar value LIFO 1987 ending inventory

Conceptually, a cost index reflecting an internally developed index can be computed as follows where a sample of the ending inventory is priced at current-year costs and at base-year costs:

Cost index = $\dfrac{\text{Sample of current year = inventory}}{\text{Sample of base year = inventory}}$

A LIFO reserve is a term used to represent the unrealized holding gain in ending inventory, i.e., the difference between FIFO historical cost of ending inventory less LIFO historical cost. The LIFO reserve can be added to the LIFO inventory shown in the balance sheet to approximate the company's FIFO inventory value. Changes in LIFO reserve from year to year are equivalent to the before-tax effect on earnings of using LIFO instead of FIFO. A LIFO liquidation problem can also arise. If during periods of rising prices an enterprise liquidates an inventory layer consisting of old costs, earnings would be increased since current revenues would be matched with costs from a period when unit costs were lower than current replacement costs. The effect of such a liquidation on earnings must be disclosed.

If the utility of the inventory is less than its acquisition cost, it is usually considered necessary to measure the inventory at its lower market value. This represents an application of the accounting concept of conservatism. Such a situation could occur as a result of physical deterioration, obsolescence, or a change in price levels. In such a situation, the difference between cost and its lower market should be recognized as a loss of the current period. This is generally done by stating such goods at a lower level, commonly designated as "market." "Market" is defined as replacement cost. However, replacement cost must fall between an upper (a ceiling) and lower limit (a floor) before it is used. The upper limit is net realizable value (selling price less cost to complete and dispose). The lower limit is net realizable value less a normal markup. The upper and lower limits are used only if replacement cost falls outside the range. The application of lower of cost or market requires the following procedures:

1. Determine market; use replacement cost if between the floor or the ceiling, or, if not, use the floor or the ceiling.

2. Compare cost and market, as determined in step 1, and make the required adjustment if market is below cost.

The application of lower of cost or market is illustrated here in five cases. Market is indicated by parentheses; the correct lower-of-cost-or-market valuation is underlined.

	1	2	3	4	5
Cost	50	60	50	60	70
Market:					
Replacement cost	(60)	(55)	51	50	68
Ceiling	66	66	66	66	(66)
Floor	52	52	(52)	(52)	52

Exhibit I-7 shows how the lower-of-cost-or-market method can be applied to inventory: item by item, category by category, or total inventory.

Accountants have developed the retail inventory method and the gross profit method for estimating inventory costs. These methods are useful when inventory valuations are needed for interim financial statements and where a physical inventory count would be too expensive, inconvenient, or impossible (e.g., for interim periods or after a fire). A retail inventory method is widely used by retail concerns to estimate their inventory. When this method is used, records of inventory purchases are maintained at both cost and retail. A cost percentage is computed by dividing the goods available for sale at cost by the goods available for sale at retail. This cost per-

Exhibit I–7

Applying the Lower-of-Cost-or-Market Inventory Method—Three Approaches

Item	Quantity	Unit Cost	Unit Market	Total Cost	Total Market	Lower of Cost or Market Item-by-Item	by Category	Total Inventory
A	10	$50	$80	$ 500	$ 800	$ 500		
B	20	60	50	1,200	1,000	1,000		
C	30	70	70	2,100	2,100	2,100		
Men's Clothing Category				$ 3,800	$ 3,900		$ 3,800	
X	40	80	80	$ 3,200	$ 3,200	3,200		
Y	50	90	80	4,500	4,000	4,000		
Women's Clothing Category				$ 7,700	$ 7,200		7,200	
Total Inventory				$11,500	$11,100			$11,100
Inventory valuation						$10,800	$11,000	$11,100

centage is then applied to the ending inventory at retail to compute the ending inventory at cost. Special terminology applicable to the retail method includes:

1. Original retail—the initial sales price, including the original increase over cost referred to as the markon.

2. Additional markups—increases that raise sales prices above original retail.

3. Markup cancellations—decreases in additional markups that do not reduce sales prices below original retail.

4. Net markups—additional markups less markup cancellations.

5. Markdowns—decreases that reduce sales prices below original retail.

6. Markdown cancellations—decreases in the markdowns that do not raise the sale prices above original retail.

7. Net markdowns—markdowns less markdown cancellations.

Exhibit I-8 illustrates the conventional retail method. This
procedure provides an inventory valuation in terms of the
lower-of-cost-or-market method of inventory valuation. Other
procedures are available.

Exhibit I-8
Conventional Retail Inventory Method

	Cost	Retail	
Beginning inventory	$18,000	$ 24,000	
Purchases	62,700	100,000	
Additional markups		13,000	
Markup cancellations		(2,500)	
Goods available for sale	$80,700	$134,500	= 60%
Cost percentage ($80,700 ÷ $134,500) = 60%			
Deduct: Sales		$100,000	
Markdowns		12,800	
Markdown cancellations		(800)	
		$112,000	
Ending inventory at retail		$ 22,500	
Ending inventory at estimated cost ($22,500 × 60%)	$13,500		

The gross margin method involves adding the beginning
inventory at cost to the net purchases at cost to compute cost
of goods available for sale during the period. Net sales for the
period are multiplied by a gross margin on sales percentage.
This amount is subtracted from cost of goods available for sales
to produce an estimate of the ending inventory. To illustrate
this procedure, assume that the following data except for the
estimated cost of ending inventory are available. The enter-

prise's gross margin rate is 20 percent.

Beginning inventory at cost	$100,000
Add: Net purchases for the period	600,000
Cost of goods available for sale	$700,000
Deduct:	
Net sales for the period $800,000	
Less: Estimated gross margin	
($8000,000 × 20%) 160,000	
Estimated cost of goods sold	640,000
Estimated cost of ending inventory	$ 60,000

The gross margin method provides an "estimate" of the inventory. A physical inventory should be taken at least once a year to verify the amount of inventory on hand. Where an enterprise deals with merchandise that has different gross margin rates, the method should be applied to each line of merchandise.

See also Allocation; Retail method; Lower of cost or market; Inventory profit; Contribution margin analysis; Break-even analysis; Direct costing and absorption costing; Construction-type contracts; Consignment; Inventory model.

REFERENCE
Chasteen, Larry G., et al., *Intermediate Accounting* (Random House, N.Y., 1984).

INVENTORY MODEL
The control of inventory involves two major considerations:

1. What is the optimal size for a purchase order?

2. When should the order be placed?

When considering the optimal order size, a manager knows that:

1. certain expenses tend to increase with an increase in order size, for example, storage-space cost, insurance, taxes, risk of spoilage or theft, interest on money invested to finance the inventory, etc.; and

2. other expenses tend to decrease with an increase in order size, for example, cost of clerical work associated with purchasing and receiving and paying bills, freight expense, etc.

As order size increases, the cost of ordering inventory decreases while the cost of carrying inventory increases. Exhibit I-9 illustrates the relationship between order size and inventory-handling costs. The optimal order size is the order size at which the ordering-cost and carrying-cost curves intersect. This relationship can be expressed in the following formula:

$$\text{Economic order size} = \sqrt{2AP/S}$$

where A = annual quantity used in units; P = cost of placing an order; and S = annual cost of carrying one unit in stock for one year. To illustrate this concept, assume that a company uses 3,600 units of inventory each year. The cost of placing an order is $8, and the cost to carry one unit in inventory for one year is $1:

$$\text{Economic order size} = \sqrt{(2)(8)(3,600)/\$1}$$

$$= 240 \text{ units.}$$

The next issue to consider is when inventory should be ordered. If the lead time (the time between placing an order and receiving delivery), the economic order size, and the average usage are known, the time issue can be resolved. For example, in the illustration the demand is 3,600 units per year or approximately 10 units per day. One order of 240 units will last for about 24 days. The time between orders will have to be about 24 days. The order should be placed so that the new order will arrive just as the last one is used up. Suppose it takes 14 days from the time an order is placed until the goods arrive. In this case, each order should be placed 10 days after the last one has arrived, so that the new goods will arrive on the 24th day after the arrival of the previous order.

See also Inventory; Planning and control.

REFERENCE
Moscove, Stephen A., et al., *Cost Accounting* (Houghton Mifflin, Boston, 1985).

Exhibit I–9
Economic Order Model for Inventory

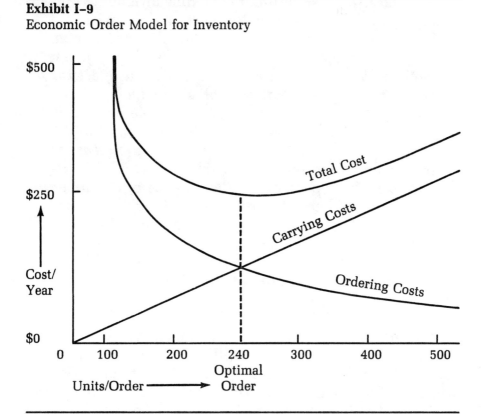

I

INVENTORY PROFIT

The Securities and Exchange Commission recommends that publicly owned companies disclose the amount of profit included in the income statement which will not recur due to increased replacement cost of inventories caused by inflation. Such profits are normally referred to as inventory profits (paper profits). The SEC supported this recommendation with the following arguments:

"The most significant and immediate impact of price fluctuations on financial statements is normally felt in cost of goods sold in the income statement. In periods of rising prices, historical cost methods result in the inclusion of "inventory profits" in reported earnings. "Inventory profits" result from holding inventories during a period of rising inventory costs and are measured by the difference between the historical cost of an item and its replacement cost at the time it is sold. Different methods of accounting for inventories can affect the degree to which "inventory profits" are included and identifiable in current income, but no method based upon historical cost eliminates or discloses this "profit" explicitly. Such "profits" do not reflect an increase in the economic earning power of a business and they are not normally repeatable in the absence of continued price-level increase. Accordingly, where such "profits" are material in income statements presented, disclosure of their impact on reported earnings and the trend of reported earnings is important information for investors assessing the quality of earnings."

"Inventory profit" comes from holding inventory in periods of rising prices rather than from selling inventory. The reported net income under FIFO during periods of rising prices is usually larger than under LIFO because LIFO charges the latest, higher cost of inventory to cost of goods sold. The excess of

FIFO's net income attributable to this factor over LIFO's net income represents "inventory profit." The cost of goods sold under LIFO approximates the replacement cost of the inventory sold and thus minimizes "inventory profit." "Inventory profit" arises primarily when old, low inventory costs (FIFO costs) are matched against current selling prices. It is the difference between the old, low inventory costs and current replacement cost of inventory that creates "inventory profit."

See also Inventory.

INVESTMENT TAX CREDITS
The Revenue Act of 1962 allowed companies to reduce their federal income taxes by an investment tax credit equal to a specific percentage of the cost of certain depreciable properties. A major purpose of this legislation was to encourage investments in productive facilities and to stimulate economic growth.

In accounting for the investment tax credit, the central issue is when the tax credit should affect income. Two acceptable methods are currently used to account for the tax credit. The flow-through method requires that the tax credit reduce income taxes in the year the credit is taken for tax purposes. The cost reduction, or deferral, method requires that the credit be allocated over the life of the asset and used to reduce income taxes over the life of the asset; the tax effect of the investment tax credit is postponed to future periods.

The Internal Revenue Code treats the credit as a direct reduction of taxes payable for the year in which the credit arises. The Tax Reform Act of 1986 repealed the investment tax credit.

See also Income taxes.

REFERENCE
Hoffman, William H., ed., *Corporations, Partnerships, Estates, and Trusts* (West Publishing Co., St. Paul, MN, 1986).

I

INVESTMENTS

Investments include temporary and long-term investments in equity securities and bonds. Other investments include real estate investments, special purpose funds, interests in life insurance contracts, advances to subsidiaries that are of a permanent nature, deposits made to guarantee contract performance, and equity interests in partnerships, trusts, and estates.

A temporary investment in equity securities or bonds is a security that is readily marketable and one which management intends to convert into cash within the current operating cycle or a year, whichever is longer. All other investments in equity securities and bonds are long-term or permanent investments. Temporary investments are usually classified as current assets in the balance sheet. Long-term investments are classified in the investment category, which usually follows the current asset section on the statement. Long-term investments are usually acquired for income, growth potential, safety of capital, or to obtain control over another company.

The method of accounting for long-term investments in equity securities generally depends upon the extent of ownership held by one corporation in the common stock of another. The equity, or cost, method of accounting is used for investments in excess of 50 percent equity interest, and consolidated financial statements are normally prepared. For external reporting purposes, the investment account must reflect the equity method for all subsidiaries that are not consolidated. Investments involving ownership interest of from 20 to 50 percent are usually accounted for by the equity method of accounting, unless evidence exists of an inability of the investor to exercise significant influence over the investee. Investments of less than 20 percent in marketable equity securities are usually accounted for at the lower of cost or market. In this case, the securities portfolio is presented at the lower of its aggregated cost or market value. When the lower of cost or market method is used, the current portfolio is accounted for separately from the noncurrent portfolio. Short-term marketable debt securities are generally accounted for at cost. Long-term debt securities are usually accounted for at cost adjusted for any discount or premium amortization.

When the cost method of accounting is used, investments are maintained in the records at acquisition cost; cash dividends received from the investee are accounted for as investment income. When the equity method is used, the investment is originally recorded at cost and subsequently adjusted by the investor's proportionate share of the investee's earnings/losses and dividend payments. Income earned by the investee increases the investment account while losses and dividends decrease the account.

See also Equity method of accounting; Cost method; Lower of cost or market; Consolidated financial statements; Joint venture.

REFERENCE

Seidler, Lee, and Carmichael, D. R., eds. *Accountants' Handbook* (John Wiley & Sons, N.Y., 1981).

JOINT PRODUCTS AND BY-PRODUCTS
Joint costs are costs of simultaneously producing or acquiring two or more products (joint products) that are produced or acquired together. Joint products resulting from the single-production process usually require further processing. Typically, none of the joint products have a relative value of such a size that it can be designated a major product. To illustrate the allocation problem associated with joint products, assume that the joint cost of producing Product A and Product B in a common manufacturing process is $90,000 (the joint costs up to the split-off point). It is now necessary to determine the inventory value of Products A and B. The relative sales value method of allocating the $90,000 to Products A and B is widely used. Assume that the 20,000 units of Product A have a sales value of $100,000 and Product B a sales value of $200,000. The $90,000 would be allocated to Products A and B in the amounts of $30,000 (one-third) and $60,000 (two-thirds), respectively. This can be illustrated as follows:

Joint cost, $90,000

Product A, $30,000

Product B, $60,000

Split-off point

J

Joint costs are sometimes allocated on a physical measure basis. Under this method, total joint costs are allocated to the joint products on the basis of some unit of product output, such as units, pounds, tons, or square feet.

By-products are those products emerging at the split-off point that have minor sales value as compared with those of the major products. In many operations, by-products are the same as scrap. By-products frequently are not allocated to any of the total joint costs incurred in the process. If additional costs are incurred after the split-off to process further the by-products, these costs are usually assigned to the by-product.

See also Allocation; Cost accounting.

JOINT VENTURE
A joint venture is an association of two or more individuals or businesses established for a special purpose. Joint ventures are sometimes used for developing real estate tracts, exploring for natural resources, underwriting and selling an issue of corporate securities, and similar undertakings. They are usually formed to share risks associated with a particular business undertaking, to accumulate capital, and to attract special skills to a project. In recent years, many joint ventures have been incorporated for ease in raising large amounts of capital and to limit liability. Investments in joint ventures are usually accounted for by the equity method of accounting.

See also Equity method of accounting; Partnership.

JOURNAL
A journal is a chronological record of events and transactions. The process of recording events and transactions in a journal is called journalizing. A journal is often referred to as a book

of original entry because events and transactions are typically initially recorded therein using the double-entry system of accounting.

All events and transactions could be recorded in a general journal. A general journal entry consists of the transaction date, the accounts and amounts to be debited and credited, and an explanation of the event or transaction. A typical general journal entry is shown here:

Jan. 15   Cash   500
                 Sales   500
                 Sold merchandise for cash.

In addition to the general journal, special journals are often used to facilitate the recording of a large number of similar transactions. Typical special journals are described here:

Type of special journal	Nature of transactions recorded
Sales journal	Sales of merchandise on credit
Purchases journal	Purchases of merchandise on credit
Cash receipts journal	All receipts of cash from any source
Cash payments journal	All payments of cash for any purpose

The general journal would be used to record any event or transaction that could not be recorded in a special journal. Adjusting, closing, and reversing entries would be recorded in the general journal.

The relationship of a journal to a ledger is shown in Exhibit J-1.

See also Double-entry system; Accounting system; Account; Ledger.

Exhibit J–1

Relationship of General Journal to General Ledger

GENERAL JOURNAL   Page 1

Date		Explanation	Ref.	Debit	Credit
19X1					
Jan.	5	Cash	1101	200,000	
		Common Stock	3110		200,000
		To record the issuance			
		of 1,000 shares of			
		no-par common stock			

Cash   Account No. 1101

Date		Explanation	Ref.	Debit		Date	Explanation	Ref.	Credit
19X1									
Jan.	5		J1	200,000					

Common Stock   Account No. 3110

Date		Explanation	Ref.	Debit		Date		Explanation	Ref.	Credit
						19X1				
						Jan.	5		J1	200,000

L

LEASES

A lease is a contract whereby real or personal property is provided by a lessor/owner to a lessee/renter for a specified period of time in exchange for compensation in the form of rent. Leases are usually entered into by a lessee primarily to acquire the right to use or control an asset.

Lease classifications for financial accounting and reporting purposes can be summarized as to type and accounting method by lessee and lessor:

Type	Lessee	Lessor
Noncapitalized (no sale or purchase of asset assumed)	Operating lease	Operating lease
Capitalized (sale and purchase of asset assumed)	Capital lease	Sales-type lease Direct-financing lease Leveraged lease

The lessee classifies a lease as a capital lease if the lease meets any one of the following criteria:

1. The lease transfers ownership of the property to the lessee by the end of the lease term.

2. The lease contains an option to purchase the leased property at a bargain price.

3. The lease term is equal to or greater than 75 percent of the estimated economic life of the leased property.

4. The present value of rental and other minimum lease payments equals or exceeds 90 percent of the fair value of the leased property less any investment tax credit retained by the lessor.

If none of these criteria is met, the lease is an operating lease.

For the lessor, a lease must meet one of the four criteria specified for the lessee and both of the following criteria:

1. Collectibility of the minimum lease payments is reasonably predictable.

2. No important uncertainties surround the amount of unreimbursable costs yet to be incurred by the lessor under the lease.

If these criteria are not met, the lease is an operating lease.

An operating lease merely requires the recognition of the rental agreement requiring periodic payments for the use of an asset during that period. Rent expense or rent income is recognized on the income statement of the lessee and lessor, respectively. No new assets or liabilities are recorded.

A capital lease is, in substance, the purchase of an asset and the incurrence of a liability. A capital lease transfers substantially all of the ownership privileges, including the benefits and risks of property ownership, and represents in economic substance but not in legal form a purchase or sale of an asset. Such leases should be accounted for by the lessee as the acquisition of an asset and the incurrence of a liability. The lessor accounts for the lease as a sale or as a financing arrangement. A sales-type lease usually results in a manufacturer's or dealer's profit to the lessor and transfers substantially all of the benefits and risks associated with the property to the lessee. In a sales-type lease, the fair value of the leased property is different from its carrying amount. A direct financing lease is a capital lease that does not result in a manufacturer's or dealer's profit or loss to the lessor, but does transfer substantially all ownership benefits and risks to the lessee. This is so because the cost or carrying value of the leased property at the inception of the lease is not materially different from the fair market value of the property. Revenue to the lessor consists of interest revenue from the financing arrangement.

The lessee would record a capital lease involving property having a fair value of $100,000 as follows:

Equipment	100,000	
Liability Under Lease		100,000

When the annual lease payment is made in subsequent periods, each lease payment consists of (1) a reduction of the liability under lease and (2) a financing cost (interest expense). A typical entry assumes the following form:

Interest Expense	xxxxx	
Liability Under Lease	xxxxx	
Cash		xxxxxx

The lessor would record a sales-type lease where the property had a carrying value of $25,000, a sales price of $75,000 (the present value of the minimum lease payments receivable from the lessee), and a gross investment in the lease of $95,000 as follows:

Lease Payments Receivable	95,000	
Cost of Goods Sold	25,000	
Equipment		25,000
Sales		75,000
Unearned Interest Revenue		20,000

The unearned interest revenue is earned during the life of the lease. The profit recognized in this sales-type lease is $50,000

(= $75,000 sales minus the $25,000 cost of goods sold). The lessor would record a direct financing lease where the equipment is valued at $95,000 and minimum lease payments are $110,000 as follows:

Lease Payments Receivable	110,000	
Equipment		95,000
Unearned Interest Revenue		15,000

The unearned interest revenue is amortized to interest revenue over the life of the lease.

A leveraged lease is a three-party lease involving a lessee, a lessor, and a long-term creditor, usually a bank or other financial institution. The long-term creditor provides nonrecourse financing to the lessor. The financing provides the lessor with substantial leverage in the transaction. For example, a contractor might agree to build an office building and lease it to a company. To finance the construction of the building, a bank lends money to the contractor (lessor). The contractor uses a relatively small amount of his own funds. The lessor-owner's return on the investment comes from lease rentals, investment tax credit, and income tax benefit from depreciation on the total cost of the property and interest expense deductions on the debt, and other expenses. The lessor classifies the leveraged lease as a direct financing lease.

A sale-leaseback occurs when an owner sells property and then leases the same property back. The seller-lessee usually has a tax advantage in that the entire lease payment can be deducted, which can include interest and amortization of the cost of land and partially depreciated other real property. The sale-leaseback is often used when financing is a problem. From an accounting point of view, any profit or loss incurred by the seller-lessee from the sale of the asset under a capital lease is deferred and amortized over the lease term or the economic life of the asset. If the lease is an operating lease, any profit or loss on the sale should be deferred and amortized in proportion to the rental payments over the period the asset is used by the lessee.

See also Liabilities; Substance over form.

REFERENCE
Seidler, Lee, and Carmichael, D. R., eds. *Accountants' Handbook* (John Wiley & Sons, N.Y., 1981).

LEDGER

A ledger (or general ledger) is a book or file of ledger accounts which are usually numbered to provide easy access and for cross-referencing purposes. Typical ledger accounts include cash, accounts receivable, inventory, and accounts payable. A list of a firm's general ledger accounts with their corresponding numbers is called a chart of accounts. In an accounting system, events and transactions are initially recorded chronologically in a journal and then are transferred (or posted) to a ledger account. At the end of an accounting period, a trial balance is taken from the general ledger from which financial statements are prepared.

In addition to a general ledger, many firms have subsidiary ledgers which are used to record details of certain general ledger accounts. For example, a company having many credit customers may have an Accounts Receivable account in the general ledger and maintain a subsidiary accounts receivable ledger to record data about individual customers. The Accounts Receivable account in the general ledger is called a control account because its balance should equal the total of the individual account balances in the subsidiary ledger. A subsidiary account is often used to support accounts receivable, accounts payable, inventory, plant assets, capital stock, selling expenses, and general and administrative expenses. A subsidiary ledger could be created for any general ledger account.

The use of subsidiary ledgers and control accounts can reduce substantially the number of general ledger accounts, reduce the probability of errors, improve the probability of locating errors that do occur, and allow for the division of labor where persons can be assigned to the various subsidiary ledgers.

See also Accounting system; Account; Chart of Accounts; Journal; Trial balance.

LEGAL CAPITAL

Many state laws require corporations to maintain a minimum level of stockholders' equity to prohibit the corporation from distributing assets to shareholders to the extent that it would impair this minimum. Legal capital is defined by state law. The par value of shares issued and outstanding of par value stock is often the legal capital. If a corporation issues no-par stock, legal capital may be (1) total consideration paid in for the shares, (2) a minimum amount required by state incorporation laws, or (3) an amount established by the board of directors. Legal capital does not refer to the market value or book value per share.

See also Capital; Capital stock.

LEVERAGE

Leverage is used to explain a firm's ability to use fixed-cost assets or funds to magnify the returns to its owners. Leverage exists whenever a company has fixed costs. There are three types of leverage in financial management: operating, financial, and total leverage. Financial leverage is a financing technique that uses borrowed funds or preferred stock (items involving fixed financial costs) to improve the return on an equity investment. As long as a higher rate of return can be earned on assets than is paid for the capital used to acquire the assets, the rate of return to owners can be increased. This is referred to as positive financial leverage. Financial leverage is used in many business transactions, especially where real estate and financing by bonds or preferred stock instead

342

of common stock are involved. Financial leverage is concerned with the relationship between the firm's earnings before interest and taxes (EBIT) and the earnings available to common stockholders or other owners. Financial leverage is often referred to as "trading on the equity." Operating leverage is based on the relationship between a firm's sales revenue and its earnings before interest and taxes. Operating leverage arises when an enterprise has a relatively large amount of fixed costs in its total costs. Total leverage reflects the impact of operating and financial leverage on the total risk of the firm (the degree of uncertainty associated with the firm's ability to cover its fixed-payment obligations).

Financial leverage arises as a result of fixed financial charges related to the presence of bonds or preferred stock. Such charges do not vary with the firm's earnings before interest and taxes. The effect of financial leverage is that an increase in the firm's earnings before interest and taxes results in a greater than proportional increase in the firm's earnings per share. A decrease in the firm's earnings before interest and taxes results in a more than proportional decrease in the firm's earnings per share. The degree of financial leverage (DFL) can be measured by the following formula:

$$\text{Degree of financial leverage (DFL)} = \frac{\text{Percentage change in earnings per share}}{\text{Percentage change in earnings before interest and taxes}}$$

The degree of financial leverage indicates how large a change in earnings per share will result from a given percentage change in earnings before interest and taxes. Whenever the degree of financial leverage is greater than one, financial leverage exists. The higher this quotient, the larger the degree of financial leverage.

To illustrate the application of financial leverage, assume that an investor is considering the purchase of real estate with a selling price of $100,000. The investment will produce a net income of $15,000 annually. The investor has the option of acquiring the investment for cash or borrowed funds obtainable at the rate of 14 percent interest to leverage the investment. The effect of several leveraged options is illustrated in Exhibit L-1.

Exhibit L–1
Financial Leverage

	Option 1 Cash purchase (100% equity)	Option 2 Leverage 1:1 (50% borrowed; 50% equity)	Option 3 Leverage 4:1 (80% borrowed; 20% equity)
Acquisition price of asset	$100,000	$100,000	$100,000
Equity in investment	100,000	50,000	20,000
Income from investment before interest	15,000	15,000	15,000
Less: Interest on borrowed funds at 14%		(7,000)	(11,200)
Cash return	15,000	8,000	3,800
$\dfrac{\text{Cash return}}{\text{Equity investment}}$	$\dfrac{15,000}{100,000} = 15\%$	$\dfrac{8,000}{50,000} = 16\%$	$\dfrac{3,800}{20,000} = 19\%$

The example illustrates an investment where the financial leverage was positive. When the after-tax cost of borrowing exceeds the cash return that can be earned on the asset, negative financial leverage results. At this point, leverage cannot increase the rate of return to common stock equity.

Since debt financing incurs fixed interest charges, the ratio of debt to equity is considered a measure of financial leverage. This ratio indicates the relationship between the funds on which fixed financial charges must be paid and the total funds invested in the firm. The higher the debt to equity ratio, the higher the financial leverage and the greater the increase of operating profits and losses on earnings per share.

When an investor uses borrowed funds to acquire real estate or any other asset, any increase in property value belongs to the equity investor. The investor's equity increases substantially with only a modest increase in property value. To illustrate this concept, assume that an investor has an option to purchase real estate for $100,000 cash or by using 90 percent financing. The investor holds the property for 10 years and the property increases at 4 percent per year. The percentage increase in equity growth differs dramatically when borrowed funds are used:

	Cash Purchase	90% Financing
Acquisition price	$100,000	$100,000
Equity investment	100,000	10,000
Investment value at end of 10 years	140,000	140,000
Percentage increase in equity growth: Equity growth / Original equity	40%	400%

Operating leverage refers to the extent that fixed costs are utilized in the production process during an operating cycle. Operating leverage can also be used to measure the impact on earnings per share of having different levels of fixed to variable costs in manufacturing products. Earnings before interest and taxes are related to changes in the variable cost to fixed cost relationship. As fixed operating costs are added by the firm, the potential operating profits and losses are magnified, and are ultimately reflected in the variation in earnings per share of stock. For example, a book publisher's cost of producing another book is below the average cost of producing the book; hence, the gross margin (sales less cost of goods sold) per book is relatively large. An enterprise with a large percentage increase in income relative to its increase in unit sales can expect to have large operating leverage. The degree of operating leverage (DOP) can be measured by the following formula:

Degree of operating leverage $=$ Percentage change in earnings before
(DOP) $\dfrac{\text{interest and taxes}}{\text{Percentage change in sales}}$

The degree of operating leverage indicates how large a change in operating profit will result from a given percentage change in sales. As long as the degree of operating leverage is greater than one, there is positive operating leverage.

The degree of total or combined leverage (DTL) is computed as follows:

Degree of total leverage $=$ $\dfrac{\text{Percentage change in earnings per share}}{\text{Percentage change in sales}}$
(DTL)

Whenever the percentage change in earnings per share resulting from a given percentage change in sales exceeds the percentage change in sales, total leverage is positive. The total or combined leverage for a company equals the *product* of the operating and financial leverages (DTL = DOL × DFL). Total leverage indicates a firm's ability to use both operating and financial fixed costs to magnify the effect of changes in sales on a firm's earnings per share.

Exhibit L-2 illustrates the application of leverages to a firm's income statement. In this illustration, note that fixed expenses and interest expense remain unchanged. Note the section of the statement involved in the computation of operating leverage, financial leverage, and total leverage. Also note that what provides the leverage is fixed expenses and interest expenses which remain unchanged. When operating, financial, and total leverages increase, the risks the firm assumes also increase since the total risk of the firm is related to the firm's ability to cover fixed operating and financial costs. In the illustration, note that the total or combined leverage of 2.0 is the result of multiplying 1.2 (DOL) by 1.67 (DFL). For this illustration, if sales increase by 1 percent, EBIT will increase by 1.2 percent. If EBIT increases by 10 percent, net income will increase by

16.7 percent. With total leverage of 2.0, to increase net income by 10 percent, sales must increase by 5 percent. Leverage analysis is an extension of break-even analysis and uses the same basic information: price, quantity, variable expenses, and fixed expenses.

Exhibit L–2
Financial, Operating, and Total Leverage

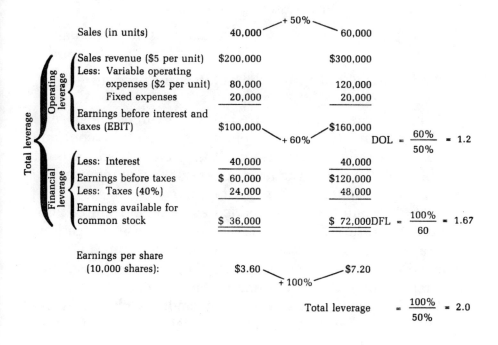

See also Break-even analysis; Financial statement analysis.

REFERENCES
Brigham, Eugene F., and Gapenski, Louis C., *Financial Management* (The Dryden Press, Chicago, 1985).
Pringle, John J., and Harris, Robert S., *Essentials of Managerial Finance* (Scott, Foresman and Company, Glenview, IL, 1984).

LIABILITIES

Liabilities are probable future sacrifices of economic benefits arising from present obligations of a particular entity to transfer assets or provide services to other entities in the future as a result of past transactions or events. This definition makes a distinction between owners' equity and liabilities and emphasizes economic obligation rather than legal debt. Three essential characteristics of an accounting liability are:

1. A duty or obligation to pay exists.

2. The duty is virtually unavoidable by a particular entity.

3. The event obligating the enterprise has occurred.

Liabilities are usually incurred to acquire funds, goods, and services required to operate an enterprise. Liabilities continue as liabilities of the enterprise until they are settled, or until another event or circumstance discharges them or removes the enterprise's responsibility to settle them.

Liabilities are usually classified as either current or noncurrent liabilities. Current liabilities are those obligations whose liquidation is reasonably expected to require the use of existing resources properly classified as current assets, or the creation of other current liabilities. This definition of current liabilities emphasizes a short-term creditors' claim to working capital rather than to the due date for classification purposes. Accounts payable, dividends payable, salaries payable, and taxes payable are examples of current liabilities. Liabilities which are not current liabilities are referred to as noncurrent or long-term liabilities. Bonds payable and mortgages payable are examples of long-term liabilities.

Liabilities are usually measured at historical proceeds, which is the amount of cash, or its equivalent, received when the obligation was incurred. Some liabilities are reported at current market value, such as those involving marketable commodities and securities including the obligations of writers of options or common shares who do not own the underlying commodities or securities. Other liabilities are recorded at their net settlement value, such as those arising from warranty obligations. Net settlement value is the nondiscounted amounts of cash, or its equivalent, expected to be paid to liquidate an obligation, including direct costs to make that payment. In other cases, the discounted value of future cash flows is used to record the amount of a liability. Long-term payables are often reported at their present value.

Contractual liabilities arise from events which are either expressly or implicitly contractual in nature. Some obligations are imposed on business enterprises by government or courts (such as taxes and fines), while others relate to nonreciprocal transfers from a business enterprise to owners or others (such as cash dividends and donations). A constructive liability is one which is implied from an arrangement, such as vacation pay and bonuses. Equitable obligations are neither contractual nor constructive obligations, but obligations arising from fairness, ethical and moral principles, or equity. An example of an ethical obligation is the responsibility of a monopoly supplier to deliver goods or services to dependent customers. Equitable liabilities are not currently recognized in financial statements. Contingent liabilities arise from an existing situation, or set of circumstances involving uncertainty as to possible gain or loss to an enterprise, that will ultimately be resolved when one or more future events will occur or fail to occur. Only contingent losses are recognized. A contingent liability is accrued if (1) it is probable that a liability has occurred, or an asset has been impaired and (2) it can be reliably measured. Examples of contingent liabilities include product warranties and pending litigation.

Deferred liabilities are often found on financial statements. Deferred credits include (1) prepaid or unearned revenue involving a contractual obligation to provide a future good or service, such as for rent or interest received in advance, and (2) obligations arising from accounting principles which defer income recognition of the item, such as investment tax credits and deferred tax credits. The second type of deferred liabilities imposes no duty on the firm to transfer assets in the future. Such items arise from past transactions and are currently deferred from the income statement.

Accounting liabilities can also be classified as follows:

1. Obligations with fixed payment dates and amounts (notes payable, bonds payable, and interest payable).

2. Obligations with fixed payment amounts but estimated payment dates (accounts payable, salaries payable, taxes payable).

3. Obligations for which both timing and amount of payment must be estimated (warranties and bonuses).

4. Obligations arising from advances from customers on unexecuted contracts and agreements (rental and subscription fees received in advance).

Obligations under mutually unexecuted contracts (executory contracts) such as those arising from purchase and employment commitments are usually not recognized as accounting liabilities. Certain contingent obligations which do not meet the two requirements listed earlier for contingent liabilities are not recognized as accounting liabilities (loan guarantees).

See also Current liabilities; Contingencies; Deferred charges (credits); Recognition; Measurement; Income taxes; Elements of financial statements; Payroll taxes; Property taxes; Off-balance sheet items.

REFERENCES
SFAC No. 3, Elements of Financial Statements of Business Enterprises (FASB, 1981).
SFAC No. 5, Recognition and Measurement in Financial Statements of Business Enterprises (FASB, 1984).

LIQUIDATION

Liquidation is one relief procedure available to an insolvent debtor. Liquidation has as its basic purpose the realization of assets and the liquidation of liabilities rather than the continuation of the business as in a reorganization. Insolvency refers to the inability of a debtor to pay its obligations as they come due. Chapter 7, Bankruptcy Reform Act of 1979, outlines the procedures for corporate liquidation. Chapter 7 is the basic liquidation procedure and is sometimes referred to as ordinary bankruptcy. Chapter 7 is available to most debtors other than a government unit, bank, insurance company, or railroad.

Liquidation can be started by a voluntary petition (debtor initiates the petition) or involuntary petition (creditors initiate the petition). In a liquidation, an interim trustee is appointed. Unsecured creditors have a right to elect a permanent trustee. In most cases, the interim trustee becomes the permanent trustee. The trustee liquidates the debtor's non-exempt property as soon as possible "with the best interests of parties in interest." The trustee proceeds to distribute the available proceeds to the debtor's creditors according to priorities assigned in Chapter 7. After the property of the debtor has been converted into cash and a proper distribution has been made to creditors and others, the debtor receives a discharge. The court will grant the debtor a discharge unless certain conditions are present. Nonindividuals do not receive a discharge in a Chapter 7 case. Nonindividual debtors normally file a voluntary Chapter 7 petition to provide for an orderly liquidation of their assets and distribution of proceeds to their creditors.

The term *liquidation* is sometimes used to refer to a situation where a business such as a partnership liquidates, winds up, or settles the affairs of the partnership, with the partnership terminating when the liquidation has been completed. In partnership liquidations, partnership assets are realized, liabilities paid, and distributions of cash, if any, are made to the partners.

Liquidation is sometimes used to refer to the settlement of

L

liabilities while realization refers to the process of converting noncash assets into cash.

See also Reorganization; Bankruptcy; Solvency and insolvency; Partnership.

REFERENCE
Ginsberg, Robert E., *Bankruptcy* (Prentice-Hall, Englewood Cliffs, NJ, 1985).

LIQUIDITY

Liquidity describes the amount of time required to convert an asset into cash or pay a liability. For noncurrent assets, liquidity generally refers to marketability. Cash is a highly liquid asset. Property, plant, and equipment would ordinarily be very non-liquid assets. Liquidity is important in evaluating the timing of cash inflows and outflows. The liquidity of an enterprise is a major indicator of its ability to meet its debts when they mature.

Liquidity ratios are often used to measure a firm's liquidity. These ratios typically relate to the enterprise's working capital—its current assets and current liabilities. Current assets include cash, short-term marketable securities, receivables, inventories, and prepaid items. Current liabilities include such items as accounts payable, taxes, interest payable, and other such short-term payables. Major liquidity ratios include the current ratio and acid-test ratio computed as follows:

$$\text{Current ratio} = \frac{\text{Current assets}}{\text{Current liabilities}}$$

$$\text{Acid-test ratio} = \frac{\text{Quick assets}}{\text{Current liabilities}}$$

Quick assets include cash, short-term marketable securities, and accounts receivable. Inventories are excluded because there may be some delay in converting them into cash. Prepaid expenses are excluded because they cannot be converted into cash. The acid-test ratio is a more severe test of a company's short-term ability to pay its debts than is the current ratio.

See also Ratios; Financial statement analysis.

LOSSES

Losses are decreases in equity (net assets) from peripheral or incidental transactions of an entity and from other transactions and other events and circumstances affecting the entity during a period except those that result from expenses or distributions to owners. Losses can arise from such transactions and events as the sale of investments in marketable securities and from the disposition of used equipment. Losses can be classified as "operating" or "nonoperating," depending on their relation to the enterprise's major ongoing or central operations.

See also Expenses; Elements of financial statements; Interim financial reports; Extraordinary item.

REFERENCE
SFAC No. 1, Elements of Financial Statements of Business Enterprises (FASB, 1981).

LOWER OF COST OR MARKET

Inventory and equity marketable securities are frequently valued in the financial statements at lower of cost or market. In applying the lower-of-cost-or-market method, the cost of the ending inventory, or portfolio of marketable equity securities, is determined by an appropriate method, and is compared with market value at the end of the period. If market value is less than cost, an adjusting entry is made to record the loss and restate the inventory or securities. For inventory applications, market in "lower cost or market" is interpreted as replacement cost with upper and lower limits that cannot be exceeded. For example, market or replacement cost should not exceed the net realizable value (i.e., estimated selling price in the ordinary course of business less reasonably predictable costs of completion and disposal); and market should not be less than net realizable value reduced by an allowance for an approximately normal profit margin.

The lower-of-cost-or-market method can be applied to each inventory item, to the major classes or categories of inventory items, or to the inventory as a whole. The entry on Inventory in this book shows the computations involved when the lower-of-cost-or-market inventory method is used.

When applied to marketable equity securities, the lower-of-cost-or-market method is applied separately to short-term and long-term portfolios of securities. Losses in market value related to the short-term portfolio are reported as part of income from continuing operations for the period. Losses in market value related to the long-term portfolio are reflected directly in the shareholders' equity section of the balance sheet in an owners' equity contra account.

The lower-of-cost-or-market method is a conservative accounting method that avoids valuing inventory or marketable equity securities on the balance sheet at more than replacement cost. The method is somewhat inconsistent in that market decreases are recognized, while market increases are not recognized. However, most accountants prefer to reflect the loss in the utility of an asset in the period the impairment is first recognized and can be estimated while gains should be recognized only when realized.

See also Inventory; Investments.

MANAGEMENT ADVISORY SERVICES

Management advisory services, or simply advisory services, consist of advice and assistance on organization, personnel, planning, operations, controls, etc., provided by accountants to clients. Such services provide advice and technical assistance to help clients improve their operations. Accountants must adhere to general professional standards when providing such services associated with forecasts, such as professional competence, due care, planning and supervision, and sufficient relevant data. Technical standards are established for management advisory service engagements. For example, for an audit client a practitioner shall not assume the role of management or any role that might impair objectivity. Responsibilities for management advisory services are now found primarily in AICPA Statements for Management Advisory Services (SSMAS), which became effective in 1982.

See Audit; Financial planning.

MATCHING PRINCIPLE

The matching principle is an accounting principle that requires that revenues generated and expenses incurred in earning those revenues be reported in the same income statement. In other words, total expenses involved in obtaining the revenues of a period should be computed and matched against the revenues recorded in the period. In this way, sacrifices (expenses) are matched against benefits or accomplishments (revenues). Revenues are recognized according to the realization principle. Expenses are determined in accordance with the matching principle.

General guidelines associated with applying the matching principle include the following:

1. Associating cause and effect.

2. Systematic and rational allocation.

3. Immediate recognition.

These guidelines are discussed under the topic "Expense."

See also Expense; Revenue; Accounting principles; Accounting assumptions; Accounting basis; Recognition; Realization.

MATERIALITY

Materiality refers to the magnitude or significance of something that would be of interest to an informed investor or creditor in making evaluations and decisions. Materiality implies significance, substance, importance, and consequence. Although materiality is primarily quantitative in nature, it is not exclusively so. Magnitude alone, without considering the nature of the item and the circumstances surrounding the decision being made, generally is not a sufficient basis for making a materiality decision. An item is material for accounting purposes if the omission or misstatement of it, in light of surrounding circumstances, makes it probable that the judgment of a reasonable person relying on the information would have been changed or influenced by the omission or misstatements. Factors which can assist in determining whether an item is material or not include:

1. The circumstances surrounding an item and its characteristics, such as the economic substance of an item versus its legal form, whether the item is unusual or infrequent, whether it is the result of voluntary or involuntary actions by management, whether it is for a temporary or permanent condition, and the sensitivity of the situation to the firm and to its investors and creditors.

2. The magnitude and financial effect of the item, i.e., the absolute magnitude, its effect on net income, or its relation to the trend of an enterprise's earnings or year-to-year change in earnings.

3. The cumulative financial effect of the item or situation, e.g., the error on one inventory card may not be material whereas the cumulative effect of all such errors could be material.

Materiality judgments are concerned with levels or thresholds. Immaterial items which have little or no consequences to statement users can be handled as expediency, fairness, and professional judgment require. The Financial Accounting Board decided not to establish materiality rules in Statement of Financial Accounting Concepts No. 2, but rather left the decision on materiality up to the judgment of those who have all of the facts. The FASB stated that "no general standards of materiality could be formulated to take into account all the considerations that enter into an experienced human judgment," and that when the Board imposes materiality rules, it is "substituting generalized collective judgments for specific individual judgment, and there is no reason to believe that collective judgements are always superior." The FASB did qualify the above by stating that

M

materiality rules may be written into some standards, which, in fact, has been done.

See also Qualitative characteristics of accounting information; Accounting assumptions; Materiality; Accounting principles; Accounting principles overload.

REFERENCE
SSFAC No. 2, Qualitative Characteristics of Accounting Information (FASB, 1981).

MEASUREMENT

Measurement is the assignment of numbers to objects, events, or situations in accord with some rule or guideline. The property of the objects, events, or situations which determines the assignment of numbers is called the measurable attribute (or magnitude). The number assigned is called its measure (the amount of its magnitude). The rule or guideline defines both the magnitude and the measure.

In accounting, assets and liabilities currently reported in financial statements are measured by different attributes, depending on the nature of the item and the relevance and reliability of the attribute measured. Five different attributes of assets and liabilities are used in present accounting practice:

1. The historical cost of an asset is the amount of cash or its equivalent paid to acquire it. Historical cost for a liability is the historical proceeds received when the liability is incurred.

2. Current cost of an asset is the amount of cash or other consideration that would be required today to obtain the same asset or its equivalent. For liabilities, current proceeds is the amount that would be received today if the same obligation were incurred.

3. Current exit value is the amount of cash or its equivalent that would be received currently if an asset were sold under conditions of orderly liquidation. For liabilities, current exit value is the amount of cash that would have to be paid currently to eliminate the liability.

4. Expected exit value is the nondiscounted cash flows associated with the expected sale or conversion of an asset at some future date. For liabilities, expected exit value is the amount of cash expected to be paid to settle the liability in the due course of business.

5. Present value of expected cash flows is the cash flows associated with the expected sale or conversion of an asset at some future date discounted at an appropriate rate of interest. For liabilities, present value of expected cash flows is the discounted amount of cash expected to be paid to settle the liability in the due course of business.

Historical cost (or historical exchange price) method underlies the conventional accounting system. Inventories, property, plant, and equipment are often recorded at historical or acquisition cost. Current cost is also used in measuring inventories. Current exit value is usually used for marketable equity securities. Expected exit value is often used for accounts receivable and accounts payable. Present value of expected cash flows is frequently used for long-term receivables and payables.

The monetary unit of measurement used in current practice is nominal units of money, unadjusted for changes in purchasing power of money over time.

See also Statement of financial position; Current value accounting; Cost principle; Asset/liability and revenue/expense assumption; Asset; Liability.

REFERENCES
SFAC No. 5, Recognition and Measurement in Financial Statements of Business Enterprises (FASB, 1984).
Staubus, George J., "An Induced Theory of Accounting Measurement" (*The Accounting Review*, Vol. LX, no. 1, January 1985).

MONETARY ASSETS AND LIABILITIES.

Monetary assets and liabilities are items whose balances are fixed in terms of number of dollars regardless of changes in the general price level. All other items not representing a right to receive or an obligation to pay a fixed sum are nonmonetary items. Monetary items include cash, receivables, certain marketable securities, accounts payable, and bonds payable. In periods of inflation (periods of rising prices), persons holding monetary assets tend to lose purchasing power, while persons holding monetary liabilities tend to gain purchasing power.

See also Constant dollar accounting; Foreign operations and exchanges.

MONEY MARKET

Money markets refer to financial markets in which short-term debt instruments such as Treasury bills, commercial paper, and certificates of deposit are traded. Money market certificates are a special type of certificate of deposit issued by banks, savings and loans, mutual savings banks, and credit unions. Money market funds are portfolios of liquid short-term securities in which shares or interests can be acquired. They usually operate like a passbook savings account or a checking account. Investors usually receive interest at rates higher than the federally restricted rates paid by banks, savings and loans, mutual savings banks, and credit unions.

See also Financial markets.

MORTGAGE

A mortgage is a contract in which a lender (mortgagee) obtains legal title or a lien on the property of the borrower (the mortgagor) with the stipulation that the title reverts to the borrower when the loan is repaid. The property serves as security for the loan. If the mortgagor defaults on the principal or interest payments, the mortgagee can usually foreclose and force a sale of the property for his benefit. The mortgagee receives the proceeds from the sale to the extent required to satisfy his loan. If the proceeds are not sufficient to satisfy the loan, the mortgagee becomes an unsecured creditor of the borrower for the balance.

See also Bonds; Liabilities.

N

NATURAL RESOURCES

Natural resources (or wasting assets) are those economic resources that are exhausted as the physical units representing these resources are removed, processed, and sold. Natural resources include oil and gas reserves, timber, coal, sulphur, iron, copper, and silver ore. Natural resources are also considered long-term inventories acquired for resale or use in production over a period of years.

Natural resources are initially recorded in the accounts at their acquisition cost. The periodic allocation of the cost of a natural resource to the income statement is called depletion. Depletion reflects the physical exhaustion of a natural resource. Depreciation reflects the exhaustion of the service potential of a tangible fixed asset, such as property plant and equipment.

The cost of a natural resource minus any residual value is systematically depleted as the natural resource is transformed into inventory. The depletion charge is usually computed by the unit-of-production method as follows:

Step 1. Compute the depletion charge per unit:

$$\frac{\text{Cost—Salvage value of the natural resource}}{\text{Estimated number of units in the natural resource}}$$

Step 2. Compute the depletion charge for the period:

Unit depletion charge × Number of units converted during the period

The Internal Revenue Code authorizes the use of percentage depletion for income tax purposes. According to the Code, a percentage of gross income from the property is charged against operations in arriving at taxable income. Percentage depletion is a function of gross income rather than of production. Percentage depletion is allowable even after the cost of the asset has been fully recovered.

See also Successful effort accounting; Depreciation; Amortization; Allocation.

REFERENCE
Touche Ross & Co., *Oil and Gas Accounting: What Producers Must Know* (Touche Ross & Co., N.Y., 1980).

NET ASSETS
Net assets of an enterprise is the excess of total assets over total liabilities as reported on the balance sheet. Net assets also equals owners' equity. Equity is defined as the residual interest in the assets of an entity that remains after deducting its liabilities. In a business enterprise, the equity is the ownership interest. The relationship between net assets and ownership interest can be illustrated as follows:

Assets – Liabilities = Net assets
Assets – Liabilities = Equity (or ownership interest)
Therefore,
Net assets = Equity (or ownership interest)

See also Accounting equation; Stockholders' equity; Capital.

NET OPERATING LOSS DEDUCTION

The net operating loss deduction is a deduction allowed for income tax purposes that enables taxpayers who incur a loss in a bad year relief from taxes paid in the three years immediately preceding and/or the seven years following the loss year. The taxpayer receives refunds for income taxes paid in those years. The tax effect of a loss carryback is measurable and currently realizable by means of a refund. It is correct to recognize such refunds in the loss period. The realization of the tax benefits from loss carryforwards is usually less certain, and should only be recognized in the loss period when realization is assured beyond reasonable doubt. If the realization of such benefits occurs in a later period, the benefit is shown as an extraordinary item on the income statement.

See also Income taxes.

REFERENCE
Hoffman, William H., ed. *Corporations, Partnerships, Estates, and Trusts* (West, St. Paul, MN, 1986).

NONMONETARY EXCHANGES

A nonmometary exchange is a reciprocal transfer between an enterprise and another entity in which the enterprise acquires nonmonetary assets by surrendering nonmonetary assets. Nonmonetary exchanges can also include services and liabilities. Monetary assets are fixed in terms of dollars and are usually contractual claims to a fixed amount of money. All other assets are nonmonetary. Nonmonetary assets include inventory, property, plant, and equipment. The cost of a nonmonetary asset acquired in a nonmonetary exchange is the fair value of the asset surrendered to obtain it, and a gain or loss should be recognized on the exchange. The gain or loss is computed by comparing the fair value of the asset surrendered to its book value. If a small amount of monetary consideration (referred to as boot) is given or received, the cost of the asset acquired can be computed as follows:

Cost = Fair value of asset surrendered + Boot given or – Boot received

When the nonmonetary exchange involves similar productive assets, the general rule stated above for recognizing gains and losses is modified. Similar productive assets are ones that are of the same general type, that perform the same function, or that are employed in the same line of business, such as a delivery truck for another delivery truck. When similar productive assets are exchanged, the exchange is not essentially the culmination of the earning process—the earnings expected from the original asset have not been completely realized but will be continued by the acquired asset. When similar productive assets are exchanged, the assets acquired are recorded at the book value of the asset surrendered, unless boot is involved in the exchange. The payor of the boot recognizes no gain on the exchange (losses are always recognized). The recipient of the boot recognizes gain on the exchange to the extent that the boot exceeds a proportionate share of the book value of the asset surrendered (losses are always recognized). Because boot has been received, the earning process is considered to have been completed to that extent and some gain can be recognized. When boot is received or paid, the book value of the similar productive asset acquired can be computed as follows:

Payor of boot:
  Cost = Lower of book or fair value of asset surrendered – Boot paid

Recipient of the boot:
  Cost = Lower of book or fair value of asset surrendered – Boot
      received + Gain recognized

See also Cost principle; Property, plant, and equipment.

NONPROFIT ENTERPRISES

Nonbusiness enterprise or organization is a term often used to refer to governmental units as well as to all other nonprofit organizations. The major distinguishing characteristics of nonbusiness organizations, according to the Financial Accounting Standards Board, include:

1. Receipts of significant amounts of resources from resource providers who do not expect to receive either repayment or economic benefits proportionate to resources provided.

2. Operating purposes that are other than to provide goods or services at a profit or profit equivalent.

3. Absence of defined ownership interests that can be sold, transferred, or redeemed, or that convey entitlement to a share of a residual distribution of resources in the event of liquidation of the organization.

Nonbusiness organizations include most human service organizations, churches, foundations, and private nonprofit hospitals and schools that receive a significant portion of their financial resources from sources other than the sale of goods and services. Nonprofit organizations can be distinguished by a difference in the source of their financial resources. One type includes organizations whose financial resources are obtained primarily from revenues from the sale of goods and services. Another type obtains a significant amount of its resources from sources other than from the sale of goods and services, e.g., grants, donations.

Major users of financial statements of nonbusiness organizations include resource providers, constituents, governing and oversight bodies, and managers. The types of information required by users of financial statements of nonbusiness organizations include:

1. Information useful in making resource allocation decisions.

2. Information useful in assessing services and ability to provide services.

3. Information useful in assessing management stewardship and performance, including information about service efforts and accomplishments.

4. Information about economic resources, obligations, net resources, and changes in these elements.

5. Information about the liquidity and solvency of the entity.

6. Managers' explanations and interpretations.

Generally accepted accounting principles (GAAP) applicable to most nonbusiness organizations are reflected in the AICPA's Statement of Position 78-10, Accounting Principles and Reporting Practices for Certain Nonprofit Organizations. Refer to entry Generally Accepted Accounting Principles for guidance on GAAP for colleges and universities, hospitals, voluntary health and welfare organizations, and governments.

See also Objectives of financial reporting by nonbusiness organizations; Governmental accounting; Generally accepted accounting principles; Fiduciary.

REFERENCE
SFAC No. 4, Objectives of Financial Reporting by Nonbusiness Organizations (FASB, 1981).

NOTES RECEIVABLE
A negotiable promissory note is an unconditional promise in writing made by one person to another engaging to pay on demand or at a fixed or determinable future time a sum of money to order or to bearer. Negotiability of the note makes the instrument readily transferable and increases its usefulness since the seller can discount it or use it as collateral for a loan.

The person promising to pay is the maker of the note; the person to be paid is the payee. Promissory notes may be either interest- or noninterest-bearing.

If a note is not paid at maturity, it is said to have been dishonored. If the payee of a note sells it prior to maturity, the transaction is referred to as discounting a note. The note can be discounted either "with recourse" or "without recourse." When a note is discounted "with recourse," the payee is contingently liable for the payment of the note if it is dishonored at maturity by the maker. To illustrate the discounting of a note receivable, assume that a $1,000, 90-day, 4 percent note dated September 3 is discounted at a bank on October 3 (60 days from maturity). The bank discount rate is 8 percent. The cash proceeds from the discounting is computed as follows:

1. Compute the maturity value of the note:
   $1,000 × 0.04 × 90/360 = $10 interest plus $1,000 face value = $1,010

2. Calculate the discount charged by the note buyer on the maturity value of the note for the number of days from the date of discount to the date of maturity:
   $1,010 × 0.08 × 60/360 = $13.47

3. Calculate the proceeds that the company receives from the discounted note:
   $1,010 - $13.47 = $996.53

If a "with recourse" discounted note is dishonored by the maker at maturity, the endorser is required to make good on the note, pay any interest due at maturity, and pay a protest (collection) fee.

See also Receivables.

NOTES TO FINANCIAL STATEMENTS

Notes or footnotes to financial statements are procedures used to present additional information not included in the accounts on the financial statements. Generally accepted accounting principles consider notes to be an integral part of financial statements. Accounting principles require that certain information be disclosed in notes, such as narrative discussion, additional monetary disclosures, and supplementary schedules. One of the notes typically describes the major accounting policies used in preparing the financial statements (for example, inventory cost-flow assumptions, depreciation method). The notes to financial statements are usually factual rather than interpretative.

See also Financial Statements; Accounting policies; Financial statement analysis.

OBJECTIVES OF FINANCIAL REPORTING

FASB Concepts Statement No. 1, Objectives of Financial Reporting by Business Enterprises, describes the broad purpose of financial reporting, including financial statements. The objectives in Statement No. 1 apply to general purpose external financial reporting and are directed toward the common interests of many users. The objectives arise primarily from the needs of external users who lack the authority to obtain the information they want and must rely on information management communicates to them. According to Statement No. 1, financial reporting should provide:

Information that is useful to present and potential investors and creditors and other users in making rational investment, credit, and similar decisions.

Information to help investors, creditors, and others assess the amounts, timing, and uncertainty of prospective net cash inflows to the related enterprise because their prospects for receiving cash from investments, from loans to, or from other participation in the enterprise depend significantly on its cash flow prospects.

Information about the economic resources of an enterprise, the claims to those resources (obligations of the enterprise to transfer resources to other entities and owners' equity), and the effects of transactions, events, and circumstances that change resources and claims to those resources.

Concepts Statement No. 1 also gives specific guidance about the kinds of information the financial reporting should provide:

Information about an enterprise's economic resources, obligations, and owners' equity.

Information about an enterprise's performance provided by measures of earnings and comprehensive income and their components measured by accrual accounting.

Information about how an enterprise obtains and spends cash, about its borrowing and repayment of borrowing, about its capital (equity) transactions, including cash dividends and other distributions of enterprise resources to owners, and about other factors that may affect an enterprise's liquidity or solvency.

Information about how management of an enterprise has discharged its stewardship responsibility to owners (stockholders) for the use of enterprise resources entrusted to it.

Statement No. 1 emphasizes that earnings information is the primary focus of financial reporting. According to this statement, earnings should be measured with accrual accounting. This requires that the financial effects of economic transactions, events, and circumstances should be reported in the period when they occur instead of when cash is incoming.

The statement indicates that management is responsible for the custody and use of the entity's resources and that financial reporting should provide information concerning that stewardship function. Financial reporting also requires that reports should include management's explanations and interpretations that would be of benefit to external users in addition to quantitative information.

See also Conceptual framework of accounting; Financial Accounting Standards Board; Financial reporting; Financial accounting.

REFERENCE
SFAC No. 1, Objectives of Financial Reporting by Business Enterprises (FASB, 1978).

OBJECTIVES OF FINANCIAL REPORTING BY NONBUSINESS ORGANIZATIONS

FASB Statement of Financial Accounting No. 4, Objectives of Financial Reporting by Nonbusiness Organizations, establishes the following broad objectives of financial reporting by nonbusiness organizations:

Financial reporting by nonbusiness organizations should provide information that is useful to present and potential resource providers and other users in making rational decisions about the allocation of resources to those organizations.

Financial reporting should provide information to help present and potential resource providers and other users in assessing the services that a nonbusiness organization provides and its ability to continue to provide those services.

Financial reporting should provide information that is useful to present and potential resource providers and other users in assessing how managers of a nonbusiness organization have discharged their stewardship responsibilities and about other aspects of their performance.

O

Financial reporting should provide information about the economic resources, obligations, and net resources of an organization, and the effects of transactions, events, and circumstances that change resources and interests in those resources.

Financial reporting should provide information about the performance of an organization during a period. Periodic measurement of the changes in the amount and nature of the net resources of a nonbusiness organization and information about the service efforts and accomplishments of an organization together represent the information most useful in assessing its performance.

Financial reporting should provide information about how an organization obtains and spends cash or other liquid resources, about its borrowing and repayment of borrowing, and about other factors that may affect an organization's liquidity.

Financial reporting should include explanations and interpretations to help users understand financial information provided.

The objectives arise from the common interests of those who provide resources to nonbusiness organizations, in the services those organizations provide, and their continuing ability to provide services. The objectives apply to general purpose external financial reporting.

See also Nonprofit enterprise; Conceptual framework of accounting.

REFERENCE
SFAC No. 4, Objectives of Financial Reporting by Nonbusiness Organizations (FASB, 1981).

OBJECTIVITY
Objectivity, or verifiability, is the ability to perform an accounting function without bias. The measurement that results from

an objective application of accounting principles and methods should be capable of duplication by another person. In auditing, objectivity refers to an auditor's ability to be impartial in the performance of an audit. Where there is considerable uncertainty in the measurement process, the measurement method that is most objective (least subjective) should usually be followed. For example, the cost of a building arrived at in an arm's-length transaction is usually more objective than an appraisal value by a real estate appraiser.

See also Arm's-length transaction; Accounting assumptions.

OFF-BALANCE SHEET ITEMS

Off-balance sheet items generally refer to the application of procedures that provide financing without adding debt on a balance sheet, thus not affecting financial ratios or borrowing capacity of an enterprise. Accounting for leases by a lessee sometimes enables the lessee to disguise what is in fact a long-term borrowing to finance the purchase of a leased asset as an operating lease, thereby avoiding having to report a long-term liability on the financial statements.

See also Defeasance; Product financing arrangements; Liability; Full disclosure.

OFFSETTING LIABILITIES AGAINST ASSETS

Generally accepted accounting principles do not usually allow the offsetting of a liability against an asset so that only the net amount is reported in the balance sheet. In such cases, disclosure by footnotes or a caption notation is usually required.

If a legal right of offset exists, offsetting is allowed. For example, a company with an overdraft in a bank account at a bank could offset the overdraft against a cash balance in another account at the same bank. Such would not be the case if the bank accounts were at different banks. In rare cases, certain government securities could be purchased which could be used exclusively for paying taxes. Such securities could be offset against tax liabilities. APB Opinion No. 11 requires that the net current and net noncurrent amounts of deferred tax charges and credits be reported, which is in essence an offsetting.

OPERATING CYCLE

The operating cycle of a business is the time between the acquisition of inventory and the conversion of the inventory back into cash. The operating cycle of a business is also referred to as the "cash cycle"and the "earnings cycle." For some industries such as a distillery, the operating cycle may extend 10 years or longer. For a grocer, the operating cycle would be measured in days. The normal operating cycle of a business is crucial in determining whether assets and liabilities are current or noncurrent. For example, current assets include cash and other assets that are expected to be turned into cash, sold, or exchanged within the normal operating cycle of the enterprise or one year, whichever is longer. Current liabilities are liabilities that come due within the normal operating cycle or one year, whichever is longer. Exhibit O-1 illustrates the normal operating cycle of a business.

Exhibit O–1
Normal Operating Cycle of a Business

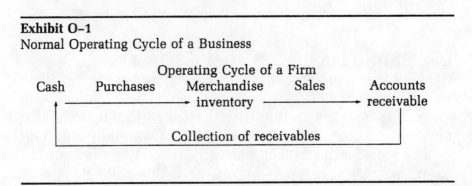

See also Current assets; Current liabilities; Working capital.

OPINION

An audit opinion expresses the auditor's conclusion concerning the financial statements. Audit opinions can be unqualified, qualified, adverse, or a disclaimer (the auditor cannot express an opinion). Reporting standards for auditing require that the auditor comment in a report on whether the financial statements are presented in accordance with generally accepted accounting principles, the accounting principles have been consistently applied from period to period, and the disclosures in the financial statements are reasonably adequate.

If an unqualified opinion is not warranted, the auditor may be required to modify the opinions. Such situations arise because the statements do not conform to generally accepted accounting principles, uncertainties exist concerning a contingency on the statements, limitations have been imposed on the scope of the auditor's examination, accounting principles have not been consistently applied, other auditors have performed a part of the examination, or the auditor wants to explain or emphasize a particular matter. Exhibit A-10 relates the cause of variations in an opinion with the type of opinion.

See also Audit.

REFERENCE
Taylor, Donald H., and Glezen, G. William, *Auditing* (John Wiley & Sons, N.Y., 1982).

ORGANIZATION COSTS

Organization costs are costs related to getting an enterprise started. Organization costs are incurred during the formation of the enterprise and prior to income-producing operations. Expenditures usually classified as organization costs include such items as promoters', attorneys', and accountants' fees, underwriters' commissions, securities registration and listing fees, printing costs, etc. Such costs are ordinarily capitalized as an intangible asset or deferred charge and amortized (written off) over a period of time not to exceed 40 years. Expenditures relating to the organization of the enterprise are assumed to benefit the future and are considered assets in that without them the company could not have been started. In practice, some accountants treat organization costs as a reduction of contributed capital. This treatment is justified on the grounds that organization charges reflect a reduction of the receipts associated with the financing of the corporation.

See also Intangible assets; Corporation.

OTHER COMPREHENSIVE METHODS OF ACCOUNTING
Financial statements prepared in accordance with other comprehensive bases of accounting (OCBOA) are not prepared according to generally accepted accounting principles (GAAP). Four criteria exist for financial statements prepared according to OCBOA:

1. A basis of accounting that the reporting entity uses to comply with the requirements of financial reporting provisions of a government regulatory agency to whose jurisdiction the entity is subject. Examples are a basis of accounting used by railroad companies reporting to the Interstate Commerce Commission and insurance companies reporting to a state insurance company.

2. A basis of accounting that the reporting entity uses or expects to use to file its income tax return for the period covered by the financial statements.

3. The cash receipts and disbursements basis of accounting and modifications of the cash basis having substantial support, such as recording depreciation on fixed assets or accruing income taxes.

4. A definite set of criteria having substantial support that is applied to all material items appearing in

financial statements, such as the price-level basis of accounting.

Accountants generally apply certain guidelines when determining the appropriate basis of accounting where GAAP are not required:

1. Does the additional cost of preparing GAAP exceed the benefits?
2. Do financial statements prepared under OCBOA differ substantially from those prepared according to GAAP?

In such circumstances, the auditor's report should include an explanatory paragraph that

1. states, or preferably refers to the note to the financial statements that states, the basis of presentation of the financial statements on which the auditor is reporting;
2. refers to the note to the financial statements that describes how the basis of presentation differs from GAAP; and
3. states that the financial statements are not intended to be presented in conformity with GAAP.

Cash basis and tax basis statements do not report financial position and results of operations in accordance with GAAP. It is recommended that they not be referred to as "balance sheet" or "income statement" without some modifications. Titles such as "statement of assets and liabilities on a cash basis," "statement of cash revenues received and expenses paid," and "balance sheet—modified cash basis" are often used.

See also Accounting basis; Income tax accounting; Audit; Special reports; Generally accepted accounting principles; Accounting principles.

REFERENCE
AICPA, *AICPA Audit and Accounting Manual* (AICPA).

OWNERS' EQUITY

See Shareholders' equity.

P

PARTNERSHIP

A partnership is an association of two or more individuals as co-owners to carry on a business for profit. Written articles of copartnership are ordinarily used to identify the rights and responsibilities of the partners, the nature and scope of the partnership, and relationships with outside parties. The partnership agreement usually includes descriptions of the following: asset valuation, admission of new partners, withdrawal of partners, division of profit and loss, liquidation of the business, and related matters.

Partnerships are treated as separate accounting entities from the partners. A partner's capital interest in a partnership is a claim against the net assets of the partnership as reflected in the partner's capital account. A partner's interest in profit and loss determines how the partner's capital interest changes as a result of subsequent operations. Profit-and-loss agreements usually are arranged to reward the partners for their contribution of resources or abilities to the partnership. These profit-and-loss sharing arrangements frequently include the following or a combination thereof:

1. Fixed ratio.

2. A ratio based on capital balances.

3. "Interest" on capital investment.

4. "Salaries" for time devoted to the partnership or a bonus as a percentage of income.

Partners' salaries and interest on capital are not expenses used in computing partnership net income. They are methods of allocating partnership net income among the partners. If the partnership agreement does not specify how profits and losses are to be divided, they are divided equally among the partners.

In a general partnership, all partners are jointly liable for the debts of the firm. Each partner is an agent of the partnership within the scope of the business and can legally bind the partnership. In most states, the Uniform Partnership Act provides the legal rights and duties of partners and partnerships. A limited partnership consists of at least one general partner and one or more limited partners. The general partner(s) manages the enterprise and has responsibilities as described in the partnership agreement. The limited partner(s) contributes capital to the firm. Their personal liability is generally limited to their investment. They share in the profits and losses but have no voice in directing operations.

Advantages associated with the partnership form of business organization include the ease of formation and dissolution, its ability to pool capital and personal talents and skills, its nontaxable status for income tax purposes, and the relative freedom and flexibility partners enjoy in business matters. Disadvantages associated with partnerships include its limited life, the ability of a partner to commit the partnership in contractual matters, the unlimited personal liability of partners, and the difficulties of raising large sums of capital and of transferring ownership interests as contrasted with the corporate form of business organization.

The Uniform Partnership Act defines dissolution of a partnership as "the change in the relationship of the partners caused by any partner ceasing to be associated in the carrying on as distinguished from the winding up of the business." Legal dissolution can be the result of:

1. Agreement among the partners.
2. The express will of a partner if no term is specified in the partnership agreement.
3. Death of a partner.
4. Bankruptcy of a partner or the partnership.
5. Court decree.
6. Admission of a partner.

The admission of a new partner or the withdrawal or death of a partner dissolves the partnership but does not necessarily cause partnership operations to cease. A person may become a partner in an existing partnership (1) by purchasing an interest from one or more of the existing partners and (2) by investing cash or noncash assets in the partnership. A person can be admitted to a partnership only with the consent of all continuing partners in the new partnership enterprise.

When a partnership is in the process of liquidation, partnership assets are distributed according to the following **order:**

1. To creditors other than partners.
2. To partners other than for capital and profit.
3. To partners in respect of capital.
4. To partners in respect of profits.

If the partnership is insolvent and one or more partners are also insolvent, the claims against the separate property of partners rank in the following order:

1. Those owing to separate creditors.
2. Those owing to partnership creditors.
3. Those owing to partners by way of contribution.

A partnership is not assessed an income tax on earnings. Partnership income is allocated to the partners and is reported on the partners' tax returns. The tax bases for assets contributed by the partners to the partnership are the same tax bases that applied to the individual partner making the contribution. The tax basis of a partner's interest in capital of a partnership is the sum of the tax bases of the assets contributed by the partner, increased by the personal liabilities of other partners which the partner assumes, and decreased by the partner's personal liabilities assumed by other partners. The sum of the tax bases of the partnership assets equals the sum of the tax bases of the partners' separate interests in capital.

See also Corporation; Joint venture; Tax shelter.

REFERENCE
Haried, Andrew A., et al., *Advanced Accounting* (John Wiley & Sons, N.Y., 1985).

PAYROLL TAXES
The federal Social Security Act provides for a variety of programs for qualified individuals and families including (1) a federal old-age and survivors' benefits program with medical care for the aged, and (2) a joint federal-state unemployment insurance program. Benefits are based upon the average earnings of the worker during the period of employment in covered industries. Funds to support these programs come from payroll taxes imposed under the Federal Insurance Contribution Act (F.I.C.A.) and the Federal Unemployment Tax Act. Social security taxes are imposed on both employer, employees, and the self-employed. The tax is collected by the employer who deducts it from the employee's gross pay and remits it to the government along with the employer's share. Both parties are taxed at the same rate based on the employee's gross pay up to an annual maximum limit.

Employers are also subject to another payroll tax which supports a system of unemployment insurance. This tax is levied by the federal government in cooperation with state governments. The federal tax is the Federal Unemployment Tax Act (FUTA). A rate is applied against income earned by covered employees up to a specified amount. The employer is allowed a credit against the federal tax for unemployment taxes paid to the state. In some states, employers with favorable employment records are entitled to a reduction in taxes.

Employers are required to withhold from employees' pay an amount estimated for federal income taxes. Employers remit the withholdings to the federal government. The amount withheld depends primarily upon the employee's earnings and the number of exemptions to which the employee is entitled to claim. Many states have income taxes and have withholding procedures similar to those used by the federal government.

See also Liabilities.

PEER REVIEW
The American Institute of Certified Public Accountants established a voluntary organization, the Division of CPA Firms (consisting of firms having an SEC practice), in 1977 to maintain and improve the quality of the accounting and auditing services performed by member firms. A peer review of a member firm, conducted by other CPAs under the auspices of the AICPA, provides considerable assurance that the firm has an appropriate quality control system for its accounting and auditing practice and that it is complying with that system. Firms are expected to undergo a peer review every three years. A major purpose of peer reviews is to recognize the public's interest in reliable financial statements. The Private Companies Practice Section of the AICPA (consisting primarily of smaller CPA firms) also has established a peer review process that is similar to that required by the Division of CPA Firms.

Peer reviewers are required to evaluate a firm's quality control system against standards and comprehensive guidelines established by the AICPA. They also test a representative sample of a firm's accounting and auditing engagements for compliance with professional standards. Reviewers are expected to determine whether a firm's policies and procedures are adequate to meet quality control standards. The reviewers issue a written report on their peer review. If the report indicates the need for corrective action, the firm is expected to indicate in writing what it will do to correct the problem. In serious cases of inadequacy, a firm may be required to undertake additional education, agree to a revisit, or submit to another peer review within a short time. Most CPA firms receive unqualified opinions.

The AICPA has identified nine basic elements of quality control for a CPA firm: independence, assignment of personnel, consultation, supervision, hiring, continuing professional education, advancement, client acceptance and continuance, and inspection. Additional criteria required include (1) assignment of responsibilities to personnel to provide for effective implementation, (2) effective communication of the policies and procedures throughout the firm, and (3) monitoring the system so that it is effective.

See also Accounting profession; Audit.

PENSIONS

A pension is an allowance, annuity, or subsidy. A pension plan is an arrangement whereby an employer agrees to provide benefits to retired employees. A pension plan may be either contributory or noncontributory. In a contributory plan, both employer and employee contribute to the fund from which benefits are to be paid. In a noncontributory plan, only the employer makes contributions to the fund. A single-employer plan is a pension plan established unilaterally by an employer. Multiemployer plans are sometimes established within an industry.

The funding aspects of pension plans are important features of any plan. Funding means to pay to a funding agency. Funding also refers to assets accumulated by a funding agency to provide retirement benefits when they come due. Pension costs that have been paid over to a funding agency are said to have been funded. A funding agency is an organization or individual, such as an insurance company or a trustee, who accumulates assets which will be used for the payment of benefits under the plan and who administers the program. Terminal funding occurs when the benefits payable to a retired employee are funded in full at the time the employee retires; there is no funding for active employees. Pay-as-you-go funding does not provide any prior funding for retirement benefits but provides resources for the pensions as they come due after retirement.

In an insured pension plan, annuities are purchased for employees under individual or group annuity contracts between an employer and an insurance company. The insurance company guarantees the payment of benefits. Noninsured plans are generally funded by a trust agreement between an employer and a trust company.

When pension benefits are no longer contingent on an employee's continued employment, the employee's benefits under the plan are said to be vested benefits. When benefits vest, an employee's pension rights cannot be reduced or taken away.

A defined benefit plan is a plan that states the benefits to be received by employees after retirement or the method of determining such benefits. A defined contribution plan is one in which the employer's contribution is determined based on a specified formula. Future benefits are limited to those that the plan can provide. A defined contribution plan specifies the amount of the periodic contributions to be paid by the plan's sponsor (and not the benefits to be received by a participant). Benefits are usually based on the amount credited to an individual's account.

An actuary is a professional who is concerned primarily with developing a pension plan that will result in a systematic accumulation of funds sufficient to meet the employer's obligations to employees upon retirement. Assumptions are made concerning such factors as mortality rates, disability rates, rate of return on investments, employee turnover, retirement ages, wage and salary rates, and other considerations. An actuarial cost method is a technique used to establish the amount of the annual cost of pension plan benefits and to determine the amount of funding required for a particular pension program. Two widely used actuarial cost methods are (1) the accrued benefit (unit credit) method and (2) the projected benefit-cost method. Under the accrued benefit method, the amount assigned to the current year represents the present value of the increase in an active employee's retirement benefits resulting from the current year's service. Funding under this method involves setting aside, in one sum, amounts required to fund in full one unit of pension benefits. The annual contribution required for the entire plan is determined by adding the single-premium sums required to purchase the benefits credited during the year for all participants. Under the projected benefit-cost method, the amount assigned to the current year usually represents a level amount that will provide for the estimated projected retirement benefits over the service lives of either the individual employees or an employee group.

Accountants are in general agreement that pension expenses should be accrued (expensed) and that they should be recognized in each period between the hiring and retiring of an employee and not solely at the time of retirement or thereafter. Pension expense for a period is the result of the following factors:

1. Service cost

2. Interest

3. Expected return on plan assets

4. Prior service cost

5. Actuarial gains and losses

The service cost component of pension expense is determined as the actuarial present value of benefits attributed by the pension benefit formula to employee service during a period. This approach computes the liability for pension expense on the basis of projected future pay. An interest component also affects pension expense since the pension liability is not paid until retirement. The interest factor consists of the interest for the period on the projected benefit obligation outstanding during the period. The expected return on pension plan assets will reduce pension expense for the period. The period of employment preceding the plan's inception date and the date the plan is amended is referred to as the prior service period. The prior service cost (for retroactive benefits) is the present value of expected future pension benefits resulting from service performed during the prior service period. Pension costs associated with the prior service period should be recognized during the service periods of employees who are expected to receive benefits under the plan. Companies are allowed to assign prior service cost on a straight-line basis over the average remaining service life of active employees expected to receive benefits under the plan. Because actuarial assumptions and estimates are made concerning the cost of a pension plan, deviations from the assumptions and estimates can result in gains and losses, i.e., experience gains and losses. Only certain gains and losses in excess of 10 percent of the larger of the projected benefit obligations or the market-related asset value of the plan need to be recognized. The resulting amount is referred to as a corridor. Any excess over the 10 percent should be amortized over the average remaining service period of active employees expected to participate in the plan. No asset or liability is recorded for prior service cost.

When the accumulated benefit obligations of a plan exceeds the fair value of plan assets, it is required that a minimum liability be immediately recognized (the pension plan is underfunded) in the general case. However, an asset would not be recognized if the fair value of the pension plan assets exceed the accumulated benefit obligation. The accounting entry to record and recognize a minimum liability will create an intangible asset as follows:

Deferred Pension Cost (an intangible asset)   XXX
  Pension Liability   XXX

FASB Statement No. 87 requires extensive disclosure in financial statements for pensions including:

1. A description of the plan, including employees covered, benefit formula, funding policy, assets in the plan, etc.

2. The components of pension expense for the period.

3. A schedule reconciling the funded status of the plan with amounts reported in the balance sheet.

See also ERISA; Annuity; Defined-benefit pension plans.

REFERENCES
Kieso, Donald E., and Weygandt, Jerry J., *Intermediate Accounting* (John Wiley & Sons, N.Y., 1986).
FASB, SFAS No. 87, Employers' *Accounting for Pension Plans* (FASB, 1985).
Employee Benefit Research Institute, Fundamentals of Employee Benefit Programs (Education and Research Fund, Washington, DC, 1985).

PERSONAL FINANCIAL STATEMENTS

The reporting entity of personal financial statements is an individual, a husband and wife, or a group of related individuals. Personal financial statements should provide adequate disclosure of relevant information relating to the financial affairs of an individual reporting entity. For each reporting entity, a statement of financial position (or balance sheet) is a required statement. The statement of financial condition is now required to present estimated current values of assets and liabilities, a provision for estimated taxes, and net worth. A provision should also be made for estimated income taxes on the differences between the estimated current values of assets, the estimated current amount of liabilities, and their respective tax bases. Comparative statements for one or more periods should be presented. A statement of changes in net worth is optional. Such a statement would disclose the major sources of increases and decreases in net worth. Increases in personal net worth arise from income, increases in estimated current value of assets, decreases in estimated current amount of liabilities, and decreases in the provision for estimated income taxes. Decreases in personal net worth arise from expenses, decreases in estimated current value of assets, increases in estimated current amount of liabilities, and increases in the provision for income taxes.

Personal financial statements should be presented on the accrual basis and not on the cash basis. A classified balance sheet is not used. Assets and liabilities are presented in the order of their liquidity and maturity, respectively. A business interest that constitutes a large part of an individual's total assets should be shown separate from other assets. Such an interest would be presented as a net amount and not as a pro rata allocation of the business's assets and liabilities. An illustration of a personal financial statement is shown in Exhibit P-1.

See also Financial statements.

REFERENCES
AICPA, AICPA *Auditing and Accounting Manual* (AICPA, 1982).
Bailard, Thomas E., et al., *Personal Money Management* (Science Research Associates, Inc., Chicago, 1986).

PLANNING AND CONTROL
Planning and control are major elements related to managing an enterprise and profit making. Planning is a process that begins with identifying "what is" and determining "what should be." Action is normally required to bridge the gap between "what is" and "what should be." In its most basic conceptualization, the planning process

Exhibit P–1
Personal Financial Statements

John and Mary Doe
Statement of Financial Condition
December 31, 1990 and 1991

Assets	1991	1990
Cash	$ 5,000	$ 3,000
Investments		
Marketable securities (Note 1)	20,000	17,000
Clix, Inc., a closely held corporation	100,000	80,000
Residence	200,000	120,000
Personal effects	30,000	25,000
Total assets	$355,000	$245,000

Liabilities and Net Worth	1991	1990
Credit cards	$ 1,500	$ 1,000
Income taxes—current year balance	5,500	4,000
Demand note payable to bank, 16%	10,000	—
Mortgage payable, 10% (Note 2)	100,000	110,000
Total	117,000	115,000
Estimated income taxes on the differences between the estimated current values of assets, the current amounts of liabilities and their tax bases (Note 3)	10,000	5,000
Net worth	228,000	125,000
Total liabilities and net worth	$355,000	$245,000

1. establishes goals and objectives, and

2. develops a decision model for selecting the means of attaining these goals and objectives.

Planning requires that choices (decisions) be made relating to:

1. goals and objectives (what you want to do and why you want to do it); and

2. the means of attaining these ends (when, where, and how to do it).

Three types of planning are basic to goal realization:

1. strategic planning (a business plan),

2. short-run planning (forecasting and budgeting), and

3. project and situation planning.

Control is primarily the acts of

1. determining that actions undertaken are in accordance with plans, and

2. using feedback to ensure that goals and objectives are being attained.

Control tells a manager how well a job is being done, how effectively goals and objectives are being achieved, and how efficiently resources are being used. Effectiveness refers to whether a goal is being achieved. Efficiency is a measure of the optimal relationship between inputs (resources used) and outputs (products or services produced). Control involves five distinct steps:

1. establish performance standards to use for evaluating performance,

2. obtain feedback information on performance,

3. determine whether any modifying action is required under the circumstances,

4. determine what action, if any, is required, and

5. take the necessary action to modify the situation.

Control is accomplished primarily through systems. In designing a control system, the goals of the control system must be integrated with activities that lead to the attainment of the enterprise's goals. Criteria for evaluating control systems are based primarily on three major concerns:

1. how the controls affect human behavior,

2. whether the benefits obtained from the controls exceed the costs of using the control system, and

3. whether the control system's procedures achieve the objectives for which it has been designed.

Controls should be developed around responsibility centers within the enterprise. A responsibility center has control over an activity of the organization, such as a department, a division, or a segment of the company. Responsibility centers should be designed so that a particular manager or group has control over an activity for a particular time period. When the responsibility center has control over costs, it is referred to as a cost center. The assembly department of a company would be considered a cost center since the manager of the department would be responsible for costs incurred in the department. If a center has control over both costs and revenues (and therefore profit), it is referred to as a profit center. An investment center is an area of responsibility which has control over revenues, costs, and assets.

The measures used for evaluating performance must relate to the objectives of the responsibility center. Control is usually more effective when what is being controlled can be quantified or measured. Variances of actual performance from budgeted performance or standards must be determined and made available to managers on a timely basis if the information derived from the analysis is to be useful. The information managers ordinarily need to control effectively can be classified as (1) score-card information, (2) attention-directing information, and (3) problem-solving information. Score-card information responds to the question: How well or poorly are we doing? Attention-directing information answers such questions as: Is the company performing according to plans? What problems or opportunities exist? What areas of the enterprise need to be changed, if any? Problem-solving information helps management resolve a particular problem: What is the problem or concern? What are the alternatives? Which alternative is preferable? The planning and control cycle can be visualized as follows:

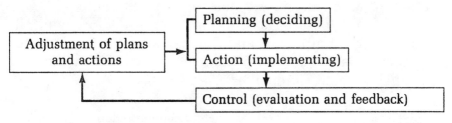

See also Budget; Internal control; Return on investment; Gross margin; Contribution margin; Financial statement analysis.

REFERENCE
Woelfel, Charles J., and Mecimore, Charles, *The Operating Executive's Handbook of Profit Planning Tools and Techniques* (Probus Publishing Co., Chicago, 1986).

POOLING OF INTERESTS
Accounting for a business combination can be accomplished by two methods: pooling-of-interests method and purchase method. APB Opinion No. 16 established twelve conditions that must be met before the pooling-of-interests method can be used to account for a business combination.

The concept behind the pooling-of-interests method is that the holders of the common stock in the combining companies continue as holders of the common stock in the combined company. The business combination is accounted for by adding together the book value of the assets and equities of the combined enterprises. The combining corporation records the assets and liabilities received from the combined companies at book values recorded on the books of the combined companies. The equity of the acquired company is combined with the equity of the acquiring company. The allocation of the acquired company's equity among common stock, other contributed capital, and retained earnings may have to be restructured as a result of the difierences in the par value of the stock issued and the par value of the stock acquired. The pooling-of-interests method can be contrasted with the purchase method of accounting for a business combination.

To illustrate pooling accounting, assume the following situation where Company A and Company B enter into a statutory consolidation and form Company C. The following data is available about Companies A and B:

	Stockholders' Equity		
	Company A	Company B	Total
Common stock	$1,000,000	$2,000,000	$3,000,000
Other paid-in capital	1,000,000	1,000,000	2,000,000
Retained earnings	2,000,000	2,000,000	4,000,000
Total	$4,000,000	$5,000,000	$9,000,000

In this case, C acquires the net assets (assets and liabilities) of A and B for stock having a par value of $2,000,000. C makes the following entry on its accounting records to record the business combination as a pooling of interests:

Net Assets (Listed)	9,000,000	
Common Stock—C Company		2,000,000
Other paid-in capital		3,000,000
Retained Earnings		4,000,000

Note that C records the assets at the amounts reported on A and B companies' books, $9,000,000. The retained earnings of A and B are carried forward to C's records and become a part of C's retained earnings. Since the par value of C's common stock issued to acquire A and B was $2,000,000 and the par value of A and B common stock was $3,000,000, C records common stock at par of $2,000,000 and records $4,000,000 other paid-in capital. The acquired company's earnings are included with the acquiring company's earnings for the full year in which the combination occurs, regardless of when the combination occurred during the year.

Because most companies present financial summaries for a number of years (comparative financial statements), these summaries are also adjusted to reflect the combined totals of the separate combining companies as if only one company had existed in all the earlier years.

See also Purchase accounting; Consolidated financial statements.

REFERENCE
Accounting Research Bulletin No. 48, Business Combinations (AICPA, Committee on Accounting Procedure, 1958).

PREFERRED STOCK
Preferred stock is a form of capital stock that possesses certain preferences or priorities over common stock. The preferences are usually associated with a prior claim to dividends and the distribution of assets upon the liquidation of the corporation. Preferred stockholders are usually not given the right to vote in corporate affairs, except under unusual circumstances. Preferred stock is usually par value preferred. Dividends on preferred stock are usually expressed as a percentage of par value; if the preferred is no-par preferred, the dividend is stated as a specific dollar amount.

Preferred stock may be noncumulative or cumulative. If the stock is noncumulative, the preferred shareholders are entitled to receive their current year's dividend on dividends declared in that year. However, the directors do not have to declare and pay dividends on any previous year which has been omitted. In contrast, cumulative preferred stock provides that dividends in arrears (dividends undeclared or passed in prior years) accumulate and must be paid to preferred shareholders before any dividends can be distributed to common stockholders. Dividends ordinarily do not become a liability of the corporation until they are declared.

Preferred stock may be participating or nonparticipating. Participating preferred stock has priority over common stock up to the basic percentage or amount stated for preferred dividends; after an equal percentage or amount is paid to the common, the preferred and common participate in additional dividends. Participating preferred stock may be classified as fully or partially participating preferred stock. If the stock is fully participating, the preferred shareholders are entitled to receive any dividends above the basic rate on a pro rata basis with the common stockholders. The pro rata amount is based on the par or stated value of each class of stock. If the preferred stock is partially participating, the preferred shareholders share the additional dividends with common shareholders only up to the participating amount, with anything above that going entirely to the common shareholders.

The following examples illustrate the cumulative and participating features of preferred stock. Assume the following information:

Preferred stock, 6%, $100 par value	$100,000
Common stock, $50 par value, 4,000 shares	$200,000

Case 1. Preferred stock is cumulative and nonparticipating. Dividends on preferred stock are three years in arrears (100,000 × .06 × 3 = $18,000). The directors declare a $60,000 dividend. The dividend would be allocated among the common and preferred as follows:

	Preferred	Common
Preferred stock:		
Dividend in arrears for three years	$18,000	
Current dividends	6,000	
Common stock:		
Balance available		
($60,000 – $24,000)		$36,000
Total dividend	$24,000	$36,000

Case 2. Preferred stock is cumulative and fully participating. Dividends are three years in arrears. The directors declare a $48,000 dividend.

	Preferred	Common
Preferred stock:		
Dividends in arrears for three years	$18,000	
Current dividends	6,000	
Common stock:		
Matching 6% dividend for current year		$12,000
Balance		
[$48,00 – ($24,000 + $12,000) = $12,000]		
100,000/300,000 × $12,000	4,000	
200,000/300,000 × $12,000		8,000
Total dividend	$28,000	$20,000

Preferred stock usually has a preference over common stock as to assets available for distribution upon the dissolution of the corporation. For example, a $100 par value preferred stock may have a liquidating value of $105 per share. The preferred would be entitled to receive $105 per share before the common should the corporation be liquidated. Companies must disclose the aggregate liquidating value of preferred stock on financial statements if one is specified.

Additional features of preferred stock can include convertible rights and callable provisions. Convertible preferred stock provides the option to the preferred shareholder to convert or exchange his preferred shares for other securities of the corporation, generally common stock. The conversion feature is included as a provision in some preferred stock contracts in order to make the purchase of the preferred stock more attractive. The call provision in preferred stock contracts establishes a call price at which the corporation may repurchase the stock from a stockholder.

See also Capital stock; Stockholders' equity.

PREPAID EXPENSE

Prepaid expenses are expenses of a future period that have been paid in advance—for example, prepaid rent or insurance. Prepaid expenses are classified as current assets even though they will never be converted into cash as would the typical current assets. Current asset classification for prepaid expenses is justified on the basis that if the expenditure for the item had not occurred, cash would have to be expended in the future.

See also Current asset.

PRESENT VALUE

Present value is the net amount of discounted expected cash flows relating to an asset or liability. Stated another way, present value is the principal that must be invested at time period zero to produce the known future value. The process of converting the future value to the present value is referred to as discounting. Present value problems can assume this form: If $1,688.96 is to be received four years in the future, what is its present value if the discount rate is 14 percent? Using a formula approach, the present value in this illustration can be computed by using the following formula:

$$p = f\left[\frac{1}{(1 + i)^n}\right]$$

where p = present value of any given future amount due in the future

   f = a future amount
   i = interest rate
   n = number of periods

In the example, the present value of $1,688.96 received at the end of four years discounted at 14% is $1,000 calculated as follows:

$$p = (\$1,688.96)\left[\frac{1}{(1 + .14)^4}\right] = \$1,000$$

The present value of an annuity is the present value of a series of equal rents made in the future. It is the amount that must be invested now and, if left to earn compound interest, will provide for the receipt or payment of a series of equal rents at regular intervals. Over a period of time, the present value balance increases periodically for interest and decreases periodically for each rent paid or received. To illustrate the present value of an annuity concept, assume that you are considering an investment that will provide you with annual cash income of $1,200 each year for five years. The first cash income will occur at the end of the current year. What is the present value of this investment at an interest rate (rate of return) of 10 percent? The following formula can be used to make the computation:

$$PV = \left[\frac{1 - \frac{1}{(1 + i)^n}}{i}\right]$$

PV = $4,548.95

where PV = present value of an ordinary annuity
n = number of rents
i = interest (discount) rate

Tables are available that make present value computations relatively easy. Present value of 1 and present value of an annuity of 1 tables are presented in Exhibit P-1 and P-2, respectively.

See also Interest; Annuity; Future value.

REFERENCE
Woelfel, Charles J., *The Desktop Guide to Money, Time, Interest and Yields* (Probus, Chicago, 1986).

Exhibit P-2
Present Value of 1

PRESENT VALUE OF 1: $p = \dfrac{1}{(1+i)^n}$

n	1.5%	4.0%	4.5%	5.0%	5.5%	6.0%	7.0%
1	0.985222	0.961538	0.956938	0.952381	0.947867	0.943396	0.934579
2	0.970662	0.924556	0.915730	0.907029	0.898452	0.889996	0.873439
3	0.956317	0.888996	0.876297	0.863838	0.851614	0.839619	0.816298
4	0.942184	0.854804	0.838561	0.822702	0.807217	0.792094	0.762895
5	0.928260	0.821927	0.802451	0.783526	0.765134	0.747258	0.712986
6	0.914542	0.790315	0.767896	0.746215	0.725246	0.704961	0.666342
7	0.901027	0.759918	0.734828	0.710681	0.687437	0.665057	0.622750
8	0.887711	0.730690	0.703185	0.676839	0.651599	0.627412	0.582009
9	0.874592	0.702587	0.672904	0.644609	0.617629	0.591898	0.543934
10	0.861667	0.675564	0.643928	0.613913	0.585431	0.558395	0.508349
11	0.848933	0.649581	0.616199	0.584679	0.554911	0.526788	0.475093
12	0.836387	0.624597	0.589664	0.556837	0.525982	0.496969	0.444012
13	0.824027	0.600574	0.564272	0.530321	0.498561	0.468839	0.414964
14	0.811849	0.577475	0.539973	0.505068	0.472569	0.442301	0.387817
15	0.799852	0.555265	0.516720	0.481017	0.447933	0.417265	0.362446
16	0.788031	0.533908	0.494469	0.458112	0.424581	0.393646	0.338735
17	0.776385	0.513373	0.473176	0.436297	0.402447	0.371364	0.316574
18	0.764912	0.493628	0.452800	0.415521	0.381466	0.350344	0.295864
19	0.753607	0.474642	0.433302	0.395734	0.361579	0.330513	0.276508
20	0.742470	0.456387	0.414643	0.376889	0.342729	0.311805	0.258419
21	0.731498	0.438834	0.396787	0.358942	0.324862	0.294155	0.241513
22	0.720688	0.421955	0.379701	0.341850	0.307926	0.277505	0.225713
23	0.710037	0.405726	0.363350	0.325571	0.291873	0.261797	0.210947
24	0.699544	0.390121	0.347703	0.310068	0.276657	0.246979	0.197147
25	0.689206	0.375117	0.332731	0.295303	0.262234	0.232999	0.184249
26	0.679021	0.360689	0.318402	0.281241	0.248563	0.219810	0.172195
27	0.668986	0.346817	0.304691	0.267848	0.235605	0.207368	0.160930
28	0.659099	0.333477	0.291571	0.255094	0.223322	0.195630	0.150402
29	0.649359	0.320651	0.279015	0.242946	0.211679	0.184557	0.140563
30	0.639762	0.308319	0.267000	0.231377	0.200644	0.174110	0.131367

n	8.0%	9.0%	10.0%	12.0%	14.0%	16.0%	18.0%
1	0.925926	0.917431	0.909091	0.892857	0.877193	0.862069	0.847458
2	0.857339	0.841680	0.826446	0.797194	0.769468	0.743163	0.718184
3	0.793832	0.772183	0.751315	0.711780	0.674972	0.640658	0.608631
4	0.735030	0.708425	0.683013	0.635518	0.592080	0.552291	0.515789
5	0.680583	0.649931	0.620921	0.567427	0.519369	0.476113	0.437109
6	0.630170	0.596267	0.564474	0.506631	0.455587	0.410442	0.370432
7	0.583490	0.547034	0.513158	0.452349	0.399637	0.353830	0.313925
8	0.540269	0.501866	0.466507	0.403883	0.350559	0.305025	0.266038
9	0.500249	0.460428	0.424098	0.360610	0.307508	0.262953	0.225456
10	0.463193	0.422411	0.385543	0.321973	0.269744	0.226684	0.191064
11	0.428883	0.387533	0.350494	0.287476	0.236617	0.195417	0.161919
12	0.397114	0.355535	0.318631	0.256675	0.207559	0.168463	0.137220
13	0.367698	0.326179	0.289664	0.229174	0.182069	0.145227	0.116288
14	0.340461	0.299246	0.263331	0.204620	0.159710	0.125195	0.098549
15	0.315242	0.274538	0.239392	0.182696	0.140096	0.107927	0.083516
16	0.291890	0.251870	0.217629	0.163122	0.122892	0.093041	0.070776
17	0.270269	0.231073	0.197845	0.145644	0.107800	0.080207	0.059980
18	0.250249	0.211994	0.179859	0.130040	0.094561	0.069144	0.050830
19	0.231712	0.194490	0.163508	0.116107	0.082948	0.059607	0.043077
20	0.214548	0.178431	0.148644	0.103667	0.072762	0.051385	0.036506
21	0.198656	0.163698	0.135131	0.092560	0.063826	0.044298	0.030937
22	0.183941	0.150182	0.122846	0.082643	0.055988	0.038188	0.026218
23	0.170315	0.137781	0.111678	0.073788	0.049112	0.032920	0.022218
24	0.157699	0.126405	0.101526	0.065882	0.043081	0.028380	0.018829
25	0.146018	0.115968	0.092296	0.058823	0.037790	0.024465	0.015957
26	0.135202	0.106393	0.083905	0.052521	0.033149	0.021091	0.013523
27	0.125187	0.097608	0.076278	0.046894	0.029078	0.018182	0.011460
28	0.115914	0.089548	0.069343	0.041869	0.025507	0.015674	0.009712
29	0.107328	0.082155	0.063039	0.037383	0.022375	0.013512	0.008230
30	0.099377	0.075371	0.057309	0.033378	0.019627	0.011648	0.006975

Exhibit P-3
Present Value of an Ordinary Annuity

PRESENT VALUE OF AN ORDINARY ANNUITY OF 1: $P_0 = \dfrac{1 - \dfrac{1}{(1+i)^n}}{i}$

n	1.5%	4.0%	4.5%	5.0%	5.5%	6.0%	7.0%
1	0.985222	0.961538	0.956938	0.952381	0.947867	0.943396	0.934579
2	1.955883	1.886095	1.872668	1.859410	1.846320	1.833393	1.808018
3	2.912200	2.775091	2.748964	2.723248	2.697933	2.673012	2.624316
4	3.854385	3.629895	3.587526	3.545951	3.505150	3.465106	3.387211
5	4.782645	4.451822	4.389977	4.329477	4.270284	4.212364	4.100197
6	5.697187	5.242137	5.157872	5.075692	4.995530	4.917324	4.766540
7	6.598214	6.002055	5.892701	5.786373	5.682967	5.582381	5.389289
8	7.485925	6.732745	6.595886	6.463213	6.334566	6.209794	5.971299
9	8.360517	7.435332	7.268790	7.107822	6.952195	6.801692	6.515232
10	9.222185	8.110896	7.912718	7.721735	7.537626	7.360087	7.023582
11	10.071118	8.760477	8.528917	8.306414	8.092536	7.886875	7.498674
12	10.907505	9.385074	9.118581	8.863252	8.618518	8.383844	7.942686
13	11.731532	9.985648	9.682852	9.393573	9.117079	8.852683	8.357651
14	12.543382	10.563123	10.222825	9.898641	9.589648	9.294984	8.745468
15	13.343233	11.118387	10.739546	10.379658	10.037581	9.712249	9.107914
16	14.131264	11.652296	11.234015	10.837770	10.462162	10.105895	9.446649
17	14.907649	12.165669	11.707191	11.274066	10.864609	10.477260	9.763223
18	15.672561	12.659297	12.159992	11.689587	11.246074	10.827603	10.059087
19	16.426168	13.133939	12.593294	12.085321	11.607654	11.158116	10.335595
20	17.168639	13.590326	13.007936	12.462210	11.950382	11.469921	10.594014
21	17.900137	14.029160	13.404724	12.821153	12.275244	11.764077	10.835527
22	18.620824	14.451115	13.784425	13.163003	12.583170	12.041582	11.061240
23	19.330861	14.856842	14.147775	13.488574	12.875042	12.303379	11.272187
24	20.030405	15.246963	14.495478	13.798642	13.151699	12.550358	11.469334
25	20.719611	15.622080	14.828209	14.093945	13.413933	12.783356	11.653583
26	21.398632	15.982769	15.146611	14.375185	13.662495	13.003166	11.825779
27	22.067617	16.329586	15.451303	14.643034	13.898100	13.210534	11.986709
28	22.726717	16.663063	15.742874	14.898127	14.121402	13.406164	12.137111
29	23.376076	16.983715	16.021889	15.141074	14.333101	13.590721	12.277674
30	24.015838	17.292033	16.288889	15.372451	14.533745	13.764831	12.409041

n	8.0%	9.0%	10.0%	12.0%	14.0%	16.0%	18.0%
1	0.925926	0.917431	0.909091	0.892857	0.877193	0.862069	0.847458
2	1.783265	1.759111	1.735537	1.690051	1.646661	1.605232	1.565642
3	2.577097	2.531295	2.486852	2.401831	2.321632	2.245890	2.174273
4	3.312127	3.239720	3.169865	3.037349	2.913712	2.798181	2.690062
5	3.992710	3.889651	3.790787	3.604776	3.433081	3.274294	3.127171
6	4.622880	4.485919	4.355261	4.111407	3.888668	3.684736	3.497603
7	5.206370	5.032953	4.868419	4.563757	4.288305	4.038565	3.811528
8	5.746639	5.534819	5.334926	4.967640	4.638864	4.343591	4.077566
9	6.246888	5.995247	5.759024	5.328250	4.946372	4.606544	4.303022
10	6.710081	6.417658	6.144567	5.650223	5.216116	4.833227	4.494086
11	7.138964	6.805191	6.495061	5.937699	5.452733	5.028644	4.656005
12	7.536078	7.160725	6.813692	6.194374	5.660292	5.197107	4.793225
13	7.903776	7.486904	7.103356	6.423548	5.842362	5.342334	4.909513
14	8.244237	7.786150	7.366687	6.628168	6.002072	5.467529	5.008062
15	8.559479	8.060638	7.606080	6.810864	6.142168	5.575456	5.091578
16	8.851369	8.312558	7.823709	6.973986	6.265060	5.668497	5.162354
17	9.121635	8.543631	8.021553	7.119630	6.372859	5.748704	5.222334
18	9.371887	8.755625	8.201412	7.249670	6.467420	5.817848	5.273164
19	9.603599	8.950115	8.364920	7.345777	6.550369	5.877455	5.316241
20	9.818147	9.128546	8.513564	7.469444	6.623131	5.928841	5.352746
21	10.016803	9.292244	8.648694	7.562003	6.686957	5.973139	5.383683
22	10.200744	9.442425	8.771540	7.644646	6.742944	6.011326	5.409901
23	10.371059	9.580207	8.883218	7.718434	6.792056	6.044247	5.432120
24	10.528758	9.706612	8.984744	7.784316	6.835137	6.072627	5.450949
25	10.674776	9.822580	9.077040	7.843139	6.872927	6.097092	5.466906
26	10.809978	9.928972	9.160945	7.895660	6.906077	6.118183	5.480429
27	10.935165	10.026580	9.237223	7.942554	6.935155	6.136364	5.491889
28	11.051078	10.116128	9.306567	7.984423	6.960662	6.152038	5.501601
29	11.158406	10.198283	9.369606	8.021806	6.983037	6.165550	5.509831
30	11.257783	10.273654	9.426914	8.055184	7.002664	6.177198	5.516806

PRIOR-PERIOD ADJUSTMENTS

A few profit and loss items are reported as prior-period adjustments on financial statements and require a restatement of retained earnings. These items are the corrections of errors of a prior period and adjustments that result from the realization of income tax benefits of preacquisition operating loss carry-forwards of purchased subsidiaries.

Material errors in the financial statements of one accounting period that are discovered in a subsequent period usually involve an asset or liability and a revenue or expense of a prior year. In the year of the correction, the asset or liability account balance should be corrected and the related revenue or expense should be made directly to the retained earnings account and should not affect the income statement for the current year. For example, assume that the Blue Company discovered that it failed to record $100,000 of depreciation expense for 1990 and discovered the error in 1991. This error overstated 1990 income before income taxes by a similar amount. Assume that after considering the income tax effect of this error, the error resulted in a net overstatement of income in 1990 of $85,000. The January 1, 1991, retained earnings balance of the Blue Company is assumed to be $500,000. The correction would be disclosed on the December 31, 1991, statement of retained earnings as a prior period adjustment as shown here:

Retained earnings, as previously reported January 1, 1991	$500,000
Less: Correction of overstatement in 1990 net income due to depreciation understatement (net of $15,000 income taxes)	85,000
Adjusted retained earnings, January 1, 1991	$415,000

If comparative financial statements are presented, the prior-year statements should be restated to show the effect on net income, retained earnings, and asset or liability balances for all periods reported.

See also Accounting changes; Errors; Income statement; Consistency.

PRIVILEGED COMMUNICATIONS

Certified public accountants do not generally enjoy the same legal protection on confidentiality with regard to client relationships as that possessed by the legal and medical professions. The accountant-client privilege is not recognized at common law, nor has it been endorsed by the American Institute of Certified Public Accountants. The accounting profession is divided on this issue. Eighteen legal jurisdictions have recognized this privilege. Depending upon the state, the accountant-client privilege might be applicable under the following circumstances, which are those applicable to an attorney-client privilege: (1) the asserted holder of the privilege is or sought to become a client; (2) the person to whom the communication was made (a) is a member of the bar of a court, or his subordinate and (b) in connection with this communication is acting as a lawyer; (3) the communication relates to a fact of which the attorney was informed (a) by the client (b) without the presence of strangers (c) for the purpose of securing primarily either (i) an opinion in law or (ii) legal services or (iii) assistance in some legal proceeding, and (d) for the purpose of committing a crime or tort; and (4) the privilege has been (a) claimed and (b) not waived by the client. (United States v. United Shoe Machinery Corp., 89 F. Supp. 357, 358-59 D. Mass. 1950)

See also Accounting profession; Audit; Working papers.

PRO FORMA

A pro forma statement or presentation reports a statement or presentation that would have been shown if a different accounting principle or method had been in effect in an earlier period. For example, for certain accounting changes in the current year that affect a previous year(s), such as a change from straight-line depreciation to an accelerated depreciation method, income before extraordinary items and net income must be computed on a pro forma (as if or for the sake of form) basis for all periods presented as if the newly adopted principle had been applied during all periods affected.

See also Earnings per share; Budget.

PRODUCT FINANCING ARRANGEMENTS

Product financing arrangements are transactions in which a company sells a portion of its inventory to another entity with the intent to reacquire that inventory in the future. The purpose of such arrangements is generally a financing arrangement in which one party is able to finance the product and still retain control over its ultimate disposition. For example, Company A sells (i.e., transfers or parks) inventory to Company B and agrees to repurchase the inventory at a specified price and time. Company B uses the inventory as collateral for a bank loan. The proceeds of the bank loan are used by Company B to pay Company A for the inventory. At a later date, Company A repurchases the inventory from Company B plus related holding costs incurred by Company B; Company B uses these proceeds to repay the bank loan. For accounting purposes, Company A is financing its inventory even though legal title has passed to Company B. Company B might be interested in such an arrangement because it may want to work out a similar arrangement with Company A in the future or for other business reasons. Since the economic substance of the transaction did not involve a sale by Company A, the inventory transferred to Company B is included in Company's A's inventory even though Company B has legal title. The proceeds from the sale are recognized by Company A as a liability and not as revenue. This treatment requires Company A to report the product and liability (a financing arrangement) on its balance sheet. Exhibit P-4 illustrates a typical product financing arrangement.

See also Revenue; Off-balance sheet item; Recognition; Realization.

Exhibit P–4
Product Financing Arrangement Illustrated

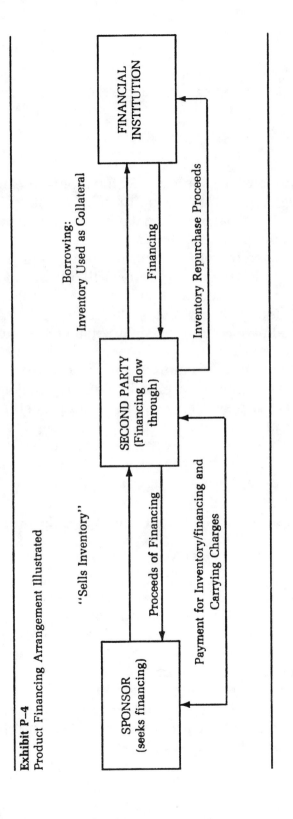

415

REFERENCE
SFAS No. 49, Accounting for Product Financing Arrangements (FASB, 1981).

PROPERTY

Any legally enforceable right which a person can acquire in something of value is a property right. Property is classified legally as either real or personal property. Real property refers to immovable property, that is, to land and anything permanently attached thereto (such as buildings, equipment, growing trees, etc.). Personal property is all other property, that is, movable property (such as automobiles, money, paintings, etc.). Personal property also includes interests evidenced by commercial paper and interests involved in the storage, shipment, sale, and financing of goods.

Eight states have community property systems. The rest are classified as common law jurisdictions. The major differences between the two systems center around property rights possessed by married persons. In a common law system, each spouse owns whatever he or she earns. In a community property system, one-half of the earnings of each spouse is considered owned by the other spouse.

See also Property, plant, and equipment; Estates and trusts.

PROPERTY, PLANT, AND EQUIPMENT

Property, plant, and equipment represent long-lived (fixed), tangible (possess physical substance) assets that are owned by business enterprises for use in operations and are not held for investment or for resale. *Property* refers to a resource such as land and can include building sites, parking areas, roads, etc. *Plant* refers to buildings, including structures, facilities, and attached appurtenances (e.g., lighting systems, air conditioning or heating systems, docks). *Equipment* includes such items as office and delivery equipment, machines, furniture and fixtures, motor vehicles, etc.

Property, plant, and equipment are usually presented in financial statements at historical (or acquisition) cost, adjusted for accumulated depreciation. Acquisition cost is the cash or cash equivalent required to acquire the asset, including expenditures required to put the asset into proper condition and location for use. Depreciation is a process that allocates the cost of a tangible long-lived asset, less salvage value, over its useful life in a systematic and rational manner. Except for land, other items included in property, plant, and equipment are subject to depreciation. Property, plant, and equipment are usually classified on the balance sheet after current assets and investments.

When assets are acquired in an exchange of one asset for another asset, such as trade-ins, the cost of the asset acquired is generally considered to be the fair market value of the surrendered asset. If the exchange is not essentially the culmination of the earning process, the exchanges should be recorded at the book value of the exchanged asset. Two examples of an exchange that does not result in the culmination of the earning process include

1. Exchange of a product or property held for sale in the ordinary course of business (inventory) for a product or property to be sold in the same line of business to facilitate sales to customers other than parties to the exchange (exchange of oil in New York for the same class of oil in California), and

2. Exchange of a productive asset not held for sale in the ordinary course of business for a similar productive asset (a drilling machine for a similar drilling machine).

Assets acquired in groups (lump-sum purchases) normally have separate purchase prices. It is necessary to allocate the total cost among the various assets acquired. For example, land, building, and equipment in the building may be acquired for a single amount. The acquisition price is usually assigned to the various assets based upon the relative market prices of the assets.

The acquisition cost of self-constructed assets includes all costs directly associated with the construction process, including direct material, direct labor, and overhead. In certain cases, interest charges during the construction of the asset are charged to the asset under construction.

Assets acquired as gifts from municipalities, citizens, and others as inducements to locate plants in certain areas have no cost but would nevertheless be recorded at their fair market value with a like amount recorded in an equity account termed *donated capital*. Natural resources may be discovered on property subsequent to the purchase of the property. The appraisal increase in the property is sometimes recorded.

Land held for speculative purposes or building and equipment no longer in use are excluded from the property, plant, and equipment category. Real estate held for resale by a real estate agency would also be excluded since it represents inventory and not property, plant, and equipment.

See also Asset; Cost principle; Nonmonetary exchanges; Depreciation; Property; Capital and revenue expenditures.

REFERENCE
Kieso, Donald E., and Weygandt, Jerry J., *Intermediate Accounting* (John Wiley & Sons, N.Y., 1986).

PROPERTY TAXES
Governmental authorities such as counties, cities, and school districts levy taxes on real and personal property. Assessed values of property are used as the basis for setting a tax rate sufficient to raise tax revenue that will meet budget requirements. Tax rates usually are determined by using a formula similar to the following:

$$\text{Tax rate} = \frac{\text{Revenue required}}{\text{Assessed property valuation}}$$

Tax rates are usually expressed as a certain number of dollars per $100 of assessed valuation.

Accountants use various methods for accruing real and personal property taxes. The preferable method is monthly accrual using the fiscal period of the taxing jurisdiction. Property taxes are usually recognized as expenses except where capitalized (as assets) while property is being developed or prepared for use.

See also Liabilities.

PROSPECTUS

A prospectus is a document that describes a new security issue. The prospectus is in the form of a circular, letter, notice, or advertisement which offers a security for sale and is filed with the Securities and Exchange Commission (SEC) as part of the registration statement. The Securities Act of 1933 was intended to provide the investing public with full and fair disclosure of information necessary to evaluate the merits of security offerings. The Act requires that a registration statement be filed with the Securities and Exchange Commission. To provide the investing public with information included in the registration statements, a prospectus is to be provided potential investors before or at the time of the sale or delivery of the securities.

See also Securities and Exchange Commission.

PROXY

A proxy is a document or authorization given by a stockholder to another person that allows that person to vote the stockholder's shares of stock in a corporate meeting. Persons are prohibited from soliciting proxies unless the stockholders have been furnished a written proxy statement or prospectus. A proxy statement discloses matters to be voted on at the next meeting of the shareholders whose proxies are solicited. Proxy solications can relate to a variety of matters, especially to obtaining voting power in connection with an annual meeting at which directors are to be elected or for a special meeting. Special meetings often relate to the authorization or issuance of securities other than for exchange, modification or exchange of securities, stock options to officers and directors, mergers, consolidations, acquisitions, and related matters. Each person solicited by management for a proxy in connection with an annual shareholders' meeting at which directors are to be elected must be furnished with an annual report to shareholders.

See also Financial markets.

PRUDENT MAN RULE
The prudent man rule is a legal concept of prudence. For example, a prudent man will not invest in speculative securities, will diversify to spread risks and avoid a catastrophic loss, and will remain relatively liquid so that distributions and payments can be made. The prudent man rule has special applications to situations involving estates and trusts.

See also Fiduciary.

PURCHASE ACCOUNTING
Purchase accounting is an accounting method that is used under certain circumstances in accounting for a business combination, e.g., a merger, consolidation, or stock acquisition. Accounting for a business combination by the purchase method follows principles normally applicable under the historical-cost method for acquisitions of assets and issuances of stock.

The cost to the purchasing entity of acquiring another company in a business combination treated as a purchase is the amount of cash disbursed or the fair value of other assets distributed or securities issued. The cost of the assets recorded on the acquired company's books is not recorded by the acquiring company as the cost of the purchased assets, as would be the case when the pooling-of-interests method is used. Since the assets acquired are recorded at their fair market value, any excess of cost over these fair values of total identifiable net assets is assigned to intangibles, such as goodwill. Goodwill is amortized over a period of years not to exceed 40. The purchase method of accounting must be used for a business combination unless all conditions prescribed for a pooling of interests are met.

In purchase accounting, postacquisition earnings of the acquired entity are combined with the surviving entity's earnings. Restatement of the financial statements of prior years is not required.

See also Pooling of interests; Business combinations; Consolidation; Equity method of accounting.

REFERENCE
Accounting Research Bulletin No. 51, Business Combinations (AICPA, Committee on Accounting Procedure, 1959).

QUALITATIVE CHARACTERISTICS OF ACCOUNTING INFORMATION

Qualitative characteristics of accounting information are those qualities or ingredients of accounting information that make it useful. The FASB's Statement of Financial Accounting Concepts No. 2, Qualitative Characteristics of Accounting Information, discusses the qualitative characteristics that make accounting information useful and are the qualities to be sought when accounting choices are made. The diagram in Exhibit Q-1 outlines what is referred to as a hierarchy of accounting information qualities. Exhibit Q-2 provides a summary of definitions used in Exhibit Q-1.

The hierarchical arrangement is used to show certain relationships among the qualities. The hierarchy shows that information useful for decision making is the most important. The primary qualities are that accounting information shall be relevant and reliable. If either of these two qualities is completely missing, the information cannot be useful. To be relevant, information must be timely, and it must have predictive value or feedback value or both. To be reliable, information must have representational faithfulness and it must be verifiable and neutral. Comparability, including consistency, is a secondary quality that interacts with relevance and reli-

426

Exhibit Q-1
Qualitative Characteristics of Accounting Information

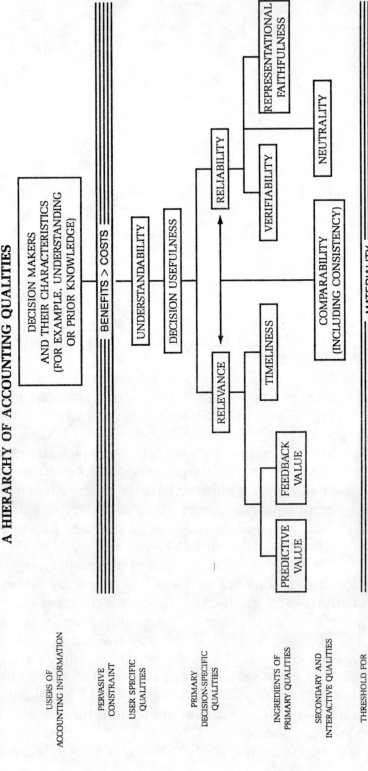

A HIERARCHY OF ACCOUNTING QUALITIES

USERS OF
ACCOUNTING INFORMATION

PERVASIVE
CONSTRAINT

USER SPECIFIC
QUALITIES

PRIMARY
DECISION-SPECIFIC
QUALITIES

INGREDIENTS OF
PRIMARY QUALITIES

SECONDARY AND
INTERACTIVE QUALITIES

THRESHOLD FOR
RECOGNITION

DECISION MAKERS
AND THEIR CHARACTERISTICS
(FOR EXAMPLE, UNDERSTANDING
OR PRIOR KNOWLEDGE)

BENEFITS > COSTS

UNDERSTANDABILITY

DECISION USEFULNESS

RELEVANCE

RELIABILITY

PREDICTIVE
VALUE

FEEDBACK
VALUE

TIMELINESS

VERIFIABILITY

REPRESENTATIONAL
FAITHFULNESS

NEUTRALITY

COMPARABILITY
(INCLUDING CONSISTENCY)

MATERIALITY

Source: Statement of Financial Accounting Concepts No. 2. "Qualitative Characteristics of Accounting Information" (Stamford. FASB. May 1980). Copyright by Financial Accounting Standards Board. High Ridge

Exhibit Q-2
Definitions: Qualitative Characteristics of Accounting Information

Bias Bias in measurement is the tendency of a measure to fall more often on one side than the other of what it represents instead of being equally likely to fall on either side. Bias in accounting mesures means a tendency to be consistently too high or too low.

Comparability The quality of information that enables users to identify similarities in and differences between two sets of economic phenomena.

Completeness The inclusion in reported information of everything material that is necessary for faithful representation of the relevant phenomena.

Conservatism A prudent reaction to uncertainty to try to insure that uncertainty and risks inherent in business situations are adequately considered.

Consistency Conformity from period to period with unchanging policies and procedures.

Feedback Value The quality of information that enables users to confirm or correct prior expectations.

Materiality The magnitude of an omission or misstatement of accounting information that, in the light of surrounding circumstances, makes it probable that the judgment of a resonable person relying on the information would have been changed or influenced by the omission or misstatement.

Neutrality Absence in reported information of bias intended to attain a predetermined result or to induce a particular mode of behavior.

Predictive Value The quality of information that helps users to increase the likelihood of correctly forecasting the outcome of past or present events.

Relevance The capacity of information to make a difference in a decision by helping users to form predictions about the outcomes of past, present, and future events or to confirm or correct prior expectations.

Reliability The quality of information that assures that information is reasonably free from error and bias and faithfully represents what it purports to represent.

Representational Faithfulness Correspondence or agreement between a measure or description and the phenomenon that it purports to represent (sometimes called validity).

Timeliness Having information available to a decision maker before it loses its capacity to influence decisions.

Understandability The quality of information that enables users to perceive its significance.

Verifiability The ability through consensus among measures to ensure that information represents what it purports to represent or that the chosen method of measurement has been used without error or bias.

Source: *Statement of Financial Accounting Concepts No. 2.* "Qualitative Characteristics of Accounting Information" (Stamford, FASB, May 1980). Copyright © by Financial Accounting Standards Board, High Ridge Park, Stamford, Connecticut 06905, U.S.A. Reprinted with permission.

Q

ability and contributes to the overall usefulness of information. Two constraints are shown on the chart: benefits must exceed costs and materiality. To be useful and worth providing, the benefits of information should exceed its cost. All of the qualities described are subject to a materiality threshold. Materiality refers to whether the magnitude of an omission or misstatement of accounting information would influence the judgment of a reasonable person relying on the information.

Information provided by financial reporting should be understandable to those who have a reasonable understanding of business and economic activities and are willing to study the information with reasonable diligence.

The hierarchy of qualitative characteristics does not rank the characteristics. If information is to be useful, all characteristics are required to a minimum degree. At times various qualities may conflict in particular circumstances, in which event trade-offs are often necessary or appropriate. For example, the most relevant information may be difficult to understand, or information that is easy to understand may not be very relevant.

See also Conceptual framework of accounting; Materiality; Consistency; Cost-benefit analysis.

REFERENCE
SFAC No. 2, Qualitative Characteristics of Accounting Information (FASB, 1981).

QUASI-REORGANIZATION
When a corporation gets into financial difficulties, it may attempt to reorganize its capital structure through formal court proceedings. To avoid the problems and expense of court proceedings, a procedure called quasi-reorganization can be undertaken that will accomplish basically the same objective. The purpose of a quasi-reorganization is to absorb a deficit (debit balance in the retained earnings account) and give the

enterprise a "fresh start." In a quasi-reorganization, a deficit is eliminated against contributed capital. If legal capital is being reduced, state approval is normally required; otherwise, only stockholders' approval is required. Once the deficit is eliminated, the corporation can proceed as though it had been legally reorganized. If the corporation operates profitably after the quasi-reorganization, dividends can be declared which would not have been possible in most states if the deficit had not been eliminated.

Subsequent to the quasi-reorganization, the new retained earnings account shown in the balance sheet must be dated to show it runs from the effective date of the readjustment. This dating should be disclosed in the statements as long as it has special significance, usually until after a post-reorganization earnings pattern has been established. A balance sheet disclosure in the stockholders' equity section could be as follows:

Retained earnings accumulated since
October 31, 1992, at which time a $500,000
deficit was eliminated as a result of a
quasi-reorganization $80,000

See also Reorganization; Bankruptcy.

REFERENCE
Chasteen, Larry G., et al., *Intermediate Accounting* (Random House, N.Y., 1984).

R

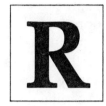

RATIOS

A ratio is an expression of a mathematical relationship between one quantity and another. The ratio of 400 to 200 is 2:1 or 2. If a ratio is to have any utility, the elements which constitute the ratio must express a meaningful relationship. For example, there is a relationship between accounts receivable and sales, between net income and total assets, and between current assets and current liabilities. Ratio analysis can disclose relationships which reveal conditions and trends that often cannot be noted by inspection of the individual components of the ratio.

Ratios are generally not significant of themselves but assume significance when they are compared with previous ratios of the same firm ratios of other enterprises in the same industry, and ratios of the industry within which the company operates.

It is helpful to organize ratios in terms of areas to be analyzed and interpreted. At least three major areas can be identified:

1. Short-term liquidity.

2. Capital structure (and long-term solvency).

3. Earnings and profitability.

Short-term liquidity refers to the ability of a firm to meet its current obligations as they mature. The relationship of current assets to current liabilities is an important indicator of the degree to which a firm is liquid. Working capital and the components of working capital also provide measures of the liquidity of a firm.

The capital structure of an enterprise consists of debt and equity funds. The sources and composition of the two types of capital determine to a considerable extent the financial stability and long-term solvency of the firm. A company's capitalization usually depends on the industry, the financial position of the company, and the philosophy of management. Long-term debt and preferred stock can add "leverage" to a company's capital structure. Capital structure ratios provide information on the debt capacity of the company and its level of financial risk.

Operating and profitability performance ratios reflect the results of the profit-seeking activities of an enterprise. Much of the data required for evaluating performance is obtained directly from the income statement, which summarizes the results of operations. However, performance should be related to the assets which produce the earnings and how outsiders (e.g., the stock market) perceive the performance and earnings of the enterprise. Measures of operating performance usually provide answers to the following questions: How much profit does the company make on each dollar of investment? How much profit does the company make on each dollar of sales? The profitability of investment usually relates to the following:

1. Return on total assets (total investment).
2. Return on invested capital (debt and equity).
3. Return on owners' investment (shareholders' equity).

The profitability of sales focuses on specific contributions of purchasing, production, administration, and overall profitability as reflected in gross profit margin, operating profit margin, and net profit margin.

434

Several important profitability ratios are sometimes referred to as "market value" ratios. Most of these ratios relate to the valuation of stock and are of considerable importance to financial analysts and stockholders. These ratios include earnings per share, dividends per share, yield on common stock, dividend payout, and book value per share of common stock. Major financial ratios are illustrated in Exhibit R-1.

See also Financial statement analysis; Leverage; Return on investment; Liquidity.

REFERENCES
Bernstein, Leopold A., *Financial Statement Analysis* (Richard D. Irwin, Homewood, IL, 1983).
Coleman, Almand, et al., *Financial Accounting and Statement Analysis: A Manager's Guide* (Robert F. Dame, Richmond, VA, 1982).

REAL ESTATE TRANSACTIONS

Real estate sales are divided into two broad accounting categories: (1) retail land sales and (2) real estate sales other than retail land sales. Retail land sales involve sales of real estate on a volume basis with relatively small downpayments. The seller usually develops the land by subdividing the property, selling the lots, and making improvements such as paving, landscaping, etc. Revenue is recognized on retail land sales when the following conditions are met: (1) the refund period has expired, (2) the cumulative payments equal or exceed 10 percent of the sales price, (3) the receivables are collectible and are not subordinate to new loans on the property, and (4) the seller either is not obligated to make improvements on the lots sold or has made progress on improvements promised. Depending upon the circumstances, revenue is recognized under one of the following methods: full accrual method, deposit method, installment method, or percentage of completion method.

Exhibit R-1
Financial Statement Ratios

Ratio	Formula	Solution to case	Interpretation
Liquidity ratios			
a. Current (or working capital) ratio	$\dfrac{\text{Current assets}}{\text{Current liabilities}}$	$\dfrac{\$430,000}{\$215,000} = 2$	Short-term debt-paying ability (i.e., dollar amount of current assets from which to obtain funds necessary to liquidate each dollar of current liabilities).
b. Acid-test (or quick) ratio	$\dfrac{\text{Quick assets, i.e., cash marketable securities, receivables}}{\text{Current liabilities}}$	$\dfrac{\$350,000}{\$215,000} = 1.6$	A more severe test of the short-term debt-paying ability than the current ratio since it excludes inventory (which awaits sale) and prepaid expenses.
c. Cash ratio	$\dfrac{\text{Cash}}{\text{Current liabilities}}$	$\dfrac{\$50,000}{\$215,000} = .23$	The severest test of short-term debt-paying ability.
Measures of the movement or turnover of current assets and liabilities			
a. Receivables turnover	$\dfrac{\text{Sales (net)}}{\text{Average receivables (net)}}$	$\dfrac{\$625,000}{\$225,000} = 2.7$	The efficiency in collecting receivables and in managing credit.
b. Age of receivables	$\dfrac{365}{\text{Receivables turnover}}$	$\dfrac{365}{2.7} = 135$	The number of days it takes on the average to collect accounts receivable; the extent of control over credit and collection.
c. Inventory turnover	$\dfrac{\text{Cost of goods sold}}{\text{Average inventory}}$	$\dfrac{\$100,000}{\$70,000} = 1.4$	Marketability of inventory, efficiency in the management of inventory, and the reasonableness of the quantity of inventory on hand.
d. Days in inventory	$\dfrac{365}{\text{Inventory turnover}}$	$\dfrac{365}{1.4} = 261$	The average number of days required to use or sell inventory (e.g., the average period that an item is held in inventory). For a manufacturing company, the number of days should correspond closely with production time.
e. Working capital turnover	$\dfrac{\text{Net sales}}{\text{Average working capital}}$	$\dfrac{\$625,000}{\$207,500} = 3$	The extent to which a company is using working capital to generate sales.
f. Number of days' purchases in ending accounts payable	$\dfrac{\text{Accounts payable}}{\text{Average daily purchases}}$	$\dfrac{\$100,000}{\$50,000} = 2$	The extent to which the company is paying its bills promptly.
Solvency ratios			
1. Measures of capital structure:			
a. Owners' equity to total assets	$\dfrac{\text{Total owners' equity}}{\text{Total assets (net)}}$	$\dfrac{\$615,000}{\$1,330,000} = .46$	Proportion of firm's assets provided by owner.

Exhibit R-1
Financial Statement Ratios (Continued)

Ratio	Formula	Solution to case	Interpretation
b. Owners' equity to total liabilities	$\dfrac{\text{Total owner's equity}}{\text{Total liabilities}}$	$\dfrac{\$615,000}{\$715,000} = .86$	Relative claims of owners and creditors to rest of firm.
c. Fixed assets to total equity	$\dfrac{\text{Total owners' equity}}{\text{Fixed assets (net)}}$	$\dfrac{\$615,000}{\$400,000} = 1.53$	Relationship of owners' investment to the company investment in fixed assets (i.e., the higher the ratio, the less owners' capital is available for working capital).
d. Book value per share of common stock	$\dfrac{\text{Common stock equity}}{\text{Number of common shares outstanding}}$	$\dfrac{\$615,000}{10,000} = \$61.50$	Net assets reported on financial statement per share of common stock.
2. Measures of debt structure (debt management):			
a. Total liabilities to total assets	$\dfrac{\text{Total liabilities}}{\text{Total assets (net)}}$	$\dfrac{\$715,000}{\$1,330,000} = .53$	Protection available to creditors and the extent to which the company is trading on equity.
b. Total liabilities to owners' equity	$\dfrac{\text{Total liabilities}}{\text{Owners' equity}}$	$\dfrac{\$715,000}{\$615,000} = 1.2$	Relationship between total debt and equity financing. "What is owed to what is owned."
Profitability (earnings) ratios			
1. Net income to sales	$\dfrac{\text{Net income}}{\text{Net sales}}$	$\dfrac{\$250,000}{\$625,000} = .4$	Profit margin per dollar of sales.
2. Operating ratio	$\dfrac{\text{Cost of goods sold} + \text{operating expenses}}{\text{Net sales}}$	$\dfrac{\$100,000 + \$150,000}{\$625,000} = .4$	Profit margin per dollar of sales.
3. Sales to total assets (or asset turnover)	$\dfrac{\text{Net sales}}{\text{Average total assets}}$	$\dfrac{\$625,000}{\$1,077,000} = .57$	Productivity of all assets in generating sales.
4. Earnings per share of common stock	$\dfrac{\text{Net income-preferred}}{\text{dividend requirements}} \Big/ \text{Average number of common stock}$	$\dfrac{\$250,000}{10,000} = \$25$	Return on common shareholders' investment per share of

Exhibit R-1
Financial Statement Ratios (Continued)

Ratio	Formula	Solution to case	Interpretation
5. Price/earnings ratio	$$\frac{\text{Market price per share of common stock}}{\text{Net income per share of common stock}}$$	$$\frac{\$75}{\$25} = \$3$$	Price paid for stock per dollar of earnings (i.e., the price of earnings). Newspaper include this information in daily stock tables.
6. Dividends yield	$$\frac{\text{Annual cash dividends per share of common stock}}{\text{Market price per share of common stock}}$$	$$\frac{\$1}{\$75} = .013$$	Cash yield or return on common stock.
7. Return on investment (or return on assets	$$\frac{\text{Net income}}{\text{Average total assets}}$$	$$\frac{\$250,000}{\$1,077,000} = .23$$	Return on investment in total assets. Sometimes net operating income is used as the numerator while intangibles and investments are excluded from the denominator.
8. Return on common stockholders' equity	$$\frac{\text{Net income}}{\text{Average common stockholders' equity}}$$	$$\frac{\$250,000}{\$470,000} = .53$$	Return on the investment by common stockholders.
9. Payout ratio	$$\frac{\text{Cash dividends}}{\text{Net income}}$$	$$\frac{\$10,000}{\$250,000} = .04$$	The extent to which a company distributes current earnings to stockholders in the form of dividends i.e., the "generosity" of the Board of Directors.
10. Cash flow from operations per share of common stock	$$\frac{\text{Net income adjusted for noncash items}}{\text{Average number of shares of common stock outstanding}}$$	$$\frac{\$395,000}{10,000} = \$39.50$$	The amount of cash generated from operations for each share of stock.

Other real estate sales refers to any real estate sale except retail land sales. A sale should be recorded upon the closing of a transaction involving a transfer of the usual risks and rewards of ownership for a consideration. Profit recognition should be deferred until specific criteria have been met, including the adequacy of the downpayment by the purchaser, the purchaser's continuing commitment to the investment, and the seller's continuing commitment for performance. If these criteria are not met, then one of the following methods should be used depending upon the circumstances: deposit method, installment method, or cost recovery method.

See also Revenue; Realization; Recognition; Installment method; Construction-type contracts.

REFERENCE
SFAS No. 66, Accounting for Sale of Real Estate (FASB, 1982).

REALIZATION
Realization refers to the process of converting noncash resources and rights into money, and is used in accounting and financial reporting to refer to sales of assets for cash or claims to cash. The terms *realized* and *unrealized* identify revenues or gains or losses on assets sold and unsold, respectively. Accrual accounting recognizes revenue as being realized when it is earned. Under accrual-basis accounting, revenue is usually realized when it is earned. Revenue is generally considered as being earned when the earning process is completed and an exchange has taken place. For example, a manufacturer makes and then sells a product. Revenue is realized when the sale takes place (and not when the product is manufactured) because the earning process is substantially completed and an exchange took place. Revenue from sales of products is often recognized at the date of sale, usually interpreted to mean the date of delivery to customers. Revenue from services rendered is recognized when services have been per-

formed and are billable. Revenue from permitting others to use enterprise resources, such as interest, rent, and royalties, is recognized as time passes or as the resources are used.

Modifications of the revenue realization principle described above include the following:

1. Revenue recognized during production. In long-term construction contracts, contractors can recognize revenue during the construction period using the percentage-of-completion method. This method can be used when the contract price is definite, when a reasonable estimate can be made of progress towards the completion of the project, and the costs incurred or to be incurred are known or can be estimated.

2. Revenue recognized at the completion of production. Revenue is sometimes recognized when production is completed. Precious minerals and some agricultural commodities trade in markets which have a readily determinable and realizable market price. Revenue could be recognized for such product when production is completed and before a sale occurs.

3. Revenue recognized when cash is collected. When considerable uncertainty exists concerning the collectibility of an account, revenue can be recognized as cash is received after the sale. The installment sales method or the cost recovery method would be appropriate for recognizing revenue under these circumstances.

See also Recognition; Measurement; Revenue; Construction-type contracts; Installment sales method; Service sales transactions; Product financing arrangement; Sales with right of return.

REFERENCE
SFAC No. 5, Recognition and Measurement in Financial Statements (FASB, 1984).

RECEIVABLES

A receivable is a claim against others for the future receipt of money, goods, or services. Receivables include accounts receivable (sometimes called trade receivables), installment sales receivable, notes receivable, receivables from officers or employees, claims against insurance companies for damages to property, and many other claims.

Accounts receivable arise from the sale of goods or services on account. A major problem associated with accounts receivable is determining what recognition should be given to the possibility that the amount owed may not be collected. The allowance method and the direct write-off method are employed to deal with uncollectible accounts. Under the allowance method, an estimate of uncollectible accounts is made at the end of each accounting period and reported in the income statement as an expense. On the balance sheet, estimated uncollectible receivables are deducted from the gross amount of accounts receivable. This deduction serves as a contra asset or valuation account. The estimated amount of uncollectible accounts is determined as a percentage of credit sales for the period, a percentage of the ending accounts receivable, or by aging the accounts receivable. The allowance method is used when there is high probability that some receivables will not be collected and when the seller can estimate the dollar amount considered to be uncollectible. When the direct write-off method is used, the account is written off and an expense is recognized in the income statement when a customer actually defaults on payment. The write-off method cannot be used when uncollectible amounts are significant and can be estimated.

See also Valuation allowance; Notes receivable; Factoring; Aging schedule.

RECOGNITION

Recognition is the process of formally including an item into the financial statements of an entity as an asset, liability, revenue, expense, or the like. Items are recognized in the statements in both words and numbers. An item and information about the item must meet four fundamental recognition criteria to be recognized, subject to a cost-benefit constraint and a materiality threshold:

1. Definition. The item must meet the definition of an element of financial statements.

2. Measurability. It has a relevant attribute measurable with sufficient reliability.

3. Relevance. The information about it is capable of making a difference in users' decisions.

4. Reliability. The information is representationally faithful, verifiable, and neutral.

The amount of revenue recognized in the financial statements is measured by different attributes (for example, historical cost, current cost, current market value, net realizable value, and present value of future cash flows).

Revenues and gains are generally not recognized as components of earnings until realized or realizable and earned. The basic rule is that revenue is recognized when the earning process is completed and an exchange has taken place. This is usually at the point of sale or when a service has been performed. Certain departures from this principle are allowed.

See also Realization; Asset; Liabilities; Revenue; Expenses; Measurement; Elements of financial statements; Qualitative characteristics of accounting information.

REFERENCE
SFAC No. 5, Recognition and Measurement in Financial Statements (FASB, 1984).

REFUNDING

Refunding refers to the replacement of an existing debt issue through the sale of a new issue. The issuing of new bonds and the cancellation of the old issue are considered two separate transactions. Retiring the old bonds results in a realized gain or loss equal to the difference between the carrying amount of the bonds and the price paid to retire the bonds. The gain or loss is recognized in the accounting period when the bonds are retired and is not deferred to be amortized in future periods.

See also Bonds.

RELATED PARTY TRANSACTIONS

For accounting purposes, related parties may be any of the following: affiliates; principal owners and close kin; management and close kin; parent companies and subsidiaries; equity method investors and investees; trusts for the benefit of employees, such as pension or profit-sharing trusts managed by or under the trusteeship of management; or any other party that can significantly influence the management or operating policies of the reporting enterprise, to the extent that it may be prevented from operating in its own best interest. Such other parties could include an officer or director of a corporation, a stockholder, and a partner or joint venturer in a partnership or venture. An affiliate is a party that controls, is controlled by, or is under common control with another enterprise, directly or indirectly. Principal owners are owners of more than 10 percent of an enterprise's voting interest. Management includes persons who have policy-making and decision-making authority within an enterprise and who are responsible for attaining an enterprise's objectives. Next of kin refers to immediate family members whom a principal owner or a member of management might control or influence or by whom they might be controlled or influenced because of the family relationship.

In related party transactions, one party is in a position to control a transaction or the effect of a transaction on another party. In such situations, a conflict of interest or transactions with insiders may occur. Examples of related party transactions that commonly occur in the normal course of business include sales, purchases, transfers of realty and personal property, services received or furnished, use of property and equipment, borrowings and lendings, and guarantees. Transactions between related parties cannot be presumed to be arm's-length transactions.

Financial statements must include disclosures of material, related party transactions, except compensation arrangements, expense allowances, and other similar items in the normal course of business. Disclosure shall include the nature of the relationship, a description of transaction(s), dollar amount of transactions, and amounts due to and from related parties. An auditor's responsibility in related party transactions is to make reasonable inquiry to determine that all material relationships are identified and disclosed and that such transactions do not violate fiduciary relationships.

See also Arm's-length transaction; Fraud; Audit; Substance over form.

REORGANIZATION
Reorganization under Chapter 11 of the Bankruptcy Reform Act of 1978 contemplates the continuation of the business enterprise and its eventual rehabilitation, rather than Chapter 7 bankruptcy, which has for its purpose the orderly liquidation and distribution of the estate to creditors according to their rank. Chapter 11 is primarily available for businesses, although individuals are eligible. The major purpose of this chapter is to allow debtors to adjust their debts, satisfy or modify liens on property, and avoid a liquidation case under Chapter 7. Filing a petition under Chapter 11 effectively stays the debtor's creditors.

A Chapter 11 process involves the following procedures:

1. proceedings are initiated either voluntarily by the debtor or involuntarily by at least three creditors with claims of at least $5,000 (where more than 12 creditors exist); fewer than three creditors with $5,000 or more in claims where less than 12 creditors exist;

2. the court may appoint a trustee who has custody of the property; a creditors' committee typically comprised of the largest creditors is established;

3. a plan of reorganization is proposed; a debtor in possession has exclusive right to file a plan during the first 120 days after the date of the order for relief; if a trustee has been appointed or if the debtor's plan has not met the 120-day deadline, other parties may file a plan; whoever proposes the plan must come forward with a disclosure statement which provides specific information about the debtor, its history and prospects, and details about the plan;

4. the court may approve or disapprove this informational document;

5. the plan and disclosure statement are submitted to those whose claims and interest are impaired by the plan;

6. finally, if the plan has been accepted by every class of impaired creditors and equity security holders, the court confirms the plan if the specified minimum criteria are satisfied, e.g., if it is in the best interests of creditors and is feasible. Confirmation of the reorganization plan discharges a nonbusiness debtor from most if not all of its debts.

See also Liquidation; Bankruptcy; Quasi-reorganization; Solvency and insolvency.

REFERENCE
Ginsberg, Robert E., *Bankruptcy* (Prentice-Hall, Englewood Cliffs, NJ, 1985).

R

RESEARCH AND DEVELOPMENT COSTS

According to the FASB, research and development costs are those costs related to developing new products or processes, services, or techniques, or modifying existing ones. Research is a planned search or critical investigation aimed at discovery of new knowledge; development refers to bringing research findings into a plan or design for further action. Development includes the conceptual formulation, design, and testing of product alternatives, construction of prototypes, and operation of pilot plants. It does not include routine or periodic alterations to existing products, production lines, manufacturing processes, and other ongoing operations.

All research and development costs should be charged to expense when incurred. This implies that the future expected value of research and development cost does not merit recognition as an asset because of the risks, uncertainties, and estimates involved.

The cost of materials, equipment, and facilities that are acquired or constructed for research and development activities and that have alternative future uses should be capitalized when acquired or constructed. However, when such equipment and facilities are used, the depreciation of such items and the materials consumed should be included as research and development costs. Activities that normally are considered research and development costs include:

Laboratory research aimed at discovery of new knowledge.
Searching for applications of new research findings or other knowledge.
Testing in search of or evaluation of product or process alternatives.
Modification of the formulation or design of a product or process.

See also Intangible assets.

REFERENCE
SFAS No. 2, Accounting for Research and Development Costs (FASB, 1974).

RESERVES

Reserve is an accounting term that is used only to describe an appropriation of retained earnings. The major purpose for appropriating retained earnings is to provide more information to the users of the financial statements. Only the board of directors can appropriate retained earnings. Reasons for appropriating retained earnings include contractual agreements requiring such appropriations (e.g., a bond indenture may place a limitation on dividends), state law (e.g., required by some states when treasury stock is acquired which could impair the capital of the company), and voluntary actions by the board to retain assets in the business for future use. The creation of a reserve is the result of an accounting entry shown below and does not set aside cash or any other asset of the company. This term has been used in the past as a valuation account (e.g., Reserve for Depreciation) and as a liability whose amount is uncertain (e.g., Reserve for Income Taxes). The term should no longer be used for such purposes.

A Reserve account for unspecified contingencies would be created by transferring an amount from Retained Earnings to the Reserve account.

Retained Earnings	50,000	
Reserve (or Appropriation) for Contingencies		50,000

When the reserve for contingencies is no longer needed, the appropriation can be returned to retained earnings:

Reserve (or Appropriation) for Contingencies	50,000	
Retained Earnings		50,000

The return of the appropriation to retained earnings increases unappropriated retained earnings without affecting the assets or current position of the company.

If an enterprise desired to set aside cash or other assets to provide for the contingencies, it could do so by establishing a fund (not a reserve). This action would represent a transaction which has economic significance. The establishment of the fund could be made as follows:

Contingency Fund (an asset)	50,000	
Cash		50,000

See also Retained earnings; Shareholders' equity.

RETAIL METHOD
The retail inventory method is a procedure that can be used to estimate inventory on a specific date. The retail method is widely used by department stores and other retail and whole-sale enterprises. In order to estimate ending inventory by the retail method, the following information must be available: beginning inventory at cost and at retail; net purchases during the period at cost and at retail values for the period. The following exhibit illustrates the computation of ending inventory, which involves computing a ratio of cost to retail of goods available for sale and then applying this ratio to the ending inventory taken at retail to convert it to the ending inventory at cost:

	At Cost	At Retail	Ratio
Inventory, January 31	$ 50,000	$ 75,000	
Purchases (net) during the period	300,000	450,000	
Goods available for sale	$350,000	525,000	0.6667
Less: January sales		425,000	
Inventory, January 31, at retail		$100,000	
Inventory, January 31, at cost:			
$100,000 × 0.6667	$66,667		

Modifications of this procedure are required when additional markups and markup cancellations and markdowns and markdown cancellations require adjustments to the computations. Markups refer to an additional markup on original sales price; markup cancellations are decreases in prices of merchandise that had been marked up above the original retail price. Markdowns are decreases below the original sale prices; markdown cancellations are decreases of markdowns arising when prices of previously marked down merchandise are increased but not to exceed the markdowns. The retail method with markups and markup cancellations and markdowns and markdown cancellations is presented in Exhibit I-8.

See also Inventory.

REFERENCE
Davidson, Sidney, et al., *Intermediate Accounting* (The Dryden Press, Chicago, 1985).

RETAINED EARNINGS
Retained earnings are earnings of the corporation which have not been distributed in the form of dividends. The major factors that affect retained earnings include:

1. Net income or loss, including income (loss) from continuing operations, discontinued operations, extraordinary gains or losses, and the cumulative effects of changes in accounting principles.

2. Dividends (cash, property, script, stock, liquidating).

3. Prior period adjustments, primarily the correction of errors of prior periods.

4. Appropriations of retained earnings (legal, contractual, and discretionary).

A *deficit* is a negative retained earnings balance. A deficit is usually the result of accumulated prior net losses or dividends in excess of earnings.

See also Statement of retained earnings; Capital; Income; Dividends; Discontinued operations; Extraordinary item; Accounting changes; Prior period adjustments; Reserves; Deficit.

RETURN ON INVESTMENT

Return on investment (ROI) is a comprehensive measure of financial performance. The basic formula for computing return on investment involves the following:

ROI = Capital turnover × Margin as a percentage of sales

$$= \frac{\text{Sales}}{\text{Capital employed}} \times \frac{\text{Net income}}{\text{Sales}}$$

The relationship of ROI to balance sheet and income statement items is shown in Exhibit R-2. Note that ROI is computed in this exhibit as follows:

ROI = TURNOVER × EARNING RATIO

where

Turnover = Sales/Capital employed

and

Earning ratio (or Margin) = Net income/Sales

Capital turnover is the ratio of sales to capital employed in generating the sales. Capital turnover is a measure of the use of assets in relation to sales. Generally, the larger the volume of sales that management can generate on a given investment in assets, the more efficient are its operations. Margin is the ratio of net income to sales.

Capital employed can be interpreted to mean (1) total assets, (2) total assets less current liabilities (that is, working capital plus noncurrent assets), or (3) stockholders' equity. When management performance is being evaluated, either the first or second concept of capital employed should be used because management should be held responsible for assets available to them. When stockholders' equity is used as the measure of capital employed, the analysis stresses the long-range ability of the firm to make use of the investments of its owners.

The ROI formula takes into account all of the items that go into the balance sheet and income statement and so represents a comprehensive overview of performance. Exhibit R-2 shows a structural outline of the relationships that make up ROI.

Exhibit R–2
Return on Investment (ROI) Relationships

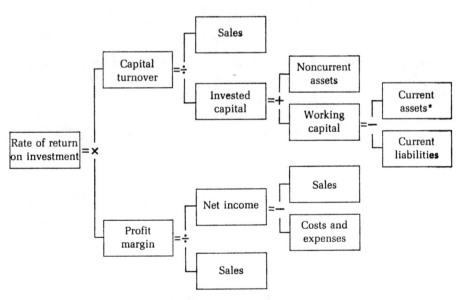

*Includes cash, accounts receivable, and inventory

To illustrate the computation of ROI, assume the following information is available:

Condensed income statement

Sales	$1,000,000
Less: Costs and expenses	800,000
Net income	$ 200,000

From the balance sheet

Working capital	$100,000
Plant and equipment	300,000
Total assets (Invested capital)	$400,000

$$\text{ROI} = \frac{\text{Net income}}{\text{Sales}} \times \frac{\text{Sales}}{\text{Invested capital}}$$

$$= \frac{\$200,000}{\$1,000,000} \times \frac{\$1,000,000}{\$400,000}$$

$$= \frac{\$200,000}{\$400,000}$$

$$= 50\%$$

Recall that the ROI formula can be restated as follows:

$$\text{ROI} = \text{Profit margin} \times \text{Capital turnover}$$

$$= 20\% \times 2.5$$

$$= 50\%$$

Various actions can be taken to improve ROI, including the following:

1. Increase total sales by increasing volume, sales price, or some combination thereof, while maintaining or improving the margin on sales.
2. Decrease expenses, thereby increasing net income.

3. Reduce the amount of capital employed (for example, reduce the inventory level, improve collection of accounts receivable) without decreasing sales.

If the chief executive officer of this firm wants to increase ROI to 60 percent next year and sales (price and/or volume) and invested capital cannot be changed, what change must occur in net income to achieve this objective?

$$\text{ROI} = 60\% = \frac{\$1,000,000}{\$400,000} \times \frac{\text{Net income (to be computed)}}{\$1,000,000}$$

$$60\% = \frac{\text{Net income}}{\$400,000}$$

Net income = $240,000 (i.e., $400,000 x 60%)

Management must focus attention on profit margin rather than on capital turnover, which is assumed to be unchangeable. Since sales cannot be increased, the improvement in net income must come from a reduction of expenses.

Advantages claimed for ROI analysis include the following:

1. Focuses management's attention upon earning the best return on total assets.
2. Serves as a measure of management's efficiency and effectiveness.
3. Integrates financial planning, budgeting, sales objectives, cost control, and profit-making activities.
4. Provides a basis for comparing companies.
5. Provides a motivational basis for management.
6. Identifies weaknesses in the utilization of assets.

See also Ratios; Financial statement analysis.

REFERENCE
Woelfel, Charles J., and Mecimore, Charles, *The Operating Executive's Handbook of Profit Planning Tools and Techniques* (Probus, Chicago, 1986).

REVENUE

Revenues represent actual or expected cash inflows (or the equivalent) that have occurred or will eventually occur as a result of the enterprise's ongoing major or central operations during the period. Gains are not revenue. Gains are increases in equity (net assets) from peripheral or incidental transactions of an entity and from all other transactions and other events and circumstances affecting the entity during a period except those that result from revenues or investments by owners.

Revenue arises primarily from one or more of the following activities:

1. Selling of products.
2. Rendering services.
3. Permitting others to use the entity's assets (leasing, renting, lending).
4. Disposing of assets other than products.

Recognition is the process of formally recording an item in the financial statements of an entity. Revenues are generally recognized when (1) the earning process is complete or virtually complete, and (2) an exchange has taken place. The earning process consists of all those activities that produce revenue, including purchasing, production, selling, delivering, administering, and others.

Revenue is usually recognized at the time of sale of a product or when services have been rendered. Revenue is sometimes recognized before the point of sale. For example, the percentage-of-completion method is sometimes used to recognize revenue from long-term construction contracts. Some long-term service contracts recognize revenue on the basis of proportional performance. Revenue is sometimes recognized after the point of sale where there is great uncertainty about the collectibility of the receivable involved in a sale. Under such circumstances, revenue can be recognized on the installment method or cost recovery method when cash is collected.

See also Income; Income statement; Elements of financial statements; Gains; Realization; Recognition; Measurement; Sales; Sales with right of return; Service sales transactions; Installment sales method; Construction-type contracts; Product financing arrangements; Real estate transactions.

REFERENCES
SFAC No. 3, Elements of Financial Statements of Business Enterprises (FASB, 1981).
SFAC No. 5, Recognition and Measurement in Financial Statements of Business Enterprises (FASB, 1984).

REVERSING ENTRIES
After the accounting records have been adjusted and closed at the end of the accounting period, reversing entries can be made on the first day of the new period to turn around (or reverse) certain adjusting entries. This accounting procedure often simplifies the recording of certain transactions in the new period. For example, assume that the following adjusting entry was made to record accrued salaries:

| December 31 | Salaries Expense | 5,000 | |
| | Salaries Payable | | 5,000 |

The reversing entry on January 1 of the new year is as follows:

| January 1 | Salaries Payable | 5,000 | |
| | Salaries Expense | | 5,000 |

See also Accounting system; Adjusting entries; Closing entries.

REVIEW

A review is defined as "performing inquiry and analytical procedures that provide the accountant with a reasonable basis for expressing limited assurance that there are no material modifications that should be made to the statements in order for them to be in conformity with generally accepted accounting principles or, if applicable, with another comprehensive basis of accounting." The objective of a review is to provide the accountant with a basis for expressing limited assurance that there are no material modifications that should be made to the financial statements.

See also Compilation; Audit.

REFERENCE
Burton, John C., et al., *Handbook of Accounting and Auditing* (Warren, Gorham & Lamont, Inc., Boston, 1981).

RULE OF 72 AND RULE OF 69

The rule of 72 refers to the computation of the time it takes for money at interest to double. It is computed as follows:

72/interest rate

For example, principal invested at 6 percent will double in approximately 12 years (72/.06).

The rule of 69 states that an amount of money invested at i percent per period will double in 69/i + .35 periods. For example, at 10 percent per period, a sum will double in 69/10% + .35 = 7.25 periods.

See also Interest.

S

S

SALES

Sales revenue includes the gross charges to customers for the goods and services provided during the accounting period. Net sales is gross sales less any sales returns or allowances available to customers and sales discounts taken by credit customers.

Sales are major business transactions involving the delivery of goods, merchandise, services, properties, and rights in exchange for cash or money equivalents, such as accounts and notes receivable. Most sales represent the normal, ongoing transactions of the enterprise. Other sales may be incidental, unusual in nature, and infrequent in occurrence. For accounting purposes, including recording and reporting, sales are usually classified as regular sales, sales from discontinued operations, or extraordinary sales on the income statement. Sales can also be classified according to the outline presented in Exhibit S-1.

See also Revenue; Sales with right of return; Real estate transactions; Service sales transactions; Sale-leaseback.

Exhibit S–1
Classification of Sales

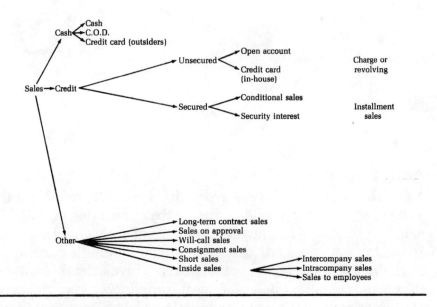

SALE-LEASEBACK

A sale-leaseback transaction is an arrangement whereby an owner sells property and then immediately leases it back from the buyer. The lessee often enters into such a lease to get working capital and for certain tax advantages that might be involved. The lessor usually enters into such an arrangement because it is a profitable investment.

From an accounting viewpoint, the sale and the leaseback are considered as a single transaction involving a secured loan. When certain conditions are met, any profit from the sale is deferred and amortized in proportion to the amortization of the leased asset, if a capital lease is involved, or in proportion to rental payments over the time the asset is used if an operating lease is involved.

See also Sales; Leases.

REFERENCE
Nikolai, Loren A., et al., *Intermediate Accounting* (Kent, Boston, 1985).

SALES WITH RIGHT OF RETURN

Sales contracts often permit the buyer to return merchandise for a full refund or allow for an adjustment to be made to the amount owed. Such contracts are common in such industries as publishing, records and tapes, and sporting goods.

Where a right to return exists, revenue is not recognized from the sale until all of the following criteria are met:

1. The sales price is fixed or determinable at the date of sale.
2. The buyer has paid or will pay the seller and the obligation is not contingent upon resale of the product.
3. The buyer's obligation to the seller would not be changed by theft or damage to the merchandise.
4. The buyer has an economic substance apart from the seller.
5. The seller does not have sufficient obligations for future performance to directly bring about the resale of the product by the buyer.
6. The amount of future returns can reasonably be estimated.

See Revenue; Sales; Realization; Recognition.

REFERENCE
SFAS No. 48, Revenue Recognition When Right of Return Exists (FASB, 1981).

S

SECURITIES AND EXCHANGE COMMISSION

The Securities and Exchange Commission (SEC) is a governmental agency established in 1934 to help regulate the securities market in the United States. The SEC has three major responsibilities: ensuring the provision of full and fair disclosure of all material facts concerning securities offered for public investment, initiating litigation for fraud cases when detected, and providing for the registration of securities offered for public investment.

The SEC is responsible for the administration and enforcement of the following acts: Securities Act of 1933, Securities Exchange Act of 1934, Public Utility Holding Company Act of 1935, Trust Indenture Act of 1939, Investment Company Act of 1940, Investment Advisers Act of 1940.

The SEC's main office is in Washington, D.C., and it has regional and branch officers in major financial centers. The SEC is directed by five commissioners appointed by the President with the approval of the Senate. The SEC is organized as shown in Exhibit S-2.

Public accountants deal primarily with the Corporate Finance Division and with the Office of the Chief Accountant. The Corporate Finance Division has primary responsibility to assure that the financial information given to the public in securities offerings is complete and not misleading. The Chief Accountant is the principal advisor to the commission on matters relating to accounting and auditing. Regulation S-X (Form and Content of Financial Statements), the Accounting Series Releases (ASRs), and a recently initiated series called Financial Reporting Releases (FRRs) are the major documents that prescribe the form, content, and methods used in reporting to the SEC. Although the SEC has developed its own rules and procedures, it has generally allowed the private sector to formulate generally accepted accounting principles.

See also Accounting organizations; Accounting principles.

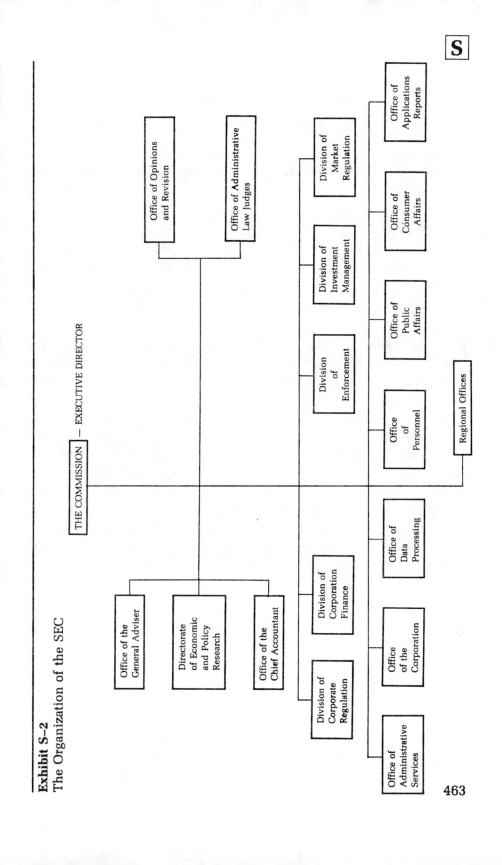

Exhibit S–2
The Organization of the SEC

S

THE COMMISSION — EXECUTIVE DIRECTOR

Office of Opinions and Revision

Office of Administrative Law Judges

Office of the General Adviser

Directorate of Economic and Policy Research

Office of the Chief Accountant

Division of Corporate Regulation

Division of Corporation Finance

Office of Administrative Services

Office of the Corporation

Office of Data Processing

Division of Enforcement

Division of Investment Management

Division of Market Regulation

Office of Personnel

Office of Public Affairs

Office of Consumer Affairs

Office of Applications Reports

Regional Offices

463

REFERENCES

Skousen, K. Fred, *An Introduction to the SEC* (South-Western, Cincinnati, OH, 1983).

Pointer, Larry Gene, and Schroeder, Richard G., *An Introduction to the Securities and Exchange Commission* (Business Publications, Plano, TX, 1986).

SEGMENTS

According to the FASB, a segment of a business is a part of an entity whose activities represent a major line of business or class of customer. A segment is a part of an enterprise that sells primarily to outsiders for a profit. Examples of a segment of a business include a subsidiary, a division, a department, a product, a market, or other separations where the activities, assets, liabilities, and operating income can be distinguished for operational and reporting purposes. Information about segments of a business, especially for diversified companies, is useful to investors of large, complex, heterogenous, publicly traded enterprises in evaluating risks, earnings, growth cycles, profit characteristics, capital requirements, and return on investments that can differ among segments of a business. The need for segment information is the result of many environmental factors, including the growth of conglomerates, acquisitions, diversifications, and foreign activities of enterprises.

A reportable segment is determined by the following procedures:

1. Identifying the enterprise's products and services.

2. Grouping the products and services into industry segments.

3. Selecting the significant industry segments by applying various tests established for this purpose.

Segment information that must be disclosed in financial statements includes an enterprise's operations in different industries, foreign operations and export sales, and major customers. Detailed information must be disclosed relating to revenues, segment's operating profit or loss, and identifiable assets along with additional information. Segment information is primarily a disaggregation of the entity's basic financial statements. Exhibit S-3 illustrates segment reporting.

REFERENCE
SFAS No. 14, Financial Reporting for Segments of a Business Enterprise (FASB, 1976).

SERVICE SALES TRANSACTIONS

Service sales transactions are transactions between a seller and a purchaser in which, for a mutually agreed price, the seller performs, agrees to perform, or agrees to maintain readiness to perform an act or acts, including permitting others to use enterprise resources that do not alone produce a tangible commodity or product as the principal intended result (FASB). Types of business that offer services include:
Advertising agencies
Computer service organizations
Employment agencies
Entertainment
Engineering firms
Retirement homes
Accounting firms
Architectural firms
Law firms
Travel agencies

Revenue from service transactions is recognized on the basis of the seller's performance. Performance is the execution of a defined act or acts or occurs with the passage of time. Four methods of recognizing revenue are:

1. Specific performance method.

2. Completed performance method.

Exhibit S-3
Segment Reporting Illustrated

ROCKWELL INTERNATIONAL

Sales and Income by segments

Years ended September 30
(In millions)

	1984		1983		1982		1981		1980	
	Sales	Income	Sales	Income	Sales	Income	Sales	Income	Sales	Income
Aerospace	$4,204	$380.7	$3,687	$335.1	$2,808	$227.1	$2,280	$201.5	$2,042	$112.8
Electronics	2,387	220.2	2,196	195.5	2,031	186.1	1,791	112.3	1,696	158.2
Automotive	1,758	214.8	1,204	44.5	1,358	49.4	1,538	17.5	1,735	92.5
General Industries	973	103.6	1,011	89.7	1,198	115.4	1,431	208.7	1,434	144.2
Total sales and operating Income	$9,322	919.3	$8,098	664.8	$7,395	578.0	$7,040	540.0	$6,907	507.5
General corporate—net		23.0		52.5		88.6		86.6		65.0
Interest expense		(42.8)		(27.2)		(35.7)		(40.5)		(46.8)
Provision for income taxes		(403.0)		(301.0)		(299.3)		(267.3)		(245.5)
Net Income		$496.5		$389.1		$331.6		$318.8		$280.2

Asset Information by segment

Business Segment	Identifiable Assets			Provision for Depreciation			Capital Expenditures		
	1984	1983	1982	1984	1983	1982	1984	1983	1982
Aerospace	$1,293	$1,055	$ 879	$ 80.8	$ 52.6	$ 28.7	$196.3	$191.9	$181.3
Electronics	1,419	1,260	1,224	97.8	78.9	67.7	199.2	135.4	110.9
Automotive	1,006	894	912	63.1	44.7	44.8	69.9	68.5	138.0
General Industries	553	623	679	31.2	31.9	29.8	38.1	32.5	52.8
Total segments	4,271	3,832	3,694	272.9	208.1	171.0	503.5	428.3	483.0
Corporate (assets—principally cash)	1,599	1,399	1,176	28.6	24.6	16.6	63.6	51.1	56.4
Total company	$5,870	$5,231	$4,870	$301.5	$232.7	$187.6	$567.1	$479.4	$539.4

Exhibit S-3
Segment Reporting Illustrated (Continued)

ROCKWELL INTERNATIONAL

Sales, Income and asset Information by geographic area

| | Sales | | | Operating Income | | | Identifiable Assets | | | | | |
| | | | | | | | Segments | | | Corporate | | |
Geographic Area	1984	1983	1982	1984	1983	1982	1984	1983	1982	1984	1983	1982
United States	$8,521	$7,371	$6,622	$845.1	$597.0	$499.9	$3,710	$3,338	$3,200	$1,436	$1,201	$ 995
Europe	423	410	466	22.4	35.0	50.5	354	283	294	75	95	84
Canada	257	196	169	41.9	30.3	24.8	110	110	100	40	44	29
Other	121	121	138	9.9	2.5	2.8	97	101	100	48	59	68
Total	$9,322	$8,098	$7,395	$919.3	$664.8	$578.0	$4,271	$3,832	$3,694	$1,599	$1,399	$1,176

United States sales include export sales of $412 million in 1984, $350 million in 1983 and $519 million in 1982.

The only customer of the company which accounted for 10% or more of consolidated sales is the United States Government and its agencies. Such sales by business segment are as follows:

Sales to United States Government

	1984	1983	1982
Aerospace	$4,180	$3,620	$2,481
Electronics	1,361	1,281	1,070
Other business segments	302	265	265
Total	$5,843	$5,166	$3,816

Included in sales to the United States Government are the following major programs:

	1984	1983	1982
B-1B	$2,389	$1,753	$ 642
Space Shuttle	1,381	1,493	1,521
Total	$3,770	$3,246	$2,163

Substantially all of these sales were made by the company's Aerospace segment.

S

3. Proportional performance method.
4. Collection method.

When performance of services consists of the execution of a single act, revenue should be recognized when that action takes place—the specific performance method. For example, when dental service consists solely of the extraction of a tooth and the tooth is pulled, revenue would be recognized at that point. When services are performed in more than a single act and the final act is so significant in relation to the service transaction taken as a whole that performance cannot be considered to have taken place until the execution of that act, revenue should be recognized only on the completion of the final act—the completed performance method. For example, revenue would be recognized by a moving company when the household furniture was transported to its destination. When performance consists of the execution of more than one act, revenue should be recognized based on the measurement of the sales value of each act—the proportional performance method. For example, recognition of revenue by an accounting firm for stages of work performed in auditing assignments, tax preparations, and related tasks would be on the proportional performance method. If a significant uncertainty exists with regard to the realization of service revenue, revenue should be recognized when cash is collected.

See Revenue; Recognition; Realization; Sales.

REFERENCE
FASB, FASB Invitation to Comment (FASB, 1978).

SHAREHOLDERS' EQUITY
The excess of assets over liabilities (or net assets) of a corporation represents shareholders' equity. This represents the book value of claims of the owners to a share in the entity's assets after debts have been settled. The claims of certain classes of owners may have priority over others, especially where there

is common and preferred stock outstanding. The preferred stock would usually have a higher priority but limited rights to share in the net assets and earnings of the corporation. Common stockholders would have a residual interest in the assets and earnings. The shareholders' equity section of a balance sheet is illustrated in Exhibit C-1. Note that both common and preferred stock are outstanding and that considerable detail is presented for both classes of stock. Retained earnings is shown as both appropriated and unappropriated. Treasury stock is disclosed as a reduction of stockholders' equity.

Shareholders' equity is increased when shares are issued by the corporation and by additional equity capital arising from earnings, and is decreased by dividends, reacquisition of stock, or losses from operations. Other transactions can also change shareholders' equity.

See also Capital; Corporation; Capital stock; Preferred stock; Retained earnings; Reserves; Statement of financial position; Capital.

REFERENCE
Miller, Paul B., et al., *Intermediate Accounting* (Richard D. Irwin, Chicago, 1985).

SOCIAL ACCOUNTING
Social accounting is a subset of accounting which assists a business to determine whether the operating goals and programs of the enterprise are beneficial to society. Social accounting reports on the social benefits and costs of doing business. The following types of social reporting occasionally are found in financial statements: grants to hospitals, the arts, minority groups, urban development, educational institutions, and charitable foundations.

See also Human resource accounting.

S

SOLVENCY AND INSOLVENCY

In a popular sense, solvency means that a business is able to pay its debts as they come due. Insolvency means that the business is unable to do so. In Section 101 of the Bankruptcy Reform Act of 1978, insolvency means a financial condition such that the sum of the entity's debts is greater than all of the entity's property at fair valuation. According to this definition, a corporation could be solvent even though it may be temporarily unable to pay currently maturing debts because of the insufficiency of liquid assets.

The ability of a firm to meet its short-term obligations as they come due is usually interpreted to refer to liquidity. Solvency and insolvency usually relate to long-term conditions.

A number of remedies are available to a firm that is in serious financial difficulty, ranging from voluntary agreements with creditors to involuntary arrangements. The courts may also become involved in the process. Nonjudicial and judicial remedies include:

Control	Nonjudicial	Judicial
Control by debtor	Extension of maturity date	Reorganization (debtor
	Composition agreement	in possession)
Control by others	Creditor committee	Reorganization (trustee
	Voluntary assignment	in possession)
		Liquidation

Composition agreements are arrangements in which creditors accept a certain percentage of their separate claims in full settlement of those claims. Debtor and creditors may enter into a contractual agreement by which control of the debtor's business is given over to a committee formed by the creditors. In a voluntary assignment, a debtor executes a voluntary assignment of property to a trust for the benefit of the creditors. Reorganizations and liquidations are judicial methods for dealing with financially distressed companies.

In liquidations, a statement of affairs is usually prepared when a bankruptcy petition is filed. The statement of affairs outlines the legal status of the various creditors and the realizable value of the assets. A statement of realization and liquidation provides information to the court, debtors, and creditors concerning the progress being made in the liquidation of the business.

See also Bankruptcy; Reorganization; Liquidation; Liquidity; Troubled debt restructuring.

REFERENCE
Ginsberg, Robert E., *Bankruptcy* (Prentice-Hall, Englewood Cliffs, NJ, 1985).

SPECIAL REPORTS

Auditors frequently are engaged to report on matters that are not financial statements prepared in conformity with generally accepted accounting principles. The American Institute of Certified Public Accountants has grouped special reports into four categories which require specific reporting procedures (SAS 14, Special Reports):

1. Reports on financial statements prepared in accordance with a comprehensive basis of accounting other than GAAP (including income tax basis, cash basis, price-level-adjusted basis, and prescribed regulatory basis).
2. Reports on specified elements, accounts, or items of a financial statement, e.g., royalties, profit participation, or a provision for income taxes.
3. Reports on compliance with aspects of a contractual agreement related to audited financial statements.
4. Reports on information presented in prescribed forms or schedules that require a prescribed form of auditor's report.

See also Other comprehensive methods of accounting.

REFERENCE
AICPA, *AICPA Audit and Accounting Manual* (AICPA, 1982).

S

SPIN-OFF, SPLIT-OFF, SPLIT-UP

A spin-off is a distribution of subsidiary stock to the share-holders of the parent corporation giving them control of the subsidiary. The distribution is similar to an ordinary dividend distribution. A split-off is similar to a spin-off except that the shareholders in the parent corporation exchange some of their parent corporation stock for the subsidiary stock. A split-off is similar to a stock redemption. A split-up is essentially the distribution of the stock of two subsidiaries to shareholders of the parent in complete liquidation of the parent.

STATEMENT OF CHANGES IN FINANCIAL POSITION

The statement of changes in financial position is a report that presents information concerning the financing and investing activities of an enterprise and the changes in its financial position for the period. Financing activities are transactions which change the firm's long-term capital structure. Such transactions include those that relate to the issuance, redemption, repayment, retirement, or reacquisition of debt, preferred stock, and common stock. Investing activities include the purchase and sale of noncurrent assets (plant and equipment), proceeds from the disposal of noncurrent assets, and outlays for the purchase of consolidated subsidiaries.

The statement of changes in financial position is considered essential for financial statement users, particularly owners and creditors, in making economic decisions. The statement of changes in financial position is considered a basic financial statement which should be presented for each period for which an income statement is presented.

The statement should disclose all important aspects of an entity's financing and investing activities regardless of whether cash or other elements of working capital are directly affected. For example, the acquisition of property by issuing securities in exchange for the property and the conversion of preferred stock or long-term debt would be disclosed in the statement.

This view of the statement of changes in financial position is referred to as the "all financial resources" concept.

The statement of changes in financial position typically summarizes sources and uses of cash or working capital (current assets minus current liabilities) along with separate disclosure of cash or nonworking capital financing and investing activities. A summary of major sources and uses of cash and working capital is presented here:

Sources	Uses
1. Profitable operations	1. Unprofitable operations
2. Disposal of noncurrent assets	2. Acquisition of noncurrent assets
3. Long-term borrowing	3. Extinguishment of long-term debt
4. Issuance of equity securities	4. Redemption of stock and dividend distributions

Exhibit S-4 summarizes major sources and uses of funds.

Exhibit S-4
Sources and Uses of Funds

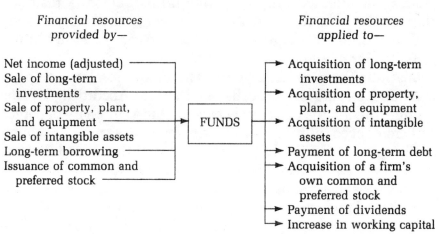

The statement can be used by owners and creditors as a basis for

1. assessing future cash flows,

2. identifying the relationship between net income and net cash flows,

3. making comparisons with earlier assessments of cash flows,

4. assessing the quality of earnings,

5. comparing information in financial statements, and

6. assessing performance of the enterprise.

See also Financial statements.

REFERENCE
APB No. 19, Reporting Changes in Financial Position (AICPA, 1971).

STATEMENT OF FINANCIAL POSITION

A statement of financial position (or balance sheet) is a report that shows the financial position of the enterprise at a particular moment of time, including the firm's economic resources (assets), economic obligations (liabilities), and the residual claims of owners (owners' equity). Assets are usually shown in the order of their liquidity (nearness to cash) and liabilities in the order of their maturity date.

Various theories have been advanced to explain the purpose and structure of the balance sheet. According to the residual theory, the balance sheet is merely a summary of debits and credit account balances after the retained earnings account has been adjusted for the income or loss of the period. In this view, the balance sheet is a "dumping ground" for account balances that cannot be assigned to the income statement. The proprietary theory of the balance sheet stresses the financial position of the owners of the enterprise as shown in this formula: Assets − Liabilities = Owners' Equity. According to this theory, the accounting entity reflects the proprietor's area of economic activity. Equity or proprietary interest represents a residual or proprietary interest in the net assets of the firm. The entity theory of the balance sheet visualizes the statement primarily as a report of values owned and owed. Creditors and owners are considered "equities" although each represents a distinguishable group in regard to claims on assets, control of the firm, and the amount of risks taken. It is the entity that owns and controls the assets of the enterprise. The business entity has an existence separate from the owners and creditors. In equation form, the entity theory appears as follows: Assets = Liabilities + Owners' Equity. According to the fund theory, the entity consists of resources (funds) which are available for a particular economic purpose subject to restraints and restrictions, often of a legal or statutory nature. Expressed in a formula, the fund theory of the balance sheet takes this form: Assets = Restrictions. A user-information theory maintains that the balance sheet should be prepared according to the uses to which it is to be put. A user-oriented statement concentrates on providing decision-making information without being concerned whether the financial statements have an interlocking relationship (or articulate) or even balance. Such statements are not currently in use, nor do they reflect generally accepted accounting principles.

The balance sheet is usually presented in one of the following formats:

1. Account form: Assets = Liabilities + Owners' equity
2. Report form: Assets – Liabilities = Owners' equity

The balance sheet discloses major classes and amounts of an entity's assets as well as major classes and amounts of its financing structure, including liabilities and equity. Major classifications used in the statement of financial position include:

1. Assets
   a. Current assets (cash, marketable securities, accounts receivable, inventory, prepaid expenses)
   b. Investments
   c. Property, plant, and equipment

    d. Intangible assets (e.g., patents, copyrights, goodwill)

    e. Deferred charges or other assets

2. Liabilities

    a. Current liabilities (accounts payable, notes payable, wages payable, accrued liabilities, unearned revenue)

    b. Long-term liabilities

3. Owners' equity

    a. Capital stock

    b. Paid-in capital in excess of par or stated value

    c. Retained earnings

Working capital is the excess of current assets over current liabilities and can be computed from data shown on the balance sheet. This significant figure is useful in determining the ability of the firm to finance current operations and to meet obligations as they mature. The relationship between current assets and current liabilities is referred to as the current ratio and is a measure of the liquidity of the enterprise.

Balance sheets are usually presented in comparative form. Comparative statements include the current year's statement and statements of one or more of the preceding accounting periods. Comparative statements are useful in evaluating and analyzing trends.

The balance sheet assists external users in assessing the firm's liquidity, financial flexibility, and operating capabilities and in evaluating the earnings performance for the period. By comparing beginning capital with ending capital, financial statement users can determine whether capital was decreased, increased, or maintained. If capital is increased, there is the possibility of dividends, which represent a return on investment. If capital is decreased or merely maintained, dividends would represent a return of capital.

Assets and liabilities reported on the balance sheet are measured by different attributes (for example, historical cost, current (replacement) cost, current market value, net realizable value, and present value of future cash flows), depending upon the nature of the item and the relevance and reliability of the attribute measured. Historical cost is the exchange price of the asset when it was acquired. Current cost is the amount of cash or its equivalent required to obtain the same asset at the balance sheet date. Current market value or exit value is the amount of cash that may be obtained at the balance sheet date from selling the asset in an orderly liquidation. Net realizable value is the amount of cash that can be obtained as a result of a future sale of an asset. Present value is the expected exit value discounted to the balance sheet date.

See also Financial statements; Measurement; Recognition; Asset; Liabilities; Current assets; Current liabilities; Prepaid expense; Liability; Working capital; Intangible assets; Investments; Property, plant, and equipment; Shareholders' equity; Capital maintenance theories.

REFERENCES
SFAC No. 3, Elements of Financial Statements of Business Enterprises (FASB, 1981).
SFAC No. 5, Recognition and Measurement in Financial Statements of Business Enterprises (FASB, 1984).

STATEMENT OF INVESTMENTS BY AND DISTRIBUTIONS TO OWNERS

A full set of financial statements for a period includes a Statement of Investments by and Distributions to Owners (or Statement of Stockholders' Equity). This statement discloses the extent to which and in what ways the equity of an entity increased or decreased from transactions with owners during the period. It reports on capital transactions rather than on income transactions with nonowners, which appear on the income statement. Investments by owners take the form of cash, goods or services, or satisfaction or conversion of the entity's liabilities. Distributions include cash dividends when declared or other cash withdrawals by owners of noncorporate entities and transactions such as reacquisitions of the entity's equity securities and distributions of noncash assets. This information is useful to investors, creditors, and other users of financial statements in assisting them in assessing the entity's financial flexibility, profitability, and risk.

See also Financial statements.

REFERENCE
SFAC No. 5, Recognition and Measurement in Financial Statements of Business Enterprises (FASB, 1984).

STATEMENT OF RETAINED EARNINGS
The retained earnings statement reconciles the beginning and ending balances in the retained earnings account. This statement can be presented as a separate statement or in a combined statement of income and retained earnings. Generally accepted accounting principles require that a retained earnings statement be present whenever comparative balance sheets and an income statement are presented. A retained earnings statement reporting a prior-period adjustment would appear as follows:

Beginning retained earnings	$100,000
Deduct: Adjustment for failure to record depreciation in a prior year	10,000
Adjusted beginning retained earnings	90,000
Add: Net income for the period	110,000
Deduct: Dividends	20,000
Retained earnings at end of year	$ 90,000

See also Prior-period adjustments; Income statement.

S

STATEMENTS OF EARNINGS AND COMPREHENSIVE INCOME

In the FASB's conceptual framework of accounting, the statement of earnings and comprehensive income is included as one component of a full set of financial statements. These statements disclose the extent to which and the ways in which the equity of an entity increased or decreased from all sources other than transactions with owners during a period. These statements report on the results of an enterprise's ongoing major or central operations, results of its incidental or peripheral transactions, and effects of other events and circumstances arising from the environment that are often partly or wholly beyond the control of the entity and its managements.

The concept of earnings is similar to net income as currently understood and disclosed on a current income statement. However, earnings do not include the cumulative effect of certain accounting adjustments of earlier periods that are recognized in the current period. Comprehensive income comprises all recognized changes in equity of an entity during a period other than those resulting from investments by owners and distributions to owners. Certain items are included in comprehensive income and excluded from earnings. Comprehensive income includes the cumulative effect of certain accounting adjustments of earlier periods and certain holding gains and losses affecting net assets, such as some changes in market values of investments in noncurrent marketable equity securities and foreign currency translation adjustments.

The relationship between earnings and comprehensive income can be illustrated as follows:

+ Revenues	100	+ Earnings	20
- Expenses	90	- Cumulative accounting adjustments	5
+ Gains	15	+ Other nonowner changes in equity	2
- Losses	5		
= Earnings	20	= Comprehensive income	17

Statements of earnings and comprehensive income do not cur-

479

rently replace the income statement.

See also Income statement; Comprehensive income.

REFERENCE
SFAC No. 5, Recognition and Measurement in Financial Statements of Business Enterprises (FASB, 1984).

STATEMENTS OF FINANCIAL ACCOUNTING CONCEPTS

Statements of Financial Accounting Concepts are a series of publications in the Financial Accounting Board's conceptual framework for financial accounting and reporting. The statements set forth objectives and fundamentals that serve as the basis for developing financial accounting and reporting standards. The objectives are intended to identify the goals and purposes of financial reporting. The fundamentals are also intended to describe the underlying concepts of financial accounting that guide the selection of transactions, events, and circumstances to be accounted for, their recognition and measurement, and the means of summarizing and communicating them to interested parties. Taken as a whole, the conceptual framework is a coherent system of interrelated objectives and fundamentals that is expected by the FASB to lead to consistent standards and that prescribes the nature, function, and limits of financial accounting and reporting. Statements of Financial Accounting Concepts do not establish standards prescribing accounting procedures or disclosure practices for particular items or events. Such standards are issued by the Board as Statements of Financial Accounting Standards.

See also Conceptual framework of accounting; Statements of Financial Accounting Standards; Financial Accounting Standards Board.

REFERENCE
FASB, Accounting Standards: Conceptual Framework of Accounting Concepts 1-5 (FASB, 1985).

STATEMENTS OF FINANCIAL ACCOUNTING STANDARDS

Statements of Financial Accounting Standards are official pronouncements of the Financial Accounting Standards Board. The Standards are considered to be generally accepted accounting principles and are binding in accounting practice. The FASB employs due process procedures in the preparation and review of proposed standards before issuing them.

Rule 203 of the Rules of Conduct of the AICPA Code of Professional Ethics covers Statements of Financial Accounting Standards:

> *"A member shall not express an opinion that financial statements are presented in conformity with generally accepted accounting principles if such statements contain any departure from an accounting principle promulgated by the body designated by Council . . . to establish such principles which has a material effect on the statements taken as a whole, unless the member can demonstrate that due to unusual circumstances the financial statements would otherwise have been misleading. In such cases, his report must describe the departure, the approximate effects thereof, if practicable, and the reasons why compliance with the principle would result in a misleading statement."*

See also Financial Accounting Standards Board; Accounting principles; Generally accepted accounting principles; Statement of financial accounting concepts; Conceptual framework of accounting.

REFERENCE
FASB, *Accounting Standards: Original Pronouncements* (McGraw-Hill, N.Y., 1985).

STOCK DIVIDENDS

A stock dividend represents a distribution of additional shares of a corporation's own stock to its stockholders without consideration on a pro rata basis (i.e., in proportion to the number of shares held). Stock dividends are usually motivated by a desire to give the shareholders some evidence of a part of their interests in accumulated corporate earnings without distributing cash or other property which the board of directors deems necessary or desirable to retain in the business.

A stock dividend does not change the enterprise's assets or shareholders' proportionate interests therein. Many shareholders look upon stock dividends as distributions of corporate earnings and usually in an amount equivalent to the fair value of the shares received, especially when the stock dividend is small (less than 20-25 percent of outstanding shares) because such dividends do not ordinarily reduce the market price of the shares. When the stock dividend is large, the market price of the shares typically declines but eventually tends to rise since a lower price can increase the demand for the shares.

When a small stock dividend is distributed, the corporation transfers from retained earnings to the category of permanent capitalization (capital stock and additional paid-in capital) an amount equal to the fair value of the additional shares issued. When a large stock dividend is distributed, the amount transferred is the amount established by legal requirements, which is usually legal capital. To illustrate the effects on the stockholders' equity section of a balance sheet when a large and a small stock dividend are distributed, assume the following information:

Common stock ($10 par, 10,000 shares outstanding)	$100,000
Additional paid-in capital in excess of par	50,000
Retained earnings	200,000
Total	$350,000

Case 1. The corporation issues a 10 percent stock dividend when the fair market value is $15 per share.

Case 2. The corporation issues a 50 percent stock dividend when legal capital is $10 per share.

The effect of the stock dividends on total stockholders' equity and the components of stockholders' equity can be summarized as follows:

	Before Dividend	Case 1	Case 2
Common stock	$100,000	$110,000	$150,000
Additional paid-in capital	50,000	55,000	75,000
Retained earnings	200,000	185,000	125,000
Total	$350,000	$350,000	$350,000

Note that total capital remained unchanged although the components of stockholders' equity changed.

The recipient of the stock dividend received no asset and so would not make any entry except a memorandum notation that shares had been received. The cost of the shares previously held would be allocated equitably to the total shares held after receipt of the stock dividend, which would be the adjusted cost per share.

See also Dividends; Retained earnings; Stock split; Legal capital.

REFERENCE
Chasteen, Larry G., et al., *Intermediate Accounting* (Random House, N.Y., 1984).

STOCK OPTIONS

A stock option is the right to purchase shares of common stock in accordance with an agreement, upon payment of a specified amount. Stock option plans are compensation schemes under which executives are granted options to purchase common stock over an extended option period at a stated price. Nonstatutory stock options are not approved by the IRS Code and do not give special tax advantages to employees. Companies sometimes grant stock appreciation rights (SAR) that allow the employee to receive cash, stock, or a combination of cash and stock based on the difference between a specified amount per share of the stock and the quoted market price per share at some future date.

In compensatory stock option plans, the excess of the market price of the stock over the exercise price is considered the compensatory portion of the plan. This amount is computed on the date that (1) the number of shares an individual employee is entitled to receive is known and (2) the option or purchase price of the shares is known. This date is referred to as the measurement date. Compensation expense is recorded as the services giving rise to the stock option are rendered.

Where stock appreciation rights are concerned, total compensation expense to be allocated is estimated by the excess of the market value over the designated price. This amount is allocated to expense over the service period.

See also Stock rights.

STOCK RIGHTS

A stock right is the privilege attached to a share of common stock to purchase a specified number of shares of common stock or a fractional share. Stock rights indicate the price at which stock can be acquired (the exercise price), the number of shares that may be acquired for each right, and the expiration date. When a corporation issues stock rights to shareholders without compensation, one right is issued for each share. The number of rights required to purchase an additional share depends upon the agreement. Between the date on which the issuance of rights is announced and the date the rights are issued, the stock to which the rights relate is purchased and sold in the market "rights on," which means that the value of the stock and the rights are united. After the rights are issued, the rights are traded separately from the stock and the stock is traded "ex-rights."

Stock warrants (or stock-purchase warrants) are securities that give to the holder the ability to buy a specified number of shares of stock at a stated price for a specified period of time. Stock warrants do not pay current income. Warrants are often used to sell bonds or stock to make the securities more attractive when they are being issued. Warrants are purchased from the issuing firm or in the marketplace for cash. Stock rights are usually issued free to current stockholders who are entitled to purchase additional shares from a pending new issue of stock in proportion to their present holdings (a preemptive right).

See also Stock options.

STOCK SPLIT

A stock split is a distribution of company's own capital stock to existing stockholders with the purpose of reducing the market price of the stock, which would hopefully increase the demand for the shares. To accomplish the stock split, the par or stated value of the stock is adjusted. For example, a $10 par value stock that is split two for one will have a $5 par value after the split. Assume that the stockholders' equity section of a corporate balance sheet indicates that the stock is split 2:1. The effect of the stock split is illustrated here:

	Before Stock Split	After Stock Split
Common stock, $10 par, $10,000 shares issued	$100,000	
Common stock, $5 par, 20,000 shares issued		$100,000
Additional paid-in capital	10,000	10,000
Retained earnings	90,000	90,000
Total	$200,000	$200,000

Note that after the stock split, the components of stockholders' equity are the same as before the split. Only the par value of the shares and the number of shares outstanding have changed.

A reverse stock split is a stock split in which the number of shares outstanding is decreased.

See also Stock dividends.

SUBSEQUENT EVENTS

Subsequent events refer to material events and transactions that occur after the balance sheet date but before the financial statements are issued. If the subsequent event provides additional evidence concerning conditions that existed on the balance sheet date and significantly affects the estimate(s) used in preparing the statements, an adjustment should be made to the statements before they are issued. For example, if a major customer's account receivable is deemed unlikely to be collected, a recognition of the loss and an increase in the allowance for uncollectible accounts should be made. If the condition did not exist on the balance sheet date but occurred after that date, the statements should not be adjusted. Disclosure should be made. For example, a lawsuit settlement after the balance sheet date would require disclosure only.

See also Full disclosure; Financial statements.

SUBSTANCE OVER FORM

Financial accounting is concerned with both the economic substance and the legal form of transactions and events. When a conflict exists between the two, information concerning the economic substance of the transaction or event is considered more relevant, reliable, and representationally faithful than legal form.

There are numerous accounting examples where substance takes precedence over the legal form of a transaction or event. For example, current accounting principles require that certain leases be reported as assets and liabilities even though the lessee does not have legal title to the property. Certain long-term notes receivable and payable are noninterest-bearing and legally have no claim to interest receipts or payments. In certain cases, accounting principles require that interest revenue and expense be recognized to reflect the time value of money. In computing earnings per share of common stock, convertible preferred stock and convertible bonds are sometimes considered common stock equivalents and used in the computation of earnings per share of common stock. In defining assets, the existence of future economic benefits is usually more important than legal ownership rights when considering whether an asset exists.

The concept of substance over form is not included as a qualitative characteristic of accounting information because it is a vague idea that is included in reliability and representational faithfulness.

The Internal Revenue Service often looks past the legal form of a transaction to its substance to determine its taxable status, especially in situations where the transaction has no valid business purpose other than saving taxes. Abusive tax shelters are a prime example of the application of substance over form by the IRS.

See also Qualitative characteristics of accounting information; Leases; Consolidated financial statements; Related party transactions; Defeasance; Product financing arrangements; Sales with right of return; Tax shelters.

SUCCESSFUL-EFFORTS ACCOUNTING
Successful-efforts accounting for oil and gas operations capitalizes such costs as exploration, drilling, and lease rentals associated with establishing the location of a natural resource only when the effort results in the discovery of a natural resource. Costs associated with unsuccessful wells are expensed. The full-cost method capitalizes the costs associated with all the wells, both successful and unsuccessful. Both methods of accounting for the cost of oil and gas properties are considered generally acceptable accounting methods and satisfy the needs of users of the financial statements. Large companies generally use successful-efforts accounting while smaller com-

panies often use the full-cost method in order to reduce current expenses and increase income. Neither method reflects the economic substance of oil and gas exploration in that they do not include the current value of the oil and gas reserves in the statements.

See also Natural resources.

REFERENCES
AICPA, *Accounting and Reporting Practices in the Oil and Gas Industry* (AICPA).
Touche Ross & Co., *Oil & Gas Accounting: What Producers Must Know* (Touche Ross & Co., 1980).

SURPLUS
The term *surplus* is generally disapproved for use in accounting. In law, surplus is defined as the excess of the net assets of a corporation over its stated capital; capital surplus refers to the surplus of the corporation other than earned surplus. In accounting, earned surplus has at times been used for retained earnings. This usage is not generally acceptable. Surplus suggests an excess that is not needed. In this sense, it is not particularly applicable to financial reporting.

See also Retained earnings; Reserves.

T

T

TAX SHELTERS

A tax shelter is an investment at risk to acquire something of value, with the expectation that it will produce income and reduce or defer taxes and that its ultimate disposition will result in the realization of gain. Tax-sheltered investments are often public offerings that have been registered with the Securities and Exchange Commission for interstate sale or with a state agency. Private offerings are not registered. Most tax shelters are structured as limited partnerships in which the investors are the limited partners. Subchapter S corporations are also used to structure a tax shelter. The tax losses generated by most tax-sheltered investments are attributable to deductions for depreciation and interest on borrowed funds that provide leverage for the investment. Investment tax credits and rehabilitation credits frequently add to the attractiveness of tax shelters.

Tax shelters have frequently been abused. An abusive tax shelter is a transaction without any economic purpose other than the generation of tax benefits. Such shelters frequently overstate the valuation of assets. The Internal Revenue Service disapproves of abusive tax shelters.

See also Partnership.

T

REFERENCE

Arthur Andersen & Co., *Tax Shelters—The Basics* (Arthur Andersen & Co., 1982).

TENANCY IN COMMON, JOINT TENANCY, AND TENANCY BY THE ENTIRETY

A tenancy in common is a form of co-ownership in which each tenant (owner) holds an undivided interest in property. The ownership interest of a tenant in common does not terminate upon the owner's prior death.

A joint tenancy is one which provides for the undivided ownership of property by two or more persons with the right of survivorship. Right of survivorship gives the surviving owner full ownership of the property.

A tenancy by the entirety is essentially a joint tenancy between husband and wife. As in a joint tenancy, upon the death of one tenant by the entirety the entire title automatically and immediately vests in the survivor.

TRANSFER PRICING

Divisions of an enterprise frequently buy and sell to one another. A price must be established for these transfers. This price is referred to as the transfer price. Various alternatives for establishing a transfer price include the following:

1. The transfer price should be set equal to the manufacturing cost of the selling division.

2. The transfer price should be the amount the selling division could sell the product for to an outside firm.

3. The transfer price should be the amount the buying division could purchase the product for from an outside firm.

4. The transfer price should be a negotiated amount agreed upon by the buying and selling divisions.

5. The transfer price should be the costs incurred to the point of transfer plus the opportunity costs for the firm as a whole. The opportunity cost would be the next best alternative for the firm. For example, if the selling division was operating at less than full capacity, the opportunity cost would be zero. If the selling division was operating at full capacity, the opportunity cost would be the lost contribution margin (selling price minus variable costs) resulting from forgoing outside sales to sell to the buying division.

The choice of method depends upon a number of factors, such as the autonomy allowed to divisions, the degree of market competition, the extent to which the goals of the division are expected to correspond to the goals of the firm, short-run supply and demand relationships, and how divisions are evaluated by the firm.

See also Cost accounting.

TREASURY STOCK

Treasury stock is a corporation's own capital stock that has been fully paid for by stockholders, legally issued, reacquired by the corporation, and held by the corporation for future reissuance. The reacquisition of the shares results in a reduction of shareholders' equity. Treasury stock is not an asset because the corporation cannot own itself. Neither can a corporation recognize a gain or a loss when reacquiring or reissuing its own stock. Treasury stock is treated as a reduction of stockholders' equity. Treasury stock does not possess voting rights or the preemptive right, nor does it share in dividend distributions or in assets at liquidation.

A corporation might reacquire its own shares for a number of reasons: to have shares to use for stock options, bonus, and stock purchase plans; to use in the conversion of convertible preferred stock or bonds; or to maintain the market price of its stock.

Treasury stock can be reported in the stockholders' equity section of the balance sheet as contra to shareholders' equity as follows:

Contributed capital:

Common stock	XXX
Additional paid-in capital	XXX
Total contributed capital	XXX
Retained earnings	XXX
Less: Treasury stock (10,000 shares at cost)	(15,000)
Total stockholders' equity	$XXXXX

See also Capital stock; Shareholders' equity.

TRIAL BALANCE

A trial balance is a list of ledger accounts and amounts. A trial balance provides evidence of the equality of total debits and credits in the ledger. The equality of debits and credits on a trial balance does not prove that the correct accounts were debited or credited. Trial balances can be taken at various times during the accounting cycle and therefore provide unadjusted, adjusted, and postclosing trial balances. A condensed trial balance would appear as follows:

	Debits	Credits
Assets	XXX	
Liabilities		XXX
Owners' equity		XXX
Revenues		XXX
Expenses	XXX	
Total	XXX	XXX

Note that assets and expense accounts usually have debit balances; revenue, liability, and owners' equity accounts usually have credit balances. This is a result of the basic rules for double-entry accounting.

See also Double-entry system; Ledger; Accounting system; Work sheet.

TROUBLED DEBT RESTRUCTURING

A troubled debt restructuring is a debt restructuring if the creditor, for reasons related to the debtor's financial difficulties, grants a concession to the debtor that it would not otherwise consider at a point earlier than the scheduled maturity date. The two principal types of debt restructuring are a transfer of assets or equity interest from a debtor to a creditor in full settlement of a debt and a modification of terms. Modifications of terms include such arrangements as interest-rate reductions or maturity-date extensions. Debtors experience gains and creditors recognize losses on troubled debt restructurings.

The accounting procedures for troubled debt restructurings can be summarized as follows for the debtor and creditor:

Form of Restructure	Accounting for Debtor and Creditor
1. Settlement of debt:	
a. Transfer of assets.	a. Debtor recognizes gain; creditor recognizes loss on restructure. Debtor recognizes gain or loss on asset transfer.
b. Granting an equity interest.	b. Debtor recognizes gain; creditor recognizes loss on restructure.
2. Modified terms; debt continues:	
a. Carrying amount of debt is less than total future cash.	a. No gain or loss is recognized on restructure.
b. Carrying amount of debt is greater than total future cash flows.	b. No gain or loss is recognized on restructure. No interest expense or income is recognized over the remaining life of the debt.

See also Bankruptcy; Liquidation; Reorganization; Quasi-reorganization; Solvency and insolvency.

REFERENCE

SFAS No. 15, Accounting by Debtors and Creditors for Troubled Debt Restructuring (FASB, 1977).

U

U.S. RULE AND MERCHANTS' RULE

According to the U.S. Rule, interest is computed on the unpaid balance of a debt. The payment is first applied to interest. The excess payment reduces the balance of the debt.

The merchants' rule is a method for allowing interest credit on partial payments made on an installment basis. One variation of the merchants' rule requires that both debt and all partial payments are considered to earn interest up to the final date. The final amount due is their difference.

See also Interest.

VALUE

The term *value* is used in accounting accompanied by an adjective: book value, par value, no-par value, stated value, appraisal value, fair market value, disposal value, salvage value, scrap value, exit value, entry value, discovery value, replacement value, maturity value, carrying value, and others.

VALUE ADDED STATEMENT

Value added refers to a portion of the selling price of a commodity or service attributable to a stage of production. A value added statement is used by many British companies to report on the wealth-creation process. Value added represents the income of shareholders, suppliers of debt capital, employees, and governments. Value added can also be conceptualized as sales revenue minus the cost of materials and services which were brought in from outside suppliers. The value added statement can be presented in the following format:

Sources:		
Sales		$500,000
Less: Brought-in materials, services	$100,000	
Depreciation	50,000	150,000
Total value added		$350,000

Applied as follows:

To wages	$200,000
To interest (banks and other lenders)	25,000
To taxes	75,000
To dividends	30,000
To retained earnings	20,000
Total value added	$350,000

The statement is supposed to present a broader view of a company's objectives than the more traditional financial statements. The statement is apparently useful for improving attitudes, motivation, and behavior since it shows the contributions made by various contributors. Less attention is given to profits and more to human accomplishments. Various value added ratios can provide diagnostic and predictive data which can be used for interindustry and international comparisons. Such ratios include: Value added/Payroll; Value added/ Taxation; Value added/Interest; Value added/Dividends.

A value added tax (VAT) is a tax levied on the value added to a commodity or service at each stage of production and distribution. A value added tax is essentially a sales tax on earlier completed transactions. Such a tax avoids the compounding effects of successive taxes on sales.

See also Wealth; Financial statements.

REFERENCE
Sinha, Gokul, *Value Added Income* (Book World, Calcutta, India, 1983).

VOUCHER SYSTEM
A voucher system is an accounting system developed to control cash payments and promote efficiency by eliminating the special purchases journal and the accounts payable subsidiary ledger. In a voucher system, each cash disbursement must be authorized by a voucher. A voucher is a serially numbered document that includes all pertinent information about the requested disbursement. The voucher must be signed by one

authorized to approve cash disbursements. Supporting documents for the expenditure, such as purchase invoices, freight bills, or receiving documents, must be attached to the voucher. After the voucher is authorized, it is filed in an unpaid voucher file which replaces the accounts payable subsidiary ledger. A voucher register and a check register are two journals used in the voucher system. A voucher register is a special journal used to record all liabilities approved for payment. A check register is used to record cash disbursements.

In a voucher system, individuals who are authorized to approve vouchers do not prepare or sign checks or have access to the voucher and cash registers. The individual who signs checks is allowed to do so only when a voucher for the payment has been authorized.

See also Internal control; Cash; Accounting system.

REFERENCE
Needles, Belverd E., et al., *Principles of Accounting* (Houghton Mifflin, Boston, 1981).

WATERED STOCK AND SECRET RESERVES

Watered stock exists when the actual value of the assets behind the stock is less than the fair market value assigned to the stock. These misstatements may be intentional or unintentional. When stock is watered, both assets and capital items are overstated in the financial statements. Watered stock could also be the result of understating liabilities and overstating capital stock. Watered stock usually arises from granting a block of stock to a promoter for services provided when the services are overvalued in relation to the promoter's services. The term *watered stock* comes from a practice followed by cattlemen of increasing the weight of their stock by watering their stock close to salt deposits after a long drive before taking them to market.

Secret reserves exist when there is an understatement of assets or an overstatement of liabilities and a corresponding understatement of capital. Secret reserves can be the result of taking excessive depreciation charges or provisions for uncollectible accounts and by other actions which understate assets or overstate liabilities. Both "watered stock" and "secret reserves" are unacceptable because financial statements would be misleading.

See also Stockholders' equity; Capital.

WEALTH
Broadly speaking, wealth consists of things of value (economic goods) owned. An economic good is an object that is material, useful, scarce, and transferable. Wealth is a stock concept; it is the total value of economic goods and services at one period of time. Wealth of an enterprise is ordinarily considered to be disclosed on the balance sheet. Wealth is closely related to income. Income is a flow concept. Income represents the total value of economic goods and services produced or sold over a period of time. Income is ordinarily disclosed on the income statement of an enterprise. Real income is the value of the economic goods and services produced. Money income received by the owners of the factors of production represents compensation in dollars for their productive contribution. J. R. Hicks, in *Value and Capital*, defined income as follows:

> *"We ought to define a man's income as the maximum value which he can consume during a week, and still expect to be as well off at the end of the week as he was at the beginning."*

For this definition to become useful, one must specify what is meant by "well-offness" as it relates to financial capital or physical capital, historical cost or current cost, historical/constant dollar income, or current cost/constant dollar income.

See also Income; Economics; Capital; Capital maintenance theories; Constant dollar accounting; Income statement; Statement of financial position.

WORK SHEET
A work sheet or working paper is a document, usually a columnar sheet of paper, that is used by an accountant to facilitate

the accountant's summarizing, analyzing, and recording activities. A special work sheet is used by accountants to enter the trial balance of the general ledger and summarize the information required for making adjusting and closing entries and preparing the financial statements at the close of an accounting period. A ten-column work sheet is illustrated in Exhibit W-1. Work sheets are frequently used as schedules for computing or supporting items appearing on the financial statements, especially those that may require adjustment.

See also Accounting system; Audit; Trial balance.

WORKING CAPITAL
Working capital is the excess of current assets over current liabilities. Working capital is sometimes defined as current assets. Net working capital would then refer to the excess of current assets over current liabilities. Adequate working capital is necessary for the business if it is to pay its debts as they come due. Creditors often consider working capital to constitute a margin of safety for paying short-term debts. The working capital cycle of a business is illustrated in Exhibit O-1.

See also Statement of financial position; Current asset; Current liabilities; Operating cycle; Ratios.

WORKING PAPERS
Working papers are the records maintained by independent auditors of the procedures followed, tests performed, information obtained, and conclusions reached relating to an audit. The working papers include the audit program, descriptions of procedures performed and their results, and comments and observations describing the auditor's judgments concerning the evidence and conclusions. The working papers serve to support the audit report and assist the auditor in conducting

Exhibit W-1

An example of a work sheet with adjusting entries

Z COMPANY
Work Sheet
For the Year Ended December 31, 19□1

Account Title	Trial Balance Debit	Trial Balance Credit	Adjustments Debit	Adjustments Credit	Adjusted Trial Balance Debit	Adjusted Trial Balance Credit	Income Statement Debit	Income Statement Credit	Balance Sheet Debit	Balance Sheet Credit
Cash	9,000				9,000				9,000	
Accounts Receivable	80,000				80,000				80,000	
Allowance for Doubtful Receivables		1,000		(e) 2,000		3,000				3,000
Prepaid Insurance	1,000			(a) 750	250				250	
Equipment	100,000				100,000				100,000	
Accumulated Depreciation		30,000		(b) 10,000		40,000				40,000
Notes Payable		10,000				10,000				10,000
Accounts Payable		20,000				20,000				20,000
Income Taxes Payable		2,000				2,000				2,000
Common Stock		60,000				60,000				60,000
Retained Earnings		40,000				40,000				40,000
Dividends	1,000				1,000				1,000	
Sale of Services		100,000				100,000		100,000		
Salaries Expense	60,000		(d) 5,000		65,000		65,000			
Rent Expense	10,000				10,000		10,000			
Income Tax Expense	2,000				2,000		2,000			
	263,000	263,000								
Insurance Expense			(a) 750		750		750			
Depreciation Expense			(b) 10,000		10,000		10,000			
Interest Expense			(c) 100		100		100			
Accrued Salaries Payable				(d) 5,000		5,000				5,000
Bad Debts Expense			(e) 2,000		2,000		2,000			
			17,850	17,850	280,100	180,100	89,850	100,000	190,250	180,100
Net Income for Year							10,150			10,150
							100,000	100,000	190,250	190,250

and supervising the audit engagement. Professional standards require that the auditor maintain detailed working papers. Working papers are owned by the accountant and should be retained as evidence to establish the nature, extent, and propriety of the services provided a client.

Auditors must prepare audit working papers to properly conduct and support an audit. The working papers should be sufficiently detailed and documented to show that the financial statements and other information being reported upon were in agreement with or reconciled with the client's records. General guidelines concerning the contents of working papers include the following:

1. The work has been adequately planned, supervised, and reviewed.

2. The internal control system has been examined and evaluated as a basis to determine what reliance can be placed thereon and to determine the extent of tests required.

3. The audit evidence obtained, procedures followed, and tests performed are sufficient to express an opinion.

Working papers prepared by an auditor in connection with an audit of a client's financial statements are usually considered the property of the auditor, although state laws vary. Because of the confidential nature of the information contained in working papers, the auditor is expected to maintain control over the working papers at all times.

See also Audit; Privileged communications.

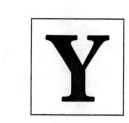

YIELD

The effective yield, or yield to maturity, is the interest rate that will reduce the bond's interest and maturity value payments to a present value that equals its price. The present value exceeds the maturity value when the nominal rate exceeds the effective rate. The amount of the excess is the premium. The present value falls below maturity value when the nominal rate is lower than the effective rate. The difference between the market and maturity values is referred to as a discount. The effective yield of a bond can be illustrated as follows. A bond with a nominal interest rate of 4 percent that is bought at 95 ($950) and matures in one year will actually yield to maturity approximately 9.41 percent: 4 percent of $1,000 (face value of the bond) produces $40 interest per year; the appreciation on the bond between purchase price and maturity value ($1,000) equals $50. The total return on the investment is $90. The yield is computed as follows: $90/$950 = 9.41 percent (approximate). Tables are available to compute the effective yield on bonds. See Exhibit Y-1 for a table that illustrates bond yields.

The yield on common stock is a financial ratio computed by dividing the annual dividends per common share by the latest market price per common share. This yield represents

Exhibit Y–1
Bond Prices and Yields

Ten-Year Bond Prices

Yield Rate %	Coupon Rate %				
	3	3.5	4	4.5	5
2	109.02	113.53	118.05	122.56	127.07
2.5	104.40	108.80	113.20	117.60	122.00
3	100.00	104.29	108.58	112.88	117.17
3.5	95.81	100.00	104.19	108.38	112.56
4	91.82	95.91	100.00	104.09	108.18
4.5	88.03	92.02	96.01	100.00	103.99
5	84.41	88.31	92.21	96.10	100.00
5.5	80.97	84.77	88.58	92.39	96.19
6	77.68	81.40	85.12	88.84	92.56

the rate of return on the market value of common stock. Yield also refers to the rate of return on an investment.

See Bonds; Ratios; Rate of return; Present value; Interest.

REFERENCES
Kellison, Stephen G., *The Theory of Interest* (Richard D. Irwin., Homewood, IL, 1970).
Woelfel, Charles J., and Mecimore, Charles, *The Operating Executive's Handbook of Profit Planning Tools and Techniques* (Probus, Chicago, 1986).